# THE POLITICAL ECONOMY
## OF IMPERIALISM

# THE POLITICAL ECONOMY OF IMPERIALISM
## Critical Appraisals

*Edited by*

**Ronald H. Chilcote**

ROWMAN & LITTLEFIELD PUBLISHERS, INC.
*Lanham • Boulder • New York • Oxford*

ROWMAN & LITTLEFIELD PUBLISHERS, INC.

Published in the United States of America
by Rowman & Littlefield Publishers, Inc.
4720 Boston Way, Lanham, Maryland 20706
http://www.rowmanlittlefield.com

12 Hid's Copse Road, Cumnor Hill, Oxford OX2 9JJ, England

Copyright © 2000 by Rowman & Littlefield Publishers, Inc.
Originally published in 1999 by Kluwer Academic Publishers.

British Library Cataloguing in Publication Information Available

**Library of Congress Cataloging-in-Publication Data**

The political economy of imperialism : critical appraisals / [edited by] Ronald H. Chilcote.
    p.  cm.
    Originally published: Boston : Kluwer Academic Publishers, © 1999.
    Includes bibliographical references and index.
    ISBN 0-7425-1010-7 (pbk.)
    1. Imperialism—Economic aspects.   2. Capitalism.   3. Economic development.   I.
Chilcote, Ronald H.

  JC359.P58   2000
  338.9—dc21
                                     00-059065

Printed in the United States of America

# CONTENTS

# PREFACE

This book brings together important essays by distinguished scholars who have devoted attention to the study of imperialism and development. It complements an anthology entitled *Imperialism: Theoretical Directions* (Humanity Press, 2000), which consists of previously published essays on important theoretical perspectives, issues, and debates surrounding these themes. Both projects relate to a lengthy chapter, "Theories of Imperialism," in my book *Theories of Comparative Political Economy* (Westview Press, 2000). These projects represent a culmination of many years of teaching in both economics and political science. During that time I taught two political science courses on development and underdevelopment, but I was unable to convince my colleagues of the usefulness of a course on imperialism that linked historical issues and debates with the more recent developmental literature. When I was welcomed into economics in 1990, my colleagues endorsed a graduate seminar on the political economy of imperialism. This volume evolved out of that experience as an effort to encourage new analysis that reflects on past contributions as well as on the prospects for imperialism in the contemporary world.

I appreciate the support of colleagues who understood the usefulness of this approach and especially the students who participated in the seminars, confronted the material, and became sensitive to the issues and debates through weekly discussion and position papers and whose comprehension led to some modest theoretical breakthroughs. I want to thank Elvia Ramiriz, a graduate student in sociology at the University of California, Riverside, for her assistance in the initial phase of organizing this volume. I am grateful for the dedicated efforts of Krista Eissfeldt, who ultimately brought this project to rest, and to my wife, Frances, who stepped in to assist with coordination of the final proofs, especially bibliographical references. I wish to acknowledge the modest financial support of the Research Committee of the UCR Academic Senate. Finally, thanks to Jennifer Knerr for encouragement and ensuring the publication of this paperback edition with Rowman & Littlefield.

# INTRODUCTION

# Ronald H. Chilcote

This volume emanates from several concerns and interests. First, it departs from the fundamental premise that capitalism in its evolving and consolidated forms underlies questions and theories of imperialism and development. Second, it assumes that the foundations for a theory of imperialism and development trace to early classical writings on political economy, and, in particular, to David Ricardo, Adam Smith, and Karl Marx. Marx, for example, analyzed the logic of the capitalist system, drawing largely upon the European experience, especially in England. He focused on capitalism in terms of accumulation, commodification, circulation, and production, maximization of profit, and so on. Third, this volume acknowledges that both positive and negative consequences accompanied the penetration of capitalism and the development of the forces and means of production thoughout the world. Marx and Engels, for instance, assessed these impacts for Ireland and India: whereas capitalism was expected to sweep away the legacy of precapitalist social formations and promote progress in India, protective measures might permit autonomus development in Ireland in the face of its dominant neighbor, England (Mohri, 1989).

Understandings of imperialism at the turn of the century emphasized the repercussions of advanced capitalism for imperial Europe and the outlying colonies. Most interpretations condemned imperialism, yet the prevailing ideas about development emanating from the advanced capitalist centers traditionally tended to assume that eventually these positive trends could be diffused to the less developed and poorer nations of the world. After the Second World War and with the fall of empires and the imperial schemes of England, France, Portugal, and other European countries, the newly emerging nations of Africa, Asia, and Latin America began to question diffusionist and capitalist development. Their criticism drew from the literature of imperialism in the search for understanding about their poverty, exploitation, and lack of development. The links between explanations of imperialism and underdevelopment were not always clear, however, and indeed after 1945, intellectuals worked hard at promoting new alternative ideas and theories.

The classical writers of imperialism wrote about the exploitation of the noncapitalist world. The contemporary writers of underdevelopment and dependency also dwelled on social formations outside the advanced capitalist world. For both classical and contemporary writers, their theories of capitalism were founded on the experience of the noncapitalist, precapitalist, or emerging capitalist world. The former tended to emphasize external dimensions of international production and trade, and the latter attempted to direct attention to internal aspects. Sometimes their offerings were polemical rather than substantive and theoretical, but the language of their discourse, whether worked around imperialism or developmental questions, became synonymous with either the progressive or negative implications of capitalism. Where the discourse around imperialism became polemical, many political economists turned to development and to questions of underdevelopment and dependency and in the process sometimes skirted attention from fundamental issues of capitalism.

During the late 1970s and the 1980s, the discourse changed as authoritarian regimes collapsed, first in southern Europe and in the southern cone of South America where dictatorships had reigned, and, second, in Eastern Europe and the Soviet Union where bureaucratic socialist experiments succumbed. Even before these changes both the World Bank and the International Monetary Fund had come to exercise considerable control over struggling domestic economies in many parts of the world. Accompanying the political openings most nations turned away from possible solutions to build autonomous capitalist or socialist development from within and moved toward the world economy by divesting the state of public enterprise and opening up trade to the outside world. During the 1990s the language of development and imperialism began to assimilate the term *globalization* to express the pervasive and expansive world economy, but fundamentally the principal concern was with capitalism and its impact. Whether we examine transnational or multinational corporations, international political economy, or finance capital, it is important to recognize that the world economy and the global system are inherently capitalist, and have been so at least since Marx's time.[1]

This volume departs from this assumption, and this introduction seeks to guide the reader into the essays that follow. They cluster in three major ways. First, the bulk of them review the literature on imperialism and reinterpret its contemporary importance in understanding world historical developments since the nineteenth century. Second, several essays critically assess how capitalism is a foundation for both imperialist and development theory. Third, some essays delve into contemporary issues of imperialism and look at and critically assess alternative theoretical formulations such as globalization.

**Imperialism, Its Historical Legacy and Contemporary Significance**

*Imperialism* derives from the Latin word *imperator*, which connotated autocratic power and centralized government. In its broad meaning, *imperialism* involves "the domination by one country or group of people over others in ways that benefit the former usually at the expense of the latter" (Griffin and Gurley, 1985: 1091). Imperialism during Roman times reinforced the traditional local ruling hierarchies, while modern imperialism generated a new basis of power among subject populations. In France, for example, during the 1830s imperialism was associated with those who wished to restore the Napoleonic Empire, and after 1848 it was used pejoratively to describe the pretensions of Napoleon Bonaparte. During the 1870s it was employed as a characterization of the practices of expanding British colonialism, and by the end of the century it was commonplace in descriptions of the dominance of one nation over another (Cohen, 1973: 10–11).

The traditional or old meaning of *imperialism* was tied to mercantile capitalism and the early phase of industrial capitalism. Imperialism under early mercantilism was based, from about 1500 to 1800, on the dominance of Spain, with its control of precious metals in South America, and to a lesser extent, Portugal, through its commercial points of contact in Africa, Asia, and Latin America and its trade in spices, slaves, and ivory. The Portuguese hegemony succumbed largely to Spain during the late sixteenth and early seventeenth centuries when the monarchies were unified under Spanish control. As Spain and Portugal lost control over maritime traffic, the Dutch, then the English, and finally the French expanded their influence as slaves moved from Africa to the Americas, sugar from the Americas to Europe, and manufactured goods from Europe to Africa.

This old imperialism was supplanted by an understanding of the new imperialism, usually referring to the intense rivalry of the advanced European nations, symbolized in the scramble for Africa and the Berlin Conference of 1885 but more conspicuous at the turn of this century. Some of the problems evident in this transition include the link between industrial capitalism of the late eighteenth century in Britain and primitive accumulation; the division of labor between primary-producing underdeveloped states and industrialized states; the cause of U.S. and European expansion at the end of the nineteenth century; the origin of export capital from Europe; the role of the large firm as an accumulator of capital and the impact on imperialism; the relationship of neocolonialism and the old colonialism; and the similarity of Soviet imperialism to capitalist imperialism (Barratt Brown, 1974).

This historical context and the various interpretations provide a backdrop for some of the now classical conceptualizations of imperialism. The major thinkers include the following:

J.A. Hobson, the English liberal who emphasized underconsumptionism as an explanation.
Rudolf Hilferding, the Austrian Marxist economist who elaborated on finance capital.
Nicolai Bukharin, the Russian Marxist theorist who linked accumulation to world capitalism.
Karl Kautsky, the Marxist theoretician who advocated a theory of ultra-imperialism and envisioned a peaceful resolution through progressive capitalism.
V. I. Lenin, the Russian Marxist and revolutionary who stressed monopoly capital.
Rosa Luxemburg, a German Marxist who analyzed accumulation in the hinterland.
Joseph Schumpeter, an economist who envisioned the withering away of imperialism with the advance of industrial capitalism.

All these thinkers were antiimperialist, but they differed in their views of capitalism and socialism. Lenin, influenced by Hobson, and sharing with Hilferding and Bukharin what has become characterized as a classical Marxist understanding of imperialism, emphasized the merger of industrial and bank capital into finance capital, the expansion of capital exports, and the increase in military production and militarism. Although their perspectives differed in other respects, Hobson, Kautsky, and Shumpeter all envisioned the containment and eventual eroding away of imperialism through either reform or the natural evolution of the capitalist system, whereas the others employed an analysis critical of capitalism and favoring a socialist outcome as a means of eradicating imperialism altogether.

Four of the essays in this volume retrospectively examine the nature and impact of imperialism upon the world order, especially in the late nineteenth and twentieth centuries. A brief summary of their respective positions may help to guide the reader into theoretical and practical issues around the experience of imperialism.

The essay by Gregory Nowell turns to a critical assessment and a moderate defense of Hobson, an early writer on imperialism about whom Nowell has written extensively elsewhere. He delves into the logic of Hobsonian imperialism and suggests this concept is useful for understanding capitalism in the past and in the present. A principal attention is the notion of underconsumption, which Hobson used as a basis for his argument that England desist from its imperial exploits abroad and instead concentrate on building a market at home to consume any excess of commodity production. Nowell elaborates on insights as well as problems in both the economic and political Hobsonian conception. He evaluates the objections to Hobson, as drawn out in the criticisms of Nemmers, Gallagher and Robinson, Edelstein, and Fieldhouse. Here he sets the framework for a defense of Hobson, and he argues for a post-Hobsonian view involving "a demand-enhancing effect to a military complex" as well as a "lack of correlation between territories acquired and the economic incentives to acquire them." Further, he suggests that cartelization combined with free trade and banking concentration in Great Britain may have undermined domestic investment. He goes on to suggest that writers like Giovani Arrighi and Immanuel Wallerstein successfully transcended the Hobsoniam imperialist model and also that both the Keynesian and Neo-Keynsian traditions were able to transcend the Hobsonian theory of underconsumption.

Author of many past works on imperialism, Michael Barratt Brown offers a retrospective on his earlier thinking. He reaffirms his view of imperialism as an expansion of industrial capitalism throughout the world, seeing it as an extension of the competitive process of accumulation of industrial capital. This imperialism took two forms, with European groups within and outside Europe building their own systems of capital accumulation and with dependent European colonies providing raw materials for Europe. Whereas some Europeans in the United States and in the British dominions began as settlers and freed themselves for independent accumulation of capital, capitalism in the Third World was largely in the form of merchant capitalism, mixed with precapitalist, feudal, or semifeudal formations.

Turning to criticism of his own extensive work on imperialism and to the rise and fall of development studies in general, Barratt Brown reaffirms that his earlier judgments were by and large valid. First, empire and imperialism were primarily responses to economic questions, although he acknowledges that he might have more adequately dealt with the social and cultural impacts of empire, as illustrated in writers such as Basil Davidson, who did address the impact of colonialism upon

African culture, for example. Second, geographical explanations for imperialism can be based on social, economic, and political development of resources, and account for the rise of Europe and the decline of Africa. In answer to the question of why European and not Asian differences in agriculture were especially important, with the irrigated river agriculture of Asia resulting in highly centralized power and the need to defend against nomadic invasion, which interfered with development, and the rain-fed agriculture of Europe resulting in decentralized economic power and facilitation of economic development. Third, the competitive struggle among national enterprises was essential, and, together with state support, constituted the foundation for the new imperialism in the late nineteenth century. Here he attempts to disprove the thesis that the British empire after 1860 was the result of the power and pressure of commercial and not of industrial capital. He also contends with the view that "a gentlemanly capitalism" in the nineteenth century was the consequence of a smooth transition from an earlier merchant and landowning oligarchy to an elite of finance capital. Finally, he notes the continuity of imperialism in post-1940s development and exploitation of former colonial peoples, based on the perpetuation of colonial trading relationship and regimes supported by the rise of elites of trading or landowning families in the former colonies, which ensured the supply of raw materials for the industries of the former colonial powers. Here he delves into corruption, direct forms of economic exploitation, and foreign debt. He concludes that capitalist development has caused more damage than benefit to its beneficiaries. History is not at an end, and new systems of production and distribution (other than capitalism) must be found if life on earth is to continue. Further, the peoples of the South were held back by the imperialist process, but the peoples of the North did not necessarily gain. Economic advances came largely from their own labor productivity and extension of industrial capitalism rather than in retarding development in the colonies. He sees some improvement in human development everywhere despite the inequalities brought about through imperialism, and new powerful forces are evolving not only to raise consciousness of injustice but to seek sustainable growth and find alternative forms of trade based on equal exchange.

The interpretative overview of imperialism offered by Michael Howard and J.E. King begins with Marx and his original rough formulation around the notion that coercion complements capitalist accumulation, turns to classical imperialism and monopolization of capital and the drive for hegemonic stability, and concludes with attention to the neo-Marxists André Gunder Frank and Paul Baran who offered, "a novel turn" and "an important advance" over earlier conceptions of imperialism by focusing on the interactions between core and periphery. Howard and King suggest that these advances exposed some of the erroneous assumptions in Marx's vision, but they also go on to criticize the neo-Marxists as well, especially their failure to analyze the Soviet mode of production or their preference for autonomous development along Soviet lines. Despite these lapses, Howard and King end with reference to differences, tensions, even violent conflicts rather than the assumed integration and unification that appears underway today, and they suggest that a "new classic era of imperialism and a continuation of neoimperialism cannot be readily dismissed as a dystopian fantasy."

In his historical overview and reassessment of theories of imperialism, Anthony Brewer addresses three major questions: why Europe was able to gain a dominant position and why it imposed a colonial form over territory that was ethnically and culturally different from Europe; to what extent the impacts of empire were responsible for differences in wealth between different parts of the world; and given the collapse of colonial empires, what remains of imperialism today. In answering these questions, he focuses on the British experience in particular. He looks at gains and losses in the imperial experience, and he suggests that while colonialism may have excluded the colonies from the benefits of technological advances, the former imperialist powers did not become wealthy simply because they were imperialist. His assessment of impacts is somewhat ambivalent as he questions the evidence supporting the view that imperialism was progressive, and he seems to lean in the direction that the colonies suffered because the benefits of modernity did not reach them in most cases, although the benefits of technological development were apparent in some cases. The fall of empire, he believes, was due to the fragility of the imperial presence and the cost of maintaining imperialism, along with the independence struggles and the drive for nation-state and democracy. The post-independence period was not accompanied by mitigation of the gap between rich and poor countries in the world economy. There is little evidence, he claims, that the world economy is slanted against the poorer countries. He is unwilling to position himself alongside the view that it is unclear what might have happened in the Third World in the absence of imperialism: "All the evidence suggests that the long-run effect of empire on the development of the imperialist centers was small." What is new today is that the world economy is fully capitalist, much like Europe was early in the century. Despite the brutality of imperialism, unevenness in development, and setbacks and crises, it is also clear that the backward areas are able to catch up to the advances of Europe.

**Imperialism and Development Theory**

Past ideas and theories about imperialism, some of them dating to the nineteenth century, recyle and reappear in attention given to development and underdevelopment after the Second World War. Scanty evidence for this proposition runs through the historical literature, and few contemporary writers explicitly search for earlier ideas and build theory on past debates.

An exception to this practice, an overview by Anthony Brewer (1990), builds on the earlier theoretical contributions of the classical thinkers, links imperialism to the developmental literature, and traces the evolution of development-underdevelopment theory after the Second World War. Brewer effectively illustrates these themes through a look at the ideas and contributions of particular Marxist thinkers, including Marx, Luxemburg, Hobson, Hilferding, Bukharin, and Lenin among the classical thinkers, and Baran, Frank, Amin, Wallerstein, Emmanuel, and Rey among contemporary thinkers.

Giovanni Arrighi also contributes to an understanding of ties between theories of imperialism and development. He has explored the limits and ambiguities of the imperialism in the thought of J. A. Hobson and attempted to reconstruct the term through an examination of Lenin (Arrighi, 1978 and 1983). More recently, he delved into the rise and decline of dominant states over the past seven hundred years, drawing on the proposition that finance capital is not necessarily a particular stage of world capitalism, as Hilferding, Lenin, and others had claimed, but in fact it is an ever-persistent and recurring phenomenon that has characterized capitalism from its beginnings in medieval times to contemporary times. Rather than confining his analysis to the more traditional conceptualization of the twentieth century, Arrighi recasts his historical overview to incorporate a historical analysis of the strategies and successes and declines of Genoa, Holland, Great Britain, and the United States. His synthesis and analytical overview awaken the reader to rethink historical development over a lengthy period of history and a series of case studies of developmental rise and decline (Arrighi, 1994).

Among other writings that lend credence to our proposition around the link between imperialism and development, Prabhat Patnaik (1995b) questioned what had become of imperialism in essays on both imperialism and development. Writing from a somewhat orthodox Marxist perspective, Bill Warren (1980) has stressed the need for an expansion of imperialism and advocated penetration of a progressive capitalism into backward areas and the imposition of the capitalist mode of production on precapitalist or early capitalist areas.

During the decades of the sixties and seventies, intellectuals in the Third World and especially in Africa and Latin America worked out perspectives that moved away from the prevailing eurocentricity that reflected many views on imperialism and Western dominance. Among the many innovative contributions of past theory, first, the early studies, especially the work of Paul Baran (1957), which tended to focus on conditions of backwardness, inequality, exploitation, and underdevelopment and to challenge traditional conservative and radical interpretations by emphasizing the role of capitalism rather than relying upon the interpretation of feudalism and dual society (Stern, 1988). Theory benefited from innovative questioning of late capitalism and the problems of development and underdevelopment. Two thinkers who departed from imperialism were Ruy Mauro Marini (1978), who worked out a theory of subimperialism, based on the expansionist plans and actions of the Brazilian military during the dictatorship in the 1964–1985 period; and Fernando Henrique Cardoso (1972), who derived his notion of associated dependent capitalist development in part from a reading of Lenin (Palma, 1978, delves into Lenin's thought in search for the roots of a theory of underdevelopment).

Other historical considerations may be helpful in understanding the theoretical relationship of imperialism to development. First, identification of historical stages may be helfpul. Traditionally the old meaning of imperialism was related to mercantile capitalism and the early phase of industrial capitalism. Harry Magdoff (1969 and 1978) divided it into three periods: from the late 1400s to the mid 1600s, an era when Europe exploited the resources of newly discovered regions; 1650 to 1770, a period of slave labor and search for commodities on behalf of the leading European powers; and 1770 to about 1870 when England turned to Africa and Asia after losing its American colonies. The old meaning, however, was eclipsed by an understanding of the new imperialism at the time of intense rivalry among advanced European nations in the scramble for Africa at the end of the nineteenth century.

The new imperialism signified a shift from dominance over trade to control of industrial transformation associated with the industrial revolution and the push of Europe toward manufacturing, which necessitated extraction of raw materials in the periphery and expansion of the world market. The early phase of the new imperialism involved primarily Great Britain and eventually the United States as dominant powers. A later phase, at the end of the Second World War, was signified by the rise of transnational and multinational corporations, whose influence extended beyond the national borders of the dominant nations.

A similar periodization occasionally appears in the developmental literature. For example, Theotônio dos Santos elaborated on a somewhat comparable schema based on historical forms of dependency: colonial dependency when trade monopolies were established over the land, mines, and labor of colonial societies; financial industrial dependency that accompanied the period of imperialism at the end of the nineteenth century and allowed the domination of big capital in the hegemonic centers and its expansion abroad; a new type of dependency that appeared after the Second World War when capital investment by multinational corporations and industry turned to the internal markets of underdeveloped countries. He described this new dependency as conditioned by the relationship of dominant to dependent countries so that the expansion of the dominant country could have a positive or negative impact on the development of the dependent one (Dos Santos, 1970).

Second, structural dichotomies appear within imperialist and development theories: political (metropole and satellite), geographical (core and periphery), and economic (development and underdevelopment). The characterization of metropole and satellite is rampant in the early literature on colonialism and imperialism, with *colony* usually substituted for *satellite* as terminology. This language is in Hobson, Lenin, and most writers of imperialism, and it was picked up by André Gunder Frank in his interpretation of backwardness in many parts of the world as a consequence of capitalist development of underdevelopment (1966). Frank argued that the contradictions of capitalism led to the expropriation of economic surplus, which generated development in the metropolitan centers and underdevelopment in the peripheral satellites. The thesis has much in common with the impact of capital accumulation and imperialism on primitive and noncapitalist economies, as analyzed by Rosa Luxemburg, but clearly it derived from Paul Baran's classic study, which influenced Latin American intellectuals and others to elaborate on what he called the morphology of backwardness and to produce a plethora of writing on dependency and underevelopment. Baran concluded that "the colonial and dependent countries had no recourse to such sources of primary accumulation of capital as were available to the advanced capitalist countries" and that "development in the age of monopoly capitalism and imperialism faced obstacles that had little in common with those encountered two or three hundred years ago" (1957: 16). This idea became the basis of a series of important regional studies by Frank (1967) on Latin America, Walter Rodney (1974) on Africa, Malcolm Caldwell (1977) on Asia, and Manning Marable (1983) on Black America.

The language of metropole and satellite underlies the eclectic theory worked out by Mexican political sociologist, Pablo González Casanova (1969). Internal colonialism involved dominant and marginal groups within a single society. His theory discounted external imperialism because Mexico had asserted its autonomy from foreign control with the nationalization of foreign oil interests in 1938, but it recognized that domination of capital was evident internally, as represented by the monopoly of the ruling metropole in Mexico City over the marginalized Indian communities. The underdevelopment of the marginal satellites was the consequence of their exploitation by and dependence on the developing metropole. During the 1960s and 1970s this idea was also applied by U.S. scholars to backward conditions in North American ghettos and barrios.

Gradually the older language of *metropole* and *satellite* or *colony* evolved into *core* and *periphery*, the commonplace contemporary terminology in distinguishing advanced industrial nations from less-developed and poor nations struggling in the Third World. These structural distinctions were incorporated in a shift from external to internal emphasis, in particular among Latin American intellectuals, who adopted the new language and shifted from the traditional preoccupation with imperialism to a concern with capitalism and its devastation. For example, economist Raúl Prebisch was one of the first to turn attention from the advanced capitalist nations and to divide the world into a center and periphery. His approach is usually referred to as inward-directed development, suggesting the possibility of warding off foreign capital and implementing autonomous or domestic capitalist development through the imposition of tariff barriers, building of an infrastructure for the local economy, and import substitution to stimulate production. The colonial historian, Sergio Bagú, developed his ideas through lectures in the United States from 1944 to 1946. He emphasized that Europe dominated international markets and shaped the structure of colonial economies in a dependent relationship. In 1947 law professor Silvio Frondizi began to focus on dependency and underdevelopment in elaborating on the impact on Argentina of two imperialisms, British commercial imperialism and U.S. industrial imperialism.

A third historical consideration arises from the plethora of literature concerned with the international implications of unequal or uneven development. In his dissection of capitalism Marx observed discrepancies in the developmental process. In his analysis of Russia during the late nineteenth century, Lenin (1899) found evidence of capitalism alongside feudalism, and later in his treatise on imperialism (1916) he elaborated on monopoly as the highest stage of capitalism. Drawing upon the thought of classical political economy, Samir Amin in his ambitious study of world accumulation (1974) envisioned the world as comprised of developed and underdeveloped societies, some of which were capitalist and others socialist, yet all of them integrated into a commercial and financial capitalist network on a world-scale. Later Amin (1976) analyzed unequal development in terms of disarticulation of different sectors of an economy, domination from the outside, and dependence caused by large foreign industrial business. Other writers also employed similar terminology, including Arrighi Emmanuel (1972a) whose theory of unequal exchange and imperialism portrayed capitalist production relations as penetrating a world economy whose units are distinguished by differences in specialization in the international division of labor and by unequal wage levels. Ernest Mandel presented a theory of late capitalism (1975) based on the consequence of an integrated international system necessitating the transfer of surplus from underdeveloped to industrialized. His thought adhered to the Trotskyist theory of combined and uneven development, arguing that the most backward and the most modern forms of economic activity and exploitation are found in variable forms in different countries, but they may be linked or combined in their development, especially under the impact of imperialism. A combined and uneven social formation could be evident in the period of transition from a precapitalist to a full capitalist economy so that elements of feudalism and capitalism might coexist.

Finally, the use of *center* or *metropole* and *periphery* or *satellite* in these theoretical formulations was usually associated with an emphasis on market and relations of exchange rather than production, and most assumed that capitalism rather than feudalism or other precapitalist social formations had predominated in the periphery since the colonial period. Usually they were distinguishable by their allegiances, either (in the case of Prebisch) to a peaceful path through reformist capitalism or (in the case of Frank) to a revolutionary path toward socialism. Another difference appeared in writings arguing that lack of development was attributable to underconsumptionism, an idea emanating early on in Hobson and emulated in many writings focused on market and commercial considerations, for example Frank in his reliance upon mercantile capitalism to demonstrate its underdevelopment of peripheral areas or Paul Sweezy, who combined critical assessments of imperialism with capitalist development and was accused of assimilating underconsumption into his argument (Brenner, 1977). Those advocating a revolutionary path also tended to replicate past debates based on idealistic assumptions that projected the possibility of skipping the capitalist stage altogether enroute to socialism (for example, the Russian Noradniks during the late nineteenth century).

Some authors in the present volume draw on these similarities in their attention to imperialism and development. John Willoughby, for example, reviews early contributions to theories of capitalist development, beginning with Adam Smith, Ricardo, and other classical thinkers, and moving on to the thinking of Marx, Lenin, and Luxembourg, distinguishing their differing perspectives and suggesting how they influenced early dependency theory. Much of the essay focuses on Marx's attention to coercion in the promotion of capitalism and to Lenin's concern with exploitation in his theoretical and empirical work on Russia. In his attention to early Marxian discussion of the capitalist development process, Willoughby, sets out to discover old traditions that pose issues in new and creative ways. While there are many theoretical advances today, it is also clear that the thought of the early revolutionaries continues to shape many of the criticisms and debates confronting development economics during contemporary times.

With critical attention to the theme of Euro-Marxism, James Blaut systematically explores prevailing thinking on a number of issues essential to understanding problems of development everywhere. He identifies two fundamental thrusts, one emanating from diffusionist European interpretations and the other the nondiffusionist and Marxist school. The former gives priority to Europe in historical progress and to European influence on the non–European world; the latter opposes these preferences. Blaut shows how the diffusionist current remains influential with its emphasis after the Second World War being in the form of modernization theory. He delves into various models of Eurocentric and diffusionist theory in contemporary Marxism, and he demonstrates the strong European bias through examination of particular theorists and critics. In a section on colonialism he draws out the opposing views and shows how "Euro-Marxists tend either to support, or to have mixed feelings about, colonialism, the most catastrophic diffusion process of modern times." His ensuing discussion contrasts globalization with imperialism. He criticizes the globalization perspective for viewing the Third World as precapitalist and the beneficiary of industrialization and modernization along with the concomitant improvement of people's living conditions when in fact very little material development has occurred: "Genuine industrialization is emerging in very few regions." However, the Marxist theory of imperialism offers a radically different view and sees capitalism as destructive. Scholars of imperialism see globalization an neocolonialism and capitalism as having become global long ago but along with increasing immiseration. His analysis shows that Eurocentrism in Marxist theory must be eradicated, so that Marxism can become more significant in understanding capitalism and its impacts.

In his review of the waves of imperialist theory, Ronaldo Munck critically assesses the limitations of dependency. His essay examines imperialism, the interlude of dependency and its impasses, and the rise of globalization. He characterizes imperialism as modernization theory, and dependency as strongly stagnationist. He proceeds to a deconstruction of dependency by focusing on its reformist, radical, and post-developmental tendencies, and he offers ideas useful for the search to elaborate a new theory of imperialism. He shows how the ideas of Latin American intellectuals represented "one of the most significant interventions of a Third World discourse in a Western paradigm in the whole post-colonial era." He identifies a typology of views in the dependency approach: reformist along lines of economists Celso Furtado and Osvaldo Sunkel, radical in the thought of Theotônio dos Santos and Ruy Mauro Marini, and methodological in the historical-structural analysis of Fernando Henrique Cardoso. His review of globalization suggests it's "conceptual inflation" equal to that of dependency in the past. He considers it a "poor guide for critical analysis of the world around us" but possibly useful in understanding "the current phase of imperialism." He offers ideas useful for the search to elaborate a new theory of imperialism and sees the possibility of resistance to globalization leading to some empowerment of opposition forces. He suggests closer attention to the cultural implications of globalization and the formulation of a post-dependency model, with attention to social movements, feminism, and alternative development strategies. He even envisions the possibility of a renewal of a dependency whose spirit carries on in potentially creative ways.

**Imperialism or Globalization?**

Efforts in recent years to transcend a theory of imperialism have stirred up debate and sometimes obscured attention to imperialism altogether. In an effort to clear up some of the confusion, I now briefly discuss and critically assess four theories that focus on the international implications of capitalism: world systems, internationalization of capital, post-imperialism, and globalization.

The first of these theories, world systems, was influenced by the French historian, Fernand Braudel, and his well-known work, *Civilisation matérielle, économie et capitalisme* (1979), which deals with historical development of capitalism from the fifteenth to nineteenth centuries. Modeling his activities after Braudel, Immanuel Wallerstein defined the world system in terms of a core area (Northwestern Europe with its highly skilled labor in agricultural production), a periphery (Eastern Europe and the early Western Hemisphere with its slavery and coerced cash-crop labor and exports of grains, cotton, sugar, and so on), and a semi-periphery (Mediterranean Europe with its agricultural sharecropping). These three categories (core, periphery, semiperiphery) thus represent three paths toward capitalist development. In his four-volume work, *The Modern World-System* (1974 and later), Wallerstein relates this historical development to a network of exchange relations in which surplus tends to be transferred from periphery to core, but it is conceptualized in terms of the world system as a whole rather than its particular parts and internal structure. Wallerstein set out to explore the early roots of capitalism, its transition from feudalism, and its evolution. In personal communication he explained his theory as being neither Marxist nor influenced by dependency theory. It is presented as unrelated to Marx or Lenin, and imperialism is not a principal concern, but systems theory seems to be an effort to transcend earlier ideas with a new conceptualization. The idea of world system has been criticized on many levels, in particular by Brenner (1977) for the implication that the transition from feudalism to capitalism was smooth and linear, but overall it has also had significant impact on historical and social analysis to the extent that not only a school but a massive body of work on world systems is available in books and in the quarterly, *Review*, edited by Wallerstein.

A second body of theory, known as internationalization of capital, was elaborated by Christian Palloix in *L'Internalisation du capital* (1975). Palloix extended the categories of Marx's capital so as to pemit an analysis of the movement of capital and class struggle on an international level. Concepts such as international valorization, modes of international accumulation of capital, an internationalization of the productive and financial system become relevant. Much of the emphasis in this approach is on the progressive aspects of capitalism, also a concern of Bill Warren, who argued (1980) that Lenin had distorted the Marxist assumption that capitalism could move forward in precapitalist countries. He believed that theories of underdevelopment were simply postwar versions of Lenin's earlier treatment of imperialism and ideas emanating from Third World nationalists and revolutionaries. Warren believed that the prospects for capitalist development in many underdeveloped countries were favorable, both in capitalist agriculture and industry. The concern of Warren with imperialism is less tied to the thinkers of imperialism and their ideas after Marx than to Marx and the progressive nature of capitalism, which will eventually spread and transform relations of production everywhere.

Yet a third effort at theory is embodied in an effort to move beyond imperialist and dependency explanations of capitalist underdevelopment in the direction of a post-imperialism. Becker et al. (1987) argued that global institutions tend to promote the integration of diverse national interests on a new international basis by offering access to capital resources and technologies; this necessitates the location of both foreign labor and management in the dependent country as well as local participation in the ownership of the corporation. In such a situation two segments of a new social class appear: privileged nationals or a managerial bourgeoisie and the foreign nationals who manage the businesses and transnational organizations. This coalescing of dominant class elements across national boundaries suggests the rise of an international oligarchy. A theory of post-imperialism serves as an alternative to a determinist Leninist understanding of imperialism and to dependency orthodoxy, according to Becker. However, international capital has dominated situations in the Third World, and there is little evidence to affirm that a managerial national bourgeoisie will emerge as hegemonic or that other classes will decline or that the national bourgeoisie will favor democracy or authoritarianism.

Finally, debate around the idea of globalization has directed attention away from imperialism and left the general impression that the rapidly advancing capitalist world is emerging unified and harmonious. The debate has evolved in popular and progressive periodicals, for example, *Z Magazine* (see Herman, 1997) and in the independent socialist *Monthly Review* (see Piven and Cloward, 1998, and Tabb, 1997) and also is examined in William Robinson's (1996) look at globalization and hegemony. The attention to globalization, like other attempts to innovate and move in new directions, tends to obsure attention to imperialism. In the present volume, Samir Amin and James Petras confront this dilemma.

Affirming that globalism dates to ancient times and its form is driven by class struggles, Amin shows how the term is neither linked to the logic of capitalism nor to imperialism. In ancient times globalization provided opportunity for backward regions to catch up with advanced ones. During modern times, in contrast, globalization means expanding and polarizing capitalism to promote inequality. He argues that globalization is "an ideological discourse used to legitimize the strategies of imperialist capital." That is, imperialism is detached from its earlier colonial form, and imperialist conflict appears to have faded away as the United States emerges as a kind of superimperialist power. The present system, he goes on, is largely based on finance capital, in both its national and global dimensions. Dominant capital seeks to implement similar policies everywhere in order to reduce social expenditures, divest the state of many of its activities, and benefit the wealthy. While manifesting a deep resentment to these current capitalist practices, Amin despairs socialist thought that shares in the illusion of a way out within capitalism.

He believes that this description of globalism is nothing less than imperialism, envisioned as the highest phase and a permanent feature of capitalism. He sees the push of dominant class neoliberalism as ultimately undermining regional organizations and unity and provoking a growing protest among the popular classes. He goes on to identify five monopolies that "shape the polarizing globalization of contemporary imperialism": new technologies, financial flows, natural resources, communication and media, and weapons of mass destruction.

Amin sees this model of globalization as fragile, and the inhuman conditions that impact people everywhere will inevitably spur on fronts of popular struggle against monopolies and imperialism. These movements will evolve through a progressive nationalism willing to promote regional cooperation opposed to the dominant powers. All this constitutes what he calls 'an authentic polycentric world" that imposes on capital the adjustments necessary to meet human requirements in a lengthy transition from global capitalism to global socialism.

These sentiments are also expressed by Prabhat Patnaik who notes that Marx wrote separately on colonialism and external conquest and did not link this with his lifetime of theoretical analysis of capitalism viewed as if it were a closed system. He takes exception with the "bourgeois internationalist" perspective that conceptualizes a dual economy of progressive metropolitan capitalism as distinct from backward internal precapitalist structures. Instead he understands these two sectors as one integrated whole. Like Petras and others he contests the notion that globalism is a manifestation of progressive capitalism that somehow will resolve the inequalities of much of the contemporary world and bring harmony. He delves into the consequences of globalism, its tendency to be divisive and break up the integrity of each nation and region. He calls for resistance to "bourgeois internationalism" through progressive forces struggling for a democratic national agenda in the Third World.

James Petras deals with the popular notion that globalization implies that a new world order has replaced the flows of capital, trade and investment, institutions, and power historically associated with the nation-state. In his concern with globalization theories, Petras poses the notion of imperialism as a traditional means to contextualize the flows of capital and locating the dynamics of capitalism in a setting of unequal power between conflicting states, classes, and markets. He critically assesses the basic premises of the globalization theorists, disclaiming its promise as an innovative development and a theory imbued with explanatory power. He shows that globalization theory serves an ideological rationalization for class inequalities and for obscuring many realities of the present world. Specifically, he highlights the analytical weaknesses of the concept globalization and the strengths of imperialism as he compares and contrasts the utility of such terms as *power, agency, class inequalities, flows of income and investment.*

He sees globalization as an imperial and a class phenomenon. Its advocates are the agrobusiness and financial classes, importers, mineral exporters, large manufacturers or sweatshop owners, with support from a subordinate group of high-level state functionaries, academics, and publicists; and the commercial classes also advocate globalist free trade. Its adversaries include the peasant and working class movements. Thus, the definition of a globalist policy is based on the centrality of class struggle.

Petras goes on to compare past and present globalism. Globalism, he feels was more significant in the past during periods when export classes predominated, such as during the sixteenth and seventeenth centuries in the relationships between imperialist centers and the newly colonized countries. The major difference between past and present is that contemporary capitalism has spread everywhere and prevails as the single economic system. Further, a new feature of globalism today is the greater volume of capital flow, transfers of wealth across boundaries, large organizational networks, the transmission of information, and the deepening and extension of the international division of labor. He debunks the notion of the inevitability and continuity of globalism. Its advocates, he believes, fall back on technological determinism and fail to recognize past contradictions, especially the "demise of globalist expansion in the past."

His extensive rebuttal takes us through a multitude of premises of the globalization thesis, and then ends with attention to the resistance to globalization, observed in a variety of social forces that begin in defense of rights and interests threatened by the globalist ruling classes. Thus, they protest the loss of employment, privatization of public enterprises, cuts in social security programs, pensions, and other social services, lessening of living standards, cutting of educational programs, and so on. These forces also combine in coalition with other environmental, gender, and ethnic struggles. He sees this resistance as a new alternative in the form of local projects of insurgent groups and movements in struggle. As such he sees them as different from nongovernmental organizations in that "they are part of a large political project of social transformation" in their confrontation with the globalist state and classes, and they are internally democratic and united in their struggle for a social economy that combines sustainable growth and economic democracy.

**Summing Up**

Howard and King question the homogenizing and harmonizing integration of the world order and see potential disruptions and a kind of new imperialism as a possibility in the future. Amin foresees a similar response to such a world order under the dominance of the United States and argues that unless there are accommodation and adjustments in favor of people everywhere and mitigation of inhuman conditions, movements of popular struggle will rise up against imperialism. Petras joins in exposing these contradictions. In this sense, they differ from the view of Brewer and Barratt Brown who see progressive tendencies in the historical process of imperialism.

While Howard and King critically tie the ideas of imperialism to many of the notions that evolved in development economics, questioning all of them in the process, other authors, notably Munck and Willoughby, accept some of the developmental ideas and at the same time link them to imperialist theory. Brewer and Barratt Brown locate their analysis in the British experience, albeit coming to quite different positions on major issues of imperialism, while Nowell in a favorable yet critical appraisal of Hobson, also departs essentially from a European perspective. Amin, Patnaik, Petras, and to some extent Munck, reflect Third World criticism of Eurocentric understandings tied to dominant ideological views of globalism. While a socialist outcome may be implied in most of the assessments in this volume, only Amin suggests the possibility of a historical transition from global capitalism to global socialism.

## Note

<sup></sup>

[1] This introductory essay complements some of my other work through which many of these themes run. Excerpts from the extensive writings of all these thinkers serve to show the reader different lines of political thinking around imperialism and the affinity of imperialism to capitalism itself. Returning to these early and traditional understandings, the reader can adequately cope with contemporary understandings of imperialism and further begin to note how the early debates on imperialism frequently reflect contemporary debates on developmental questions and issues. An expanded essay on imperialism and development is in Ronald H. Chilcote, Chapter 5, "Theories of Imperialism," *Theories of Comparative Political Economy* (Boulder: Westview Press, Forthcoming). A selection of previously published writings on imperialism and development is in a companion volume, Ronald H. Chilcote (ed.), *Imperialism*, Humanity Press (forthcoming).

# *PART I*

---

**IMPERIALISM: ITS LEGACY AND
CONTEMPORARY SIGNIFICANCE**

# PART II

# CHAPTER 1

## WHATEVER HAPPENED TO IMPERIALISM?

## M. C. Howard and J. E. King

### 1. Imperialisms

During the last two centuries the term *imperialism* appears in a wide variety of usages. Underlying this diversity, however, a common theme is evident. A reference to imperialism has signified processes through which distinct economies have been incorporated into overarching structures of power, thereby enhancing the integration of their disciplinary systems, resulting in their operating as a more coordinated whole. Typically, amalgamations occur on unequal terms involving unidirectional mechanisms of domination and subjugation, and usually *imperialism* becomes synonymous with the use of extra-economic coercion in international or intercultural relations (as distinct from its exercise in extending political control in circumstances of cultural homogeneity).

The economic analysis of imperialism has been confined largely to the work of Marxian theorists. Both classical and neoclassical economists have argued that the use of force brings deadweight losses — net costs for which there are no corresponding net benefits. Consequently, rational decisionmakers will recognize the superiority of contract as a means of acquisition because all parties may benefit more through voluntary exchange than violent conflict. Thus, while the reality of imperialism has rarely been denied, it has been widely thought to be outside the boundaries of orthodox economic analysis, which limits itself to the logic of rationally acquisitive action.[1] Schumpeter (1919) is, perhaps, the best known embodiment of this perspective, tracing imperialist expansion in the modern era to a tenacious feudal overhang. The idea still has a large following, even among radicals, but it has never been the predominant strand in Marxian political economy.[2]

Marxian theorists' principal concern has been to understand capitalist imperialism, not the imperialisms of other types of economic system. But since the dynamism of this mode of production has been historically unique, Marxists have altered their emphasis repeatedly. We classify the theories into three types — original, classical and neo — and critically review composite portraits of each in sections 2, 3, 4, and 5. The second and third are understandable products of the preceding theory and are, therefore, traceable back to Marx's original formulation. Moreover, all three contain enduring insights and in this minimal sense we can say that theories of imperialism exhibit intellectual progress. True, analysis has tended to lag behind events and could be charged with *ex post* rationalization. Yet this is a characteristic widely evident in all economic theory. Rarely do we find anywhere a reasoned conjecture put forward well in advance of the first appearance of those phenomena it can be used to explain. It is also difficult to devalue the economic importance of imperialism. No economist of any school has ever seriously denied that the gains from trade encourage ever wider integration. Nonetheless, imperialisms have contributed mightily to creating the differences in comparative advantage, scale economies, and institutional complexes that are commonly recognized to be the proximate causes of trade flows.

Marx's original analysis of imperialism focuses on the peculiarities of English colonization, but he views them as exemplifying a general, universalizing quality of capitalism. By hindsight, his ideas can be regarded as most relevant to *Pax Britannica*. With its erosion and the appearance of pronounced hostilities between advanced capitalist states, culminating in two world wars, Marx's original position becomes augmented (not jettisoned) by the formulation of classic theories of imperialism in Hilferding (1910), Bukharin (1915), and Lenin (1916a). All three stress the emergence of monopolization within developed national capitalisms, which is held responsible for altering the motive forces of imperialist aggression and their immediate targets. They wane in influence as Soviet-American bipolarity emerges and tensions between advanced capitalisms are tamed under *Pax Americana*, both phenomena being understandable outcomes of the classic era. Now the principal concern of Marxian theorists turns toward explaining the retarded transformative impact of capitalism in the Third World. The main thesis of Baran (1957) and Frank (1967) becomes the underdevelopment of the periphery, with exit from dependency on the world economy seen as a prerequisite for autonomous and rapid development. Both maintained that economic mechanisms alone cannot suffice to hold peripheral areas within capitalist circuits of exchange, and that large doses of extra-economic coercion are essential.

Dependency theory still retains adherents, but their ranks were depleted with waves of capitalist restructuring within the Third World after 1960, the stagnation of the Soviet economy in the 1970s, and its collapse in the 1980s. All three occurrences weakened the structures containing global capitalist expansion. New Marxian ideas have come to the fore to incorporate these seismic shifts, although we view them, along with their proponents such as Warren (1980) and Harris (1987), as a return to Marx. Since a great deal has been learned over the last century, contemporary theorists go beyond replicating ideas propounded in the 1850s. Nonetheless, Marx's main theme — that Western capitalism would create a world in its own image and generalize economic growth in doing so — takes on renewed vigor. The principal analytic problem becomes one of explaining how a fully capitalized world and, therefore, a less imperialist world, continues to exhibit properties that make Marxism relevant. We provide some of our own thoughts on this matter in Section 6.

## 2. Marx's Model of Capitalism

Marx treated modern imperialism in two forms. His analysis of the primitive accumulation of capital points to the role colonization played in the creation of capitalism as a mode of production in Western Europe, and principally in England. Once established, he argues, capitalist imperialism proper is an indispensable medium through which capitalist relations are spread beyond the initial heartlands. In both cases, what Marx says is intimately connected to his conception of those characteristics that constitute a capitalist economic system. Appreciating this point is fundamentally important, not only for assessing Marx's claims about imperialism, but also for evaluating the amendments, reversals, and elaborations they have inspired. Therefore we begin by outlining the model in terms of which the original theories of imperialism were formulated and, with changing emphases, many Marxists have thought subsequently.[3]

Five elements are definitive: impersonal markets, universal dependence on exchange, generalized acquisitiveness, rationalized organizations, and the insulation of economic activity from politics and culture. As we will explain shortly, it is the coexistence of these attributes that is critical to their growth-promoting capacity, but we begin by describing each separately before explaining how they interact.

First, in capitalism, productive enterprises typically produce for impersonal markets rather than operating under customary regulation for a local clientele, which has been the prevalent form of exchange throughout history. Impersonality need not imply that market relationships between buyers and sellers are fleeting, only that they are not integrally connected with kinship and communal ties, and that the main bond is the cash nexus. Thus people can easily form new contractual relationships if and when they deem it in their interests to do so. Second, the provision of inputs such as labor and land is marketized, along with that of produced goods and services. Contracts for inputs in exchange for wage payments and rents govern their allocation between different productive activities, and mobility between sectors encounters minimal natural and legal constraints. This implies, *inter alia*, that people depend on markets for meeting the bulk of their consumption needs, so that self-provisioning is insignificant. All this is in sharp contrast to bondage relationships, including slavery and serfdom, where laborers are legally tied to a lord or to land, or to both, and where many household requirements are met through home production or within small kinship networks. Third, the dominant motivation governing productive enterprises is the acquisition of wealth in the abstract, which is usually measured in monetary terms. Many types of precapitalist property owners were orientated, instead, toward the accumulation of a narrow subset of resources such as land or particular goods like horses, retainers, and palaces. In other words, productive enterprises in capitalism seek to maximize profits, and are relatively unconcerned with the actual commodities they buy and sell to do so. Fourth, in the pursuit of profits these productive establishments are rationally organized, rather than being circumscribed by traditional principles centered on family, kinship, and clientage. Profit maximization implies cost minimization, therefore, inputs are employed on the basis of their productivity, and combined together in efficient proportions. Market dependence and contractual relationships provide the flexibility that allows an alteration in the mix of factors of production, so as to facilitate adjustment to new opportunities for profit.

Finally, economic, political, and cultural organizations tend to be insulated from each other. In particular, the fusion of property ownership in land with public authority evident in feudal systems is absent, while churches lack the significant political influence and wealth typical of their position in precapitalist societies. Instead the state specializes in the exercise of political power, backed by a monopoly in the use of legitimate coercion, and does so by administering formal and predictable laws in accordance with liberal principles of justice. These specify the rights of various kinds of property owners, including workers, whose principal assets are capacities to perform different types of labor. Subject to some important qualifications, rights to exclusive control, benefit, and disposal, are legalized, so that those who do not own what they require have to gain access through market exchange based on contracts. Religious organizations are also regulated, and confined to propounding ideas and exacting rituals that have little autonomous significance for economic and political activities. However, it is important not to misunderstand this last characteristic of capitalism. There is a separation of spheres of activity in the sense that economic, political, and cultural functions are highly specialized, but this does not imply that they cease to affect each other. While acquisitiveness is the dominant economic force and is allowed free rein, the fact that people feel the need to infuse what they do with transcendental significance means that cultural ideas, including those of religion, will tend to harmonize with material interests. And the maintenance of liberal property rights is likely to require their legitimization through cultural sanctification and the minimization of political influence by those classes who do relatively badly in capitalist conditions. Thus claiming that political, economic, and cultural organizations are separated from each other does not imply the absence of cultural and political supports for capitalist economic activity, just as other types of economic systems are buttressed by noneconomic structures.

Such a system is highly peculiar when measured by the norms of history. It involves a strong but bounded political authority, well developed civil liberties but limits to popular influence, pronounced acquisitiveness but restrained hedonism and honest transacting. All this illuminates what has become very evident in the twentieth century: capitalist relations have proved to be markedly less exportable than most Marxists (and liberals) have believed. Nonetheless, this is a contentious matter to which we return in sections 3, 5, and 6. What is not disputable, though, is the capacity of capitalist institutions to facilitate economic growth. The historically unique form of acquisitiveness of capitalist enterprises provides the drive to develop productive power, and it does so in general, rather than concentrating advance in just a few sectors. This is strongly reinforced by competition between enterprises, and by the relatively open access to their control by those who can marshal the assets and accept the risks of the market environment, which is continually subject to innovation and technological change. Inventiveness is itself promoted by conditions of cognitive freedom; in particular no productively relevant knowledge can be inhibited by the charge of heresy, since religious organizations are politically weak. Moreover, any technical change that is widely adopted tends to be genuinely productive because economic activities are validated by market demands, and the costs of mistakes are concentrated upon those who undertake the wrong investments. Consequently, there is always a strong incentive for people to form their expectations rationally, taking into account all the relevant information currently available. At the same time, contractual freedom and market dependence provide the adaptabilities required for the rational organization of production in the light of the full array of available technologies. There are no legally enforceable distinctions of status in the form of caste, estate, and guild prohibitions that systematically limit the efficient combination of inputs. Liberal property rights support this arrangement even when the results might weaken social cohesion, and any democratic participation that could seriously threaten these rights is usually constrained by repression, ideological conditioning, and constitutional impediments. What Schumpeter (1942) called the "creative destruction" of rapid innovation becomes very evident as existing investments, and enduring relationships are destroyed economically by newer, more productive ones.

The five defining characteristics of capitalism thus form a syndrome of mutual support and reinforcement. Economic systems historically preceding capitalism lacked one or more of these characteristics, and Marx believed this to account for their general state of productive stagnation. When they did prove capable of raising productive power it was achieved only at a slow rate, and reversals occurred easily in the face of natural catastrophes, population increases, conservative action by political authorities, and the predacity of enemies. Capitalist systems are exceptional in exhibiting a sustained and pronounced tendency toward raising productivity, which has so far proved immune to any long-term retreat. Those readers who continue to doubt this will find the growth statistics presented in Tables 1 and 2 thoroughly puzzling.

### 3. The Original Marxian Account of Imperialism

Marx's account of primitive accumulation locates those historical events that engendered the commodification of labor and land in Western Europe, and which led to the accumulation of nonlanded property allowing the employment of labor and land under capitalist relations of production. He claims imperial conquest to be important, but makes it clear that colonization did not conform to capitalist principles of expansion. Instead tribute, pillage, and the creation of new bondage relationships typical of precapitalist forms of imperialism predominated. There is no inconsistency here because Marx's purpose is to focus on the origins of capitalism in Europe, not to explain either its functioning or its geographical spread once it is established. Nor does it matter much for understanding the modern world economy whether or not he was correct in what he said.[4] Clearly, given Marx's conception of capitalism in section 2, there must be powerful forces bringing about a break from the dominant structural relations of the past. And he explicitly limited his historical comments to the transition from feudalism to capitalism within Europe, denying them any universal relevance.[5]

By contrast, the validity or falsity of Marx's treatment of capitalist imperialism proper is of momentous importance. The following propositions form the core of his writings on this issue.[6] It is the general acquisitiveness of capitalism that propels geographic extension, rather than its own contradictions or particular conjunctural events. These may play a role in explaining capitalist imperialism but only with regard to its specific forms and precise chronology. Sometimes capitalism can enter into existing exchange relationships in precapitalist economies and, by its superior efficiency, transform them into capitalist exchange relations. More frequently, capitalist penetration is impeded or wholly blocked by the operation of precapitalist systems, and in these cases some form of imperial domination and forceful restructuring along capitalist lines is essential for expansion to succeed. In both circumstances the impact of capitalism will act ultimately as a solvent on established modes of production, as well as creating the basis for modernity — economic, cultural, and political. Destruction tends to precede reconstruction, not only for obvious reasons of sequencing but because imperialism initially exhibits many precapitalist features, reflecting the imperfect transformation of metropolitan centers, and these wither only as capitalism purifies on its home ground. Thus, while many of the phenomena associated with precapitalist forms of imperialism, including tribute and outright theft, remain evident for long periods, their significance for Marx is totally different from that in precapitalist imperialisms. Ultimately, as genuinely capitalist extensions to new territories is taking place, a duplication of European achievement will occur, including sustainable economic growth.

None of these forecasts are finely grained predictions, and analogues to the ideas of contemporary growth theory — absolute and conditional convergence, path dependent growth trajectories, growth clubs, differentiated sources of growth, and so forth — are absent from Marx's writings. Moreover, some of the relevant empirical evidence is difficult to interpret (as we comment upon more fully in section 5). But, this said, much of what has occurred in the last 150 years is consistent with Marx's expectations. The five characteristics he took to be definitive of capitalism, which we summarized in section 2, have both purified in the initial capitalist societies and spread widely beyond them.[7] They have also been associated with fast economic growth (measured by historical standards), as attested by Reynolds (1985) and the data reproduced in Tables 1 & 2. Other variables indicate that progress (in the Marxian sense) has been far-reaching, especially improvement in life expectancy, literacy and urbanization, and the decline in famines and plagues.[8] Inequalities between different areas of the globe remain staggeringly large, but for the most part they can be attributed to uneven development.

Nevertheless, even the most sympathetic reading of history is not wholly in accord with Marx's theory of imperialism. His most obvious failure lay in appreciating the diversity of precapitalist modes of production. Indian conditions were taken as paradigmatic, and what he believed to be the unchanging nature of Asiatic societies was generalized to all non–Europeans. This view was typical of nineteenth century European intellectuals and was neither conceptually coherent or empirically accurate.[9] These deficiencies, though, are of minor significance for Marx's theory of imperialism, since circumstances favorable to the endogenous development of capitalism outside of Western Europe appear to have been nonexistent or exceptionally weak, and virtually all noncapitalist forms of economy impeded transformation by peace-

**Table 1. Gross Domestic Product per Capita, 1820–1989 ($ at 1985 U.S. relative prices\*)**

|  | 1820 | 1870 | 1890 | 1913 | 1950 | 1973 | 1989 |
|---|---|---|---|---|---|---|---|
| *Panel A: Advanced Capitalist Economies* | | | | | | | |
| Austria | 1048 | 1442 | 1892 | 2683 | 2869 | 8697 | 12519 |
| Australia | 1250 | 3143 | 3949 | 4553 | 5970 | 10369 | 13538 |
| Belgium | 1025 | 2089 | 2654 | 3267 | 4229 | 9417 | 12875 |
| Canada | n.a. | 1330 | 1846 | 3515 | 6112 | 11835 | 17236 |
| Denmark | 980 | 1543 | 1944 | 3014 | 5227 | 10527 | 13822 |
| Finland | 639 | 933 | 1130 | 1727 | 3481 | 9073 | 14015 |
| France | 1059 | 1582 | 1955 | 2746 | 4176 | 10351 | 13952 |
| Germany | 902 | 1251 | 1660 | 2506 | 3295 | 10124 | 13752 |
| Italy | 965 | 1216 | 1352 | 2079 | 2840 | 8631 | 12989 |
| Japan | 609 | 640 | 842 | 1153 | 1620 | 9524 | 15336 |
| Netherlands | 1308 | 2065 | 2568 | 3179 | 4708 | 10271 | 12669 |
| Norway | 856 | 1190 | 1477 | 2079 | 4541 | 9347 | 15202 |
| Sweden | 1008 | 1401 | 1757 | 2607 | 5673 | 11362 | 14824 |
| UK | 1450 | 2693 | 3383 | 4152 | 5651 | 10079 | 13519 |
| USA | 1219 | 2244 | 3101 | 4846 | 8605 | 14093 | 18282 |
| *Panel B: Other European Countries* | | | | | | | |
| Greece | n.a. | n.a. | n.a. | 1211 | 1456 | 5781 | 7564 |
| Ireland | n.a. | n.a. | n.a. | 2003 | 2600 | 5248 | 8285 |
| Portugal | n.a. | 833 | 950 | 967 | 1608 | 5598 | 7387 |
| Spain | 900 | 1221 | 1355 | 2212 | 2405 | 7581 | 10881 |
| *Panel C: Latin American Countries* | | | | | | | |
| Argentina | n.a. | 1039 | 1515 | 2370 | 3112 | 4972 | 4080 |
| Brazil | 556 | 615 | 641 | 697 | 1434 | 3356 | 4402 |
| Chile | n.a. | n.a. | 1073 | 1735 | 3255 | 4281 | 5406 |
| Colombia | n.a. | n.a. | n.a. | 1078 | 1876 | 2996 | 3979 |
| Mexico | 584 | 700 | 762 | 1121 | 1594 | 3202 | 3728 |
| Peru | n.a. | n.a. | n.a. | 1099 | 1809 | 3160 | 2601 |
| *Panel D: Asian Countries* | | | | | | | |
| Bangladesh | n.a. | n.a. | n.a. | 519 | 463 | 391 | 551 |
| China | 497 | 497 | 526 | 557 | 454 | 1039 | 2538 |
| India | 490 | 490 | 521 | 559 | 502 | 719 | 1093 |
| Indonesia | 533 | 585 | 640 | 710 | 650 | 1056 | 1790 |
| Korea | n.a. | n.a. | 680 | 819 | 757 | 2404 | 6503 |
| Pakistan | n.a. | n.a. | n.a. | 611 | 545 | 823 | 1283 |
| Taiwan | n.a. | n.a. | 564 | 608 | 706 | 2803 | 7252 |
| Thailand | n.a. | 741 | 801 | 876 | 874 | 1794 | 4008 |

**Table 1.** *Continued*

|  | 1820 | 1870 | 1890 | 1913 | 1950 | 1973 | 1989 |
|---|---|---|---|---|---|---|---|
| *Panel E: African Countries* | | | | | | | |
| Cote d'Invoire | n.a. | n.a. | n.a. | n.a. | 888 | 1699 | 1401 |
| Ghana | n.a. | n.a. | n.a. | 484 | 733 | 724 | 575 |
| Kenya | n.a. | n.a. | n.a. | n.a. | 438 | 794 | 886 |
| Morocco | n.a. | n.a. | n.a. | n.a. | 1105 | 1293 | 1844 |
| Nigeria | n.a. | n.a. | n.a. | n.a. | 608 | 1040 | 823 |
| South Africa | n.a. | n.a. | n.a. | 2037 | 3204 | 5466 | 5627 |
| Tanzania | n.a. | n.a. | n.a. | n.a. | 334 | 578 | 463 |

Source: Maddison (1994), Table 2.1, p. 93.

Notes: n.a. denotes not available; * Computed in terms of 1985 U.S. dollars utilizing U.S. prices.

ful methods. Thus, even though Marx's understanding of the non–Western world was seriously flawed, the deficiencies fail to inflict serious damage on his claim that imperialism was a precondition for the universalization of capitalism.

Marx's underestimation of the complexity of conflict inherent in capitalist imperialism is a more serious deficiency. While he did not share in two great illusions of classical economic liberalism — that the use of force was premodern and unproductive — he did adhere to Cobdenite beliefs about the anachronism of large-scale violence in resolving disputes between advanced capitalisms. This explains why Marx theorized much more about capitalism than particular capitalisms, believing the spread of modernity to be an expression of a transnationalism rather than an internationalism. And he looked forward to the erosion of all forms of particularistic identity, including allegiances to national economic systems, national states, and national cultures. Ever deeper and wider integration would then follow essentially peaceful channels, and could dispense with all forms of imperialism once capitalist conditions became general.[10] Marx seems to have had no inkling that leading capitalist powers would turn the weapons of imperialism against one another. No doubt he was influenced by the relatively peaceful conditions of the "long nineteenth century," and he died before military rivalry became evident. Engels lived on, recognized it, and was horrified by the impending disaster of industrialized warfare.[11]

### 4. Classic Theories of Imperialism

While Marx's political economy failed to encompass the modern interstate system and, indeed, said little about capitalist states at all, the classic Marxian theorists of

**Table 2. Rate of Growth of GDP per Capita, 1820–1989 (Annual Average Percentage Compound Rates of Growth)**

| | 1820–1870 | 1870–1913 | 1913–1950 | 1950–1973 | 1973–1989 |
|---|---|---|---|---|---|
| *Panel A: Advanced Capitalist Economies* | | | | | |
| Austria | 0.6 | 1.5 | 0.2 | 4.9 | 2.3 |
| Australia | 1.9 | 0.9 | 0.7 | 2.4 | 1.7 |
| Belgium | 1.4 | 1.0 | 0.7 | 3.5 | 2.0 |
| Canada | n.a. | 2.3 | 1.5 | 2.9 | 2.4 |
| Denmark | 0.9 | 1.6 | 1.5 | 3.1 | 1.7 |
| Finland | 0.8 | 1.4 | 1.9 | 4.3 | 2.8 |
| France | 0.8 | 1.3 | 1.1 | 4.0 | 1.9 |
| Germany | 0.7 | 1.6 | 0.7 | 5.0 | 1.9 |
| Italy | 0.4 | 1.3 | 0.8 | 5.0 | 2.6 |
| Japan | 0.1 | 1.4 | 0.9 | 8.0 | 3.0 |
| Netherlands | 0.9 | 1.0 | 1.1 | 3.4 | 1.3 |
| Norway | 0.7 | 1.3 | 2.1 | 3.2 | 3.1 |
| Sweden | 0.7 | 1.5 | 2.1 | 3.1 | 1.7 |
| UK | 1.2 | 1.0 | 0.8 | 2.5 | 1.9 |
| USA | 1.2 | 1.8 | 1.6 | 2.2 | 1.6 |
| *Panel B: Other European Countries* | | | | | |
| Greece | n.a. | n.a. | 1.4 | 3.1 | 1.3 |
| Ireland | n.a. | n.a. | 0.7 | 3.1 | 2.9 |
| Portugal | n.a. | 0.3 | 1.4 | 5.6 | 1.7 |
| Spain | 0.6 | 1.4 | 0.2 | 5.1 | 1.8 |
| *Panel C: Latin American Countries* | | | | | |
| Argentina | n.a. | 1.9 | 0.7 | 2.1 | −1.2 |
| Brazil | 0.2 | 0.3 | 2.0 | 3.8 | 1.7 |
| Chile | n.a. | n.a. | 1.7 | 1.2 | 1.5 |
| Colombia | n.a. | n.a. | 1.5 | 2.1 | 1.8 |
| Mexico | 0.4 | 1.1 | 1.0 | 3.1 | 1.0 |
| Peru | n.a. | n.a. | 1.4 | 2.5 | −1.2 |
| *Panel D: Asian Countries* | | | | | |
| Bangladesh | n.a. | n.a. | −0.3 | −0.7 | 2.2 |
| China | 0.0 | 0.3 | −0.5 | 3.7 | 5.7 |
| India | 0.0 | 0.3 | −0.3 | 1.6 | 2.7 |
| Indonesia | 0.2 | 0.5 | −0.2 | 2.1 | 3.4 |
| Korea | n.a. | n.a. | −0.2 | 5.2 | 6.4 |
| Pakistan | n.a. | n.a. | −0.3 | 1.8 | 2.8 |
| Taiwan | n.a. | n.a. | 0.4 | 6.2 | 6.1 |
| Thailand | n.a. | 0.4 | 0.0 | 3.2 | 5.2 |

**Table 2.** *Continued*

|  | 1820–1870 | 1870–1913 | 1913–1950 | 1950–1973 | 1973–1989 |
|---|---|---|---|---|---|
| *Panel E: African Countries* | | | | | |
| Cote d'Invoire | n.a. | n.a. | n.a. | 2.9 | −1.2 |
| Ghana | n.a. | n.a. | 1.1 | −0.1 | −1.4 |
| Kenya | n.a. | n.a. | n.a. | 2.6 | 0.7 |
| Morocco | n.a. | n.a. | n.a. | 0.7 | 2.2 |
| Nigeria | n.a. | n.a. | n.a. | 2.4 | −1.5 |
| South Africa | n.a. | n.a. | 1.2 | 2.3 | 0.2 |
| Tanzania | n.a. | n.a. | n.a. | 2.4 | −1.4 |

Source:  Maddison (1994), Table 2.2, p. 97.

Notes:  n.a. denotes not available; * Computed in terms of 1985 U.S. dollars utilizing U.S. prices.

imperialism believed the lacuna could be filled from within Marxian political economy by elaborating on the centralization of capital. The first to do this was Hilferding (1910) and all other classic texts (bar those of Rosa Luxemburg and her followers) were heavily indebted to his pioneering work. This was certainly true of Bukharin (1915) and Lenin (1916a), as they themselves acknowledged, even though they gave Hilferding's ideas their most radical interpretation.

None of the classic writings (including those of Luxemburg) denied what Marx had said about imperialism, but their focus shifted toward explaining intracapitalist imperialist conflicts.[12] The basic ideas of Hilferding, Bukharin, and Lenin were broadly similar. Monopolization within advanced capitalisms had increasingly fused economic and political structures, aligning each national bourgeoisie with its state and undermining previously vibrant cosmopolitan dispositions and liberal institutions. Capitalist acquisitiveness remained resonant, but it was now projected overwhelmingly outwards to the external world economy. Faced with a substantially colonized globe, it turned toward supporting strategies aimed at the integration of other developed capitalisms within the jurisdictions or hegemonic sphere of particular national states. According to classic Marxists a new structural incompatibility within capitalism had matured. The economic forces promoting enhanced integration remained undiminished, but they were divided between sovereign political authorities who could only continue to grow rapidly at each other's expense. The further development of the productive forces was fettered by the boundaries of existing states, or their empires, and a resolution of this contradiction demanded intraimperialist warfare.

This was a conclusion denied by Karl Kautsky, "the pope of Marxism," prior to the First World War, and his reasoning was both orthodox and acute. Even under monopoly capitalism, he argued, it would be prudent for the great powers to construct an ultraimperialism, agreeing to exploit the world jointly by apportioning economic space to their capitalists in line with their relative strengths. Of course, Kautsky faced the problem of explaining the onset of hostilities in 1914. He did so by pointing to the doggedness with which militaristic, precapitalist classes held on to political power. Many other social democrats agreed, supporting their national cause as the most progressive, or least unprogressive.[13] Thus it was a difference over the meaning of imperialism that helped divide European Marxism.

The chief rebuttal to Kautsky came from Lenin, who maintained that wars of hegemonic succession and redivision were inevitable because national capitalisms grew unevenly. In particular, the control of the world economy exercised by Britain and France had outstripped their relative productive significance. Both Germany and Japan, whose capitalist development had dramatically accelerated in the preceding half century, found their future advance impeded. They resorted to aggression as the only secure way of redistributing the property of other powers and subordinating them to the requirements of their own accumulation processes. And, Lenin continued, whatever the outcome of World War I incessant processes of uneven development would act to destabilize any postwar settlement.[14] Not surprisingly, given the actual events of the first half of the twentieth century, these ideas have proved to be very influential even with non–Marxists, like Fischer (1974), Gilpin (1981), and Kennedy (1989). However, Lenin's arguments could have been considerably strengthened as, indeed, could the conclusions derived from analyzing monopoly capital.

Any capitalist class under competitive or monopolized conditions derives significant economic support from regulation within a national state and a national culture. The protection of property rights internally and externally are but the most obvious benefits. Advantages are also derived from the creation of a homogenized symbolic system, including a single language, the provision of common infrastructural facilities, and the establishment of particular institutional networks facilitating interaction via contracts. Monopoly capital may form especially intimate relations with domestic political authorities, and the unevenness of development between national capitalisms is likely to enhance political, institutional, and cultural differences between them.[15] But the more enduring factors in underpinning "habitat preference" for capitalists remain in operation through all stages of capitalist development, providing a material foundation for national allegiances, and movements to extend the hegemonic scope of national arrangements.[16] Neither the centralization of capital nor uneven development, then, are likely to be tangential to explaining intraimperialist conflicts, but it should not be supposed that they constitute the radical rupture from the competitive capitalist conditions of the time of Marx that was assumed by virtually all the classical theorists of imperialism. Moreover, both Marxists and liberals can be sharply criticized for failing to recognize the enduring economic bases for parochialism and aggression.

However, in their reassessment of the state, Hilferding (1910) and Bukharin (1915) did point the way in which some of these considerations could be incorporated into Marxism. They recognized the enormous advance in the technology of surveillance and monitoring, together with extended capacities for rational organization, that had been developed by capitalist states. Bukharin went so far as to talk in terms of the state as a New Leviathan, regarding it as the predominant structure within advanced capitalisms because it exercised a pervasive management role over the whole of civil society. This included institutionalizing and otherwise assimilating working class collectivities to national purposes. Indeed, much of what Bukharin wrote appears to be more consistent with political realism than Marxian economics. Modern states were treated as unit actors coping in a world where the balance of power had broken down. And this suggested that all forms of imperialism might not only involve economic integration driven by the imperatives of capitalistic acquisitiveness but also have something to do with the agendas of states *acting as states*. No Marxist could ever embrace this idea completely, as the work of Rosenberg (1994, 1996) shows. But it has been influential with historical sociologists, like Giddens (1981, 1987), Mann (1986, 1993), and Skocpol (1979, 1992), who accept much of Marx's analysis of capitalism but argue that it locates only one dynamic among others stemming from the rival imperatives of power and culture.

Bukharin, together with Lenin over whom he exercised a great intellectual influence after 1914, used their new analysis of the state to justify a novel sequencing in the process of historical transformation.[17] Whereas Marx had thought in terms of capitalist economic development underpinning revolution, they added war as an intermediate variable. Explicit here was a recognition of the class conciliation orchestrated by state administrations that penetrated deeply into the social and economic structures of advanced capitalist nations. Only by disrupting this domestic integration was a successful revolutionary transformation feasible. Furthermore, Lenin recognized that modern states could not be easily overpowered by revolutionaries unless their internal repressive capacities had broken down. And it is difficult to underestimate the importance of these insights. From Bismarck's time every violent conflict between great powers has brought revolutionary upsurge to the losers and massive socioeconomic change to the victors.[18] Since the theory of monopoly capital and uneven development was thought to make imperialist wars inevitable, there is here some confirmation of Marxian orthodoxy. But in achieving this, the classical theories of imperialism exposed the problem of the entities to which economic determinism applied. Was it the world system, or nationally integrated capitalist economies? Clearly, since it was the structure of the world economy that was held responsible for transformative wars, the distribution of productive capacity, and not simply the overall level of development of the productive forces, became a key factor. This meant, though, that another set of variables entered the determining base, and the relatively simple propositions of Marx's formulation of historical materialism became less secure.

The theoretical justification of the Russian Revolution as being in conformity with the materialist conception of history came from the Bukharin-Lenin analysis of imperialism. The Russian empire was simply the weakest link that had snapped first. But, of course, in doing so it created a wholly new world to which Marxian theories of imperialism had to adapt. They responded by telescoping state and nation into class. During the interwar years, Comintern theorists argued that imperialism had brought a new unity to the oppressed everywhere (workers, peasants, and even the national bourgeoisie of colonized territories), and that the Soviet Union was the leader of the antiimperialist bloc. This was reinforced by claiming that imperialism as Marx had understood it had become a parasitic endeavor and was no longer a progressive developmental force. Thus the interstate system dovetailed with the structure of exploitation and resistance in the world economy, and state rivalry had become nothing more than an expression of the class struggle.[19] While this was a clear departure from Marx's ideas, some of his own comments on nationalism could be used to justify its direct continuity with the original theory of imperialism.[20]

## 5. Neoimperialism

As the classical theories comprehended the era of imperialism, it seemed to have ended in the postwar years, which saw a pacification of relations between great capitalist powers and extensive decolonization. Neither phenomenon, however, was actually incompatible with what the theorists of imperialism had proposed. The two world wars brought the dominance of a single national capitalism, that of the United States, which behaved in a hegemonic manner by restructuring the world economy in its own interests. The break up of European empires through decolonization was part of this grand strategy and reflected the partial success of the imperialist project as defined by Marx. Once colonies were integrated into the circuits of capitalist exchange there was a lessened incentive to maintain external political control, and this helps to explain the ease with which most independence movements achieved national sovereignty.[21] However, since peace between advanced capitalisms and the extension of the state system to peripheral areas elevated the importance of the "dull compulsion of economic forces" over extraeconomic coercion, they both raised the prospect of the ending of the imperialist epoch.

The only scope for any counterargument appeared to lie in adapting established theories to the conditions of bipolarity by amending and elaborating on the ideas proffered by Comintern strategists during the interwar years. And this became the hallmark of neo–Marxism, which constitutes the third phase of imperialist analysis. The objective remained what it had always been — to understand the processes of economic integration that capitalism demanded — but the focus now shifted back to the peripheral areas of the word economy. The new problem for core states was to maintain Third World incorporation into the circuits of capital, contain the expansion of Sovietized economies, and break down virtually all forms of protection, traditional and modern, that had been erected against market forces. Neo–Marxists believed that modernization along Western lines was impossible to emulate, requiring advanced capitalist powers to apply force repeatedly in order to secure the adherence of underdeveloped areas. Economic discipline alone would never suffice, because the immiseration processes of capitalist development were now overwhelmingly concentrated outside the metropolitan centers. Following upon the amendments introduced by classical theorists of imperialism, neo–Marxists accepted that the laws of motion enunciated by Marx no longer applied without qualification to the internal operation of advanced capitalisms. Wages had risen far above subsistence levels, welfare policies involved significant redistributions of income, and the working class was no longer excluded from political decision-making processes. It was widely believed that the pauperization properties inherent in capitalist development had become relocated to the Third World, and thus exploitation on an international scale became the central concern of the neo–Marxists. Evident here is a more general notion of path dependency that was lacking in classical Marxism. For Marx capitalisms in different parts of the world economy were runners on the same track. Some started earlier, and some traveled more quickly, but the greater their interaction the faster the overall pace, and there was no particular economic significance attached to international inequality providing it was generated capitalistically. The neo–Marxists questioned all this. Early starters were favored by some accident, which provided the initial impetus, but they changed the environment for those that followed, creating bipolar paths of development and underdevelopment.

The new theories also took a novel turn in arguing that it was Marx's analysis of primitive accumulation that had actually proved to be more general than his treatment of capitalist imperialism proper. But there was also some continuity with the classical theories in the appeal to notions of monopoly capital. Combining them, neo–Marxists such as Baran (1957) and Frank (1967) argued that imperialisms of the past had structured the world economy into a form where underdevelopment was reproduced in the periphery, whose continued exploitation was essential to core economies' own accumulation. This diagnosis was accompanied by a radical revision in politics, too. Instead of economic development leading to revolution, revolution was now seen as a prerequisite for economic development (along Soviet lines). Remaining within the orbit of capitalism could generate only dependent development in which growth occurred solely in response to the needs of developed capitalisms. Autonomous economic progress was considered to be impossible because peripheral economies had been distorted in order to facilitate the exploitative requirements of advanced capitalisms.[22]

In analyzing this underdevelopment, neo–Marxists made an important advance over preceding conceptions of imperialism by moving beyond the binary opposition of extraeconomic coercion and "the dull compulsion of economic forces." Capitalist enterprises in the core economies enjoy market power, and capitalist states act as economic managers. This relegates the market forces/coercion dichotomy to the extremes of a continuum where the power of particular decision-makers fuses with market processes. Strategic interaction is neither pure coercion nor the unadulterated market dependence of atomistic competition. It is, instead, a combination in which the asymmetries of domination and subjugation occur *within* economic relations. Marx recognized this repeatedly but was unwilling or unable to treat it theoretically, except in the context of the labor process. Classical theories necessarily had to come to terms with the added complexity of monopoly capital but they failed to encompass core-periphery interaction, which was not their principal concern. The neo–Marxists did, and the context in which they wrote made it essential for them to do so.

The incorporation of the domestic working class into the institutions of advanced capitalist economies, and the exercise of American hegemony over other core states through formal military alliances and international economic agreements, meant that disputes within and between these economies were settled primarily through the exercise of what Nye (1990) calls *soft cooperative power*. For the greater part, the periphery remained excluded from the networks involved in its exercise. The civilizing process became much more evident within the core but was rarely extended much beyond it. Thus decolonization and the achievement of statehood within the periphery disguised a very real divide between the two sectors of the world economy. The formulas of liberal modernization theory, including the doctrine of comparative advantage, did not capture all the important issues. Of at least equal relevance was inclusion within the resulting webs of interaction supporting cooperative agreements specifying the rules of engagement in the world economy. But this could be attained only by possessing sufficient political and economic weight, and exclusion deprived those in the periphery of the influence needed to shape the context best designed to attain it.

At the same time, the prominence accorded to the multidimensional nature of power in neo–Marxism also muddied the waters. For Marx and the classics, the nature of capitalist imperialism was a relatively clearcut matter involving the use of force to engender economic integration, and this was seen to be distinct from the coordination achieved via competitive markets. Once it was recognized that large economic and political agents could exercise power solely through market activities the clarity of this distinction vanished. Now it was possible to describe the actions of multinational corporations, core states, international organizations, and institutionalized agreements as imperialistic, even if the use of violence was absent. Not surprisingly, *imperialism* tended to become a term of abuse rather than an analytic category, applicable to all relationships between unequals in which there was any evidence of differential advantage. This was not simply a manifestation of sloppy thinking. Power and domination have proved to be the most difficult of phenomena to elucidate precisely. Significant advances have been made by Marxists like Gramsci (1988), and by those heavily influenced by Marxism, such as Bourdieu (1986), Lukes (1973), and Foucault (1979). However, as yet, their work has had much more influence on cultural studies of imperialism and has rarely been brought into its economic analysis.[23]

So far as the empirical evidence goes, neo–Marxian economists' descriptions of Third World conditions are less easily dismissed than has often been supposed (including by ourselves in the past,[24] and despite what we have said here in section 3). While the growth statistics in Tables 1 & 2 show that economic advance has been widespread, they also reveal what Pritchett (1997) calls *Divergence, Big Time*. Since the 1820s, advanced capitalisms as a group have experienced pronounced convergence toward equal per capita GDPs. Simultaneously, the polarization characteristics of the growth process appear to have dominated the spread effects, in that this group has pulled farther ahead of the peripheral economies taken as a whole. In 1820, the average income ratio between Europe and Africa was 2.5:1; it is closer to 10:1 now. The gap between the United States, the richest nation in the sample, and India, the focus of Marx's analysis of imperialism and one of the poorest economies for which complete data are available, has widened from a ratio of 3:1 to almost 18:1. The rich economies of the world remain a small group concentrated in North America, Western Europe, and Australasia. Japan is the only country devoid of European roots that has successfully joined the small set of advanced capitalisms.

Corresponding to the record of economic growth, political and military interventions by advanced capitalist powers have quashed many attempts to break
with the *status quo*. This has gone well beyond countering Soviet expansionism,
targeting a wide variety of movements aiming at some form of independent
national development.[25] Appealing to today's conventional wisdom (more accurately described as the Washington consensus), which claims these to have been
wholly wrong-headed strategies that were bound to fail, is jejune. Most attempts
were incapacitated before they got off the ground and have therefore not become
subjects for empirical refutation. Those that overcame Western opposition were
often quarantined outside the world economy, and forced to rely overwhelmingly
on domestic resources, rather than being allowed to create the comparative advantages and scale economies that have always been regarded as the rationale for
Listian strategies.[26] More generally, the historical record of what are now advanced
capitalist economies points to the importance of both modernizing revolutions
(from below or from above) and the adoption of protectionist policies as prerequi-
sites for successfully entering into the world economy.[27] One factor that distinguishes most of the East Asian growth miracles is that they were permitted a
measure of independence in economic policy *and* relatively free access to the
markets of advanced capitalisms, as part of deliberate strategies adopted by core
states to help contain the spread of Sovietization. Their experience also points to a
paradox, which is evident in the history of all advanced capitalisms. It was the external security problems faced by rulers in these countries that provided them with
incentives to favor domestic capitalist development over noncapitalist exploitation.[28] Moreover, the institutions that enabled high-speed growth among the East
Asian NICs suggest that, while capitalist relations of production may be necessary,
they are unlikely to be sufficient for rapid accumulation. As Amsden (1989), Evans
(1995), and Wade (1990) argue, economic management by states involving both
administrative autonomy and the construction of networks of communication and
exchange between public officials and private capital seems to have been crucially
important. On this Marxism, like social science in general, can say very little because
there is no well-developed theory of state bureaucracies.[29] Furthermore, Marx's
model of capitalism outlined in section 2 has proved misleading because of its liberal
bias in favor of minimalist, arms-length, state-capital interaction in the formulation
of internal economic policy.

At the same time, neo–Marxian accounts of underdevelopment highlighted some
of the other erroneous presumptions in Marx's original scenario. Neither capitalist
acquisitiveness nor expanded trade always promote enhanced productivity. Instead,
they can strengthen extraeconomic coercion, where profits are squeezed from producers operating within relatively stagnant technologies.[30] The establishment of the
full complement of capitalist relations of production was frequently hindered by the
legacy of imperial control. The most obvious examples of this occurred where political development ran ahead of the economic. Colonists frequently laid a foundation
for domestic elites to appropriate resources easily through the apparatus of modern
states precisely because they were unconstrained by local capitalist classes. Accumulation via the enforcement of secure property rights then took second place to
directly unproductive profit seeking activities.[31] All in all, the characteristics of cap-

italism, which we enumerated in section 2, have proved to be less of an organic unity than most Marxian theorists and liberal economists had assumed. Hence the stress we placed on the peculiarity of these characteristics appearing together.

Thus neoimperialist writings are contradicted neither by the growth statistics nor by the impossibility of providing theoretical justification for them. Their true weakness lies in what their authors saw as the pivotal factor explaining underdevelopment in the periphery and development in the core. While ideas similar to the arguments outlined above were expressed by Baran, Frank, and their followers, everything was subordinated to what was seen as the primary force — surplus transfer from the South to the North, usually through some form of monopolization.[32] Intuitively, this cannot be dismissed as incoherent, but no convincing account was ever provided of why, once extracted, surplus was not used to finance accumulation in the periphery but was instead retained in the core to increase investment and consumption there. Moreover, the paltry size of even the maximum feasible transfer of surplus cannot account for very much of the current prosperity in advanced capitalisms. The first laws of accumulation are arithmetic, and with core economies now constituting close to three-quarters of world output, and with capital-output ratios of around 3:1, exploitation of other economies obviously falls far short of their reproductive requirements.[33] The overriding problem of most peripheral economies has been the incapacity to produce a surplus, or productively utilize it, rather than having it siphoned off externally. It is difficult to resist the conclusion that what misled the neo–Marxists was the manner in which they applied Marxian theory. The identification of nations and states with classes implied that wealth and poverty were intimately related to international exploitation.

There are here two further misunderstandings. As we have already mentioned, historical materialism has always been ambiguous as to those variables to which its categories apply, and many neo–Marxists took full advantage of this to claim that capitalism was a world system *and only a world system*. For them, national economies were equally capitalist in being parts of a capitalist whole, and the absence of rapid convergence in the periphery was depicted as the result of the overarching capitalist structure, not as a failure of capitalist relations of production to become firmly established outside of core economies. Furthermore, however it is interpreted, there is here a weakness evident in historical materialism. Peripheral economies did not adapt optimally to the technological potential for raising labour productivity. Instead, noncapitalist methods of squeezing resources from producers were all too frequently promoted by rulers over capital accumulation. Historical materialists have erroneously presumed that once a technology appropriate to capitalist development has come into existence it will engender corresponding property rights, and well-developed states would emerge to make them secure. Neither has proved to be universally true, as the parlous condition of much of the Third World shows. There are powerful intervening variables distorting the hypothesized relations between the productive forces and the productive relations, and between the productive relations and forms of political power.

Another deficiency evident in neo–Marxism was its failure to analyze the Soviet mode of production materialistically, along with a similar silence with regard to the paler versions of this system inscribed in import substitution industrializations.

Neither Baran (1957) nor Frank (1967) nor most of their followers could be legitimately described as being uncritical of Stalinism and nationalist elites in the Third World. But they all seemed to presume that the problems were predominately political or ideological, and that there was nothing in the nature of these economic systems that brought about waste and degeneration. Rapid development was regarded as a relatively simple matter of accumulating surplus and installing mass production technologies. Exactly how political rulers were to be restrained from terrorizing their societies, economic agents deterred from corruption, and mechanisms instituted for maintaining efficiency in those peripheral economies that rejected the world market and followed their strategy of growth was never addressed. Again, Marx's own ideas may bear some responsibility for this. After all, he had drawn a distinction between prehistory and socialism that suggested all of these problems would be confined to the period before the revolution and no longer pose a problem once the break with capitalism had been made.

Since the early 1970s, neo–Marxists have been subjected to an avalanche of criticism.[34] Some critics have themselves been on shaky ground, interpreting the growth record as obviously inconsistent with ideas of underdevelopment, and glossing over the ways in which imperialism degraded the export of capitalist relations. Great weight was placed on the growth miracles of the NICs, without much attention being given to whether the structure of the world economy would allow them to become much more widespread. Domestic systems of power in peripheral economies were seen as the chief constraint on vibrant capitalist development, without acknowledging that imperial control had contributed substantially to bringing these systems of power into being. But the proponents of underdevelopment were seriously disadvantaged by the weaknesses inherent in their surplus transfer explanations. This was made much worse as their preferred strategy for autonomous development along Soviet lines was thoroughly undermined when the projects of advanced capitalisms for containment, reversal, and extended incorporation triumphed in the 1980s and 1990s.

## 6. Peering into the Future: The Closing Years of Imperialism or a New Beginning?

The general tenor of Marxian critics like Warren (1973, 1980) and Harris (1987, 1990) has been to proclaim a return to Marx. The logic of their position implies that imperialism has a predominantly historical significance: a capitalist world system has been created, coordination is primarily economic, and cultural homogenization is proceeding apace. They also presume that the means of violence have developed to the point where their full employment could serve no rational economic purpose, and cooperation is likely to predominate in further integration. Admittedly, remnants of imperialism can be found. The world economy is dominated by the activities of advanced capitalisms and they control the institutions of regulation. The rules they enact are largely designed to meet their interests and have been savagely disruptive in emerging markets, as is evident in IMF shock therapies and World Bank structural adjustment programs, which are often backed by threats of extraeconomic coercion.[35] Overt military disciplining of rogue states is still occasionally required.

But, while it is possible to weave all this into a story depicting imperialism as alive and kicking, according to this perspective it has paled compared to the record of the past 150 years. The specifically Marxian contribution to understanding economic integration appears to have withered in relative significance.

It is reasonable to project it withering further. Such is the grand design of American strategic planners mapping out the structures they desire for the future world system. Backward capitalisms are to be purified of precapitalist remnants and illiberal practices. Relations between advanced capitalisms will be further regularized with regard to both economic interaction and military cooperation. Technologies for global surveillance and the projection of military force on a worldwide scale, which are already exceedingly well-developed, will improve and be used to generalize the conditions of law and order presently characterizing the territories of the core. If such schemes are successful, it is conceivable that intraimperialist wars will not recur and that the economics of growth convergence will operate much more widely and strongly than they have done hitherto. Current trends already show the erosion of institutional differences between capitalisms, and they would be reinforced. International organizations could augment their powers and evolve into agencies of world government. The remaining barriers to capital mobility might disappear entirely as property rights become secure, so that the comparative advantages of what are now peripheral economies could constitute powerful bases for rapid development. Marx's model of capitalism would then be truly universalized and his economic forecasts unambiguously fulfilled. Moreover, the critique of capitalism in terms of alienation, injustice, and exploitation would have to deal with fewer complexities, and the forces of opposition could become less divided.[36]

It is also very easy to construct a diametrically different scenario. Uneven development continues in a context of separate states, many of which remain exceedingly powerful and particularistic. Much integration is still to be accomplished, and the lack of jurisdictional unification means that distinct political authorities meet at many points of friction. If environmental degradation is anywhere near as strong as the green movements claim, a global Ricardian stagnation could materialize in the twenty-first century, but this is more likely to induce violent conflicts than bring about an unchanging stationary state. The armed resolution of differences may be inevitable, as several eminent theorists of international relations forewarn,[37] and what they say can be recast in the Marxian framework of Rosenberg (1994, 1996) and Wallerstein (1983, 1984). The factors underpinning growth divergence appear to be very strong and not easily reversed. If scale economies and polarization forces remain potent, the marked inequalities present in the world economy could increase further. Since most of the periphery is of marginal significance to advanced capitalisms and large NICs alike, few resources are likely to be expended in aiding its development. Thus a new classic era of imperialism and a continuation of neoimperialism cannot be readily dismissed as a dystopian fantasy.

## Notes

[1] With the emergence of informational economics and the added importance attributable to private knowledge and transactions costs, contemporary neoclassical economists are better able to explain violent conflict as an outcome of rational choice. See Howard and Kumar (1999).

[2] See, for example, Hirschman (1982), Mayer (1981), Moore (1966) and Trotsky (1971).

[3] What we say is an accurate portrayal of Marx's model of capitalist, as is attested by the readings in Howard and King (1976: 86–93). However, we do simplify and exaggerate and use the terminology of historical sociologists like Weber (1948, 1983). Our purpose in doing so is to stress how peculiar is a fully developed capitalist system. Marx's views on this issue are discussed by Lefort (1978).

[4] See O'Brien (1982).

[5] See Blackstock and Hoselitz (1953: 217).

[6] See Avineri (1969), Howard and King (1985: 225–37), and Marx and Engels (1850–1888).

[7] Hobsbawm (1962, 1977a, 1987, 1995), Warren (1980), Von Laue (1987).

[8] Hauchler and Kennedy (1993), Madison (1995), and Usher (1998).

[9] Anderson (1974a: 462–549), Howard and King (1985: 225–37), Wolf (1982).

[10] Of course, Marx imagined that violent conflict would continue in the form of class-based antagonisms, but he expected these to replace other forms of solidarity, and the consciousness of the proletariat was considered to be an embryonic universalism, not a new particularism. It is also true that Marx was very well aware of the transformative impact of wars in the past. See Giddens (1981) and Linklater (1990). However, it is clear that he believed non-class based violence would decline with capitalist development, for much the same reasons as those given by liberal theorists of his own time. Thus, while it possible to claim that there are anticipations of classical theories of imperialism in Marx's writings, this requires that his understanding of the historical specificity of capitalism be ignored or devalued.

[11] Howard and King (1989: 15–16, 91–3).

[12] This is made very clear by Etherington (1982) in response to the many historians who insist on reading them as explanations of nineteenth century colonization.

[13] Howard and King (1989: 93, 123–4, 247–8, 252, 274).

[14] Howard and King (1989: 243–66).

[15] Feldstein and Horioka (1980), Gerschenkron (1966), Hampden-Turner and Trompenaars (1993).

[16] Theorists of modern nationalism, like Gellner (1983), stress precisely these considerations. Bourdieu (1986) provides a complementary understanding in terms of an extended conception of capital. In the language of game theory, there are club goods which support path dependent development, locking in most economic activities to the jurisdictions of national states; see Aghion and Howitt (1998), Arthur (1994), Lucas (1995) and North (1990).

[17] Howard and King (1989: 243–66).

[18] Porter (1994) and Skocpol (1979).

[19] Howard and King (1989: 243–66, 1992: 24–47), Kubálková and Cruikshank (1989), Light (1988).

[20] Linklater (1990). However, similar considerations to those outlined in note 10 apply.

[21] It was the most advanced capitalisms that resisted decolonization least; Britain and the United States accepted the political independence of their colonies more willingly than did France and Portugal.

[22] Marx's writings on Ireland can be regarded as an anticipation of this idea; see Marx and Engels (1844–1894). However, similar considerations to those outlined in Note 10 apply.

[23] See, however, Hargreaves Heap (1989), Hargreaves Heap and Varoufakis (1995), and Rothschild (1971).

[24] Howard and King (1992: 205–24).

[25] Chomsky (1991, 1993, 1996), Kolko (1988).

[26] Backhaus (1992), Bairoch (1993), Krugman (1991, 1995). The point we are making is not simply that Cuban, Nicaraguan and Vietnamese revolutionaries, to pick but three examples, would have performed very much better economically if they had not been resisted with such ferocity by Western capitalist powers. More generally, the empirical evidence on relative growth rates is not akin to that given by nature, or the result of freely chosen strategies of industrialization. It has been constructed by the activity of imperialism.

[27] Bairoch (1993) and Skocpol (1994).

[28] Bertram (1990), Hall (1986), Kennedy (1989), Mann (1988), Rosenberg and Birdzell (1986), Sen (1995), Skocpol (1979), and Tilly (1992).

[29] Nonetheless, some useful work is accumulating. See Evans (1995), Evans, Rueschemeyer and Skocpol (1985), Jessop (1990), North (1981), Olson (1993), and Udehn (1996). The best that can be said for the literature on 'public choice' is that it should never be forgotten but ultimately fails to explain why not all political authorities degenerate into Mobutuism (on which, see note 31 below).

[30] Howard and King (1992: 205–24).

[31] Evans (1995: 43) provides an extreme but telling illustration "Once Joseph Mobutu Sese Seko gained control over Zaire in 1965, he and his coterie within the Zairian state apparatus systematically looted Zaire's vast deposits of copper, cobalt and diamonds, extracting vast personal fortunes visibly manifested not only in luxuriant life-styles at home but also in multiple European mansions and Swiss bank accounts of undetermined magnitudes. In return for their taxes. Zaïrians could not even count on their government to provide minimal infrastructure. After fifteen years of Mobutu's rule, the road net, for example, had "simply disintegrated". In the first twenty-five years under Mobutu, Zaire GNP per capita declined at a rate of 2 percent per year... gradually moving this resource-rich country toward the very bottom of the world hierarchy of nations and leaving the country's population in misery as bad or worse than that which they suffered under the Belgium colonial regime ... the government's effectiveness at repression substantially exceeded its effectiveness at road building. State response to the ... (killing of a tax collector in Bandundu Province in 1978, for example) ... took the form of two detachments of soldiers who killed seven hundred of the local people. Later fourteen men were hanged as "ring leaders" in the tax collector's death ..." See also Alavi (1972), Bairoch (1993), Bardhan (1997), Bhagwati (1982), and Lucas (1995).

[32] Emmanuel (1972a) appeals to unequal exchange under what appear to be competitive conditions. Nonetheless, it is market power in the labour markets of core economies (rather than the monopolization in product markets favoured by Baran (1957) and Frank (1967)) which drives his results, which, in any case, are not very robust. See Howard and King (1992: 186–204).

[33] How far the exploitation of colonies contributed to accumulation in core economies during earlier periods is discussed by Griffin and Gurley (1985: 1105–9).

[34] Howard and King (1992: 205–24).

[35] George (1988). Programs of shock therapy and structural adjustment which have been implemented in response to debt crises have been successful in restoring macroeconomic stability, reversing current account deficits and forcing privatization and deregulation, but so far as accelerating economic growth and reducing inequality are concerned the record to date has been disastrous.

[36] Brzezinski (1996), Gergin and Stanislaw (1998), Gompert and Larrabee (1997), Friedman and Friedman (1996), Fukuyama (1992) and World Bank (1997). Projects aimed at eliminating non-capitalist forms of economy and politics in peripheral areas rest upon considerations more substantial than liberal proselytizing. Growing interdependence requires the enforcement of harmonized rules and, therefore, better developed capitalist relations of production and liberal states. Put crudely, but not inaccurately, capitalists in advanced countries find it increasingly costly to expand business in jurisdictions run by crooks and thugs, especially where problems of political legitimacy promise future disorder. See, for example, Kapstein (1996).

[37] Bernstein and Munro (1997), Friedman and Lebard (1991), Garten (1992), Huntington (1996), Kennedy (1989, 1993), and Mearsheimer (1990).

# CHAPTER 2

## IMPERIALISM REVISITED

## Michael Barratt Brown

An invitation to revisit arguments about the nature of imperialism, which began for me 40 years ago, is an opportunity for both self-criticism and self-justification. One can answer one's critics and accept or reject their criticisms. One can take into account new knowledge and new theories and the modifications in one's own ideas that have resulted. I have tried in this essay to do all these things, and in the end to decide how far the core ideas, which I developed, have stood up to the test of time. So, in this essay, I start from my earliest historical studies of the British Empire and end with my most recent association with practical work among those who have suffered most from the unequal relations established by imperialism.

On this view, imperialism is in effect the expansion of capitalism worldwide, but the expansion has taken more than one form. In one, the system of industrial capital accumulation was simply reproduced. New groups of people in new places began to work the system, exploiting labor to make profits and accumulating capital. Exchanges took place between them on roughly equal terms, making allowances for later development. This is what happened in the spread of capitalism throughout Europe, to the United States and the British dominions of European settlers, and then to Japan and most recently to East Asia (Barratt Brown, 1974: ch. 6). In another form, colonies were established, not in the original sense of settlements, but as dependent territories, required by extra-economic pressure, including enslavement, to supply only those goods or services, needed to assist accumulation in the capitalist centers (Barratt Brown, 1974: 96). As Geoff Kay has argued they were "not exploited enough," in the sense that labor productivity was not increased by machinery to yield a larger surplus for accumulation locally (Kay, 1975).

In fact, some European peoples, those in the United States and the British dominions, all began as colonies in both senses but freed themselves for independent accumulation of industrial capital. Elsewhere, in what we call the Third World, even after political independence, capitalist accumulation has been largely restricted to the form of merchant capitalism (Barratt Brown, 1974: 186). This was also what happened when Spanish and Portuguese colonies in Latin America were freed. Only merchant capitalism emerged in association with precapitalist — feudal or semi-feudal — formations (Barratt Brown, 1974: 258). Japan and parts of East Asia and

China, away from the Treaty ports, escaped direct colonial rule and this has allowed industrial capitalism to develop (Barratt Brown, 1963: 56). Under colonial rule, only merchant capital tied in to the colonial trade was encouraged, and merchant capitalists along with land-owning groups provided the postcolonial rulers (Barratt Brown, 1974: 260–1; Barratt Brown, 1963: 180).

It appears to be very difficult for merchant capitalists to evolve into industrial capitalists. In Britain in the seventeenth century, it took a major struggle for the outsiders to oust the merchant monopolists (Barratt Brown, 1963: 33). Merchants buy at one price and sell at another and have little experience of the processes of production, least of all of industrial production. They tend even to hold in some contempt those who get their fingers dirty in mines or factories or laboratories, and this has been particularly the case with the elites that succeeded colonial governments. The Industrial Revolution, especially in Britain, was a real revolution because a new class of industrial capitalists emerged along with the new technology as well as a new kind of working class (Barratt Brown, 1963: 43). Of course, many second and third generation industrial capitalists set themselves up as landed gentry, marrying their childen into the older merchant and landowning classes. But their wealth came from industrial capital and from their investment in the extension throughout the empires of industrial capital in industry, mining, plantations, railways, and shipping (Barratt Brown, 1988: 29).

Because of this class question, a further thesis that emerged from my studies concerned the very different involvement of the several economic classes in the age of imperialism. There was no question in my mind that the economic pressures made the running in the British Empire — from Robert Clive and Jardine Matheson and the East India Company through to Joseph Chamberlain and Cecil Rhodes and the British South Africa Company (Barratt Brown, 1963: 43–4). But industrialists worked together with merchants and aristocrats as traders and colonial governors and drew their capital from a wide range of the British middle classes. What became clear was that the benefits of empire for the working classes were few and far between though some trade unionists became imperialists. Empire for those with imperial investments or official posts in the colonies was one thing; it was something quite different for the working people who had to fight the colonial wars and face unemployment when the purchasing power of exploited colonial peoples collapsed (Barratt Brown, 1972b: 81).

Similarly, in the colonies and most especially in India colonial rule was often indirect rule through local princes and chiefs and a civil service and officer corps, educated and incorporated at Oxford and Cambridge and Sandhurst and their equivalents in France and Belgium (Barratt Brown, 1963: 178–9). By contrast, most of the people of the colonies were treated as less than human, driven into mines and plantations to pay the poll tax, conscripted into the imperial armies or for indentured labor in distant lands, at best exploited as small farmers through colonial state marketing boards (Barratt Brown, 1963: 160). The concept of Europe or North America as a whole exploiting the colonies as a whole, or of the core exploiting the periphery, does not appear in my books, since it is not only a wholly un-Marxist concept, but conflicts with the facts. At the center and in the colonies there are and always were both exploiters and exploited, both rich and poor; and the gap between the two is generally the wider the poorer on average is the economy of the country concerned (Barratt Brown, 1972b: 88). India has always provided the most obvious examples, but Latin America shows disparities that are no less considerable (Barratt Brown, 1974: 321–2; UNDP, 1997: 42–3 and 610).

## Where My Views Have Been Criticized

Criticism of my early work concentrated on four main issues:

1. My emphasis on the economics of imperialism and my neglect of both political and cultural factors, (Fieldhouse, 1973) and also, a more recent criticism, my neglect of the importance of geographical factors (Diamond, 1997).

2. My insistence that imperialism was a product of industrial rather than of merchant, commercial capitalism, or at most of a combination, but under industrial and not commercial pressures for higher productivity (Cain & Hopkins, 1993a).

3. My argument that most of the people of the colonial powers, in the core countries, benefited little from imperialism; (Alavi, 1964: 104) and as a corollary my questioning whether economic development at the center was at the expense of underdevelopment in the colonies, such underdevelopment, in my view, even holding it back (Frank, 1966).

4. My assumption that the idea of progress is not beyond question and that overall economic development has advanced rather than retarded the fulfillment of human capacities in general (Shanin, 1997: 65–72).

Most of the criticism has raised important questions and doubts in my own mind about the conclusions of my several studies. Much academic and practical work in the last two decades has helped in unraveling the economic changes and the social and political events that took place during the age of imperialism, when European people came to dominate the whole world, and then in making sense of the years that followed the achievement of political independence by the peoples who had been subjected to colonial rule (Davidson, 1978; Davis & Huttenback, 1986; Edelstein, 1982; Hobsbawm, 1987; Landes, 1966; McCloskey & Floud, 1981; Pollard & Holmes, 1972).

Since my early writing, we have seen the rise and fall of development theory (Leys, 1996) and the burgeoning of development studies, which has ended in a major onslaught on the whole concept of development and on the idea of progress itself (Wolfgang Sachs, 1992; Bawtree and Rahnema, 1997). This has been associated with an attempt to revise the whole body of Marxist thought, which has been the foundation of my own studies. Not only has Marx's distinction, following Hegel, been questioned of the historic succession of several stages or epochs in human development, but even the concept of capitalism has been dismissed in the belief that history is now at an end (Fukuyama, 1992). Much of this is the result of the collapse of the Soviet Union and of the so-called socialist experiments that were associated with it. The increasing recognition of the ecological limits to economic growth has also demanded a revision of earlier expectations about technological advance (Brundtland, 1987).

I had already abandoned my belief in the Soviet Union as a socialist formation when I wrote the first edition of *After Imperialism*, but I still accepted that a planned

economy made subject to democratic controls was the way forward for all peoples
(Barratt Brown, 1963: 482). I have already made my *mea culpa* in this respect
(Barratt Brown, 1995: xiiiff). I underestimated the strength of the competitive
instinct in human nature and its capacity to override the cooperative instinct. It was
clear that humanity had evolved through a balance of the two (Comfort, 1976:
16–19). Feminists would say the balance between the masculine and the feminine
had become impossibly weighted towards the masculine. The work of the anthro-
pologists, which I came to study especially in Africa, indicated to me that the harsh
natural environment of the African continent had always demanded for human survival a much greater emphasis on cooperation than the more benign conditions of
Europe and North America (Achebe *et al.*, 1990). Indeed, these latter conditions
had encouraged a degree of human competitiveness that had resulted in enormous
technological advances but now threatened the very survival of the human race and
of the planet itself.

I have examined some of this new work in the books I have written since the
1970s about the several political economies in the world today and especially in my
studies of Africa (Barratt Brown, 1995 and 1996). I have come to the rather surprising, and perhaps arrogant, conclusion that I do not need to alter very much of
what I originally wrote. I have in many respects been confirmed in my earlier judgments by new studies and by personal experience. In several particular cases I have
responded to my critics already. To some I responded in the long preface to the
Merlin 1970 edition of *After Imperialism* (Barratt Brown, 1970) but this essay gives
me the chance to respond in a more comprehensive manner, and to confess where
I was in error and consider the cause of my errors.

**Political and Cultural Imperialism**

I feel quite unrepentant in my insistence that empire and imperialism were always
answers to economic questions. I am happy to accept that for most of the nineteenth
century, British imperial activities were a kind of free trade imperialism. Indeed,
that was how I described capitalism and empire in the years 1824–1870 (Barratt
Brown, 1963: 51). Capitalists in Britain, as the first industrial power, had a competitive advantage over all other capitalist groups and could use free trade to break
down all reistance to British goods and capital, just as the United States was to do
later when it established world hegemony. After 1870, interstate rivalry, which
forced the partition of Africa and much else, was at base an economic competition
— for markets and sources of raw materials. Joseph Chamberlain's campaign for
imperial preference was about protecting British industry. His defeat resulted
chiefly because British capital was invested worldwide and not just in the British
Empire (Barratt Brown, 1963: 101).

Of course, I do not deny, and I do not think I ever did deny, that political ambitions entered into the motivation for imperial ventures. I reaffirmed this in responding in the second edition of *After Imperialism* to criticisms from D.K. Fieldhouse
(Barratt Brown, 1970: xi–xii). In the first edition, I emphasized both Disraeli's political agenda over India and the pressure for expansion from the colonies themselves
— both from governors and settlers — a point that has been taken up subsequently

(Emmanuel, 1972b). But the home government did not disown Disraeli's "prancing proconsuls" in India nor the British occupation of Egypt nor Rhodes's land grab in southern Africa. The route to India through the Suez Canal was a lifeline for British investment in Asia. Political control over territories overseas was necessary for British capital *pace* Dr. Fieldhouse, precisely because of rising competition from United States, German, and French capital (Barratt Brown, 1974: 186).

I am much less sure that I adequately dealt with the social and cultural impact of empire on the consciousness both of the conquered and the conquerors. I did try both in the first edition of *After Imperialism* (Barratt Brown, 1963: 18), in the Preface to the second edition (Barratt Brown, 1970: xliii), and at the end of *Economics of Imperialism* (Barratt Brown, 1974: 328-9) to emphasize the moral much more than the economic corruption of empire for the metropolitan working class. But Edward Said's great work, *Culture and Imperialism*, showed me how much I had missed, as an English middle class intellectual myself, of the total corruption of British society by the nineteenth century experience of imperial power (Said, 1993). I had even more seriously missed a proper understanding of the colonial experience for the people of the colonies. The appalling implications of the slave trade, indentured labor, and labor in the southern African mines and on plantations everywhere I had understood insofar as one who has not experienced such misery can ever understand.

It required, however, the work of the new generation of African historians, introduced to me and interpreted for me by Basil Davidson (Davidson, 1992: 47; Davidson, 1995: 79) to realize the much deeper impact of colonial domination upon African culture. The attempt was made by the colonial rulers to denigrate, or indeed actually to wipe out, African memories, and to substitute an artificially created tradition of chiefs and tribal rivalries (Ranger, 1983) quite alien to the indigenous democratic controls and interethnic bonds of the great empires of real African history. Much the same treatment had been served out to preconquest American history. Indian history was too obvious on the ground to be thus obliterated. It could not reasonably be said of any of the great Indian monuments, as it was of Great Zimbabwe, that these buildings could not have been built by local people. Nor was there in India or in China the possibility of pretending, as was done with Egypt until Martin Bernal corrected our distorted vision, that Egypt was not really part of Africa, and Greek civilization was not in origin African (Bernal, 1987).

I have tried to make good my failings in the past in understanding the cultural implications of imperialism in my last book on Africa, *Africa's Choices: After 30 Years of the World Bank* (Barratt Brown, 1995) and in my Leeds University African Studies lecture (Barratt Brown, 1997). It is clear to me now that indigenous cultural characteristics have had a far greater influence on economic development than I had allowed for. The successful marriage of capitalist ethos with indigenous culture in Japan and China and much of East Asia stands in stark contrast with its absolute failure in Africa (Barratt Brown, 1995-2: 44). It was always a mistake to lump together all nonindustrialised countries, as W.W. Rostow did, by calling them "traditional societies" and assuming that they would all follow the same stages of development (Rostow, 1970: 4). I tried to avoid that mistake, but I did assume that the results of economic development would not be so dissimilar. I am rather more doubtful today, but I am clear that increased productivity lies at the center of development, just as it was for imperialism.

## Geographical Explanations of the North-South Divide

An American evolutionary biologist, Jared Diamond, has advanced the novel thesis that the cause of the great division in the world between more developed and less developed parts goes back to the original geographical endowment of the continents, and particularly of the flora and fauna susceptible to domestication (Diamond, 1997: chs. 9 & 10). The great Eurasian continent spreading for 5000 miles east and west without major climatic divisions not only happened to contain far more plants and large mammals that could easily be turned to human use by selective breeding but also allowed for their cross-continental dispersion with no great obstacles of deserts or tropical forests to impede this.

Diamond thus explicitly excludes any racial explanation for differences in development but does make a quite peculiar distinction between straight-haired peoples whom he calls "white" and curly-haired peoples whom he calls "black" (Diamond, 1997: 379, fig. 19.1). This allows him to include the early civilization of Egypt in Eurasia rather than in Africa — an extraordinary distortion of facts that most Egyptian and classical scholars were prone to until corrected by Martin Bernal's *Black Athena* (Bernal, 1987).

It is central to Diamond's argument that the production and accumulation of a food surplus, whether by agriculture or by animal husbandry, made possible the division of labor and the development of complex societies, from which evolved centralized forms of government and organized religions. No one will deny this, but this happened on the American and African continents as well as on the Eurasian, in spite of their poorer natural endowment. Diamond gives scant credit to the pre-conquest empires of Central and South America, despite the many historical works on the Mayas, Aztecs, and Incas, and none to the precolonial African empires, despite all Davidson's and other Africanists' recent works (Davidson, 1984).

Diamond, moreover, goes on to say, "Descendants of those societies that had achieved centralized government and organized religion *earliest* ended up dominating the modern world" (emphasis added — MBB) (Diamond, 1997: 266-7).

This is simply not true. Sumeria, Egypt, China, and India do not dominate the modern world. China may come to do so, but the North American descendants who dominate the modern world cannot be said to be direct descendants of the earliest civilizations, even if the conclusions of Bernal and others are accepted that Greek and therefore Roman civilization had its origins in the Nile valley (Bernal, 1987; Davidson, 1984). Indeed, this is presumably the last thing that Diamond could accept because it would mean that the African continent (and not some extension into Africa of western Asia) after all, despite its apparently poor natural endowment, achieved one of the earliest forms of centralized government and organized religion. We have to find reasons why the first great civilizations collapsed in Sumeria, Egypt, India, and China and why Europeans came to dominate the world.

I have found no arguments that would lead me to abandon the view that over-centralization based upon irrigated agriculture was the cause of the decline of the early civilisations and that the more decentralized forms of government based on rain-fed agriculture were the cause of the rise of Europe and also of Japan (Barratt Brown, 1963: 29–30). Diamond argues that centralized government in China preceded irrigation (Diamond, 1997: 283–4) and there have been other critics of the thesis of Oriental despotism and an Asiatic hydraulic mode of production (Anderson, 1974a: 487). In *After Imperialism* I had supplemented Karl Wittwogel's hydraulics with Owen Lattimore's understanding of the need for defence against nomadic invasion (Lattimore, 1951). Why else were the capital cities of the earliest empires not at the center of agriculture but at the frontiers with nomadic peoples — Thebes, Persepolis, Delhi, Beijing? And I added Muscovy, where there was no irrigation but constant threat of invasion. The Mongols do not fit into Diamond's thesis. They only adopted the centralized government and organized religion of the peoples they conquered, but their cavalry nearly overran Europe, and it was, as Diamond shows, Pisarro's horses that overwhelmed the massed armies of Atahualpa at Cajamarca (Diamond, 1997: 77).

It would seem that I too have a geographical explanation for the rise of Europe and the decline of Africa, indigenous America, and Asia. But mine is based upon social, economic, and political development of resources that seem to me to be provide a much richer explanation than the results of plant and animal breeding. In fact, Diamond adds another geographical explanation for China's failure to develop (Diamond, 1997: 414–5). This is the long unbroken coast line with only three offshore islands, to be compared with Europe's indented coasts and many islands and inland seas, which encouraged competitive trade and seafaring. Diamond does know about the spread of Chinese trade all along the islands of the West Indies and even across the Indian Ocean to Madagascar and East Africa prior to the arrival of Vasco da Gama, by which time this Chinese trade had ceased. But he regards the suspension of the Chinese fleets in the fifteenth century as "the result of a typical aberration of local politics that could happen anywhere in the world: a typical power struggle between two factions at the Chinese court (the eunuchs and their opponents). The former faction had been identified with the sending and captaining of fleets" (Diamond, 1997: 412).

That was just the point and something that did not "happen anywhere in the world." The two factions were specifically called "the sea party" and the "inland party" (Levathes, 1994). The wealth of a trading merchant class was challenging the traditional power of the imperial tribute from the land collected along the canal system from the whole of China's vast territory. The merchants lost because of the sheer scale of agricultural tribute. By 1512 the emperor had ordered the destruction of all ocean going junks — four times the size of anything Europe could then show — and forbidden all sailing beyond coastal waters. Chinese development was held back for nearly four centuries. Into the space created European adventurers could move freely and Japan could develop in her own way.

The geographical explanation for imperialism is not only subject to refutation by the actual facts of history, but it needs to be refuted because it leads to a deterministic view of the fate of the peoples of these continents which are said to have been poorly endowed with natural resources and also to total omission of the effects of European conquests, enslavement, and colonization. Thus reviews of Diamond's book have emphasized Africa's lack of resources and consequent failure to develop. One, under the heading of "Why Rhino-Mounted Bantu Never Sacked Rome," forgetting that elephant-mounted North Africans very nearly did, began with a quotation from Aimé Césaire, and continued:

> Not only did Africa south of the Sahara fail to invent gunpowder, gas and electricity; they failed to invent, or even acquire in pre-colonial times, writing, the yoke, the plough and the wheel (Leroi, 1997).

Diamond manages to draw the line between his "white Africa" and "black Africa" well south of the Sahara to run from the Guinea coast sloping southwards and eastwards to the Horn to include Ethiopians among the whites (Diamond, 1997: 379). A less tendentious definition of sub-Saharan Africa would have to include Timbuktu and the great city of Khano at the southern end of the camel trail across the desert where the caravans arrived and departed. According to Basil Davidson:

> Along well worn trails there are caravan markers — roughly sketched carts pulled by donkeys or horses — that were engraved in very ancient times, probably before 500 BC. The Phoenicians who founded Carthage obtained gold from West Africa (Davidson, 1984: 90).

And nobody doubts that the alphabetic scripts of Meroe and the Sabaean scripts of Axum in what is now Ethiopia were indigenous and not copied from Western Asian or Egyptian writing (Davidson, 1984: 37–9).

Unfortunately, the prejudice against African capacities is easily fueled. No sooner had Diamond's book begun circulating but the director of the Harvard Institute for International Development was writing in the London *Economist* on "The Limits of Convergence, Nature, Nurture and Growth":

> Temperate climes have generally supported higher densities of population and thus a more extensive division of labor than tropical regions.

He wrote and concluded.

> that we should begin to accept as normal a situation in which Africa and other tropical regions are fed by temperate zone exports...the blocking by the rich countries of labour-intensive manufactured exports from the poor will have to end (Jeffrey Sachs, 1997: 21).

He did not explain that the food exports are so heavily subsidized by Northern governments, to keep agrobusiness consuming oil and fertilizer and other chemicals, that African and their fellow tropical farmers are unable to compete with them and are being driven off the land into the shanty towns (C. Robinson, 1989: 38; UNDP,

1997: 87). There, some will find work to supply the cheap labor for labor-intensive manufactured inputs into the big northern companies production synergy. Imperialism hasn't changed very much, because only a very few of the one-time colonies when they achieved independence had the capability for industrial development that would enable their own capitalists to start on the road of independent capital accumulation. It was not their natural endowment that was holding them back but the weakening under colonial rule of their indigenous strengths. And that weakness I confess that I had undestimated (Barratt Brown, 1995–2: 171).

**Empire and Industrial Capitalism**

The major revision of Marxist theories of imperialism has revolved around the significance of the Industrial Revolution in Britain and the emergence of an industrial capitalism and an industrial working class at the end of the eighteenth century and around the connection between the expansion of industrial capitalism and empire building. In the mid-1980s Perry Anderson (Anderson, 1987) and Geoffey Ingham (Ingham, 1984) from rather different perspectives seized upon some studies by W.D. Rubinstein (Rubinstein, 1987) of nineteenth century wealth in London and combined these with what they learned from a series of articles published in 1980 in the *Economic History Review* by P. J. Cain and A. G. Hopkins: "The Political Economy of British Expansion Overseas, 1870–1914" (Cain and Hopkins, 1986, 1987). Cain and Hopkins proposed that British capitalism was what they called a "gentlemanly capitalism" and the empire an expansion of the predominantly commercial form of British capitalism. This fits nicely into the picture Perry Anderson and Tom Nairn had drawn earlier of a British society that had never had a real capitalist revolution or a real industrial revolution and therefore unlike other European societies on the continent no real industrial bourgeoisie and no real working class (Anderson and Nairn, 1964). The great arch of English state institutions was presented as a seamless whole reaching out from the Norman Conquest to modern times, personified in the monarchy and still represented in Her Majesty's Privy Council and in the continuing prerogatives of the House of Lords (Corrigan and Sayer, 1985).

This picture failed to recognize the almost total replacement of the Norman aristocracy by Henry VIII's nominees who combined merchant and land-owning interests, the new alliances they formed when they were challenged by outsiders throughout the seventeenth century, and the new balance of power between land and capital that followed the English Revolution and was confirmed by the "Glorious Revolution" of 1688 (Hill, 1972). By placing William of Orange on the throne, the new ruling class was firmly established. Thereafter, wealth from the land could never again challenge wealth first from commerce and then from industry. The founding of the Bank of England in 1700 was an indication of the new power of the state. But British colonial possessions had already been established throughout the seventeenth century in North America, the West Indies, West Africa, and India. Cromwell's Navigation Acts and associated acts had already determined the nature of the colonial relationship. The colonies were to supply raw materials and their industrial development was to be restricted and all trade was to be carried in British ships.

"It was the intention in settling our plantations in America," wrote the English Commissioner for Trade and Plantations in 1699, "that the people there should be employed in such things as are not the product of England to which they belong" (Lipson, 1934: 173).

There was a long build up of industrial development in Britain, but there was an undoubted acceleration of economic growth in the last quarter of the eighteenth century, which, together with the application of new technology gave substance to the idea of an Industrial Revolution. But the real revolution consisted in the emergence of a new class of industrial capitalists (Dobb, 1946). The Industrial Revolution was not made by merchants or landowners, although the wealth of both was involved. The new manufacturing class, which had pioneered the technological changes involved, soon formed alliances with the older ruling classes. They found their national political leader in Sir Robert Peel, textile manufacturer, Prime Minister between 1834 an 1846, repealer of the Corn Laws that protected English agriculture from cheaper foreign food, essential to keep down the costs of industrial labor, the introducer of an income tax in lieu of duties on the sales of goods, creator of a police force and a national postal service and progenitor of the Bank Charter Acts and company laws that gave British owners of capital their crucial legal protections at home and overseas (Semmell, 1970).

The administration of Sir Robert Peel, who more than anyone created the Conservative Party, has to be recalled in order to counter the revisionist argument that the UK continued to be ruled by landed aristocrats throughout the nineteenth century and that industrial capital had little or no influence on British government policy until well into the twentieth century. The essential argument of Anderson and Ingram, however, is not only that the old aristocracy continued in power, but that the combination of merchant capital and a landed interest accounted for Britain's wealth in the nineteenth century and that the British Empire was above all an instrument for managing their commercial interests and not primarily an extension of British *industrial* capitalism (Anderson, 1987: 4; Ingham, 1984: 97).

**Commerce and Industry**

In my response to Perry Anderson in a *New Left Review* article of 1987 (Barratt Brown, 1988) and to Ingham in a further response in *New Left Review* (Barratt Brown, 1989), I rehearsed the facts, which I still believe totally disproved their thesis. Since then Cain and Hopkins have expanded their *Economic History Review* articles into a two-volume work, *British Imperialism* (Cain and Hopkins, 1993a and 1993b). The following is a summary of their theses:

> The industrial revolution was only one aspect of the economic development of an already successful mercantile capitalist system without any fundamental transformation in the nature of property ownership or the source of political power. British banks emerged from merchant trading with very limited links to industry. Commercial activity grew faster than industrial output in Britain throughout the nineteenth century. The wealth and power of the

City far exceeded that of industry, which was neglected infavor of commercial services particulary after the 1850s. Commercial earnings covered the widening gap between exports and imports. London's spreading commercial and banking network created the pressure for the great expansion of empire in the second half of the nineteenth century. This expansion, beginning only after the 1850s, provided colonial employments, expecially in India, which became "a superb arena for gentlemanly endeavor . . . for the performance of duty, and for the achievement of honor." Far from being a sign of failing powers, Britain's industrial decline was but the obverse of the thrusting strength of the City of London as the world's financial center, a strength that is not diminished today as services become as important as trade in the world economy (Cain and Hopkins, 1993b: 29–40; 1993a: 300–309).

The message for today that the British economy, having had its industry largely wiped out by Mrs. Thatcher's government can, as Mrs. Thatcher hoped, rely now on its service industries need not detain us, except to note that income from services in the world economy is grossly overstated. Far from being equal to the value of the trade in goods, the trade in services represents about 20 percent of world trade in the 1990s (excluding that is interest and investment income which would add another 15 percent, but is not really a service income) (UNCTAD, 1996: 224–262).

Some of the assertions of Cain and Hopkins, like those of Anderson and Ingham, can be challenged with statistics, which I shall deploy in a moment. I have already called upon Peel's legislation and particularly the Bank Charter Acts and Company Acts to justify the claim that there was indeed a fundamental transformation in the nature of property ownership, and in the repeal of the Corn Laws, which protected the landowning agricultural interest, a transformation in the source of political power. The fact that the aristocracy continued to dominate British cabinets right down to the time of MacMillan's cabinet of 1962 does not mean that this was where the power lay in British politics. It has to be remembered that most of the members of the House of Lords by 1914 had peerages that did not go back beyond a hundred years (Whitaker's, 1963: 222). Far more important in nineteenth-century Britain was the political power of local government. The magnificent town halls of Britain's larger cities outside London bear witness (Daunton, 1989). Joseph Chamberlain was not the only cabinet minister to make his name as well as his money outside the City of London (Saville, 1988).

It is fashionable among the revisionists to put references to Britain's Industrial Revolution not only in lowercase but in inverted commas (Arrighi, 1994: 192, 199, 208). The inventors of the new technology — Newcomen, Trevethick, Boulton, and Watt, Arkwright and Hargreaves, Stephenson and Brunel — were not just craftsmen but entrepreneurs who pioneered a new type of capitalism. It is impossible to imagine such men who made the Industrial Revolution as just one aspect of a succesful mercantile capitalist system (Court, 1938). The argument about the origins of the nation's wealth in the nineteenth century will be examined below.

There is one assertion by Cain and Hopkins that has been so often repeated although totally false that is must be taken up here. This is that British banking derived from mercantile and aristocratic origins and always had weak links with industry. Nearly all the British banks in fact originated in industry and from among the new industrial capitalists — and nonlandowning, nonconformists at that (Hamilton, 1947: 224). The Quaker forge masters in the Midlands founded Lloyds; Quaker clothiers in East Anglia and their cousins, brewers and silversmiths in London, founded Barclays; and the Quaker Gilletts founded Barclays DCO; Quaker and other Bristol ship owners founded what became National Provincial. Even the merchant banking houses that financed the central core of the City of London's overseas interests had industrial origins — J. P. Morgan started as copper smelters in Swansea, the Barings were initially in the west country cloth industry, the Hoares were shipowners from southern Ireland. Nathan Rothschild first came to Manchester to finance the trade in cotton goods, James Morrison, made his money from a textile warehouse in London, which marketed goods from the mills of Lancashire (Saville, 1988). Of course they built large houses in the country, and the villagers of Earlham would have been surprised to hear their landlord Gurney referred to, as Cain and Hopkins have it, as an "upstart," when they comment on the crash of Overend and Gurney in 1866 and seek to explain why the Bank of England failed to rescue it as it rescued Barings a few years later (Cain and Hopkins, 1987: 5). Joseph Gurney, the Quaker founder of the bank, had established what came to be called in the Napoleonic era, the "Banker's Bank" (Lubbock, 1922). Some upstart!

The picture that emerges is of much closer links between industry and commerce than the Cain and Hopkins thesis would allow for. The first reason for this is that industry was much more important in the national economy in the nineteenth century than they indicate. Manufacturing and mining overtook agriculture in share of the national income in 1820, not as they say in 1850, and continued to rise until the share reached 40 percent in 1901 when trade and transport totalled 23 percent and government services and the professions amounted to 10 percent (Deane and Cole, 1964: 175). Some 45 percent of the whole output of British manufactures, moreover, was being exported from 1870 to 1914, exports during this period trebling in volume (Deane and Cole, 1964: 29). From about the 1860s, the marketing of British industrial exports was financed with trade credit from London and sold through a large army of commission agents spead aross the world, less than half in the empire. The City's role became increasingly important as the proportion of capital goods in Britain's exports increased in the last quarter of the nineteenth century (Deane and Cole, 1964: 31, Table 9).

Competition was growing with the United States and Germany. Steel output in both had reached a figure double that of the UK by 1913, and in that year German exports equalled in value those from the UK. Ominously, they achieved that level again in 1938 (Svennilson, 1954: 260). It was this competition that led Chamberlain to campaign for imperial preference, but many British manfacturers were happy to import cheap German steel. The City of London was as divided as industry on the issue of tariff reform but most financial houses quite rightly saw the whole world as Britain's market (Barratt Brown, 1963: 106–7). What Chamberlain was right about was the need to spend more on health and education in Britain and to raise the purchasing power of the masses of the people, if Britain's competitive position in the world was to be maintained (Landes, 1966: 561). A recent study of the quality of life in the British industrial revolution concludes that "quite modest [3% of GDP per year] public spending increases could have enhanced the quality of life and at the same time have been justified in terms of rate of return" (Crafts, 1997: 617).

There is thus a question whether the empire was a cost or benefit to the British economy, but in David Landes' words:

> the competitive struggle of national enterprises was the most impor-
> tant single factor among the preconditions for the new imperialism
> (Landes, 1969).

**The Basis of a "Gentlemanly Capitalism"**

Such competing national enterprises were bound to require state backing. The British state, contrary to all the myths of a "night-watchman state," and "a lightly taxed state" (Cain and Hopkins, 1993: 150) was involved not only in the business of supporting sterling and guaranteeing loans but of seizing territories, encouraging settler capitalists, fighting the Boers for control over South Africa's gold, maintaining large armed forces overseas, patroling the seven seas with the British navy, and running a public expenditure budget at twice the level of the average for other industrial powers in the years up to 1914 (Peacock and Wiseman, 1961: 166; Davis and Huttenback, 1986: 160–5). The Cain-Hopkins thesis, taken from Rubinstein and endorsed by Anderson, has to claim that all this was necessary not for protecting direct British investments or the export trade but for maintaining "England's role as the clearing house of the world . . . for the multilateral transactions of the many political units of the world's space" (Cain and Hopkins, 1986: 489).

Thus it is the central conclusion of the Cain-Hopkins thesis that the new imperialism arose "neither in the 'inner logic' of the development of industrial capitalism nor in the simple facts of mere acquisition of new possessions" . . . but was "an overseas manifestation of a reconstructed form of gentlemanly capitalism centred upon the City of London and the service economy of the home counties." "The growth of the service sector, including the financial institutions centred upon London, was the chief influence upon Britain's presence overseas after 1850" (Cain and Hopkins, 1987: 10–11). With less than one-third of the national income and less than a fifth of foreign earnings derived from services (Deane and Cole, 1964: 175; Imlah, 1958: Tables 4, 13, 14, 20–21; Barratt Brown, 1988: 28), it was, apparently, an extraordinary case of the tail wagging the dog.

There is no doubt that British industry slipped back in the last quarter of the nineteenth century. Declining shares of world output and trade were inevitable, as the products of new industrial countries entered world markets. But there was a widely recognized setback to economic growth in the 1884–6 slump in profits, prices, and export volumes, and three great Commissions of Inquiry into the Depression of Trade and Industry were launched (Barratt Brown, 1963: 81). By the end of the century, growth had recovered despite cyclical setbacks, and exports grew steadily to a volume in 1913 three times that of 1870 (Deane and Cole, 1964: 311, Table 83).

Between 1870 and 1913, employment in the UK grew from 13 to 20 million (Feinstein, 1972). This does not look like the "hundred years of decline" or the *fin de siecle* or "figures" of Britain's "descent" in Anderson's imagery (Anderson, 1987: 41).

There are at least five propositions in the Cain-Hopkins thesis of "gentlemanly capitalism" and of an empire based on the service sector that can be tested from the statistical evidence:

1. that by the middle of the nineteenth century the balance on the trade account in UK earnings from overseas was surpassed by the balance on the services account
2. that by the end of the nineteenth century the stock of UK overseas investment was mainly in commerce and government stocks and not in production
3. that the flow of UK capital after 1870 was greater into investment overseas than investment at home
4. that by the middle of the nineteenth century wealth in the UK was largely derived from activities in London
5. that during the nineteenth century power was increasingly concentrated in the hands of a mercantile/landlord "gentlemanly capitalist' elite

It is the factual correctness of all these statements that can be challenged, to disprove the proposition that the British empire as it was established after 1860 was the result of the power and pressure of commercial and not of industrial capital.

The first fact to be recognized is that by far the greater part of the British empire had already been established by the 1850s (Barratt Brown, 1974: 110, Table 4). Additions thereafter added much territory, as boundaries were extended from established bases, but the populations and economic assets involved were relatively small, with the important exception of Egypt and the Suez Canal (Barratt Brown, 1974: 186–7, Table 16). The second fact to be examined is the definition applied to commerce and services. Both Anderson and Ingham include brewing and shipping as commercial activities and the income from overseas investment in the figure for services, although most of the investment was not in services (Barratt Brown, 1989: 126).

Without these various inclusions, the claims of Cain and Hopkins for the preponderance of commerce over industry in Britain's foreign earnings cannot be substantiated. And Imlah's calculations of the UK balance of payments showed the growth of exports and of shipping (a necessary part of production, as Marx recognized, contrary to Ingham's claims) (Marx, 1978: 225–8) as being faster than the growth of business services even after 1870 (Imlah, 1958: Tables 4, 13, 14, 20–21; Barratt Brown, 1987: 28). Nor can it be claimed that most of the overseas investment was in government stocks. The Chatham House study of UK accumulated overseas investment in 1913 shows the following proportions: Government stock, 30 percent (21 percent in the Empire); railways, 41 percent (12 percent in the Empire), public utilities, 5 percent; commerce and industry, 6 percent; mines and other raw materials, 10 percent; banks and finance, 8 percent (Royal Institute of

International Affairs, 1937: pp. 153–4; Barratt Brown, 1963: 153). There is no way in which a majority can be found here to be in government and commerce.

Movements of UK capital investment from the 1860s to 1913 were more remarkable for the changes in their relationship to the national income than for the changes in the relationship between home and foreign investment. On average, over the years from 1865 to 1913, according to Feinstein's figures, home investment took 5.7 percent of national income and overseas investment 5.1 percent, the latter generally taking a larger proportion when the total was high. It was particularly high in the late 1860s and in the last years before the First World War (Barratt Brown, 1974: 176, Table 13, taken from Feinstein, 1972). It is not, therefore, easy to argue that industry at home was starved of capital as a result of overseas investment, easier to suppose that reduced purchasing power at home, the result of growing income inequalities, was forcing UK capital to invest overseas. To this should be added the educational weaknesses already referred to and the absence of entrepreneurial skills, especially in writing off old plant and investing in new technology at home (Landes, 1966: 567). Shortage of capital was very rarely quoted as a problem in developing industry in nineteenth century Britain (Pollard and Holmes, 1972: 503).

It has already been shown that throughout the nineteenth century the greater part of the national income was derived from manufacturing, mining, and agriculture. Of course, there were always rich pickings to be had in the City of London. The studies of W. D. Rubinstein (Rubinstein, 1987), which revealed that the wealthiest persons in Britain in the nineteenth century derived their wealth from land and commerce and not from industry, have been taken by Anderson and Ingham to indicate that British capital was gaining more from commerce than from industry and this was perpetuating the subordination of industry in Britain to land and commerce (Anderson, 1987: 35; Ingham, 1984: 30–32). This is the core of their argument, but Rubinstein's figures have been questioned by Daunton on the ground that the use of probate returns will not reveal the value of private industrial undertakings that would be passed on from father to son well before death (Daunton, 1989: 128).

The argument is, however, about power as well as about personal wealth; and the revisionary thesis, especially in the hands of Geoffrey Ingham is that there was from 1850 onward a City-Bank-Treasury nexus that came to dominate British government and policy-making at home and overseas (Ingham, 1984: 127–34). This, according to Ingham, was all concerned with maintaining the power of the pound sterling, not just for investment overseas but for holding the whole capitalist system together, through the City as a clearinghouse for multilateral exchanges worldwide. The role of the Treasury was to ensure that government spending was kept under control, so that there should be no danger of inflation that would raise questions about the value of the pound. The Bank of England managed interest rates to the same end, and the City provided the mechanisms for all the different kinds of financial exchange generated by economic activity everywhere — and took its commissions. The nexus was operated by a class of aristocratic financiers, gentlemanly capitalists, far removed from the gyrations of industrial capital (Cain and Hopkins, 1993: 125).

There is a certain measure of truth in this picture, although, as we noted earlier, very few of the peerages dated from before the 1870s. In any case, it does not establish a case for this nexus as providing either the central motivation for British imperialism or the apparent subordination of industry to finance in Britain. Without British industry and its exports and its overseas investments, demand for the pound sterling, for insurance, trade credit, and all the other city services would have been negligible. There is a fundamental misunderstanding in much of the revisionist argument about the nature of the oveseas investment. It was throughout the nineteenth century almost entirely the reinvestment of past profits in future activities, and was not most of it in a sense new money (Barratt Brown, 1974: 173; Knapp, 1957: 438). According to O'Brien (O'Brien, 1988: 171) 35 percent of the value of the stock of assets held by British capitalists overseas by 1900 has been shown to have been direct company investment, mainly made by very large vertically integrated companies like the oil companies, Lever Bros., Coates & Patons, Brunner Mond, etc., through the application of retained profits.

Looking at political power in nineteenth-century Britain, the seats of power at the center in government and in the City of London have to be seen against seats of power in the provinces. Local government meant something at that time, especially in the major new industrial cities of the North and Midlands. Joseph Chamberlain's period of office as Mayor of Birmingham is quoted by the historian, John Saville, as "only the most spectacular illustration of a political process that was going on all over urban society" (Saville, 1988: 38). When the National Liberal Federation was founded in 1877 with Gladstone's presence and blessing, its headquarters were significantly in Birmingham, and its first president was Chamberlain.

In addition to the metal-working industries, textile mills, coal mines and shipyards of the Midlands and the North of England, both Scotland and Wales were major centers of coal mining, steel-making, and ship building. Many rich men from the North and the Midlands spanned the whole range of industry and finance, with an agricultural interest as well. Such a man was Alexander Henderson, the first Lord Faringdon, who owned an ironworks in Staffordshire, stood for Parliament for a Staffordhire seat, financed the Manchester Ship Canal, was involved in the Great Central Railway and the flotation of the Imperial Tobacco Company, and retired to farm in Oxfordshire (Daunton, 1989: 140). My grandfather, who was a Lancashire man, used to say that "Brass were made in't north and spent in't south."

The whole picture of a gentlemanly capitalism in the UK in the nineteenth century is based on the assumption that there was a smooth transition from an earlier merchant and landowning oligarchy to an elite of finance capital. The country houses of England are supposed to prove this. The middle classes that provided the brokers and agents in the City and the colonial officers in the empire have to be assumed to have come via the public schools and ancient universities from the landed gentry. In terms of sheer numbers, this is an absurd assumption. The class that disappeared in the nineteenth century was that of the yeomanry and smaller tenants (Cole and Postgate, 1946: 70–1). This must have been where the new middle class came from, and we know who built the country houses. According to Franklin the great majority were built by manufacturers — not the stately homes of the Dukes and Marquises, of course, but the thousands of smaller estates (Franklin, in Saville, 1988).

**How Old Is the North-South Divide?**

This has been a long exegesis to reestablish industrial capitalism as the source of imperialism and it leaves a further revision still unanswered. This is that the division of the world between rich and poor, north and south, core and periphery was already established long before the Industrial Revolution, which was on this view a quite minor event in the history of capitalist world systems. Andre Gunder Frank goes back further and writes in his 1991 memoir, "The Underdevelopment of Development":

> I now find the "same continuing world system," including its center periphery structure, hegemony-rivalry competition, and cyclical ups and downs has been evolving (?developing) for five thousand years at least ... In this world system, sectors, regions and peoples *temporarily and cyclically* assume leading and hegemonic central (core) positions of social and technological 'development.' They then have to cede their pride of place to new ones to replace them (Frank, 1991):

This perspective, like Diamond's, takes such an Olympian view of world history as to make any recent analysis or comparison largely vacuous. Giovanni Arrighi takes a somewhat shorter span of history, covering not 5000 but only 500 years. He calls his book, published in 1994, the *Long Twentieth Century*, but he sees this as a continuation of the "Long Fifteenth to Sixteenth," "Long Seventeenth," and "Long Nineteenth Centuries." The age of Venice was followed by the Genoese, then by the Dutch, the British, the United States, and perhaps next the Japanese (Arrighi, 1994: 364, Fig. 10). In each rise and fall he finds an empire that began with productive labor ending up with financial speculation. He suggests that there is no real contradiction between my views and those of Anderson and Ingham; we are speaking about different periods and about different aspects of one "systemic cycle of capital accumulation."
    "It was, Arrighi writes,

> precisely by being both industrial and imperial in ways that neither Venice nor the United Provinces [the Dutch] had ever been that Britain could exercise the functions of world commercial and financial entrepot on a much grander scale than its predecessors ever dreamed of doing (Arrighi, 1994: 176).

Now this World System is just the kind of explanation for imperialism that I do not accept as correct for the nineteenth-century British Empire. When an entrepot is not simply a warehouse for temporary storage of goods in transit — and a little short of 10 percent of Britain's foreign earnings in the 1890s and 1900s did come from the reexport business (Imlah quoted in Barratt Brown, 1988: 28), it is a commercial center for trading and marketing; and that could just be stretched to include capital and other money markets and exchanges. Much later, in the 1930s in Britain's case, and today in the case of the USA, one might describe some aspects of British imperialism and the hegemony of the United States in terms of financial speculation. But it would be missing the driving force behind imperialism, both British and American, from the nineteenth century onward, in the pressure to increase industrial productivity, for the expansion of industrial capital, and today of very large industrial capital, to become instead preoccupied with the marketing operations of worldwide business.

Concentrating attention on the financial operations at the imperial center has two results: first, it certainly emphasizes, if not the gentlemanly origins, certainly the supposed gentlemanly character, of those factories, mines, plantations, and small holdings; secondly, it allows a picture to emerge of an abstract core and periphery, with the periphery always exploited by the core. The reality is much more complex. Exploitation takes place in both the core and the periphery, as some of the World Systems school accept (Wallerstein, 1982). But it is a direct exploitation of labor in each case and not some apparent exploitation of the whole of the South by the whole of the North.

Evoking the hegemonic positions of whole peoples and regions, thus, only serves to conceal the underlying exploitation of labor by capital. The same is true of the generalized assault on development *per se*, without any examination of different forms of development. All are assumed to be what capitalism has engendered, although the unacceptable c-word is never mentioned (Esteva, 1992: 6–25). This is the position adopted by the self-styled post-development theorists, who claim that the age of development is over; development has failed, they believe; and those who still seek to promote development are deluded or self-interested. This is because all relationships between the developed and the developing must be by their very nature antagonistic (Rahnema in Bawtree and Rahnema, 1997: 384).

**The New Imperialism**

I accept entirely that much, even most, of the post-1940s economic development has been not only capitalist, but imperialist, in the sense of worldwide economic exploitation of whole peoples by groups of capitalists. Since the achievement of independence by the one-time colonial peoples, the methods employed have been mainly economic although extraeconomic force has been used in southern Africa and in the several military offensives by the one-time colonial powers and by the United States — in Viet Nam, Granada, Panama, Nicaragua, and in the Persian Gulf. Moreover, military dictators in excolonial countries have been supported by the one-time colonial powers and by the United States throughout Africa, Latin America, and the Caribbean to forestall or obstruct the emergence of regimes that might be less than sympathetic to the purely economic exploitation, which was continuing (Dan Smith, 1992: 148).

The main form that this continuing imperialism has taken has been in the perpetuation of the colonial trading relationship, which assigned to the colonies the supply of raw materials for the industries of the colonial powers. This was built in to the post-colonial world with the inheritance of power in the one-time colonies by regimes that represented elites of trading or land-owning families. Through taking over the colonial marketing boards and establishing joint ventures with the expatriate mining companies, they assured themselves the finance for their development projects and for their own and their followers' accumulations of wealth (Barratt Brown, 1995–2: 126). Much of this wealth was invested not in their own countries but in Swiss banks or in real estate in Florida and Hawaii. The spoliations of Marcos in the Philippines and of Mobutu in Zaire were only the most infamous examples of a general practice. It had been going on in Latin America ever since the early nineteenth century, when Spain had to cede colonial rule in the Western Hemisphere (Frank, 1971).

Apart from such corruption, which has rarely been the subject of serious criticism by the large capitalist groups in North America or Europe, the relationship has been evidently disadvantageous for the one-time colonial suppliers of primary commodities. The many different countries supplying these commodities and the millions of small suppliers of tropical products, and especially of coffee and cocoa, found themselves in a weak bargaining position faced by the quite small number of large transnational purchasing companies (Barratt Brown, 1993: 64). For the period of postwar reconstruction in the 1950s commodity prices were high, but they have been on a downward trend ever since, partly because of the development of substitutes for natural materials and partly because of the appearance on world markets of heavily subsidized Northern agricultural products competing with tropical produce (Barratt Brown and Tiffen, 1992: 30). Most of the colonies were established as producers of just two or three commodities for export and were thus heavily dependent on the income from their sale, and prevented from adding value to primary production (Barratt Brown and Tiffen, 1992).

The one-time colonies suffered further from other much more direct forms of economic exploitation. In many territories mines and plantations continued to be worked for giant transnational companies by forms of wage labor that hardly distanced them from slave and indentured labor (Barratt Brown, 1995–2: 311), but in Kay's sense was not exploitation enough to generate local accumulation (Kay, 1975). Where excolonial governments entered into joint ventures with expatriate companies, the abuse of transfer pricing, specially by the big mining companies, resulted in the local government receiving less than the world market value for its minerals (Barratt Brown and Tiffen, 1992: 102). Governments were hardly likely to complain, because they were still getting their rake-off or feared to lose the business in a competitive world.

The third form of exploitation most nearly corresponds to the World Systems view of the world. Governments of one-time colonial territories, especially those that do not have oil beneath them, borrowed heavily from Northern banks in the 1970s to pay for the higher priced oil, and for other inputs for their development projects. They had expected to be able to pay back from their primary commodity exports. But while the prices of these declined, the prices of their imported manufactured goods rose, and on top of that world interest rates soared. These countries began to build up debts, which accumulated and soon took up a large part of their foreign earnings (George, 1992: xiv–v). The bankers, from national private banks and from international financial institutions, rescheduled and issued new loans, so that the foreign debts of Third World countries, which amounted in the 1980s to under $1000 billion, had doubled by the late 1990s (George, 1992: xv). The IMF and the World Bank have, moreover, insisted that, as a condition of receiving further finance, debtor countries carry out programs of structural adjustment, which includes a requirement to step up commodity exports to pay off the foreign debt. Since all debtor countries were told to do the same, commodity stocks built up and prices fell still further (Barratt Brown, 1995–2: 88–90).

Although these forms of exploitation appear to involve the exploitation of poor countries by the rich, the benefits accrue to the big companies including the banks, and hardly at all to the consumers in the North, as a review of world coffee or cocoa prices and the current retail prices to consumers would soon reveal (Barratt Brown, 1993: 68). Indeed the general taxpayers in the North have been paying for the agricultural subsidies that have been ruining Southern farmers and have been making up for the tax concessions given by their governments to banks, which were allowed to place their losses on Third World debt in special accounts (George, 1992: 65). Nor do the elites of the Third World countries suffer unless they have to cut back on payments to their clients and find themselves challenged in military coups or local elections (Barratt Brown, 1995–2: 126).

It did not, moreover, prove to be the case that the division of the world established in the seventeenth century between what was called by the World System school "the core and the periphery" was incapable of being ended. Japan had not only emerged from the periphery, but had established a different kind of imperialism. This enabled Japan's conquered territories to develop their own processing of raw materials and later their own industries (Cumings, 1996). Local groups of capitalists in South Korea and Taiwan, and later in China, Malaysia, and Indonesia were able with Japanese finance and machinery to begin and pursue their own process of capital accumulation (Castley, 1996). This was not the merchant capitalism of trade but fully developed industrial capitalism, as Bill Warren had predicted (Warren, 1980). Some industrial development had, of course, taken place also in Latin America, but it had been checked by the extreme inequalities of income in these countries; and the recent turmoil in East Asia might suggest that the limit of East Asian capitalist development had been reached. I do not think that anyone believes that of China, but the wide inequalities of income in Indonesia do suggest that further capitalist development is unlikely without major political changes (UNDP, 1997: 43).

This still leaves unanswered the question asked by the anti-developers and post-developers, whether such capitalist development has left people whose economies have been developed any better off. It is very hard for those of us, who enjoy all the advantages of modern medicine, electric light, heating and air-conditioning, multiple printing, telecommunications, air, road and rail transport, tools and machines to do our heavy and most boring work, to say that we would be better off without all this, unless we are truly prepared to withdraw to a monastic life. It is entirely honest and logical of the post-developers to have made this clear (Rahnema, 1997: 393–4).

The point at issue for the question of imperialism is that, while capitalist development breeds inequalities, it would not have survived for so long if it had not also always increased the number of its beneficiaries without increasing the number of losers. This is not to say that history is at an end, and that capitalism can solve the world's problems. That it manifestly cannot do. The forms of capitalist development have begun to cause more damage than benefit to its very beneficiaries. The planet simply cannot sustain such damage any longer. New systems of production and distribution will have to be found if life on earth is to continue (Brundtland, 1987). But there were major advances in the nineteenth century and in the early twentieth and again in the developing countries after the 1950s (UNDP, 1997: 23). To quote the *Report*:

> Since 1960, in little more than a generation, child death rates in developing countries have been more than halved. Malnutrition rates have declined by almost a third, the proportion of children out of primary school has fallen from more than half to less than a quarter. And the share of rural families without access to safe water has fallen from nine-tenths to about a quarter (UNDP, 1997: 2).

After that, it seems somewhat idiosyncratic of the post-developers to write that "the whole system of technical assistance set up in the early 1950s to promote the 'development' of the Third World, [which] has so spectacularly failed to contribute to the well being of their populations" (Rahnema and Bawtree, 1997: p. 190). Such critics of all development really go too far when they go on to ask those of us who have been involved in such assistance to consider the "deeper motivations" prompting our work, perhaps using our advice for our own ends and "indulging a false love for an abstract humanity" (Rahnema, in Rahnema and Bawtree, 1997: 392). Instead, they say we should be trying, in Majid Rahnema's words, to discover "the redeeming power of human powerlessness" (Rahnema: 393) and enter "the meditative world of a free searcher" (Rahnema: 401). This is, as we have just seen, the logical conclusion of their position.

This has been the call throughout the ages to religious retreat, to the ashram or the monastery, to the life of prayer and asceticism. And it has produced many examples of selfless service, the copying of manuscripts, the exercise of good farming practice, the building of great churches, and, today too, much devoted work among the poor. But it is combined in Rahnema's vision, as so often before, with the elitist concept, which he takes from Confucian thought of the *jen*, who are the "authoritative persons . . . the most trusted members of the community." who have most responsibility for creating a good society, to be distinguished from the *min*, the blind masses. Through the thoughts of the *jen* must come what Rahnema calls "an aesthetic order built on the pursuit of good and harmony among difference" (Rahnema, 1997: 389–90). One is bound to recall that outside the cloisters life for the masses was mainly one of unremitting toil on the monastic lands to feed the abbott and his friars, whose abstemiousness was not always so apparent as to assure Rahnema's "harmony among difference."

Any middle-class European who has made the study of imperialism a life's work must be agonizingly aware of what colonial rule and its aftermath have meant for millions and millions of the world's people. The capitalist model of development has been built on the exploitation of labor, including very particularly the labor of the people whose lands were colonized. But how does it help for us to withdraw? It is suggested that the ex-colonial peoples would be better off without the exploitative trade relations with their erstwhile rulers (Gronemeyer, 1992: 63; see Lang and Hines, 1993: 126). But very few of these peoples are prepared to abandon the possibility of reducing the heavy toil of digging and hoeing and carrying head loads over uneven forest and mountain tracks, or of communicating with the rest of humanity through radio, TV, telephone and E-mail. These peoples need to grow cash crops and produce other goods for export to the developed countries to buy those things that they cannot produce themselves. It would indeed be one of Rahnema's examples of the arrogance of development workers if we were not to assist them to do so.

Throwing the baby out with the bath water seems perverse and is not answered by asking, as Rahnema does, why we "continue to wash the baby in dangerously polluted water" (Rahnema: 381). It is possible to criticize the capitalist model of development without having to accept that "the ideas of Progress and Development had disastrous consequences for the lives of vernacular societies" (Rahnema, 1997: 392) — *vernacular* implying that at some time in the past small village communities were so much happier places than large urban communities today. It is at best a dubious proposition, but it is hardly helpful for us now because, short of a nuclear disaster, there is no possibility of our returning to Erewhon.

Some years ago, Immanuel Wallerstein proposed

> It is undoubtedly the case that few 16th-century rural producers worked as hard or as long for so little as do rural producers in today's Third World (Wallerstein, 1982).

I never knew how one might prove or disprove such a statement, but Wallerstein has recently made very clear that it applies not only to rural producers but to all such comparisons: In "making a careful balance sheet of what has been accomplished by capitalist civilisation during its historical life," Wallerstein concludes: "My own balance sheet is negative overall, and therefore I do not consider the capitalist system to have been evidence of human progress" (Wallerstein, 1997).

And since this system is in Wallerstein's view, and here I would agree, essentially a European invention, we are all guilty of Eurocentrism in giving it so much credit. Even its science is proving self-destructive. Now, this may appear to be a strong argument, but it is based on the assumption that European scientific discoveries can only be used in a capitalist way. Marx's view of successive social formations may have been overoptimistic about the classless society that could emerge from capitalism, but the heart of his argument was about the contradictions which new technology creates for old social formations. And that could hardly be more obvious today. Whether one is optimistic about the change that will follow is not a matter of a two cultures education system, as Wallerstein suggests, but of one's experience with the men and women who can make the change.

My own personal experience of involvement in development work leaves me optimistic and wholly disinclined to take Majid Rahnema's advice and retire to a world of meditation to "discover my true limits and possibilities" (Rahnema, 1997:

393). Along with many of the post-developers, I too look to the continuing indigenous strengths of people all over the world at the grass roots, but I do not expect them to withdraw into small communities and cut themselves off from the technological advances taking place (Barratt Brown, 1995: 212). Where they have the chance of access to some of the new technology, especially for transport and communication, small-scale farmers, who still make up more than half of the populations of the Third World, have shown great capacities for working together and strengthening their bargaining position in world markets. The best known examples are the coffee farmers of Latin America, the Caribbean, and Africa who have, with the help of outside support from organizations like Twin Trading, built up their own commercial networks for selling their products in the supermarkets of Europe, North America, and Japan. A similar development — and I deliberately use the word — has taken place among cocoa and ground nut producers in Africa and among many other groups of small-scale farmers and artisans throughout the Third World (Tiffen and Zadek, 1996).

This development is in line with two trends of the times among Northern consumers — increasing consciousness of the injustice of the world marketing systems and growing fear of the unsustainable nature of the exploitation not only of people but of the land and environment by capitalist production methods. Most small-scale farmers in their cooperative associations combine practices that are both socially and environmentally responsible. They organize effectively, they work democratically, and they intercrop food and cash crops, so that they do not need to use large quantities of artificial fertilizer and chemicals in production. Together with the vast proliferation of voluntary and self-help organizations worldwide, they are showing the way toward an alternative to the exploitative hierarchies of capitalism (Barratt Brown, 1995–2: 320).

In my earlier books I put much hope in the possibilities of a "third way" for democratic governments in the First, Second and Third Worlds, subject to popular accountability, planning their trade and production in ways that would challenge the power of the giant accumulations of capital. It seemed then that mutually agreed systems of computerized calculation of demand and supply could replace the anarchy of the market (Barratt Brown, 1993: ch. 10). Such ideas proved to be politically and economically unacceptable to those in power and failed to excite the interest of ordinary people because they still implied a top-downward way of management.

Forms of cooperative organization have, however, survived in the interstices of the world economy — in the proliferation of voluntary and non-governmental organizations and in the informal and black economy. A whole new future now opens up for them as a result of the democratization of information through the new technology. The spread of knowledge through the Internet, where knowledge gives power, is changing the paramaters of the world economy (Kelly, 1997). Where international commodity agreements between governments failed to protect the producers against the giant companies, the networks of producers themselves, linked by new information systems, are succeeding (Barratt Brown, 1997: 23–4). It is once again possible to speak about the ending of imperialism.

# CHAPTER 3

## IMPERIALISM IN RETROSPECT

## Anthony Brewer

Think of a map of the world as it was at the start of the twentieth century. European empires spanned the globe, sprawling across Africa and Asia. In the Americas and Australasia, whole populations had been displaced by European migrants. Of the world's main population centers, only China and Japan remained outside European rule, and they were both profoundly shaken by contact with Europe. Now jump forward to the present. European empires have vanished, bar a few trivial remnants, but the world is still profoundly marked by their effects. Jump back to the eighteenth century, and Europe and Asia look almost like equals — Adam Smith used China as an example of a highly developed country, though he knew that all was not well with the Chinese economy. Go back further, to the fifteenth century, and Europeans were not even aware of the existence of the Americas. On a long time scale, the rise of European imperialism and its sudden collapse are among the most striking features of world history, as well as being among the most important factors shaping the world we live in.

The purpose of this paper is to reassess theories of imperialism. It is not an easy task. It is not simply that different theories come up with different answers, but that they rarely agree on the right questions to ask, on how to conceptualize the problem, or on what would constitute an acceptable answer. One way to proceed would be to take different views in turn and to try to understand each in its own terms. I have tried to do that elsewhere (Brewer, 1990), but it hardly seems possible at less than book length. The alternative is to try to formulate some relatively simple questions, and to assess the answers that have been offered.

There seem to me to be three big questions. First, why did Europe gain such a dominating position, and why did that dominance take the form of direct colonial rule over huge areas with populations ethnically and culturally very different from their European overlords? Second, how should we analyze the effects of empire on colonized areas and on the imperial powers themselves? In particular, how far was empire responsible for lasting differences in wealth between different parts of the world? Third, why did the colonial empires fall, and what remains of imperialism today?

Imperial territories took two different forms. In the Americas and Australasia the indigenous population was largely displaced by incomers from Europe or elsewhere. These colonies of settlement effectively became extensions of Europe. In most of Asia and Africa, by contrast, European settlers remained a minute fraction of the population, so Europeans ruled over overwhelmingly non–European populations. There were a few intermediate cases, like South Africa and Algeria, which proved particularly intractable in the period of decolonization. I shall not discuss colonies of settlement, intra-European empires like the Austro-Hungarian empire, or phenomena like British rule in Ireland, French rule in Brittany, or Prussian rule in the Rhineland, which should be discussed in the quite different context of nation-building. The cases that are now sometimes called *imperialism* are cases where nation-building failed, or where the boundaries of the nation were unclear. The main focus will be on the British empire, because it was by far the largest and most important.

## The historical context

Much of the discussion of imperialism is centered on the "scramble for Africa" at the end of the nineteenth century and on the period leading up to the First World War. The classical writings on imperialism date from this time, and they were naturally concerned with contemporary events (Hobson, 1902; Hilferding, 1910; Luxemburg, 1913; Bukharin, 1917; Lenin, 1917).

In a longer historical perspective, however, this emphasis on the period in which European imperialism took its final form misses the essentials. Much of the territory at stake in Africa was thinly inhabited and offered few economically useful resources. The main shape of European imperialism was established earlier. The Americas were conquered and substantially occupied by Europeans from the sixteenth century onward. In most of the Western hemisphere, imperialism had run its course by early in the nineteenth century. Even if one rules the earlier empires out of consideration, the key to the second generation of European empires was the relation between Europe and the great population centers of South and East Asia — India alone had a population roughly four times that of the whole of sub-Saharan Africa, and the British empire, much the largest of the European empires, was built around the route to India and on to China. British penetration of India developed in stages from the eighteenth century, and was substantially complete by the middle of the nineteenth century. China was never subject to direct colonial rule, but the Chinese market was broken open in the first half of the nineteenth century, long before the scramble for Africa. Any theory of imperialism must be judged against the whole historical sweep of empire.

What, if anything, was new about European overseas empires? After all, empires have existed since before the beginning of written records — there have always been peoples, cities, or states that conquered and subjugated others. This is not a trivial question. Earlier empires had profound effects — think, for example, of the legacy of the Roman empire in Europe or of Arab and Turkish empires in the Middle East. Should we look for different theories to explain the British empire and the Roman empire? I think we must, primarily because the economic context was so different.

The last few centuries in Europe have seen the emergence of capitalism, along-side the growth of empire. That is easily (and frequently) said, but it is harder to define what capitalism is or to date its appearance. Few would disagree that capitalism involves the production of goods and services for sale on the market by privately owned profit-seeking enterprises. Some Marxists would insist on adding that capitalist enterprises employ free wage-workers (though other Marxists seem happy to talk of slave plantations as capitalist). The problem is that capitalism, so defined, has never accounted for the whole of economic activity, but that a capitalist element in a mixture of forms of economic organization is very old indeed — it certainly goes back to the ancient world. The proportions differ in different places and times, but it is never an all-or-nothing question.

What is more relevant here is that a growing capitalist preponderance in parts of Europe was accompanied by a long, slow, acceleration of technical change. Output, population, and productivity started to grow at rates that were slow in absolute terms but faster than anything that had been seen before. Successive waves of technical change transformed every aspect of life. As a result, the world came to be unified into a single (very unequal) system, in a way that was quite new. Previously, uneven development and the rise and fall of empires had local or at most subcontinental effects. Now they affected the whole world.

In the sixteenth century, the time of the first European empires, European technology was not yet, in general terms, ahead of many parts of Asia, but some parts of Europe had crucial advantages in naval technology, weaponry, and navigation. The voyages of the late fifteenth and early sixteenth centuries marked the conquest of the oceans (Parry, 1981). The Indian Ocean had been crisscrossed for centuries, but the Atlantic and Pacific Oceans posed quite different problems to early navigators. It is possible to go from India to Africa simply by following the coast, while the monsoon wind patterns make it possible to cross the Indian Ocean from Asia to Africa and back, with a reliable following wind in each direction. The big oceans are different. What Columbus and other fifteenth- and sixteenth-century navigators did was to demonstrate how to use the trade winds and the westerlies to make repeatable roundtrip crossings.

The Americas were opened up to European penetration for the first time (minimal Icelandic contacts hardly count). The result was a historic tragedy, "the worst health disaster there has ever been" (Porter, 1997: 163; see also Crosby, 1986), but one that was to a large extent unavoidable, for biological, bacteriological reasons. The populations of the Old World and the New had been isolated from each other, so disease organisms had evolved separately. Once contact was established, populations were subject to new diseases to which they had no immunity. The effects were very different in the Old World and the New, seemingly because their precontact populations were so different. The larger population of the Old World had fostered a more rapid evolution of disease organisms. The effect in the New World was catastrophic. Population fell to a fraction of its precontact level. Some people still seem to believe that the Spanish conquerors exterminated whole populations or worked them to death. It should always have been obvious that the relatively minute force of Spanish invaders did not have the capacity to do this. We now know that population, and with it whole civilizations, collapsed in areas that no European had yet penetrated. The outcome would have been the same if it had been the Aztecs who made contact with Europe and not the other way round.

The ballooning of the Spanish empire is easy to explain. The Spanish wanted gold and silver. The Americas contained rich sources of these metals (and areas that did not were conquered anyway, just in case). The inhabitants of the Americas were technologically far behind those of Europe and were decimated by disease. The subordination of the Americas, and the partial replacement of the local population by newcomers (slaves included) was an immensely important historical event, but it cannot be explained in the same terms as later European empires in Africa and Asia.

European penetration into Asia on any significant scale developed much later. Even in the eighteenth century, the three great centers of human population and civilization — Europe, the Indian subcontinent, and East Asia — were still almost on a par an terms of technology and economic development, though the European economic space already spanned the world. Britain and France, among others, had control of parts of India, but one should not overstate the significance of the fact. India was not a nation but a subcontinent occupied by many states and ethnic groups. Some European powers were significant players in the politics and warfare of the subcontinent, but so were various local states and others. India had seen the rise and fall of empires, domestic and external (as Europe had). If we could stop the clock in the mid-eighteenth century, before Clive's victory at Plassey and Hasting's reforms of a decade later, European involvement in India would not look like an unusual or particularly significant fact in Indian history. Even in the early nineteenth century the British empire in India, by then immense, was not so different from the Mogul empire it replaced. It now looks special but only with hindsight.

For a long time, European contacts with Africa were restricted to the coast. Here, something must be said about the slave trade, which clearly had a devastating effect on the lives of millions of Africans. It is fairly obvious how it fits in to the story — labor was scarce in the Americas and slaves were available in Africa. Europeans controled the seas. An opportunity for profitable trade existed, so it was exploited. Europeans did not (normally) enslave Africans — Africans were enslaved by other Africans for sale to European slave traders. Slavery had long existed in Africa, albeit in quite different forms. Saying this does not in any way reduce the moral responsibility of the slave traders or minimize the moral enormity of slavery, but the purpose here is to explain what happened, not to pass judgment. The impact of the slave trade on Africa itself is difficult to assess because of the lack of written records outside areas of direct European or Middle Eastern contact, but it must have been huge. The point is that it manifested itself as a transformation in the internal affairs of Africa, without direct conquest by Europeans.

In the eighteenth century, the three great civilizations — Europe, India, and China — still confronted each other as apparent equals, but the balance had tipped. The pace of technical change was starting to accelerate significantly. The world had been mapped and the oceans conquered. The wider geographical scope for trade led to multiplied opportunities of profit, while new industries and new methods of production created new opportunities for trade. Increasing trade volumes stimulated advances in shipbuilding and navigation, increasing the European advantage. The scene was set.

### The causes of imperialism

In the "long" nineteenth century, say from the publication of the *Wealth of Nations* to the First World War, European empires spread across the globe. This is what any theory of imperialism must explain. I will survey some of the candidates briefly (for a fuller treatment, see Brewer, 1990).

A significant feature of many theories is a focus on the export of capital, rather than on simple trade in goods. A brief discussion of the historical record is a helpful preliminary. Foreign investment in the later nineteenth century was mainly portfolio investment (loans to foreign borrowers or the purchase of other kinds of financial assets). Direct investment by companies in physical assets abroad on a large scale did not take off until well into the twentieth century, after imperial expansion was effectively completed, making it unlikely that direct investment was a major driving force, even in the final burst of empire building. The focus of a theory of imperialism, then, must be on portfolio investment. Here it is worth noting that Britain was much the largest capital exporter and that the bulk of portfolio investment went to independent countries or to British dominions populated mainly by British migrants and well on the way to independence. In the later nineteenth century new British investment abroad roughly matched profits from existing overseas investments, so there was surprisingly little net effect on Britain. It is, of course, true that a growing stock of overseas assets was being built up in the process and that any interference with either side of the balance would have had major effects.

Hobson (1902) produced the first worked-out theory of imperialism. He claimed that there was a chronic tendency to underconsumption (or excessive saving) in advanced capitalist economies because workers' consumption was limited by poverty while capitalists saved a large part of their income. Hence, he argued, there was an increasing shortage of investment opportunities at home for a growing volume of saving and a growing need to invest abroad. Similar stories have been told by others. Lenin's argument seems to have been similar, although it was expressed so vaguely that it is hard to say what it amounts to. Rosa Luxemberg (1913) had a similar underconsumption theory, although she used it to argue for a need for foreign markets rather than foreign investment.

Underconsumption theories are now out of fashion. It is true that this is an area in which final conclusions are hard to reach, but Hobson's own theories were less than convincing and no one since has much improved on them. The main argument against underconsumption is that domestic investment itself adds to domestic demand, so it is perfectly possible to have high investment, low consumption, and a high rate of growth. Underconsumptionists typically think that low consumption must mean low demand and few investment opportunities. That much is certainly wrong. Whatever the judgment on the theory, the facts are against Hobson. In Britain, as just noted, foreign investment mainly involved reinvesting profits from earlier investment abroad rather than siphoning off excessive domestic saving. Most investment did not go to colonies, weakening the link between foreign investment and imperialism. Real wages were in fact rising in the last quarter of the nineteenth century, and the share of profits and saving was not. Foreign investment is undoubtedly part of the story, but claiming it as the central explanatory factor and linking it to underconsumption is implausible.

Some Marxists have linked foreign investment to Marx's "tendency for the rate of profit to fall." Lenin is sometimes named in this context, although it is difficult to find such arguments in what he actually wrote. Marx had argued that as capitalism developed, the rate of profit would tend to fall because of a rising "organic composition of capital." Some of his followers claim that investment in less-developed areas, where this tendency has yet to appear, can stave off falling profits, thus providing a motive for advanced capitalist states to conquer less-developed areas. Here it is only necessary to say that Marx's argument is now known to be faulty, and that there is no theoretical or empirical basis for such a tendency.

Another set of theories links imperialism to the rise of monopoly. Hobson used monopoly as a possible source of inequality, and hence of underconsumption. Hilferding (1910) came up with a different and perhaps more substantial argument. Bukharin (1917) followed him and made the link to imperialism more explicit. Lenin too hinted at similar arguments, taken from Bukharin and Hilferding. The Hilferding-Bukharin argument relates not to well-established monopolies but to a system in which monopoly power is still rather fragile, and takes the form of cartels (interfirm agreements) that can break down easily and that are threatened by foreign competitors. Monopoly power is immensely profitable, but it has to be backed by state support and the exclusion of foreign competition. Once this point is granted, it is easy to see a motive for imperial expansion to shut out foreign competitors.

This is a more plausible argument, at least as an explanation for the scramble for Africa at the end of the nineteenth century. As an explanation of the rise of the British empire, the largest of all, it is weak, because the main expansion of the British empire came earlier, in a period which no one would describe as monopolistic. Indeed, Britain remained relatively unmonopolized until the end of the empire-building period. The Hilferding-Bukharin story has more force as an explanation of the sudden entry of late-developing European powers into the race for territory and the sudden emergence of acute competition between European powers in the colonial arena.

The theories discussed above have several features in common. First, they were the work of Europeans who wanted to explain events in Europe in their own time, the beginning of the twentieth century. They do not explain the whole sweep of imperialism, because they were not intended to. They have little to say about developments in areas outside Europe because their authors knew little about the world outside Europe. Second, they share a common structure of argument. Capitalism faces some potentially crippling problem, which tends to worsen over time. Imperialism offers a temporary (but only temporary) solution. Hence capitalist states are forced to adopt imperialist policies. Hobson thought that a reformed, more egalitarian, capitalism could survive without imperialism. The others, all Marxists, thought that the revolutionary overthrow of capitalism was the only answer, and was imminent. None of this seems remotely plausible now that capitalism has survived and flourished without empires.

How then can the seemingly inexorable rise of European imperialism in the nineteenth century be explained? Rather than looking for a single factor that can be called the cause of imperialism, it may be better to look at the steady changes going on beneath the surface. Throughout the nineteenth century, economic and technological development continued, spreading from its original centers to other countries, all in Europe or settled by Europeans. Some acquired empires, others did not. Non–European areas (with the single exception of Japan, late in the century) were left behind. An immense amount of work by economic historians and economists has gone into describing and understanding the process of growth in different places and periods and an immense amount remains to be done, but in the broadest of outlines there is nothing surprising about Europe's lead. Before the unification of the world economy, progress in different areas went on effectively in isolation. Europe happened to be first, and it was inevitable that a gap would open. This was, of course, before full colonial penetration — the possible effects of imperialism in widening the gap will be discussed later.

The immense gap in development that had emerged by the nineteenth century obviously lies behind the phenomenon of imperialism. So too does the fact that Europe was capitalist. Development created new demands, new markets, and thus new opportunities for trade. Transport costs fell drastically, promoting trade but also cutting the cost of exerting military power at a distance. Troops as well as goods could travel on the new steamships. Investment opportunities opened up, along with opportunities to transfer new technologies to areas where they were previously unknown. Indeed, investment and technology transfer, to improve transport or set up new lines of production for export, were often a prerequisite of trade.

The world economy was steadily unified, and a massive asymmetry of economic and military power emerged. That is not enough, in itself, to explain why European dominance led to direct colonial rule, but it sets the context. International trade was in the hands of Europeans — they had the knowledge, the ships, the capital — so it was Europeans who penetrated other continents, not the reverse. Disputes inevitably arose. There was almost invariably a clash of economic, social, and legal systems. European traders and investors looked to their home governments for support. Trade had always had a political and military dimension (in medieval Europe and in other parts of the world), but the scale was far larger than ever before.

The way things developed was very different in different places. At one end of the scale, pre–Columbian societies in Central and South America were penetrated very early, collapsed completely under the onslaught, and were reduced to complete subjugation. China and Japan, by contrast, were never brought under colonial rule. Part of the explanation may lie in Europe, or at least in what Europeans stood to gain (or thought they stood to gain) in different areas. Areas thought to have gold were stormed. Other parts of the Americas were left alone for centuries because no one could see any profit in them. But the main explanation must lie in the different responses and capacities of different non–European societies.

Before the final scramble for Africa (when each European country wanted to grab its share before it was too late), European powers always preferred to do deals with local rulers when they could. It was cheaper, and costs always mattered. If necessary, they might intervene to establish a puppet regime or to station troops where they could exercise effective control. The full panoply of colonial rule was usually a last resort. Much depended on local circumstances (see Gallagher and Robinson, 1953; Robinson, 1972, 1986; Robinson and Gallagher, 1961). Direct conquest of China or Japan always looked too expensive and risky, although pressure could be exerted in cheaper ways (British bombardment of China in the Opium Wars, Commander Perry's ships threatening the same in Japan). India too might not have succumbed if history had been kinder, but the Mogul empire (itself in origin a foreign regime) was falling apart just when Britain and France were at war with each other and both had rapidly growing interests in India.

There is a sense in which the British empire really was acquired almost by accident, bit by bit, "in a fit of absence of mind." There was no plan. Each acquisition of territory was the result of contingent events and could have gone the other way. That is not the whole story, of course. The situation was such, the preconceptions and aims of policy-makers and of those who implemented policy on the ground were such, that the empire was bound to grow. Underlying everything was the economic drive (of traders, not governments) to seek out new profit opportunities and the massive asymmetry of power, which ensured that the British Government really could intervene to protect its citizens throughout the world. By the late nineteenth century there was a conscious ideology of empire, a Colonial Office planning the future of the empire (generally rather ineffectually), and so on, but that was the result, not the cause, of empire.

Despite the immense variety of routes by which particular territories were incorporated into European empires at very different dates, they ended up by the early twentieth century as parts of a fairly uniform structure, governed by colonial functionaries with standardized rôles and uniforms, guided by a common ideology of European superiority, if also of a European duty to educate their subjects and to rule justly. (There was a great deal of hypocrisy in this, of course, but it was not always entirely hypocritical.) The bureaucratization of empire was an offshoot of the bureaucratization of European states and of the magnitude of the task of governing huge areas and huge populations. There had to be rules, procedures, and precedents, but this superficial uniformity concealed a ramshackle structure of very different societies, conquered in different ways at different dates for different reasons, and destined to develop very differently.

## The effects of imperialism

It is often claimed or implied that the present inequality between rich and poor countries is the result of imperialism. I have already argued that Europe's economic and technological lead over other parts of the world predated imperialism and made it possible, but the next step must be to discuss the effect of imperialism, once established, on the gap between rich and poor areas. If the aim is to explain lasting economic differences between different areas, the focus must be on the effects of imperialism on long-run growth, both in the imperial centers and in their subject territories.

There is a very general reason why it is difficult to deal with this set of questions in a satisfactory way. To measure the effects of imperialism we must compare what actually happened with a counterfactual, what would have happened in the absence of imperialism. Since the growth of imperialism was so intimately bound up with the growth and integration of the world economy, it is difficult to see how one can conceive of a world in which there was no imperialism without falling into pure fantasy. A counterfactual is by definition something that did not happen and about which we can have no independent factual evidence. One can perhaps look at some specific aspects of the problem, such as patterns of trade or investment, and try to get some idea of the extent to which colonial control distorted the pattern. It might in principle be possible to compare areas that were conquered with areas that were not, but there were very few places that wholly escaped European control and those few may have done so because of special factors that distort the comparison. Thus, it is sometimes said that Japan succeeded economically because it was never occupied as a colony, but it could equally well be said that Japan had particular strengths that led it both to succeed in resisting Western control and also to strive to match and surpass the West.

*Gainers?*

What, if anything, did the imperial powers gain from their empires? Possible economic gains from imperialism can be gathered under four headings: (1) loot; (2) gains from unequal trade; (3) profits from investment; and (4) indirect effects, such as elimination of potential competitors. The first of these can be dealt with fairly quickly. Loot there certainly was, but things like gold and art treasures are of little long-run economic benefit. Gains from extortion and corruption could also come under this heading — some individuals in the colonial services undoubtedly became very rich, but the long-run effects on the imperial powers at a national level were marginal. The indirect effects, (4), are the hardest to pin down. I will not attempt it, beyond recording that no one has convinced me that they were an important source of long-run economic benefits for the imperial powers. I will therefore concentrate on what are almost certainly the two most important as well as the most readily measurable factors: trade and investment.

First, consider possible gains to the metropolis from unequal trade. It is worth recalling some basics of the theory of international trade. Some writings on imperialism give the impression that if one party benefits from trade it must be at the expense of the other. This, of course, is false. Trade is normally beneficial to both parties. Imperial powers doubtless gained from trade with their colonies, but so they should. The question is whether they somehow enriched themselves more than they would have done if the pattern of trade had not been affected by imperialism. The problem of finding an appropriate counterfactual raises its ugly head. There is no simple or conclusive way to deal with it.

One possible approach is to ask whether there were any ways in which imperial powers might have tried to rig the terms of trade in their favor and, if so, whether they really did try and how effective they were. Much the most common tactic was to force the colonies to trade only with the metropolis, thus excluding competitors from colonial markets and preventing colonial producers from looking for alternative buyers. How much effect this really had on the terms of trade is debatable. If there were enough competition within the metropolis-colony system, and if the metropolis were open to trade, it may have made little or no difference. Competition would keep prices in the colony in line with prices in the metropolis, itself linked to world prices by trade. Where the metropolitan market was monopolized, on the other hand, buyers in the colonies and in the metropolitan home market alike suffered the effects of monopoly pricing. Where trade with the colonies was in the hands of monopoly trading groups, matters might be worse for the colony. On balance, metropolitan states may well have gained in this way, although markets tend to resist any very large distortions. If prices for colonial exports were forced down too far, producers would switch to other crops, driving prices up again. If metropolitan products were sold at excessively high prices, it would be at the expense of low volumes of trade and hence small total gains. It should be added that colonies were also quite often given exclusive access to metropolitan markets and may have gained at the expense of metropolitan consumers and of other potential suppliers as a result.

Any quantitative estimate of metropolitan gains from trade distortion must rest on a (counterfactual) estimate of what prices should, or might, have been. Absurdly large estimates of metropolitan gains (and peripheral losses) have been proposed (e.g., Emmanuel, 1972a: 369), but they are based on unspecified or fanciful counterfactuals — I can always claim that I am being underpaid if I say that I deserve twice (or ten times) what I get. The only sensible comparison to make would be between trade as it was and free trade between independent states. Without detailed product-by-product studies (for which data is rarely available) it seems impossible to provide any accurate estimate, but I think one can safely say that the gain to the metropolitan states was small. For reasons already given, there are limits to the extent to which terms of trade can be manipulated and it is unlikely that those limits were reached in more than a small fraction of cases. Trade with colonies was small by comparison with total GNP, so the gain as a percentage of GNP was a rather small fraction of another rather small fraction. The brute fact is that precisely because the colonies were poor they were relatively minor trading partners and offered only small gains to the metropolis.

If it is argued that the metropolis made lasting gains from cheap imports, there are further factors to consider. Any gains from improved terms of trade are most unlikely to have been wholly, or even mainly, transformed into investment and hence growth. The fraction of any increase in income saved was quite small, and some of that was lost to the metropolitan economy as investment abroad. Note, in particular, that one cannot simultaneously claim that capitalist states needed outlets for investment abroad because of excessive saving and also that the metropolis gained in investment and growth from unequal trade. If savings were already too high, any gains from unequal trade could only have made matters worse. Cheap materials, it is true, may have given metropolitan manufacturers an advantage over competitors from other advanced countries — a significant motive for imperial expansion — but that would lead to a shift of competitive strength between advanced manufacturing countries, not a widening of the gap between colonies and metropolitan powers as a whole.

It can also be argued that capitalism as a whole gained by opening up areas that would not otherwise have been involved in the world economy at all. This is probably true, but note first that trade created by imperialism in this way could be beneficial to both parties, and second that there are always alternatives. If the capitalist world had been left without access to areas opened up by imperialist conquest, investment would simply have been concentrated in a smaller sphere. It is difficult to know what the consequences would have been.

Profits from investment are easier to measure, though different investigators have come up with different results. The general consensus seems to be that returns from investment abroad were roughly in line with returns at home. It would be surprising if it were otherwise, since investment flows always tend to equalize returns. Total returns from foreign investment (as opposed to the percentage rate of return) were quite small relative to profits from domestic investment. Since most foreign investment did not go to colonies, the total income from colonial investment was even smaller. The only partial exception is Britain in the years before the First World War, when foreign investment was quantitatively quite significant but, as noted before, new investment abroad roughly matched profits from earlier investments, minimizing the effect on the domestic economy. In fact, the period in which returns from foreign investment were at their peak was precisely the period in which Britain started to fall behind countries which did not invest as much abroad or have comparable imperial possessions, suggesting that possession of colonies did little to help economic growth.

One must not forget that imperialism had costs of a very prosaic sort — the costs of military forces, of colonial administration, and so on. They were substantial. There is a long tradition of opposition to colonialism in the metropolitan countries themselves, going back to Adam Smith and before, on the grounds that the benefits of imperialism (if there are any) accrue to special interest groups, while the costs fall on taxpayers as a whole. A number of writers have tried to draw up a balance sheet for the imperial enterprise as a whole, with differing results. One of the most recent concluded that imperialism was a loss-making enterprise, "neither necessary nor sufficient for the growth of the economy" (O'Brien, 1988: 200). Others may reach somewhat different conclusions, but I think it is safe to say that if there were any net gains to the imperialist powers, they were small.

Why did empire come into existence and persist if the gains were so small? I have argued that many annexations were the result of particular, perhaps transitory, local circumstances. Once the commitment had been made, it was hard to reverse without risking domino effects. Even so, the scramble for Africa suggests that empire was seen as desirable, even though in the event the territories at stake proved almost wholly unprofitable to their new masters. A number of factors seem to have been at work. First, there were special-interest groups that expected to profit, and it is a well-known result in political economy that cohesive pressure groups may be able to push through policies that are bad for the population as a whole. Second, national pride and prestige were at stake. Third, the special circumstances of the time militated in favor of imperial expansion. Those parts of the world that were potentially available for conquest by Europeans had almost all been claimed. New imperial powers, like Germany, and those whose empires were small in comparison with their aspirations as world powers, like France, knew that this might be their last chance, while Britain saw its standing and its existing territories and spheres of interest threatened. Power and status counted for more than narrowly economic gains.

There is one reason above all for thinking that the current wealth of the ex-colonial powers (along with other countries that never had a significant empire) has nothing much to do with imperialism. Real incomes, in the long run, depend on productivity. Rich countries are rich because their citizens are more productive than those of poorer countries, and the main source of increasing productivity is technical advance. It is possible to argue that empire contributed to capital accumulation (though I have argued above that its effects were probably small), but without technical advance there would have been nothing to invest in. I see no plausible way in which the possession of colonies could contribute significantly to the advance of technology. It is certain that imperial powers could not learn directly from their subject peoples because their subjects were less advanced technologically. Could it be argued that colonial markets raised the return to technical advance, and thus stimulated discovery? Hardly. There may be cases in which new developments were aimed at colonial use or colonial markets, but it is hard to think of significant examples. All the major advances were aimed in the first instance at domestic markets in the advanced centers, and were only transferred to colonial use as a by-product.

The world is richer and more populous now than it used to be because of the stream of scientific and technological discoveries over the centuries, from Galileo to the development of information technology. It is possible that colonialism excluded colonies from the benefits of technical advance — that is a different question, to be taken up below — but not that ex-imperial powers are rich because they were imperialist.

*Losers?*

If it is hard to assess the effects of imperialism on the imperial powers, it is even harder to evaluate its effects in the areas bought under imperial control, for two main reasons. First, the areas incorporated into European empires were so varied. How can one hope to say anything that will apply to areas that were still inhabited by hunter-gatherers when Europeans first intruded and to great civilizations like those of India and China? Second, precisely because the effects of imperial penetration were so far reaching, the problem of constructing a counterfactual, of saying what might have happened without imperialism, becomes almost impossible.

There are two contrasting views of the effects of colonial rule. On the one hand, it is often argued that colonialism retarded and distorted development, leaving ex-colonies poor and backward. On the other hand, it has been argued (by Marx, among others) that colonialism brought the benefits of modernity and economic development. This second view is deeply unpopular now, not because it has been disproved but because it is regarded as politically tactless. I should stress here that I am not concerned with the morality of imperialism, but only with its effects, primarily with its long-run economic effects. Whatever one thinks of the morality of imperialism, moral or political factors should not be allowed to affect the economic analysis.

What can be said? Consider first the two main headings considered before — the terms of trade and the returns on foreign investment. Metropolitan powers frequently tried to shift the terms of trade in their favor. This practice was by no means universal, and it may not always have been effective, but there can be little doubt that colonies' terms of trade were frequently worsened. The implicit (counterfactual) alternative is free trade. I have argued that the gains were no more than marginal for the metropolis, but it does not follow that the effects were equally minor in the colonies, which were typically poorer and less diversified. Even fairly small price reductions might have significant effects on the potential for growth. On the other hand, wholly new opportunities for trade emerged. Here again, the counterfactual is crucial. Some colonies may well count as gainers from new trading opportunities if the notional alternative were one in which there was no contact with Europe at all, but losers if the notional alternative were one in which new trades were introduced but on more equal terms.

The profits on foreign investment remitted to the metropolis are relatively (only relatively) easy to calculate. They were certainly positive overall, but that is not enough to justify a claim that colonies were poorer as a result. Where the profits were the result of monopoly power or of the seizure of natural resources, the case is fairly straightforward — a counterfactual in which such profits were not extracted justifies counting their extraction as a loss. Where the profits remitted represented a return on productive investment by metropolitan investors, however, the case is much less clear. What was the alternative? If it could be argued that domestic investors could have provided the required funds and collected the profits without any reduction in other forms of investment, then the profits remitted could be treated as a loss, but that case seems most unlikely. If cheaper sources of finance could have been found, the difference in interest payments would count as a cost of colonial rule. If the only alternative to foreign investment was no investment at all, as it must often have been, then there must often have been a net gain to the colony even after deducting profits remitted to the metropolis.

It is probably not worth persisting with this sort of calculation because other factors are almost certainly much more important. Consider, for example, the rubber industry in Malaya. To consider only the terms on which rubber was traded and the amount of profits repatriated by plantation owners would be to miss the point. The whole industry was a British creation. Malaya became the main producer of rubber for the world market only after a secret British mission had obtained rubber plants from the Amazon, propagated them in Britain, and sent them out to Malaya. If Malaya had remained independent, would this have happened? It seems unlikely. What is needed, then, is an assessment of the total effects of the development of the rubber industry, by comparison with some hypothetical alternative.

Malaya is a particularly obvious case, but similar developments occurred almost everywhere. The colonial powers introduced new industries and new methods of production while obstructing or even prohibiting others. They changed the legal framework, with almost unknowable effects on development, they constructed or reconstructed education systems, made key decisions about infrastructural investment, and so on. It is often argued that imperial powers excluded their colonies from key industries and thus excluded them from the benefits of continuing technological development. There are certainly many cases that fit this pattern, but there are also many in which imperialism brought new technology with it. Without a well-developed counterfactual, it is impossible to draw up a balance sheet.

It is thus easy to see how one could make a superficially strong case for claiming that imperialism was historically progressive, a bearer of modernity, but equally easy to see how one could argue the opposite, either by denying that modernity, at least in that form, was beneficial or by arguing that its benefits were willfully withheld. No one can doubt that the effects of imperialism were fundamental, but there is no plausible way of saying what might otherwise have happened.

### The fall of imperialism

The whole immense fabric of colonial empire collapsed with amazing rapidity. The independence of India and Pakistan in 1947 was the key event. Up to that moment, the map of empire had remained much as it was at the peak of imperial expansion half a century earlier. Within two decades, there was almost nothing left (except the rather special case of the Russian empire, which hung on until the fall of communism). There are two key questions to ask. First, why so sudden a collapse? Second, and more important, how large a change was it? Was the collapse of empire really a turning point, or was it, as some have claimed, merely a cloak for the continuation of imperialism by other means?

The collapse of empire is not difficult to explain, at least in general terms. I have argued that empire mostly arose for contingent reasons. It was never necessary to the imperial powers, it was always expensive, and it was never very profitable, taken as a whole, although particular territories were profitable at particular times. The balance of cost and benefit could easily shift. It was not quite that simple, of course, because more than economic costs and benefits were at stake. The apparatus of empire, once established, had a momentum of its own. Careers and investments were at stake. Psychologically, empire had become important, particularly to nations that did not like to admit that their rôle in the world was shrinking. Equally, however, political changes within the metropolis could bring antiimperialist forces to the fore. There was little sober basis for clinging on to empire.

It is important to realize that empire was always potentially fragile. It had never been, and could never be, maintained by brute force alone. The threat of overwhelming force was there, of course, but only if it almost never had to be used. In India, for example, the British presence (military and civilian combined) never exceeded 0.05% of the population. The great empires worked because they were taken for granted.

After the Second World War, however, everything changed. The dominant power was now the United States, which had not inherited a significant colonial empire or a colonial tradition on European lines because it had been busy expanding its internal frontier while others were building empires and because the native inhabitants had been effectively wiped out. (The United States had, in fact, one substantial colonial possession, the Philippines, but was already committed to allowing it independence.) With no empire of its own, the United States was generally happy to see others lose theirs, if only because it expected to gain from the establishment of looser spheres of influence.

The ideals of nationalism and democracy had spread from Europe (where their effects had been equally revolutionary) to provide ammunition for the enemies of imperialism. The status quo could not persist. Once the example of India showed the way, the whole edifice was bound to fall. Little more need be said at this level of generality. The process was sometimes appallingly destructive — witness the wars in Algeria and Vietnam and the partition of India — but in a longer historical perspective it was over very quickly. What is worth noting is that although different areas were, in reality, very different in terms of their economic, political, and social development, they achieved independence almost simultaneously. The empires may have grown piecemeal, but they collapsed like a house of cards.

**After imperialism?**

How much real difference did decolonization make? The end of formal empire did not eliminate the underlying asymmetry of wealth and power that, I have argued, underlay imperialism. So what has changed? On a military and political level, the independence of the new states is real enough. In almost all cases, the troops of the occupying power departed and new national armies took their place. The new rulers were often rather hostile to the previous colonial power and were determined to assert their independence. They took over or created the apparatus of a modern nation state.

It remains, of course, true that nation-states pursue their own interests and that stronger states exert pressure on weaker states, but there are several reasons for thinking that relatively weak states are now able to defend their independence better than they could in the nineteenth century. First, the framework of international law and of international organizations now covers the whole world and acts as a substantial, though not infallible, deterrent to aggression. Powerful countries gain from being seen to respect the independence of others. Second, powerful states will not collaborate with each other in bullying weaker states, except in exceptional circumstances. Up to the 1980s, the Soviet Union, though it had the worst record of any major state in its own behavior towards others, acted as a counterpoise to the power of capitalist states. That is no longer so, but a number of Asian states are growing in power and would certainly resist any new colonial adventures. The United States is the only power that could act as the center of a new imperialism and after the scarifying experience of the Vietnam War there is little likelihood that it will attempt to do so.

Political independence, however, did little in itself to change the economic inequality between rich and poor countries, since the fall of empire coincided with a period of sustained prosperity and growth in the advanced countries, and the gap between rich and poor in the world economy opened wider than ever. Not surprisingly, it was soon suggested that the end of formal imperial rule concealed the continuation of economic imperialism. The experience of Latin America strengthened this feeling. The Spanish empire in Central and South America had collapsed in the early nineteenth century, but where the United States had clearly matched and even overtaken Europe, Latin America remained for the most part relatively poor. A rather simplistic way of thinking, which divided the world into developed and under-developed countries (North America, Europe, and Australasia as against Latin America, Asia, and Africa), encouraged the idea that Latin America, despite its long history of independence, should be classed with the ex-colonies of Africa and Asia.

There is only space here for a very broad overview of the issues involved. I will contrast two opposed views of the postimperial world. In one, identified with what came to be called dependency theory, the world is seen as bipolar, divided into a center (the advanced countries, including the main colonial powers) and a periphery (underdeveloped countries, including ex-colonies). Relations between center and periphery are asymmetric — the center benefits, but development in the periphery is blocked or distorted, reproducing the bipolar relation. In this view, the position of a country in the world system is the main factor determining its development. Any internal factors that hinder development are the result of past and continuing participation in the world system (Andre Gunder Frank, 1969a, 1978a; for a fuller discussion see Brewer, 1990). The alternative view, which seems to me to be much closer to the truth, sees the world system as open and constantly changing. In this view, different countries face many possibilities and opportunities. Poor countries can catch up, perhaps rapidly, though there is no assurance that they will do so. Development in any particular area depends both on factors internal to that area and on opportunities for trade, but these are much too varied to be conceptualized in terms of a bipolar center/periphery system.

The factual record tells strongly against the dependency perspective. Even the most casual glance at the record shows the massive variability in rates of development across countries and across time. At one end of the scale are countries like (South) Korea, which have caught up very rapidly, while at the other end of the scale are a number of mostly small, mostly African, countries where per-capita income has fallen. In many cases, falling incomes can be linked to specific events such as civil war or other forms of disruption. There is also great variability between different periods. For example, Brazil was one of the most rapidly growing economies in the 1965–85 period, but per-capita income actually fell in the 1985–95 period. It is possible to calculate average growth rates of (say) per-capita income for different groups of countries, but they are not very relevant. (There is, incidentally, a significant bias in classifying countries by their income now, and then arguing that rich countries have experienced more rapid growth than poor countries. The bias arises because growth leads to wealth. For example, Korea, now a high-income country, started as a low-income country and became rich as a result of rapid growth. Any correlation between growth and wealth must take wealth at the beginning as its basis, though even this proves little.)

The huge variability in growth rates clearly has to be explained by factors specific to particular countries and time periods. From any point of view other than that of dependency theory there is nothing surprising about this. Different areas with very different histories, social structures, resources, and so on, naturally develop differently. There is something distinctly patronizing and Eurocentric in the very word *periphery*, and in the idea that the most important fact about peripheral economies is their relation to the center. Dependency theory remained, in a sense, an ideological prisoner of the imperialist past, unable to recognize how much the world had changed (c.f. Kiely, 1995).

It is not enough, of course, simply to reject the simplistic center/periphery division. It might still be the case that the world economy was in some way slanted against poor countries. What can be said? Consider trade policy first. The trade restrictions imposed on colonies came to an end with the fall of imperialism, though a few ex-colonies continued to benefit from preferential access to the markets of the colonial power for a few traditional products. This does not mean that trade became free. In some sectors, notably agriculture and textiles, advanced countries introduced very restrictive policies in response to political pressure from their own producers. The main losers were the advanced countries themselves, where consumers paid higher prices to divert resources from more productive uses to inefficient, declining sectors, but Third World countries also lost trading opportunities. It has to be added that Third World countries themselves have often introduced extremely restrictive trade policies, and have almost certainly suffered as a result.

As always, any assessment of the effects of trade restrictions depends on the counterfactual used for comparison. Standard trade theory suggests, in general terms, that distorted trade is better than no trade but worse than free trade. (Standard theories of the gains from trade have come under fire, but no one has offered a convincing alternative.) The one generally accepted exception to the standard case for free trade is the protection of infant industries, often cited as the justification for restrictive trade policies in the Third World. It is a valid case, but only if it allows the development of industries that really will grow to the point where they no longer need protection. By this test, restrictive policies have failed more often than they have succeeded. Detailed study of tariff policies has often revealed apparently absurd patterns of effective protection, with unreasonably high rates of protection for some activities and low or negative rates for others, in both advanced and underdeveloped economies. In sum, trade distortions may well have hindered development, but some of the most damaging and irrational restrictions have been imposed by Third World countries themselves.

Now consider capital movements. The main issues have already been discussed in the context of the colonial period. There is no general reason for independent countries, free to borrow in international markets, to regard capital inflows as dangerous or to resent the repatriation of profits by foreign investors. Capital inflows can clearly contribute to development. That does not, of course, mean that borrowing is always well judged. I shall briefly discuss two new aspects of the postcolonial period: direct investment by multinational corporations, and the debt crisis which emerged in the 1980s.

Multinationals are simply businesses that happen to operate in a number of countries. Most are based in advanced countries, although an increasing number are now based in India, Korea, and other ex-colonies. The key question about the operations of foreign multinationals in any particular country is Why is this activity carried out by a foreign firm? Local firms presumably have the edge in terms of local knowledge, so the answer must be that the multinational brings something (perhaps technical knowledge or managerial skills) that the local firms do not have. Unless the multinational has been given special privileges (which some were), any profits it makes over and above the normal return on investment reflect the market value of its firm-specific capabilities. Inward investment may represent an opportunity for local nationals to acquire some of these capabilities — one reason Japanese inward investment was welcomed in Europe in the 1980s was a hope that locals might pick up some of the secrets of the evidently successful Japanese style of management. One particular issue that has been much discussed is that of transfer pricing. It is alleged that firms manipulate the prices used to value intrafirm trade in such a way as to minimize their tax liability. It would be surprising if they did not, but it is hard to see this as a serious issue for anyone other than tax lawyers. People will always try to evade tax, and any regime of taxes and tax enforcement must take account of it. Overall, the existence of multinational companies is a reflection of the growing integration of the world economy but raises no special problems for poor countries.

The debt crisis is clearly a very serious matter for many countries. In outline, what happened is straightforward. In the 1970s a group of (Third-World) countries succeeded in exploiting their collective monopoly position and forced the price of oil up. The main losers were the main oil users, the advanced countries, but the burden also fell on those Third World countries that did not have oil of their own. These countries wanted to borrow to meet the problem, at least in the short term. Oil producers had profits that they wanted to lend, while a complex of policy responses by advanced countries led to rapid inflation and low or negative real interest rates, encouraging borrowing (on variable interest terms). The inevitable reaction came in the 1980s when real interest rates were forced up to very high levels to slow inflation, with disastrous effects for countries that had borrowed heavily. Without in any way minimizing the pain that the debt burden has imposed on some of the world's poorest people, it should be seen for what it is, the product of special circumstances, and not a structural feature of the system or a necessary consequence of borrowing in open capital markets. It has nothing to do with imperialism (or neoimperialism or neocolonialism).

In sum, there is no justification for a claim that the world economy is especially slanted against poor countries. This does not mean that development is guaranteed or that it is simple and costless — it never has been.

**Conclusions**

Imperialism was a byproduct of the emergence and development of capitalism in one part of what was then a fragmented world, and of the subsequent creation of a single world economy. Theories which link imperialism to a particular stage or feature of the development of capitalism (such as underconsumption or the rise of monopoly) are unconvincing and unnecessary. At the most general level, all that can be said is that it was inevitable that unification of the world economy would lead to clashes between incompatible economic, legal, and social systems, and equally inevitable that they would be resolved in favor of the most powerful. At a more specific level, different phases of imperialism in different areas must be analyzed individually, in terms of the interaction between many different and often conflicting forces. They cannot be reduced to mere instances of some general functional necessity of capitalist development.

The effects of imperialism were strikingly asymmetric. Colonial territories were completely transformed by colonial rule and by the impact of the new world economy. The long-run effects of imperialism on the development of colonial territories can be described in specific instances but no overall judgment on them is possible, precisely because they were so far reaching. There is no way to guess what would have happened in the absence of imperialism, and thus no meaningful basis for comparison. In particular the frequently made claim that Third World countries today are poor because they were exploited by their imperialist masters may be true or false, but we cannot know which. In the main capitalist centers, by contrast, change came from within. All the evidence suggests that the long-run effect of empire on the development of the imperialist centers was small. Capitalist countries with and without empires developed at similar rates along very similar lines. None of this, of course, is a defense of empire — the exercise of imperial power was frequently brutal, arbitrary, and humiliating, but moral outrage about the process should not be allowed to distort discussion of its long-term results.

The world economy is now fully capitalist, with only insignificant remnants of other systems. It is divided into a very large number of states that are legally equal, recognized internationally, and equipped with all the essential elements of the modern nation state. This is new. The world economy at the start of the twenty-first century is more like the European economy of a century or more ago, with many independent capitalist countries at varying levels of development, than it is like the world economy of imperialism. The history of Europe in the twentieth century reminds us that conflict, atrocities, and massive setbacks cannot be ruled out but also that relatively backward areas can catch up, as successive regions of Europe have.

# CHAPTER 4

## HOBSON'S *IMPERIALISM*: ITS HISTORICAL VALIDITY AND CONTEMPORARY RELEVANCE

### Gregory P. Nowell[1]

> This conjunction of an immense military establishment and a large arms industry is new in the American experience. The total influence — economic, political, even spiritual — is felt in every city, every State house, every office of the Federal government. We recognize the imperative need for this development. Yet we must not fail to comprehend its grave implications. Our toil, resources, and livelihood are all involved; so is the very structure of our society. In the councils of government, we must guard against the acquisition of unwarranted influence, whether sought or unsought, by the military-industrial complex. The potential for the disastrous rise of misplaced power exists and will persist.
> — President Dwight D. Eisenhower, Farewell Address,
> 17 January 1961

Hobson's *Imperialism: A Study*[2] is an enduring classic of international political economy. In spite of criticism from the right and left, in spite of the development of Keynesian economics as the sophisticated successor of underconsumption theory, in spite of world-system models of the capitalist state system, Hobson's book continues to be, by academic standards of success, enormously popular. *Imperialism* is widely available in paperback, and an Internet search reveals the book's regular appearance on syllabi. *Imperialism* may be classified as one of the great British polemical works of the last two centuries: as brilliant, profound, and passionate a statement as Burke's *Reflections on the Revolution in France* and Keynes' *Economic Consequences of the Peace*. It invites attack and defense; it polarizes its readership and comes to be read not just in terms of its historical content but in terms of the generalized applicability of its message: Was it true *then*? Is it true *now*? If so, *how* is it true now?

Conservatives such as Fieldhouse (1961) wish to show that the work was wrong *then* and by implication is wrong "now" (anytime later). Some radical theories have also bypassed elements of Hobson's three-factor analysis of imperialism, which rests first on underconsumption, second on the military-industrial complex, and third on the broad social consequences of militarization, racism, and their cultural effects.

This essay explores the logic of Hobson's *Imperialism*. I argue that the building blocks of Hobson's argument in *Imperialism* were then and are now relevant for understanding capitalism. I start with underconsumption, proceed to Hobson's political model, and thence to his critics.

## Hobson's Economics: Underconsumption, Imperfectionism, and Overseas Investment

Underconsumption's intellectual lineage starts with Mandeville, Malthus,[3] and passes through Sismondi and Rodbertus.[4] However, scholars have demonstrated that underconsumptionist ideas circulated in the British business press, were represented on British parliamentary boards of inquiry, and present in the American business press.[5] Hobson "socialized" a theory that had been used to justify imperialism. Capitalists had used overproduction to explain the need for overseas markets; working class representatives countered with underconsumption as a rationale for higher wages.

Hobson's underconsumptionist "Taproot of Imperialism" (1902: 71–109) starts with the late nineteenth century's tremendous development of industrial production. The accompanying industrial concentration exacerbated the maldistribution of wealth. With industrial concentration, employers could set their prices for labor. Individual workers had to compete with one another for jobs and had to take whatever price they could get.[6]

The asymmetric labor-capital bargaining positions led Hobson to question what economics knows as Say's Law — the theory that each act of production generates, in the aggregate, enough consuming power (wages) to purchase what is produced.[7] The Keynesian position is emphatically anti–Saysian: full employment rests on adequate investment, adequate investment depends on demand, and neither demand nor investment levels will generate full employment as anything but one out of a wide spectrum of possibilities. By contrast Hobson (p. 81) seems to accept Say's premise: "With everything that is produced a consuming power is born." If full employment of labor and capital is not reached — as should always be the case under Say's law — "the only possible explanation of this paradox is the refusal of owners of consuming power to apply that power in effective demand for commodities" (p. 83). The lack of effective demand originates in the inequalities of the wage bargain struck between workers and industry. This tendency reaches distressing proportions under the conditions of high production and concentrated industry characteristic of the late nineteenth century. In eras with less industrial concentration, industries had to compete against a larger number of other industries to hire labor power. The development of industrial concentration causes workers' consumption to lag at the same time that it greatly increases wealth in the hands of industrialists, who cannot spend it all. Hobson, as we shall see further on, concludes that a Saysian full-employment equilibrium is a condition that can only be fulfilled when the political activities of trade unions and enlightened (liberal free trade, antitrust) capitalists create the necessary government arrangèments. His conclusion resembles Keynes', that full employment is only one of many possible equilibrium conditions, but Hobson's emphasis on the politics of redistribution and a military economy differs radically (in both senses of the word) from Keynes' focus on the factors that influence investor sentiment.

The concentrated industrial conditions of the late nineteenth century favored the creation of cartels and trusts, which for Hobson substitute (p. 85) "regulation of output for reckless overproduction." Cartelization drives the prices of some mass consumption goods up, and further exacerbates the tendency of wages to lag the increase in productivity.

The concentration of wealth in the upper tier of society becomes an impediment to the consumption necessary to achieve maximum domestic investment. "The rich will never be so ingenious as to spend enough to prevent overproduction" (p. 84). This is excess savings. "If the apportionment of income were such as to evoke no excessive saving, full constant employment for capital and labor would be furnished at home" (p. 87). In the absence of redistributive policies, the rich will seek to invest abroad. Investment abroad, however, is a complicated political, cultural, military, and economic proposition. Because other capitalist nations are also undergoing the same developmental process, there will be competition for control of markets and resources. This competition takes the form of the great imperial race for territories that characterized the late-nineteenth century.

Here two elements of Hobson's thought merit consideration from the later Keynesian perspective and vocabulary. Like Keynes, Hobson argues that the rich have a lower marginal propensity to consume than workers and the poor. Income concentrated in the hands of the people with the highest marginal propensity to consume has the most stimulative effect on a domestic economy. Investment, in the Keynesian view, will not occur without a good prospect of a return. Conditions of anemic demand lead to anemic investment. To rephrase the matter from Hobson's perspective, the very fact of having concentrated income among the rich, with their lower propensity to consume, creates simultaneously the conditions for anemic investment.[8] Foreign investment provides a better alternative for the rich to achieve higher rates of return, though this alternative could condemn the working classes of England to unemployment and lower wages.

By contrast Keynes (1936) does not locate the "failure of Say's law" in the inequality of labor and capital at the bargaining table, even though he does discuss distribution of income. He locates the failure of Say's law in the operations of a money economy where investment is governed by jittery investors whose fears about the future reduce today's investment, and as a result, today's income and consumption. Keynes' view is more "intrinsically" anti–Saysian in the sense that a pure market economy has no necessary tendency to full use of resources. Hobson's more radical view points to the weak political power of the laboring and consuming classes as a macroeconomic problem. Keynes' cautious views point more to methods for ameliorating the fears of the investing classes. Hobson views the economic system as generating both actual (imperialist) political outcomes and having the theoretical potential to attain Saysian equilibrium — so long as the capitalists are not in total control. Hobson's democratic socialism is that quintessentially European position, that social democracy is needed to make capitalism work best. The inherent theoretical contradiction of this position has not kept the capitalist social democracies of later decades from achieving fairly respectable records with regard to domestic prosperity, distributional equity, and toning down their global war mongering.

Underconsumption is Hobson's explicitly defined mechanism for capital export. Perhaps part of the political neutering of Keynes' *General Theory* lies in its evasion of this issue, based as it is on a closed economy. In a closed economy uninvested funds must accumulate as idle bank balances, or more accurately, a decrease in the ratio of new bank lending to old loans being paid off. The assumption of a closed economy leads the economic theorist away from an examination of the institutional structures that govern capital export.

Hobson, by contrast, tackled exactly this. But he failed to identify the natural rate of capital export that prevailed before the imperialist age. He really has two capital export mechanisms in his book: the one identified (underconsumption) and the other only present by implication (a natural rate). It follows that we do not know to what level the rate of foreign investment must fall to be nonimperialist. Hobson makes some suggestions on this topic without being convincing. Full employment of capital and labor (pp. 87–88)

> does not imply that there would be no foreign trade. Goods that could not be produced as well or as cheaply at home would still be purchased by ordinary process of international exchange. Such international buying is wholesome, and not the blind eagerness of the producer to use every force or trick of trade or politics to find markets for his "surplus" goods.

Hobson's view accepts in part the Ricardian theory of comparative advantage, and presumably there must be some dynamic that separates out "true and necessary" foreign investment and purchases of foreign goods from the imperialist kind of foreign investment.[9]

Hobson's failure to tackle the problem of the benign levels of foreign investment and the malign investment threshold, which constitutes imperialism, has given impetus to the development of theories of imperialism, or of the imperialist capitalist world-economy, which assume that foreign investment is a constant, or at a minimum, recurring feature of all forms of capitalism and that the effort to identify capital export with Lenin's highest stage — or Hobson's cartels and combines — is misguided or futile. Major theorists have pursued the thesis that capital export is a constant feature of capitalism, although care is usually taken to sort this out into some form of phases; these writers include but are not limited to Luxembourg (1913), Amin (1974, 1980), Wallerstein (1976, 1980, 1989), and Arrighi (1978, 1994). These latter theories offer more or less open-ended views of capitalist expansion. Hobson (1902), Hilferding (1910), and Lenin (1917), see war, revolution, or (for Hobson) social reform as likely to provoke an end to imperialism. But Hobson's stance as a liberal reformer puts him on the hook, more than these other theorists, for distinguishing benign and malign foreign investment. It is a responsibility he evades.[10]

Hobson's highly qualified endorsement of Saysian equilibrium leads him to the argument that maldistribution of wealth — the ability of one class to capture a greater share of aggregate income than another — creates both unemployment (underconsumption) and foreign investment (paving the way to imperialism). His position raises the possibility that he is what Milgate and Eatwell (1983) call an imperfectionist. For imperfectionists the activities of labor unions or business cartels disturb a natural tendency towards a full-employment equilibrium, achieved by fluid adjustments of prices for goods and labor. Prices distorted by business combines or labor contracts lead to underutilization of resources. Post-Keynesian theorists worry that if the imperfectionist interpretation of Keynes is correct, Keynes is an economist for "the exceptional circumstance," when one group has managed to distort the market, rather than the rule, which governs all markets. This view leads to the neoclassical synthesis and sharply constricts the significance of Keynes' work to an unusual subset of market conditions, and therefore to a corner of orthodox economics. It is inimical to post-Keynesian theory.[11] Neoclassical Keynesians would fault Hobson's support of trade unions.

In international relations, the clearest statement of the imperfectionist theory is Mancur Olson's *Rise and Decline of Nations* (1982). Olson cannot see how Keynes makes sense other than as a theorist describing conditions of market imbalances caused by industrial cartels and labor unions. Under these conditions, prices cannot adjust and the market cannot reach full employment equilibrium, which also means that output will not reach optimal levels and the nation as a whole will be threatened with decline (Olson, 1982: 224–232). Over time nations develop the disease of organized "distributional coalitions" in the same way that cholesterol piles up in the arteries of the middle aged; Olson's remarkable thesis is that wars and (in particular losing wars) help clear out the clogged arteries, freeing nations of their plaque-like distributional coalitions, allowing prices among labor and commodities to reach their natural equilibrium levels. Therefore, defeated Germany and Japan outpaced victorious Britain and the United States in postwar growth. Wage rigidity, not demand insufficiency, is the cause of a depression; deficit spending and other Keynesian measures are policies designed to resuscitate economies choked by distributional coalitions. Olson is an imperfectionist by Milgate and Eatwell's criteria.

Is Hobson an imperfectionist like Olson? No. Olson's theses are essentially anti-union, antisocial welfare, and also anticartel, though his antitrust position seems to take a back seat to his hostility to the welfare state. Hobson's program for reforms includes redistribution, higher wages through trade unionism, antitrust and free trade policies. If he were entirely confident that there is a *market driven* tendency towards a full-employment equilibrium, he would hardly need to advocate so strenuously *a political redistribution of power*. As he puts it (p. 90): "Trade Unionism and Socialism are thus the natural enemies of Imperialism, for they take away from the 'imperialist' classes the surplus incomes which form the economic stimulus of Imperialism." Olson also advocates a redistribution of political power: the abolition of the power of such entities as trade unions. But Hobson sees the that there is no natural market equilibrium that can be distinguished from the political question of how power, and with it the ability of the working classes to consume, is distributed in society. Cutting off trade unionism abolishes the only logical counterweight to the development of oligopoly and oligarchy.[12] Without organized political struggle from the dispossessed, the entire national economy, and the state that governs it, are delivered over to the hands of a developing industrial and financial oligarchy. The combination of oligarchy/oligopoly will determine its own level of equilibrium economic activity: one that favors maldistribution of wealth, overseas investment, and the development of the military capabilities necessary to maintain the entire structure of imperialism. As Hobson asserts (p. 93),

> It is idle to attack Imperialism or Militarism . . . unless the axe is laid at the economic root of the tree, and the classes for whose interest Imperialism works are shorn of the surplus revenues which seek this outlet [foreign investment].

We thus return to that vexatious point, whether Hobson, as a liberal, should be held to identifying some preimperialist level of foreign investment that is natural.[13] At some point above this market-determined level, foreign investment becomes toxic, or imperialist. Lacking a direct explanation in *Imperialism*, we venture an answer to the question from another of Hobson's works. In the *Evolution of Modern Capitalism*,[14] Hobson considers early colonialism — as practiced by the Italian Republics, and later Spain and Portugal — to have depended primarily on the forced exploitation of serfs or slaves in a relationship that was exploitative but not exchange based, i.e., not fully capitalist (Hobson 1894: 10–11). The merchant monopolies and colonies that dominated eighteenth-century trade were in some form of intermediate development;[15] the national home economies (Britain, France, etc.) had also not achieved sufficient levels of foreign trade to be fully capitalist. "The breaking-down of international barriers and the strengthening of the industrial bonds of attachment will be seen to be one of the most important effects of the development of machine industry," Hobson says (1894: 34). But in Ireland and the American colonies, Britain's system forbade the development of manufactures (1894: 37) in a manner not characteristic of genuine capitalism. By contrast, in the late nineteenth century,

> The chief directing motive of all the modern imperialistic expansion is the pressure of capitalist industries for markets, primarily markets for investment, secondarily markets for surplus products of home industry. Where the concentration of capital has gone furthest, where a rigorous protective system prevails, this pressure is necessarily strongest. (1894: 262).[16]

Thus Hobson is acutely aware of the earlier struggles for control of international resources. But does not bestow on this long history the appellation of capitalism in the same manner as an Arrighi (1994) or a Wallerstein (1976, 1980, 1989). He idiosyncratically reserves the term *modern capitalism* for the machine age. Lenin, following the tradition of Marx, called imperialism the *highest phase* of capitalism. For Hobson, imperialism would appear to be *the phase at which capitalism begins to exist in its full form*, period. "The chief material factor in the evolution of Capitalism is machinery," he writes (1894: 27). It would follow that capitalism itself is not fully developed until its machines are. The preceding periods were dominated by merchants, had insufficient labor reserves, and had not entered the machine age, which for Hobson also means big investments in need of wide market areas, followed by industrial concentration, cartelization, protectionism, and the accumulation of excess profits, leading to foreign investments.

Hobson cannot preach a return to some earlier ideal of a natural rate of foreign investment — or equilibrium levels of investment and full employment — because he saw those eras as neither benign nor fully capitalist. There never was a time when a fully capitalist economy fully invested savings in productive new investment. Not only can there be no return to such an era, but Hobson puts forward a remarkable either-or argument: *either* a nation moves to class government, oligarchy, imperialism, and underconsumption, *or* it moves to redistributive democratic socialism, including free trade, antitrust policies, and full employment. Reaching a full employment equilibrium *requires* an organized effort by the Trade Unions to organize a social democracy, which, from a secure power base where it controlled the state, would be able to push through the political reforms upon which a full employment equilibrium would depend.

Hobson therefore cannot be an imperfectionist like Olson: Olson sees the perturbations emanating from a political structure that rests upon the supporting economic processes which, were they but left untouched, would tend towards full employment equilibrium. Hobson, by contrast, sees the achievement of a redistributive, full employment equilibrium economy as an artifact of state intervention pushed through by an organized working class.

This means that the Hobsonian economy rests on the social order and power relationships organized by the state.[17] If there is a natural rate of foreign trade and foreign investment in a Hobsonian world, it is because a social democracy has made a determination that it can indulge itself in some Ricardian efficiencies. The nonimperialist rate of overseas investment is a politically determined norm, not a mathematically determined response to a differential in comparative advantages.[18]

Although it is Hobson and Mummery's *Physiology of Industry* that has retained the attention of economists, *Imperialism's* short chapter on underconsumption breaks with the earlier work.[19] In *Imperialism* Hobson conceives of savings as a financial or monetary asset; in the *Physiology* savings were conceived as goods produced but not consumed, as given in the formula Savings = Production − Consumption.[20] But it is true nonetheless that *Imperialism* did not lead to a critique of the nonneutrality of money; and though Hobson launched an attack on the organs of finance (the stock and bond markets) more strident than Keynes', it was not predicated on an analysis of investor fears, liquidity preference, and other features of the Keynesian analysis. *Imperialism's* analysis of underconsumption differs from the *Physiology* primarily in its insistence on the asymmetries of power and wealth accumulation that characterized the development of machine production, industrial concentration, and cartelization. Endorsing trade unions and socialism, and pushing for antitrust policies, social control of investment, and redistribution of wealth, Hobson goes much harder against the interests of capital than he did when writing with Mummery. The *Physiology's* weaker reform suggestion is a tax on savings (Hobson and Mummery, 1889: 203).

More fundamentally *Imperialism* is no longer a theory of economic cycles. The *Physiology* sees underconsumption (Hobson and Mummery, 1889: 205) as chronic, but seems to mean by this recurrent: otherwise the book could not refer to periods as it does (Hobson and Mummery, 1889: 203) in recommending that in "all periods of underconsumption . . . taxation should clearly be directed so as to be the smallest check on consumption." *Imperialism*'s attack on the political power of the dominant classes does not promise abolition of the business cycle. Rather, it promotes world peace through increasing aggregate demand and through a redistribution of wealth.

Hobson's revealing insight also leads him into a blunder. The *Physiology* had already analyzed the stimulative, full employment effects of the Franco-Prussian War (Hobson and Mummery, 1889: 165–185). Hobson's blistering attack on the military-industrial complex is related to the earlier work, and he is obviously worried about the distorting effects of military spending. Hobson sees military spending as an absolute cost financially and also a moral cost. The moral cost remains; the blunder, such as it is, is his failure to see that in the face of chronic insufficient investment and demand, military expenditure could dope the economy to a higher level of aggregate income. This insight in fact would have strengthened his argument, for it lays the basis for why an arms race can be self-sustaining *regardless* of the return on foreign investment, on which so many of Hobson's critics have focused. In the now textbook formulation, $Y = C + I + G$.[21] An increase in G, in this case military expenditure, could increase national income and lead to a full employment equilibrium by creating sufficient demand to allay the investor fears explored by Keynes. Indeed, this particular thrust adds a whole dimension to the question of the empire's profitability generally, because if the empire served to provide the excuse for increased G, and therefore larger Y (aggregate national income), it may have been a paying proposition regardless of calculated returns on the actual possessions or even aggregate overseas investments.[22]

If this is so, then imperialism is not a net financial loss to the economy, regardless of calculated returns from, and expenditures related to, foreign empire. It is a thorny logical problem. On the one hand, economic concentration leads to stagnation. On the other hand, the imperialist solution may increase aggregate income even though it reinforces (by exacerbating the conditions the oligopolies and concentrations of wealth that lead to stagnation) the conditions that would decrease aggregate income. The analogous image is a driver who simultaneously applies the brakes of his vehicle and pushes down on the gas pedal. Forward movement may occur, but at great damage to the system as a whole. So it is with imperialist society.

Rationally, what is needed is a driver (an antitrust, free-trade social democratic party) that will try to run the vehicle in a manner consistent with a logical appreciation of the vehicle as a whole. What occurs in reality is that the driver in place, the imperialist elite, manages to get sufficient forward movement, and to obscure sufficiently the other damage, that all the other passengers in the vehicle are content with its progress. Polemically, Hobson tries to argue that imperialist society amounts to no forward vehicle movement. In reality, the imperialist vehicle can make forward progress, enough to satisfy the other passengers and especially the enlightened trade unionists on whose political capacity Hobson depends. The easy polemical argument, which Hobson implies is true, is that the choice is between zero miles an hour, or a very slow, unsatisfactory speed, and zipping along at a comfortable seventy. Keynesian analysis suggests that a military state might get the social employment vehicle up to sixty or even sixty-five, at which point Hobson's trade unionists might prefer dozing to trying to change the driver. Such working class acquiescence is in fact the pessimistic truth on which Max Weber focused when writing about imperialism.[23]

So assessing imperialism's practicality cannot be a simple matter of economics, and if Hobson misses or obscures the incoming-enhancing benefits of the "doped economy" implicit in the Keynesian $Y = C + I + G$, he does not lose sight of the larger issues: the costs of making the social vehicle move in this fashion are inordinately high, even if satisfactory to some of the passengers as well as the driver. Military Keynesianism creates an international political environment which by definition is unstable because it will lead to war.

The struggle for power, in its dual forms of politics and war, is *always* the underlying principle of Hobson's macroeconomic model: "the safety of nations" (p. 89) was at stake and foremost in his mind. Unlike Keynes, who mocked critics worried about a long-term structural budget deficit by reminding them that in the long run we are all dead, Hobson worried that in the *short-term*, we, or at least many of us, would end up dead as a consequence of imperialist rivalries. A full-employment militarized economy, in the context of such concerns, cannot be presented coolly as a theoretical alternative to a full employment social democratic society that prioritizes redistribution. Hobson's view of full employment equilibrium is inseparable from his views of domestic and international political stability, and a military Keynesian approach to national economic management is intrinsically untenable. Indeed, under Hobson's assumptions the politically dimensionless world of Keynes' *General Theory* is an impossibility: the fundamental cause of demand insufficiency resides in the activities of an oligarchy whose domestic and international political agenda must be understood in order to understand the intractability of the underconsumption problem.[24]

Wrestling with the business cycle, variability in demand and investment, and multiple possible employment equilibria allowed Keynes to revolutionize economics. Hobson abandoned these, in *Imperialism*, to develop a *political* economics. In the Keynesian world demand insufficiency is remedied by interest rate manipulation and demand management through deficits (and redistribution, if we stick to the text of the *General Theory*). The tools are pulled out of the economic tool box and applied and withdrawn as the need waxes and wanes.

Not so Hobson's war cycle: once started it responds not to endogenous fluctuations in national income and aggregate demand, but to perceived threats relating to other nations that are also arming and practicing imperialism. The logic of the military industrial complex is to become a permanent feature of the polity and the economy; each new boost in military production incites the opponent to do the same and vice versa. The arms race has no logical conclusion, save for war. The militarized economy, which ultimately taxes private consumption and directs public expenditure towards the oligopolistic heavy industries that have engendered underconsumption, exacerbates inequalities of wealth and leads to the paradox of enhanced underconsumptionist tendencies even in the face of demand stimulation from the war machine. The process at best mitigates the business cycle at the potential cost of war. As an economic tool it is flawed, because the elite cannot jeopardize its international position by dialing the arms race up and down according to the whims of the business cycle. The military machine becomes embedded in the economy as a whole,[25] and this fact and its deleterious consequences are far more important to Hobson than explaining, in his single macroeconomic chapter, why business cycles might persist under these conditions.[26]

Thus one of Hobson's political-economic achievements is the analytic treatment of what today we can capture in the phrase "military-industrial complex" but which for Hobson emerges as a cumulative portrait in pages 46–107 of his book. The point does not require detailed textual exegesis, and the reader may compare one of Hobson's summarizing statements (p. 106) with the text of President Eisenhower's message reproduced at the head of this essay:

> The economic root of Imperialism is the desire of strong organized industrial and financial interests to secure and develop at the public expense and by the public force private markets for their surplus goods and their surplus capital. War, militarism, and a "spirited foreign policy" are the necessary means to this end. This policy involves large increase of public expenditure.

**Hobson's Political Model**

Hobson's argument that imperialism represents a phase of advanced capitalism bears a strong resemblance to the analyses of Hilferding, Bukharin, and Lenin, that were all written in the ten to fifteen years following the publication of *Imperialism*.[27] However, if the underconsumption thesis that we have advanced is correct, we should not interpret Hobson's political model in the language of the base-superstructure common to Marxism. A more persuasive analog would be Polanyi's *Great Transformation* (1944) which broadly sees the market economy as teetering on the edge of a general social collapse, and which survives precisely because the state resorts to ever-increasing institutional innovations and manipulations of market outcomes (whether in trade or distribution of wealth) in order to keep the market going. If the Marxist sense is that the superstructure of politics rests on the base, the Hobson-Polanyi model might show the market as nested within an elaborate political apparatus or shell apart from which capitalism could not exist.[28] Hobson's portrait of elite capture of the politics of the imperialist state is similar to the Marxist line, but his solution of a free trade, antitrust, nonimperialist social democracy holds out the possibility that the state is not *necessarily* a slave to capital. "Secure popular government, in substance and in form, and you secure internationalism: retain class government, and you retain military Imperialism and international governments" (Hobson, p. 171).

Hobson anticipates Eisenhower's military-industrial complex by 59 years. The costs of imperialism are much more than the coolly calculated financial analysis that his critics have taken from the taproot chapter.[29] The interests that marshal themselves behind the imperial program include the financial community, which reaps commissions on the bonds it floats and the stocks it sells;[30] the military (as a bureaucracy), whose competition with other imperial powers leads to larger budgets; the individual soldiers, many of whom are recruited from the ranks of the unemployed and who see career paths and respectability opened to them; the educated elites, who are candidates for colonial positions overseas; the political parties, which reap generous donations in return for their parliamentary support; and the press, which is financially connected to the great houses of finance and industry.[31]

The captains of industry reap the benefits of overseas investments, as in executing a contract to build a railroad, but also get contracts to build the great, ironically named capital ships and other weapons that support the imperial program. Part of the otherwise unemployed working class gets jobs.[32] In sum, Hobson's portrait again forecasts Eisenhower's warning of a military industraial complex whose influence "economic, political, even spiritual — is felt in every city, every State house, every office of the government"; and of course goes farther than Eisenhower's worry that "we must never let the weight of this combination endanger our liberties or democratic process"[33] by arguing that the military-industrial complex is by its nature a corruptor of democratic liberty.

Pedagogy gets swept up in the tide of imperialism. National chauvinism and racism are the order of the day in the elementary schools.

> To capture the childhood of the country, to mechanize its free play into the routine of military drill, to cultivate the savage survivals of combativeness, to poison its early understanding of history by false ideals and pseudo-heroes . . . to establish . . . geocentric view of the moral universe in which the interests of humanity are subordinated to that of the country . . . to feed the always overweening pride of race (p. 217).

At the university level,

> It is needless to charge dishonesty against the teachers, who commonly think and teach according to the highest that is in them. But the actual teaching is none the less selected and controlled, wherever it is found useful to employ the arts of selection and control, by the business interest playing on the vested academic interests. . . . The real danger consists in the appointment rather than the dismissal of teachers, in the determination of what subjects will be taught . . . the subservience to rank and money, even in our older English universities, has been evinced so nakedly, and the demands for monetary aid in developing new faculties necessarily looms so large in academic eyes, that the danger here indicated is an ever-growing one . . . it is the hand of the prospective, the potential donor that fetters intellectual freedom in our colleges (pp. 218–220).[34]

Again, Hobson anticipated Eisenhower, who more pithily warned, "The prospect of domination of the nation's scholars by Federal employment, project allocations, and the power of money is ever present — and is gravely to be regarded."[35] Some American political scientists continue to see these kinds of influences in the academic community.[36]

Hobson foresees an ideological pitch that foreshadows not only totalitarian imperialism but, to a lesser degree, the fever that swept the United States during the hostage crisis in 1979–1980, or during the War against Iraq in 1990–1991. How to change imperialist society is left unsolved. The colossal conflicts he feared happened not once but twice in his lifetime. The apparent accuracy of his predictive model nonetheless has not earned him respect among scientific American political scientists, whose ideological obstinacy reflects a systemic output — and further confirmation — of Hobson's political-economic model.

**Hobson and his Critics**

This section examines some of the principal objections to Hobson, and how one might respond to them in light of present knowledge.

*Hobson contends protectionism is an essential component of imperialism, but Britain was not protectionist.* Hobson's chapter on imperialist finance (pp. 95–108) argues that the oligarchs of the military industrial complex prefer to hide the costs of imperialism. They do this by financing military expansion through bonds, which are funded by tariffs. Hobson had apparently not given thought to the income tax as an alternative funding mechanism, even though the income tax was used by Britain during the Napoleonic wars and later. However, there was a substantial protectionist movement underway, and Hobson erroneously anticipated its near-term success.[37] Protectionism is also linked to cartels. Here he is on much stronger ground: cartelization played an important role in the British economy at this time, and in fact the legal right to cartelize may have been industry's compensation for not pushing all-out for tariff protection. It is also true that Britain's principal economic dependencies either had or were moving towards protection, a major component of Hobson's argument.[38] Britain did move towards tariff protection during the 1930s.[39]

The militarized society that Hobson extrapolates from the British case seems more representative of later fascist movements. Perhaps the persistence of democratic rule showed Hobson's inability to see the strength of democratic institutions in Britain. Or perhaps it is remarkable that he could create a broadly predictive ideal type based on an analysis of an imperial country that awkwardly fit that type. However, Hobson failed to anticipate that the process of fighting a war might increase the bargaining ability of the working class, in the war's aftermath, to push for social democratic reforms, a thesis developed by Kolko (1994).

*Hobson fails to take into account money, interest rates, and capital deepening (Nemmers, 1956).* Hobson pushed his theory towards a political model of the macroeconomy, and did not develop Keynes' critique of nonneutral money in the capitalist system. Capital deepening is the notion that excess savings, as posited by

Hobson, might not occur because with high investment levels greater innovation might lead to the replacement of unproductive capital stock. High investment rates lead to technological change that "can act in the same capacity as war in destroying excessive saving" (Nemmers, 1956: 40). But this criticism fails to take into account the degree to which cartels may impede investment. Along these lines Freyer (1992) distinguishes cartels from trusts, arguing that the latter may be more efficient, but that British law and practice favored the former. Although it is true that Sylos-Labini (1956) argues that mere replacement capital in a stagnant economy will be more modern and hence increase productivity, his argument does not support Nemmers' critique. Sylos-Labini argues that labor left jobless by improved replacement capital will increase profits and at the same time decrease aggregate demand — which fits in the Hobsonian recipe. Davis and Huttenback (1986: 96) cite the modernity and high returns of the steel and armaments firm, Vickers; but the prosperity of such a firm is integral to Hobson's thesis about the military-industrial complex; he obviously never meant that all industry was stagnating for the entire period, or he could not have attributed the inequality in bargaining between labor and capital to industrial concentration and increases in productivity.

*Hobson fails to see that imperialism is also a free trade phenomenon (Gallagher and Robinson 1953).* Hobson was certainly strong enough in history to know that the British empire expanded before the 1880s and also that it had areas of informal influence. By emphasizing mid-Victorian imperialism, Gallagher and Robinson appear to be capturing only a part of the analysis and in some ways setting up a straw man. Hobson may not have adequately examined the period of mid-Victorian free trade. Nonetheless, his treatment of other periods (especially in the *Evolution of Modern Capitalism*) shows that he distinguishes between mercantile exploitation of foreign economies and imperialism. In particular, *Imperialism* rests on a combined argument about the domination of the economy by an industrial-financial oligarchy organized into a military-industrial complex. This elite's control of the economy, through the medium of cartels, protectionism, and trusts, is a *cause* of underconsumption; its organization into a foreign investment machine with an ever-increasing military apparatus is the oligarchy's *solution* to the same problem.

Could these circumstances have obtained in the period of mid-Victorian free trade? Probably not. For one, the influence of rural landlords was still strong as the nineteenth century opened; the dominance of this class is associated with primarily mercantilist forms of exploitation, which Hobson puts in a separate category from late-nineteenth century imperialism. Secondly, the state of industry was much more competitive. In the presence of many competitors capitalists have difficulty cartelizing, and as a consequence the ability to extract a surplus profit (or monopoly rent) is also reduced. The marginal propensity to consume (the ratio of income spent to income saved) for mid-Victorian society as a whole must have been higher. This means that the capitalists had less surplus and, due to competitive effects and the presence of steady demand that was not held back by inflexible (cartelized) pricing of goods, a more steady demand for their product. Under Hobsonian (and Keynesian) terms this would mean a greater propensity to invest in more production. This economy, then, however cyclical it may have been, was not faced with the kind of stagnation which would give an oligarchy both the incentive and the means to extend its control into the political sphere.[40] Hobson's argument is that the development of the military-industrial complex is an historically specific feature of late-nineteenth century capitalism. Absent the naval arms race, absent the heightened tension over zones of formal control, absent the increasing militarization and propagandization of society, the imperialism of free trade did not present the threat to the safety of nations that Hobson feared. Hobsonian imperialism depends on an international context in which other capitalist nations are in a similar phase of evolution, which spurs individual national elites/oligarchs to ever more confrontational policies. The worst of the nineteenth century's imperial wars were not much in comparison with the twentieth century wars whose basic outlines Hobson wrote about with evident anxiety.[41] Gallagher and Robinson's equation of the imperialism of the free-trade era to the highest stage imperialism that preoccupied writers like Hobson and Lenin is sustainable only so far as the role of the military-industrial complex and domestic cartelization are ignored; and this is as much to say that their analogy is no analogy at all.[42]

*The Edelstein (1982) Analysis.* This is one of the most sophisticated econometric analyses of investment behavior in the mid- to late-nineteenth century period. It pays careful attention to Hobson's excessive savings hypothesis (Edelstein, 1982: 171–195). The author analyzes closely a number of rival savings and investment hypotheses, and in this sense his book is a fair and serious effort to evaluate the forces that led to overseas investment from Britain. Edelstein (1982, p. 195) does give some limited support to Hobson's thesis, especially concluding that "a reformulated concept of over saving does seem to fit the facts of particular episodes at the origins of the 1877–90 and 1903–13 foreign investment surges,"[43] but the conclusion of his book is nonetheless rather negative. "New opportunities [in Britain] for domestic capital formation in the late-nineteenth and early-twentieth century were not stymied by any lack of funding. . . . It was probably low return domestic projects that were neglected, ones with lower returns than the typical lowest return overseas projects actually taken up" (Edelstein, 1982: 311). This perspective tends to shift the perspective away from over savings to capital flows as a result of comparative advantages.

But Edelstein's universe is not really Hobson's universe, and most especially Edelstein has missed Hobson's emphasis on industrial concentration and cartels and their effect on aggregate savings and investment. The data he presents do not really let us distinguish what is going on between the cartelized and noncartelized sectors of the economy, and he does not take into account the fact that by siphoning profits to itself cartelized industry can depress the noncartelized business sector.[44] For Hobson, heavy industry can expand or at least maintain a higher capacity utilization under the influence of government purchasing orders for weapons programs, while the depressed noncartelized sector of the economy still presents an unattractive arena for investment precisely because income is being siphoned off to make purchases from the politically and economically dominant cartelized sector. We have already seen why Hobson chose not to examine the income effects of the

military-industrial complex, but it is odd that Edelstein, seeking to analyze macroeconomic behavior on the basis of hard data, should have omitted the military-
industrial complex's impact on aggregate income and savings. Davis and Huttenback (1986: 160–163) note that Britain maintained "the highest per capita
defense expenditures in the world" and add that a reduction to the levels of
Germany and France (themselves overspending at imperialist levels in Hobson's
view) would have reduced military spending by 12% of national savings. Under
neoclassical economic assumptions, any money not spent on the military would
automatically be reinvested in other sectors of the economy. Under Keyensian
assumptions, however, not spending on the military could exacerbate a chronic
underconsumptionist slump.

Military spending could have offset Hobson's predicted demand insufficiency and
affected the outcome of Edelstein's econometrics. Hobson may not have stated the
matter clearly, but an economist writing with eighty years' advantage should not
have omitted these variables from his assessment of investor behavior.[45] The effects
of military spending may weaken underconsumption effects, in terms of empirical
data; but such a finding would strengthen Hobson's points about the institutional
and political structure of imperialism. Ironically, military spending might have
increased national aggregate income and led to greater aggregate savings that
investors would have sought to place abroad.

Finally, Edelstein pays little attention to the possibility of a British liquidity trap.
The demand stimulus from military spending, in a two-tier economy characterized
by cartelized and noncartelized industry, would benefit primarily the former. The
competitive sector of the economy would have depressed profits and not attract
investment. The growth of foreign investment could have been not so much a flight
*toward* higher returns overseas as a flight *away* from the risks of sinking money into
low-yield bonds where the risk to the asset value of the bond from an interest rate
change was greater than the near-term yield.[46] Where low interest rates fail to make
for investment because it is pushing on a string, foreign investment can represent a
push away from the risk of low yields as well as a pull from foreign investment alternatives. This would explain the paradox in Edelstein's finding (1981: 84–85) that the
risk of default was higher in Britain's domestic (and on average, lower yield) investments, compared to those overseas: ordinarily lower interest rates signal a market
assessment of lower risk, but not in a liquidity trap. The effects of concentration in
the financial sector, where the gradual consolidation of the banking sector during
the entire imperialist period favored incremental increases in reserve requirements
from 6% to 15%, created a powerful domestic deflationary tendency on the supply
of credit and money regardless of the interest rate.[47]

Edelstein's analysis, in short, tests for variables that are consistent with (some)
modern macroeconomics, but he omits many of the key variables that are a component of Hobson's analysis and in so doing also bypasses some of the distinguishing features of late-nineteenth and early-twentieth century economies
(cartelization, trustification, protection) that were central to Hobson's concerns and
those writers whom he influenced. Even Edelstein's tentative support for Hobson's
view on savings is misleading, because Edelstein associates the data fit with business cycles, whereas Hobson had abandoned underconsumption as a theory of the

business cycle and is looking to it more as the economic corollary and driving factor behind oligarchic control of a war-prone political economy.

*The Fieldhouse Critique (1961).* The author of the foreword to the American edition of *Imperialism* calls Fieldhouse's essay cogent and skillful. (Siegelman, 1965: xv) But Hobson gets little credit for having made the general prediction that scholarship would place itself at the service of imperialism, and both Fieldhouse's article and Siegelman's introduction are cold war products.[48] Fieldhouse expounds classical economics, and we find in his discussion of Hobson not even trace elements of Keynes (1936), much less Kalecki (1969/1952), Domar (1947), and Robinson (1949).[49] Fieldhouse was evidently unwilling or unable to situate Hobson's work as part of a continuing economic tradition, blithely ignoring the tribute in Keynes' *General Theory*[50] and jamming Hobson's theory into a mishmash of classical economics and erroneous interpretation. Fieldhouse misses a description of the ideological and economic operations of a military-industrial complex so obvious that only a scholar could have missed it; President Eisenhower certainly did not.

Fieldhouse compounds ideology with bad elementary math. He asserts (Fieldhouse, 1961: 198) that "rates of over 5 percent were available on other British . . . railway debentures and industrials." That is, there was some other reason why investors sought lower (in the neighborhood of 3.94 to 4.97 percent) returns abroad. It is hard to imagine a sillier point. First, he is taking a component of an average and arguing that because one component of the average is high that higher rates of return were generally available; but it is in the nature of an average to have high and low values, so to select out the high values of the British domestic securities market and compare them to average values elsewhere is ideological math mongering of the worst sort, in addition to being wrong.

It is worth examining why investors sought a greater risk premium in *some* domestic British investment over *some* foreign investment, given the low long rate pegged by the Consol. One answer: the British economy was more exposed because it had no tariff, and investors were eager to put money into countries which did. Railway returns in particular depended on the prices they could charge, which depended on the prices fetched by goods. Railways that transported tariff-protected goods were likely to fetch better profits than railways which did not,[51] and investors were right to perceive rails in protected economies such as India or the United States as lower-risk investments than the marginal British rails.[52] As for other industrials, a textile or steel firm in free-trade Great Britain clearly was at greater risk from international competition than its homolog in Germany or the United States. Firms exposed to international competition would have to pay a greater risk premium.[53] Investors would have known the difference between a railroad that was particularly exposed to competitive effects, because it was carrying a high cost product to an inefficient customer or customers, versus a railroad that was not; and they would have known which steel company might be exposed to competition and which had landed lucrative contracts building dreadnoughts. The aggregate data do not by their nature show the specific factors which account for a spread of yields.

The failure of the British economy to enact tariffs in before World War I meant not that Hobson's model was wrong but that the mechanism was under specified.

In Great Britain industry received the legal right to cartelize; cartel contracts were enforceable in court and cartel monitoring and enforcement was a recognized specialty in accounting (Freyer 1992: 3, 13, 19). This was industry's *quid pro quo* for not getting a tariff; the finance sector required free trade if Britain were to provide a market so that its worldwide creditors could earn the money to pay Britain's loans back. Moreover, established industry, particularly steel, benefited from the sales of British goods as a corollary of British finance.[54] The free trade policy was not entirely negative; but needless to say high finance had no problems with tariffs in the countries in which the investments occurred, as these tariffs protected the return on investment.[55]

The *legal cartelization* of the British economy differed from the *trustification* of economies such as the United States. The trust buys up all competitors and shuts the least efficient down. The cartel is a federation designed to protect all members, including the least efficient. The trust captures through market share and economies of scale higher profits with modernizing investment. By contrast, new investment is discouraged among cartel members because it upsets production quota allocations and makes for difficult problems, especially where legal enforcement of a cartel contract is an option. Even without tariffs, Britain had a recipe for a Hobson-type underconsumption: high prices through cartelization, an elite which captured excess profits through cartelized pricing, depressing demand; and reduced incentives to invest domestically, due to anemic demand and the high exposure to international competition, against which legal cartelization could afford only some protection. These forces make for exactly the kind of environment that would export capital.[56]

Fieldhouse attacks Hobson for building a model that depends on foreign investment and then showing as evidence relatively economically uninteresting geographic assets such as Africa and the Far East. The bulk of British overseas investment went to places like the United States, Canada, and Argentina. Here, even Hobson's supporters have gone astray.[57] In the nineteenth century the world's resources were largely unknown. The opening of the American prairies to wheat exports threatened ruin not just to Germany's Junkers but to the railroads that carried their grain to market. Such was at least part of the rationale for the "alliance of iron and rye." No one anticipated that Persia would yield oil and when it did it greatly complicated the development of Mesopotamia and was seen as a threat to existing oil export facilities in the Caucasus.[58] If I build a railroad in the United States, I do not want to see the value of its export markets threatened by rival products from Australia or Argentina or anywhere else. If I export diamonds and gold from South Africa at enormous profit, what risk do I run if someone should find a similar resource in some other part of Africa?[59] Can I afford to have that person not be me? Hobson's *Imperialism* furnishes the answer: since the imperialists can shift the cost of acquiring overseas territory on to others, and since they benefit from manufacturing the war machine, which helps to acquire these territories, and since they benefit from floating the bonds and collecting the interest thereon: why *not* acquire everything in sight? As an imperialist, it is my *best* policy for protecting *existing investments*, and especially the best policy *for making sure that a potential competitor does not acquire a resource which will allow him to compete in my cartelized markets*. This is the true nature of the struggle for international territories. If I want to protect my grain or mineral investments in Argentina or the United States from new production that could open up in a few years, it is better to acquire new real estate, as in Africa, even if I'm not sure what is there and even if, once it is acquired, I have no particular incentive to invest there, because the fruits of such investment might compete with my other investments elsewhere.

Thus it is only of minimal interest that some territory did or did not receive a given quantity of investment. Hobson was right. The trend towards investing abroad was linked to the need to acquire ever more territories abroad, because returns and prices in the international markets of the time were developing so quickly that the profitability of any one investment could not be assured if some other new investment came on line so quickly that lower prices internationally threatened the ability to recoup major capital outlays. This would be a threat to industrial capital and to the financiers who provided the liquidity to make the physical investments. Logically they should have collaborated in the imperialist enterprise; intrinsic to the undertaking was that many or most territorial acquisitions would perform poorly viewed from the perspective of total outlay versus total return.

Relevant to Fieldhouse's view of Hobson is Hobsbawm's (1987: 61) wry observation, "The disadvantage of the anti-anti-imperialist literature is that it does not actually explain that conjunction of economic and political, national, and international developments, which contemporaries around 1900 found so striking that they sought a comprehensive explanation for them. It does not explain why contemporaries felt that 'imperialism' at the time was both a novel and historically *central* development. In short, much of this literature amounts to denying facts which were obvious enough at the time and still are."[60]

## Hobson Post-Hobson

I have set forward the outlines of a defense for Hobson's *Imperialism*. These arguments go beyond Hobson's. I have argued for a demand-enhancing effect to a military-industrial complex, which Hobson failed to consider. I have set forward a new argument about the lack of correlation between territories acquired and the economic incentives to acquire them. I have argued that cartelization, combined with free trade and concentration in banking in the British metropole, may have discouraged domestic investment as much as the combination of trusts and tariffs offered by Hobson. I have raised the possibility that capital export was linked to a version of the Keynesian liquidity trap.

Are we still talking about Hobson? Yes and no. Hobson's etiology of imperialism is in the main accurate. I have extended Hobson's arguments in ways to which he himself might have been sympathetic. I do not claim to have laid a definitive interpretive framework for imperialism; mainly, I find legitimate the continuing interest in *Imperialism*, and suggest it provides a plausible framework on which to build. Hobson's core issues are oligarchy, oligopoly, their impact on the political system, their impact on the potential for social control over investment, and redistribution of income. This, I would argue, is the true Hobson, who appeals to the modern reader, not the narrowly construed explicator of colonialism.

Looking at the broad picture, the decline in the great imperial holdings of Britain, France and other countries in the post-World War II period, combined with the simultaneous evolution of these countries as redistributive welfare states, is in the main consistent with Hobson's views. So is Abraham's analysis (1986) of Weimar Germany, which links the eventual strength of militarism to the weakness of labor and internationally oriented business, in comparison to the dominance of protectionist heavy industry and agriculture. Moreover, the post-World War II United States, the one capitalist state with the most developed military-industrial complex, also had the weakest social welfare program, which as Fordham (1998, pp. 103–130) has documented, is not merely coincidence but a matter of conscious policy-making at the highest level. These are all component themes of Hobson's social analysis.

Hobson's emphasis on the need for social control over capital investment, unpopular now, was also unpopular in his time.[61] Consider the implications: suppose that the market for steel in Britain has reached a saturation point. The distribution of wages and income in the steel industry has at once concentrated income, limiting the marginal propensity to consume, and concentrating funds for investment in the hands of an elite that sees little prospect for making an adequate return by investing domestically. The same economic process concentrates political power and alters the ideological landscape. It becomes easy to see that the solution to Britain's problem is to sell more railroads overseas. The holders of today's physical assets see the safest yields in incremental markets for existing investments. They prefer this to investing in a new technology like electrification. As a result, electrification is slowed by the commitment of the investing class to find markets for existing forms of production.

Theoretically, a social democracy might opt to invest in electrification instead, providing for domestic investment, increased domestic consumption, a higher quality of life, and diminishing the need for demand enhancement that caters to entrenched interests.[62]

As this is written, the California oil industry (Chevron, ARCO, Unocal) extracts major monopoly rents (via zone pricing) from its market and is a major investor in overseas oil ventures in Russia and the Caspian sea. For two decades the industry has stifled political proposals to invest in a new, alternative fuel infrastructure and vehicles, that would have less damaging effects on the environment. The world waged war against Iraq, followed by a blockade. It is not colonies that are thus preserved, but the viability of current investments and consumption patterns in transportation.[63] All the component elements of Hobson's analysis are there, including market concentration, anti-Arab and anti-Moslem racism, surplus profits concentrated in the hands of a few, stifled domestic research and development, foreign investment, war, and a lack of any kind of democratic participation in decisions affecting aggregate income and the distribution of wealth (imputable to the wholesale corruption of the ruling parties). The whole is accompanied by a stifling ideological environment, which at every level (university, press, television, cinema) assures us that ours is the just and proper way.

Social control of investment might introduce new transportation technologies. As matters stand, the acquisition of Caspian and Russian crude supplies, which will become chains that tie the investing oil companies to fighting strenuously for the preservation of the technologically obsolescent, environmentally harmful transportation system on which they depend. Money sent overseas might be better used at home, benefiting not just Californians but world peace. Hobson's thesis that oligopolistic market control makes for capital export and no investment (or the wrong investment) continues to have relevance.

Hobson's view of a positive new liberal internationalism (Long, 1996) is less favorably viewed by radical reformers in an age where the human costs of the international division of labor are all too well known.[64] But Hobson's passionate objection (pp. 223–284) to the exploitation of the third world is not recognizably different from modern criticisms of the *maquiladoras* in Mexico or elsewhere.

Where does that leave us? The sophistication of authors like Arrighi (1994) or Wallerstein (1976, 1980, 1989) exceeds that of Hobson's imperialist model, just as the whole Keynesian and post-Keynesian traditions surpass Hobson's underconsumption theory. But given the relatively weak position of working class parties in Europe, and their virtual non-existence in the United States, there will be a continuing relevance of the Hobsonian problematique by default. Given the dominance of capitalist values, the humanitarian concerns underlying Hobson's work will be discussed within the basic framework provided by *Imperialism*, or they will not be discussed at all.[65]

The theory of state behavior known as realism, which vaunts the pursuit and maximization of power by the state above all else, continues to bear out the accuracy of Hobson's fears about the permeability of academe to imperialist ideology. In what remains his most prescient sentence, Hobson (pp. 188–189) predicted, summed up, and dismissed a half century of post-World War II American academic writing: "The notion of the world as a cock-pit of nations in which round after round shall eliminate feebler fighters and leave in the end one nation, the most efficient, to lord it on the dung-hill, has no scientific validity." Such is the American school of "realism" in international relations.[66]

Thus the modernity of Hobson's *Imperialism* and its powerful classroom appeal lie in its etiology of power. By writing with enduring clarity about international imperialism in his own time, he identified the dysfunctions resulting from the domination of international capital in our own.

*Notes*

---

[1] The author wishes to thank P.J. Cain, William Darity, Jr., Benjamin Fordham, David Skidmore, David Gibbs, and John Legge for their comments on drafts of this paper. The author thanks the many participants on the post-Keynesian theory Web site at http://csf. colorado. edu/pkt.

[2] In this paper, all citations with a page number only are to Hobson (1902). Please note in cases where an original date of publication is given, as in Hobson (1902), a more recent date of publication and publisher is given in the reference. It is to this more recent date that the page numbers refer.

[3] See brief discussion of Malthus in Hollander (1996).

[4] See Bleaney (1976) and M. Baratt Brown (1974) for very thorough evaluations of this lineage. See Perelman (1996) for late nineteenth century theory and practice. Hobson cites Wilshire (1900) the California real-estate tycoon after whom Wilshire Boulevard in Los Angeles is named.

[5] See Kadish (1994); Etherington (1983, 1984, pp. 6–39); Cain (1978, 1985).

[6] Chick (1996, p. 186) presents a similar portrait of workers as in "invidious positions in capitalism . . . except at full employment in a buoyant market." Hobson's view of the structural weakness of labor is absent from Keynes' *General Theory* (1964/1936).

[7] See discussions of Say (1803) in Henwood (1997: 202) and Kates (1996).

[8] Keynes (1936: 373) advocates redistribution but with much less enthusiasm than Hobson: "Thus our argument leads towards the conclusion that in contemporary conditions the growth of wealth, so far from being dependent on the abstinence of the rich, as is commonly supposed, is more likely to be impeded by it. One of the chief social justifications for great inequality of wealth is, therefore, removed."

[9] To point out that Hobson did not resolve this fundamental problem is only to say that he did not resolve what remains unresolved by everyone else. The various authors of a recent collection of essays (Nivola, 1997) on environmental regulation blithely assume that any increment of regulatory cost to a producer will result in an incremental incentive to invest overseas, but make no effort to show just what a normal rate of overseas investment, absent the horror of environmental regulation, would be.

[10] Hilferding (1910: 233–234) saw capitalism's potential to evolve into a total cartel. Lenin posited that imperialism was the highest stage of capitalism because the combination of exploitation and war would force the revolutionary transition to socialism. Post-World War I authors needed some version of imperialism to account for capitalism's continuation. See Baran (1957), Sweezy (1942), and Strachey (1959).

[11] See discussion in Palley (1996: 37).

[12] On this point and others there is a strong echo of Hobson in Kalecki (1952).

[13] Arrighi's brilliant *Geometry of Imperialism* (1978) stresses the inapplicability of Hobson's model to the earlier imperialist periods — as did Hobson himself.

[14] This work was first published in 1894 and revised in 1906 (the version used here). So it both precedes and antecedes *Imperialism*.

[15] Hobson concedes that there were "single examples on a tolerably large scale of capitalist organization in the later Middle Ages" (1894: 20) but he does not extend his concept of developed capitalism to the early renaissance.

[16] *Imperialism* maintains this stance: markets and manufactures are mentioned along with outlets for investment of surplus profits on p. 71, but on p. 73 he says, "Far larger and more important is the pressure of capital for external fields of investment."

[17] Post-Keynesian theory has shown more interest in the state and the distribution of power. For example Palley (1996: 11) sees post Keynesian economics as an extension of Keynes, including "a recognition that all economies are social systems, and capitalist economies therefore need to be analyzed as such." Wage inflation is seen as the "symptom of a struggle over the distribution of income" (Davidson, 1991: 89), a view held by other post-Keynesians (see Susjan and Lah, 1997; Lavoie 1992). But these views omit the specific relationship of state to society.

[18] This conclusion is very similar to Freeden (1994: 28), who writes "Hobsonian free trade was only free within the framework of rational social control and coordination . . . economic liberty involved challenging monopolies and therefore permanent measures of public control."

[19] Magnusson (1994: 149–150) makes a similar point, focusing on other elements of Hobson's argument.

[20] Hobson and Mummery (1889: 36). See also Backhouse (1994, pp. 85–86) who argues that Hobson and Mummery have an unresolved tension between savings as fully invested capital and its potential to exist in the form of hoarded money. In the Keynesian formulation, Savings = Income – Consumption (Keynes, 1964: 63).

[21] $Y = C + I + G$, or in English, (National Income) = (National Consumption) + (National Investment) + (National Government Expenditure). Macroeconomists drop the national prefix because the discussion of aggregates is assumed.

[22] See Davis and Huttenback (1986: 166–194, 306); Edlestein (1981), for example for attempts to calculate the profitability of the empire.

[23] Weber (1968, 1: 901–940).

[24] This is not to say, however, that assessing the implications of Keynesian thinking from different political perspectives has not been undertaken. See analyses by Block (1977: 107); Collins (1981: 1–20); Turgeon (1997). Keynes himself noted that it might be "politically impossible for a capitalistic democracy to organize expenditure on the scale necessary to prove my case — except under war conditions." (Cited by Collins, 1981: 12).

[25] We have not introduced M. Baratt Brown's (1974) otherwise excellent study of imperialism into this essay for several reasons. First, it develops primarily the ideas of Joan Robinson. Second, it makes no reference to Hobson at all, save in the section on Marxism; and even then it references the *Physiology*, not *Imperialism*. Finally, it ignores the role of the military-industrial complex, which, if one were building a Keynesian theory of imperialism based on the Hobsonian antecedent (and this would certainly be logical), would be an essential component of the analysis, especially insofar as demand management through military spending is a component of state behavior in the international system.

[26] The emphasis here on the military-industrial complex and its effects on aggregate demand points to problems with Edelstein's (1982) focus on economic cycles, discussed below.

[27] Arrighi (1978) claims that the Bukharin (1915), Hilferding (1981), and other Marxist theories are distinct ideotypical models. I follow Brewer (1980: 112–113) in seeing Hobson as linked to, but not directly a part of, the multiple Marxist models of imperialism.

[28] Przeworski (1990: 69–72) argues that Marx offers no Marxist theory of the state because the state is not a fundamental part of the reproduction of capital.

[29] See section on Hobson's critics.

[30] Hobson shared a general antisemitism of the period (see analysis in Arendt 1951) which shows itself in one line of *Imperialism* (1902: 57): "United by the strongest bonds of organization, situated in the

very heart of the business capital of every State, controlled, so far as Europe is concerned, chiefly by men of a single and peculiar race, who have behind them many centuries of financial experience. Hobson's *War in South Africa* (1900: 189–197) has a good deal more on Jews. But his *Evolution of Modern Capitalism* (1894) discusses the development of finance (pp. 235–272) without any reference to Jews, and sees finance as a necessary development of capitalism with no reference to ethnicity; but there are two rather neutral references to the Jewish role, relating again to South Africa (pp. 266 and 268). In *Imperialism*, Hobson concludes his analysis of finance by referring to the money lending classes (p. 109). Had he wanted to pin imperialism on the Jews, the word *classes* would have been neither present nor plural. Hobson does not meet the criteria for modern political correctness, which is disappointing given his advanced pluralist views regarding race and imperialism generally, but *Imperialism* is first and foremost a work that stresses the interest of classes. See also Magnusson (1994: 147).

[31] Bribery of the press in French imperialism is well documented; it is specifically mentioned in a source document authored by the oil magnate Calouste Gulbenkian (see Nowell, 1994: 99) and twice by Feis (1964: 133, 157–158). But Hobson meant structural interlocks of ownership rather than bribery of editors.

[32] Hobson had no concept of the multiplier effect. See Backhouse (1994).

[33] President Dwight D. Eisenhower, Farewell Address, 17 January 1961.

[34] Hobson hoped publicly funded education would avoid some of these ills, but he could not know that state legislatures could be as interfering as private donors.

[35] Eisenhower, Farewell Address, 17 January 1961.

[36] See discussion in Chilcote (1994: Chapter 2, especially pp. 40–48).

[37] See history in Brown (1943).

[38] Edelstein (1981, 1994) discusses the profitability of the tariff-protected colonies.

[39] Freyer (1992) makes a compelling argument about the impact of cartelization on the British economy. See also Macrosty (1907). Nemmers (1956: 47) acknowledges that Hobson remarkably foresees the development of protectionism.

[40] This argument fits well with Darity (1992: 164). Darity argues that the colonial economy "displayed a remarkable and unique array of intersectoral linkages of both types for Europe and especially for Britain. Hence the multiplier effects were bound to be quite substantial." But, though the mercantilist slave trade sought monopolies of sale of goods in both directions, it did not seek to impose monopolies on the production of goods in Britain. Hence the spur to investment and the strong multiplier effect. In the Hobsonian universe maldistribution and cartelization concentrate savings and discourage investment. In theory the marginal propensity to consume (for capitalists especially) would be lower and hence the multiplier weaker.

[41] Cain (1990: 34) describes World War I as a complete surprise to Hobson, which is difficult to reconcile with his authorship of *Imperialism*. Perhaps this is a case of "not only is your worst nightmare right, but it is far more right than you wanted to believe."

[42] Cottrell (1991: 42–47) offers a criticism of Gallagher and Robinson's thesis based on an economic and diplomatic evaluation that does not address the underconsumption thesis.

[43] Edelstein (1981: 83) makes the same point.

[44] A point made by Kalecki (1952: 18); Hilferding (1910: 233–234); Baran (1957: 85) and by Hobson himself (1927: 44).

[45] The omission is repeated in Edelstein (1994), in a piece that is otherwise provocative.

[46] Keynes (1936: 202). See also Darity and Horn's argument (1988) that banks are loan pushers.

[47] Beach (1935: 87–88) comments on the shift of reserve requirements between domestic lending banks that were gobbled up by foreign lending banks. Altered reserve requirements after a merger could have reduced capital available for lending by 57%. Had this happened all over the country all at once, it would have been a catastrophic deflation. Instead, it was a continual pressure resulting from banking consolidation.

[48] Magnusson (1994: 154–160) also explores Fieldhouse's critique of Hobson.

[49] See discussion by Schneider (1994: 104) who furnishes the Robinson (1949) and Domar (1947) citations and who elaborates on Hobson's relevance to the Harrod and Domar growth models.

[50] Clarke (1990) analyzes the Hobson-Keynes relationship and finds Keynes discovered Hobson largely *after* the *General Theory* had been completed. But Clarke misses a whiff of a suggestion that Keynes (1919: 12) may have picked up Hobson's influential *Imperialism* argument indirectly: "The projects and politics of militarism and imperialism, of racial and cultural rivalries, of monopolies, restrictions, and exclusion, which were to play the serpent to this paradise."

[51] Cf. Grosvenor (1885: 88, 92), who links upward movements in railroad stock prices to news of cartel agreements in the coal industry. Investors knew that the railroads would charge more for higher-priced coal, and that freights were less when a coal "combination" fell apart.

[52] Edelstein (1981: 78) shows that railroads were higher yield investments overseas than at home.

[53] Edelstein (1981: 84–85) finds that the risk of default on an investment was higher in Britain than in overseas investments.

[54] See Edelstein (1981: 90–91).

[55] Loan guarantees and land grants were important in addition to tariffs. See Cairncross (1953, p. 187).

[56] W. P. Kennedy (1987) finds anemic investment in late nineteenth century high technology in Britain, in line with the arguments developed here and by Hobson.

[57] E.g. Strachey (1959); Sweezy (1942: 303) likens colonial expansion to the economics of monopoly, but does not make the jump to the protection of investments from further productive development.

[58] See Nowell (1994: 45–79).

[59] As an illustration of how unexpectedly new resources could open up, Davis and Huttenback (1986: 60) give an example of how copper was discovered in Peru after a railroad was built to service a silver mine.

[60] Italics in original.

[61] Long (1996: 5) recounts how Hobson's antiimperialist lectures were frequently broken up by jingoistic mobs.

[62] W. P. Kennedy (1987) makes a strong argument for the general lack of investment in leading-edge technologies in Britain.

[63] Published studies of the air quality struggle per se are scant and published linkages of this struggle to the investment behavior overseas of the California firms nonexistent. An introduction to some of the issues may be found in Nowell (1990).

[64] Mander and Goldsmith's (1996) *Case Against the Global Economy* presents a variety of anti-free trade views that are superficially anti-Hobsonian but which share many of Hobson's values.

[65] The U.S. has left-wing pluralist tradition that frankly discusses the adventures and misdeeds of capitalism, and that has been resilient in spite of being marginal. Examples include Beard and Smith (1934), Schattschneider (1935), Tarbell (1936) and Key (1942). Neopluralist analyses include Gibbs (1991), Skidmore and Hudson (1993), Ferguson (1995), Fordham (1998), Boone (1992), Cox (1994), Nowell (1994) and a number of others. See essays in Cox (1996).

[66] See Long (1996: 86–90, 119–120, 243–244) for insightful analysis of realist theory in comparison to Hobson's views. Some works, such as Lebow and Risse-kappen (1995) indicate disillusionment with the dominant paradigm. It should be noted, however, that traditional realist works such as Mahan (1890) are rather more lucid in integrating economics and state power than realist epigones.

# PART II

IMPERIALISM AND DEVELOPMENT

# CHAPTER 5

## EARLY MARXIST CRITIQUES OF CAPITALIST DEVELOPMENT

## John Willoughby

### Introduction: Classical and Marxian Antecedents to Development Economics

Development economics is a post-1945 phenomenon. After World War II, some mainstream economists responded to the challenges of anticolonial nationalism and began to study those structured processes that prevented significant increases in material living standards throughout much of the Global South. By the end of the 1950s, with the substantial financial assistance of many American foundations and governmental institutions, an enormous literature on underdevelopment had emerged. Academics such as W. Arthur Lewis, Gunnar Myrdal, Ragnar Nurkse, and Albert Hirschman had attained substantial academic fame, and talented graduate students entered this field with alacrity. As a result, nearly every economics program in the Western world had at least one development expert on its faculty.

Despite the apparently recent vintage of this branch of economics, one could reasonably argue that modern economics owes its birth to development concerns. Adam Smith's "inquiry" raised many of the main themes that concerned the postwar specialists in the development field. His arguments about the importance of providing the appropriate incentive and property rights framework for growth, about the need for intensified capital accumulation, and about the stimulating effects of trade remain central to much mainstream development theory (Smith, 1910).

During the late 1940s, however, Smith was not featured in much of the new literature. This may have been because of the central role which most governments played in national economies in the aftermath of World War II as well as what seemed to many to be the manifest failure of liberal capitalism during the interwar period. Moreover, the search for economic rigor led many theorists to look upon Smith's work in *The Wealth of Nations* as brilliantly presented but intellectually mediocre (Schumpeter, 1954: 185).

For this reason, the later writings of Thomas Malthus and David Ricardo — despite their relative institutional barrenness — contributed more to the rebirth of the economics profession's analysis of growth. W. Arthur Lewis's characterizes his deservedly famous article "Economic Development with Unlimited Supplies of Labor" (Lewis, 1954) as an extension of classical economics growth theory. In addition, Ricardo's theory of comparative advantage remains central to many development accounts (Ricardo, 1951). Finally, Thomas Malthus's demographic theory had the virtue of presenting a very clear causal mechanism. That this vision of peasants and workers as unthinking reproductive rabbits provided little guidance to policymakers was not important. Malthus, at least, proposed a link between increases in material production and movements in per capita income, which could be explored and modified. The prejudicial nature of Malthus's vision meant, however, that his contribution to early development theory ceased once modern demographic science became established (Malthus, 1966).

This quick survey is not meant to imply that other classical and early neoclassical economists made no contribution to development economics. Still, with the exception of John Stuart Mill's infant industry theory (Schumpeter, 1954: 505), it is fair to say that orthodox descendants of the classical school made little effort to improve on Smith's wide-ranging attempt to link our understanding of historical evolution to economic forces. Nor were there any startling new breakthroughs in trade and growth theory before World War II, which allowed orthodox economists to move beyond Ricardo's contributions.

In contrast to this paradoxically weak classical and neoclassical tradition, Marxian theory had by the early twentieth century already developed rich analytical descriptions of the evolution of mature capitalism and the spread of capitalist social relations to backward economic territories. Even before World War I, two of the theoretical and political giants of this golden age of Marxian — Rosa Luxemburg and Vladimir Lenin — had proposed two sharply different conceptions of the prospects of capitalist development in the periphery (Lenin, 1960; Luxemburg, 1913). Moreover, the 1920s produced well-focused debates within the fledgling Soviet Union on the role of the state in promoting rapid industrialization. In these great debates, Leon Trotsky, Nikolai Bukharin, Evgeni Preobrazhensky, and others attempted to articulate how linkages should evolve between the backward rural sector and the modern industrial one. This debate not only focused on the savings generation process, but also concerned itself with the nature of the rural sector, the pattern of investment that the state should promote, the connections that should be established between agricultural exports and capital goods imports and the appropriateness of the incentive framework provided by markets (Erlich, 1960).

The criminal brutality of Stalinist collectivization and the superindustrialization drive cast these vivid debates into the historical dustbin for a time. Moreover, the Cold War, which quickly followed World War II, placed another barrier between the direct use of this early, vibrant Marxian tradition by the early mainstream development theorists in the West. Marxian academics themselves also tended to neglect the 1920s debates — although the early argument between Luxemburg and Lenin played some role in the development of radical dependency theory and the mode of production school.

Despite these weak links to modern development theory, an exploration of early Marxian discussion of the capitalist development process and of appropriate development policy is of interest. It is always useful to discover an old tradition that poses important issues in new and potentially creative ways. Recent advances in development economics have made many of the precise formulations of the early Marxians obsolete, but a study of these writings demonstrates that the issues that confronted these revolutionary intellectuals still define many of the major challenges facing development economics today. Indeed, recent critiques of the inequitable and coercive character of industrial development could still gain important insights from early Marxian development theory.

**Understanding the Capitalist Development Process: Marx, Lenin and Luxemburg**

Karl Marx provided only limited guidance to the Marxists of the next two generations who wished to understand the capitalist development process in precapitalist regions of the world economy. His own writings stressed a dialectic between the devastation of preindustrial production forms and the spread of advanced industrial technique. That this process could coexist for some time is perhaps Marx's major contribution to modern economic and sociological development theory. Economic and social dualism was key to the Marxian vision of the spread of capitalist social relations (Marx, 1972a; Marx, 1972b).

In addition to this insight, Marx also stressed the importance of political coercion in the creation of new social relations. He argued that the establishment of capitalist property relations required the forcible expropriation of those societies with communal claims to land and other productive resources. The combination of this theory of primitive accumulation with his description of social devastation and prolonged economic dualism suggests that the capitalist economic development process requires concerted political coercion (Marx, 1976). On the other hand, Marx's own theoretical discussions of capitalist evolution tended to place the primitive accumulation process during the rosy dawn of the emergence of capitalism. (The English word *primitive* does not adequately capture the meaning of the German word that Marx used, *ursprungliche*. The term *ursprungliche Akkumulation* suggests original or beginning accumulation.) This ambiguity meant that those Marxists following in the master's footsteps could reasonably disagree about the centrality of state violence in the development process. Such an emphasis on coercion could also call into question Marx's own belief that the development process was ultimately progressive.

It is not surprising that debates over these issues emerged most vividly in prerevolutionary Russia. Radical populists argued that capitalism was destroying egalitarian communal structures of peasant organization. Moreover, they maintained that this process was occurring because capital accumulation produced beyond its limited market. The problem of underconsumption, according to this school of thought, was particularly acute in environments of mass impoverishment, and this acute contradiction led to aggressive capitalist attacks on collectivist peasant life.

This perspective did not win universal approval among prerevolutionary Russian radicals. In particular, the young Vladimir Ilyich Lenin was vociferous in rejecting the argument that capitalism faced underconsumption problems or that there was much of anything progressive that existed within communal pre-capitalist economic forms. Lenin made his most impressive defense of Marxian orthodoxy in his earliest major work *The Development of Capitalism in Russia* (Lenin, 1960). This work stands out not only because of the later fame of the author, but because of Lenin's ability to combine careful empirical research with well-argued Marxian theory.

Lenin began by elaborating Marx's original argument that capitalism differentiates the peasantry further and dispossesses many from the land. He classified the position of the rural population according to its relations to a variety of surplus extracting processes. (Indeed, this conceptualization of exploitation bears striking resemblance to the much later and more abstract work of John Roemer (1982.) Despite this acknowledgment of the harsh intensification of capitalist inequality, the young Lenin dismissed contemptuously the fundamental tenets of Russian radical populism. First, the future Bolshevik leader used the reproduction schemes developed by Marx in Volume II of *Capital* to deny that there existed any chronic problem of underconsumption associated with the emergence of capitalism in pre-capitalist societies. Second, Lenin vigorously maintained that the destruction of precapitalist peasant life is ultimately progressive and should be welcomed by Marxists.

This latter argument recalls Bill Warren's controversial, 1970s arguments that Marxists should welcome imperialism's progressive role as a pioneer of capitalism (Warren, 1980). Since Lenin's later work often suggested that capitalism had become parasitic and reactionary, it is useful to quote extensively one important passage of this earlier work:

> One has only to picture to oneself the amazing fragmentation of the small producers, an inevitable consequence of patriarchal agriculture, to become convinced of the progressiveness of capitalism, which is shattering to the very foundations the ancient forms of economy and life, with their age-old immobility and routine, destroying the settled life of the peasants who vegetated behind their medieval partitions, and creating new social classes striving of necessity towards contact, unification, and active participation in the whole of the economic (and not only economic) life of the country, and of the whole world (Lenin, 1960: 382).

Later on in *The Development of Capitalism* Lenin extended this position by arguing forcefully for the integration of women and children into production on the grounds that such participation "stimulates [women's and children's] development and increases their independence, in other words, creates conditions of life that are incomparably superior to the patriarchal immobility of pre-capitalist relations" (Lenin, 1960: 546–7). It was clear to Lenin that Russian Marxists should embrace this future and agitate for the most progressive development of capitalism possible. The task of Marxists in prerevolutionary Russian was to confront the feudal-dominated political order in order to create those political economic conditions associated with the capitalist social order, which would permit an effective revolutionary proletariat to emerge and eventually overthrow capitalism.

Part of the young Lenin's consciously ironic commitment to bourgeois society rested on his assessment that capitalism could raise the social productivity of Russian producers and thus allow workers and peasants to achieve much higher cultural standards of life. He believed — as most Marxists of the Second International did — that capitalist growth could take place in ways that permitted its expanded reproduction. He spent much space in the early section of *The Development of Capitalism in Russia* defending this perspective by applying Marx's expanded reproduction schemes to the Russian case. Lenin attempted to demonstrate that it was possible for output values to be provided in the correct sectoral proportions so that commodities produced under capitalist conditions in the capital goods and consumption goods sectors (Departments I and II) could unproblematically exchange with constant and variable capital produced within the peasant economy.

This is one of the first attempts to develop a model that linked a modern, capitalist sector with a premodern rural one. The technique ultimately proved to be unsuccessful in that it required arbitrary and unrealistic assumptions about how resources might flow between various sectors of the economy (Robinson, 1951). Still, this Marxist method can be seen as a forerunner to both a more aggregative Keynesian or Kaleckian approach to macroeconomic analysis and a more detailed input-output analysis of economic linkages. For our purposes, the expanded reproduction method is important because almost all the theorists used it to argue for or against capitalism's inherent tendency towards breakdown and violence.

Rosa Luxemburg is the prewar Marxian theorist most associated with what can fairly be called an alarmist perspective on capitalism's barbaric tendencies. She argued that primitive accumulation is always necessary for capitalism because it must break down precapitalist forms in order to open up markets for inevitably surplus consumer goods (or variable capital) and to acquire through coercion deficient capital goods (or constant capital). The details of Luxemburg's argument about the impossibility of expanded reproduction through fair capitalist exchange are generally dismissed by even the most sympathetic commentators. Still, there is no doubt that Luxemburg was the first major Marxist theorist to describe with some precision what used to be called by Andre Gunder Frank "the development of underdevelopment" (Frank, 1969b).

Luxemburg's most impressive achievement is her stylized description of the stages of precapitalist breakdown. She insisted that

> Capitalism must . . . always and everywhere fight a battle of annihilihation against every historical form of natural economy that it encounters, whether this is slave economy, feudalism, primitive communism, or patriarchal peasant economy. The principal methods in this struggle are political force (revolution, war), oppressive taxation by the state, and cheap goods (Luxemburg, 1913: 369).

She argued that after precapitalist economic structures — or, in her terms, natural economic forms — dissolve, capitalism continues its destructive evolution by disintegrating simple commodity production and the related peasant societies upon which this economic process rested.

For Luxemburg, there was little that could be considered progressive by this swallowing up process. The social unraveling Luxemburg described does not pave the way for sustained rises in material cultural standards. One reason that the liberation of producers from traditional shackles fails to improve living conditions is the intense role that militarism plays in the expansion of international capitalist accumulation networks. Luxemburg remarked that

> The case of Egypt, just as that of China and, more recently, Morocco, shows militarism as the executor of the accumulation of capital, lurking behind international loans, railroad building, irrigation systems, and similar works of civilization. The Oriental states cannot develop from natural to commodity economy and further to capitalist economy fast enough and are swallowed up by international capital (Luxemburg, 1913: 439).

The implication is that the peoples of the East trade traditional shackles for new one forged by Western militarism and imperialism.

Lenin never accepted the theoretical model which Luxemburg developed to explained the rapacious nature of capital accumulation. He never accepted the proposition that capitalism could only expand through the continued exercise of violence against precapitalist forms. On the other hand, the postrevolutionary Lenin did articulate arguments about the parasitic nature of monopoly capitalism, which led him to similar conclusions. The global expansion of Western capitalism against the peoples of the East had ushered in an era of superexploitation, war, and stagnation (Lenin, 1939: 99). If there were to be peaceful development, then socialist governments would have to discover the appropriate policies that would liberate impoverished producers from capitalist and precapitalist chains.

## The Bolshevik Revolution and the Failure of War Communism

One difficulty that many contemporary mainstream and radical theorists face in evaluating the early Marxian contributions to development is that many forget that revolutionary Marxists of the early twentieth century judged the success of their policies through a different prism than even most contemporary radicals do. The primary goal of Lenin, Luxemburg, and others in this tradition — no matter what their disagreements were — was the establishment of a new socialist order. Moreover, Lenin and his comrades did not justify socialism as a more efficient and just path to material abundance. Rather, the hypothesized greater ease of establishing socialist property relations and governance in an environment of material abundance was the justification for promoting material development. Creating societies, which permitted producers to regulate their own economic and political lives, was the goal of revolutionary socialist activists, not the expansion of material social productivity as such.

The tenacity of this tradition is most clear during the War Communist policy of the postrevolutionary civil war. Between 1918 and 1920, the industrial economy of prerevolutionary Russia disintegrated. Ties between the rural hinterland and the cities were cut, and hundreds of thousands of urban dwellers attempted to return to the villages they or their ancestors had relatively recently left. The money supply exploded, and the resulting monetary instability meant that the Bolshevik authorities had to physically requisition food supplies and raw materials — sometimes with violence. The few workers remaining in essential industries received in-kind bundles of goods as wage payments. Factories operated according to government command without receiving monetary compensation (Nove, 1969: 46–82).

Such conditions impoverished most of the Russian people even more profoundly than the economic dislocation of World War I. By 1920, famine stalked the land. No responsible political leader could embrace such conditions. Nevertheless, many of the most influential leaders of the revolution celebrated the seemingly egalitarian and collectivist institutions of War Communism even though this period was associated with extraordinary devastation. It was not that the Bolsheviks looked favorably on the rapid depopulation of the major cities or looming mass starvation. Rather, left Communists such as Nikolai Bukharin and Evgeni Preobrazhensky argued that the disappearance of money as a usable means of exchange and the resulting organization of a state-directed barter economy might permit the new state to establish advanced communist social forms no longer based on the pursuit of individual self-interest or capital accumulation (Filtzer, 1979: xiv; Tarbuck, 1989: 85–9).

Trotsky was one of the first major Bolshevik leaders to question this attempt to establish a Communist state without first creating the conditions which would permit a flourishing proletariat (Deutscher, 1954: 497). It was the Kronstadt rebellion, however, which forced Lenin to promulgate market-oriented policies, which became popularly known as NEP. Most Bolsheviks interpreted the structural adjustment-like efforts to permit private market trading, to introduce a predictable taxation system, to limit subsidies to state industries, and to back a new currency with gold as a defeat. Lenin frankly admitted that this turn to capitalist incentives could only be justified if it permitted the growth of an urban, industrial economy (Nove, 1969: 120).

The call for an alliance between peasants and workers only partially masked Lenin's impatience with Russia's rural backwardness. The early Bolshevik goal was to create as quickly as possible those conditions which would eventually establish a socialist order. Given the enormous scale and relative weight of Russian agriculture, it is not surprising that the political economic linkages between rural and urban economic activity became the primary object of study of those activists and economists concerned with building the conditions for socialism.

**Rural-Urban Articulations and the Theory and Practice of Primitive Socialist Accumulation**

Evgeni Preobrazhensky deserves recognition as the first socialist economist to attempt to develop a theory of socialist development. His concern was not to prove that socialist economic development was more rapid and sustained than capitalist economic development. Rather, he wished to develop policies which would strengthen the state industrial sector so that capitalist development would not engulf the fledgling Bolshevik state. As with the Marxists before him, economic development had an important political as well as social dimension.

Preobrazhensky clearly recognized that he was entering uncharted territory. He began one of his first commentaries on the New Economic Policy by noting that not one of the more industrial European or American nations "is in a positions to show industrially backward Soviet Russian the image of its immediate future." Because of the Bolshevik revolution, "human society is now [only] able to dimly perceive the 'natural laws of its movement' in the upcoming period" (Preobrazhensky, 1979: 4). The problem centered on understanding the evolution of large-scale industry under state or Soviet control and its relationship to an increasingly commercialized peasant economy.

Will the petty-commodity production of the rural sector emerge into capitalist enterprise? To this question, Preobrazhensky answered yes. There was little doubt in his mind that Lenin's original model of rural capitalist development still applied and that the increasing enrichment of segments of the peasantry provided the state with a development opportunity. Nevertheless, Preobrazhensky worried that the growth of kulak capitalism would result in the state sector becoming engulfed by emboldened domestic and foreign capitalist interests. A key problem for him was to determine how the state should react to this danger.

It is clear that Preobrazhensky's worry about the stability of the Soviet state under conditions of NEP was not unusual. Bolshevik discussions of their position during the 1920s reflected unease with both ruling over a predominately rural society of peasants and existing within a hostile capitalist world order (S. Cohen, 1973: 181). The key to survival for almost all the leadership was to promote the most rapid growth of Soviet industry possible, while preventing the peasantry from establishing autonomous accumulation circuits.

This is especially clear in Preobrazhensky 1922 article "The Economic Policy of the Proletariat in a Peasant Country." Here, he argued that the Soviet state faced three economic tasks:

1. To increase the output of large-scale industry on the basis of an incentive system, which ensured the maximum productivity of labor.
2. To increase the country's agricultural output in cooperation with the peasantry while gaining "control over petty production in the way that capital has always done so, namely through trade and credit."
3. To transform the technological base of petty peasant production (Preobrazhensky, 1979: 22).

We can see from these three challenges that the logic of the Bolshevik weak political position led the leadership to articulate tasks which led Lenin and his comrades away from the prerevolutionary goal of establishing socialist political economic relations and towards those issues which concern mainstream development economists. Thus, Preobrazhensky dismissed rather quickly the viability of any attempt to establish payment systems which did not link pay to productive effort. Instead, the article focused on policies such as the state monopoly of trade and credit. Proeobrazehnsky optimistically asserted that such measures would permit the proletariat (i.e., the state) to control and monitor economic activity as well as to integrate peasant trade with the production of state industry. Such measures would then make the planning process that much easier.

One theme that emerged in Preobrazhensky's attempts to describe those state policies, which would best link the state industrial and rural peasant sectors most effectively, was the growing conviction that extraeconomic measures needed to be taken to speed up the pace of industrial accumulation. It is here that Preobrazhensky began to emphasize more and more forcefully the need to promote what he called primitive socialist accumulation. By explicitly recalling Marx's emphasis that capitalist development required the coercive reorganization of property relations, Preobrazhensky seemed to be making the claim that any process of noncapitalist material development would require state-backed coercion. The term implies that the state must use force against parts of the population to establish socialist property relations.

Preobrazhensky's introduction of this grandiose, politically charged term unfortunately obscured his rather modest argument for the limited use of state power to push the development process in channels more favorable to the proletariat. He argued that planning authorities should establish control over credit, manipulate the terms of trade between agriculture and industry, and establish more onerous (but still predictable) taxation methods to extract more resources from the peasantry for industrial investment projects.

His arguments for such coercive measures gained salience because it soon became clear that the New Economic Policy was only partially successful. NEP did quickly restore commercial relations between town and country. The agricultural sector did rebound from the period of devastating famine to reach prewar levels of production by 1925. Industrial production also began to recover. These successes, however, could not mask what came to be known as the scissors crisis. The more rapid recovery of agricultural production combined with the monopolistic economic practices of the new state enterprises led to a sharp deterioration of the terms of trade for the agricultural sector (Nove, 1969: 93–6).

The initial reaction of Nikolai Bukharin — the most enthusiastic backer of NEP's pro-peasant pronouncements — called for the deepening of NEP by reducing the prices of industrial goods and allowing private capitalists to compete against the state industrial trusts. Preobrazhensky, on the other hand, reacted to this crisis by advocating intensified industrialization organized through a state-sponsored investment plan and financed through rising industrial prices and "tax increases for the well-to-do elements of the countryside" (Preobrazhensky, 1979: 47). Funds collected would be applied to high priority industrial projects determined by planning authorities. This was proposed for political and economic reasons. The political reason concerned fear that the success of peasant-based capitalism would undermine the socialist project. His economic argument for state-directed industrialization was based on a more complex assessment of specific Soviet economic conditions and his general understanding of the demands of industrial accumulation.

Preobrazhensky began his economic analysis by correctly noting that the more egalitarian nature of Russian agriculture after the revolutionary land seizures of 1917 and 1918 meant that there was an increased demand for consumer goods which industry could not yet meet. One of his biggest fears was that this would lead to added pressures to import more consumer goods rather than scarce means of production. Preobrazhensky argued that balanced industrial growth required the joint development of heavy and light industry. Planners should be in a position to anticipate future industrial requirements and funnel resources to sectors that would be unprofitable if markets were left to allocate investment resources without state intervention. The short-time horizon of market-oriented entrepreneurs could be overcome by a planning process that focused on those projects that required large investments in fixed capital.

Preobrazhensky was well aware that a shift of resources which would tie up capital in large-scale projects could also threaten the living standards of the main allies of the state — the urban working class. In one revealing passage, he wrote:

> The rise [in wages] does not promise to be particularly rapid in the next few years either, because industry, after accumulating circulating capital (which is still in extremely short supply), will begin restoring fixed capital and resume urban construction, tasks that will require "primitive socialist accumulation," not only at the expense of the petit bourgeois classes through taxation but also at the expense of wages (Preobrazhensky, 1979: 26).

Preobrazhensky was also well aware that cheaper consumption goods and agricultural inputs could be imported. However, he suggested in an analysis (which both anticipates dependency theory and partially describes the reality Russia has faced since the collapse of the Soviet State) that if trade were unrestricted, Soviet

> industry would be eliminated because of its unprofitability and uselessness from the capitalist standpoint. . . . Agriculture . . . would suffer severely . . . from the transformation of the entire country into an agrarian semicolony of world capital (Preobrazhensky, 1979: 64–5).

The fear that the immature state sector would disintegrate in the face of superior capitalist enterprise and imperial coercion ran through all of Preobrazhensky's writings. He insisted that a state attempting to construct socialism must "divert the flow [or resources] from the channels of primitive . . . NEP accumulation to the mill of primitive socialist accumulation.") Such policies could subordinate capitalist accumulation to the "forms of large-scale socialist economy" (Preobrazhensky, 1979: 30). The economic argument for such a policy was that planned socialist development would ultimately raise the living standards and participatory potential of workers more effectively than reliance on peasant-based capitalism and the world market. Nevertheless, Preobrazhensky frankly admitted that the development process he envisaged would be plagued by conflicting goals of raising real wages versus promoting the accumulation of capital goods, rationalizing production versus reducing unemployment, and integrating with the world market versus developing domestic technological capabilities (Preobrazhensky, 1979: 230). One of Preobrazhensky's most impressive achievements was his clear recognition of the severe trade-offs, which any development policy-maker must face.

This work provided the theoretical basis for Trotsky's increasingly intense criticism of the New Economic Policy (Deutscher, 1959: 99–103). After Lenin's death in early 1924, debate over the future of the Soviet state and economy became more strident. Disputes over economic policy became vehicles for the struggle for political power. The most eloquent defender of NEP was Nikolai Bukharin — who had earlier been the most passionate defender of the War Communist period. Despite this inconsistent theoretical past, Bukharin never wavered from his perspective that the new economy would best prosper if the private peasant sector were allowed to grow. Bukharin's calls for the development of socialism through the enrichment of peasantry suggested a slower pace of development and investment in industry which would provide the rural sector with necessary inputs and desired consumer goods.

One central reason for the disagreement between Bukharin and Preobrazhensky was Bukharin's increasing worry that increased surplus extraction from the countryside would upset the delicate social equilibrium, which seemed to be maintaining the Soviet state in power. On the economic level, he was convinced that the fragile incentives supporting agricultural production and marketing would become disrupted by a strategy of intensified "primitive socialist accumulation." Moreover, Bukharin, unlike Preobrazhensky, was less confident that the state enterprises could actually organize economically productive investment projects. He regularly proposed instead measures which would force the lowering of prices and increase competitive pressures by allowing private traders and rich peasants to compete with the state sector (Tarbuck, 1989: 142–44).

In a sense, these disputes between the right and left of the new Soviet Communist Party reflect disputes among development theorists that became important during the beginning of development economics during the 1950s and 1960s.

1. To what extent should the state plan development in order to overcome the short time horizon enforced by capitalist competition?
2. To what extent does integration into the world economy doom peripheral economies to become permanent semi-colonies of industrialized Western states?
3. What should be the appropriate mix be between heavy and light industrial investment?
4. To what extent should the state turn the terms of trade against the rural sector in order to stimulate industry?

There are important differences between these early Marxian discussions and the early period of development economics. Modern development theory has explored the theoretical and practical implications of these policy options much more rigorously. On the other hand, the early theorists were clearer in articulating political as well as economic goals when advocating particular development planners. Preobrazhensky's early works did not consistently suggest that socialist planning would produce more rapid increases in material production. Rather, he argued that state-sponsored "primitive socialist accumulation" would maintain the Soviet state system more effectively and allow the coming increases in material abundance (as well as anticipated political transformation in Western Europe) to lay the basis for a new socialist order. One the other hand, Bukharin feared Preobrazhensky's approach because he was both skeptical of its economic effectiveness and worried by its political ramifications.

There were points of some agreement between Bukharin and Preobrazhensky. Although Bukharin was reluctant to rein in the entrepreneurial energy of the kulak and Preobrazhensky was skeptical of peasant cooperatives' ability to resist the influence of the rich peasant, both did support a more aggressive effort to encourage the creation of marketing, credit and productive cooperatives in the countryside. Preobrazhensky argued that such institutions could allow the state to monitor productive and trading activity more effectively while giving more incentives to interact voluntarily with the state sector. Bukharin similarly believed that there were economic and political benefits to be won from the encouragement of voluntary resource pooling. Not only might the peasantry gain from economies of scale and scope, but the establishment of cooperatives would limit the ability of individual rich peasant household to establish exploitative credit and labor relations with poorer members of the village community (Erlich, 1960: 164).

Stalin's collectivization project beginning in the Fall of 1928 put a halt to the possibility of reaching a reasonable synthetic policy which could have raised the rate of industrialization while maintaining the basic market incentive structures facing the Russian peasants. In one sense, Stalin's emphasis on rapid industrialization and the harsh extraction of surplus from the peasantry made Preobrazhenshky's advocacy of state coercion seem prophetic. Given the violent nature of collectivization, the term *primitive socialist accumulation* was no longer metaphorical. Perhaps for these reasons, Preobrazhensky abandoned the embattled Trotskyist camp to support Stalin's Great Turn.

In reality, Stalinist policy destroyed Preobrazhensky's hope of state-sponsored industrialization, which could integrate a contained peasant capitalism with a development project that promised the not-too-distant rise in working class living standards. Far from being an adventurist radical, Preobrazhensky's 1920s proposals seem cautious, even conservative, in the aftermath of mid-twentieth century Stalinist and Maoist excesses.

He himself came to realize that Stalin's industrialization drive was not promoting the rational material development of Russian life. In an act of extraordinary bravery given the perilous times of the early 1930s, Preobrazhensky submitted an article critiquing Stalin's overemphasis on the production of Department I or capital goods. He called for a new emphasis on consumption goods production and predicted that failure to correct the imbalances in the Soviet economy would lead to a permanently hypertrophied heavy industrial sector (Filtzer, 1979: xlii–xlvii). As sensible as this critique was and as plausible as Bukharin's commitment to a slower-paced industrialization process was, both Preobrazhensky the super-industrializer and Bukharin the NEP advocate paid for their commitments to economic realities with their lives.

### Evaluating the Early Marxian Development Theories

One of the most striking aspects of the early Marxian discussions of state policy is that Bukharin, Lenin, Preobrazhensky, Trotsky, and others were just as likely to justify their policies for their political efficacy as they were for their economic development potential. Success fundamentally meant finding those policies, which would strengthen the proletarian state. It was assumed that substantial increases in the economic productivity of labor was one essential feature of success, but the early Bolsheviks explicitly recognized that growth of a capitalist sort might doom the communist project. Indeed, both Bukharin Preobrazhensky at times suggested that there might be a trade-off between creating an institutional environment favorable for the emergence of socialism and per capita increases in material production. Recognizing the crucial importance (for the Bolsheviks) of maintaining the Soviet state provides a good framework for understanding Stalin's initial decision to collectivize agriculture and undertake his massive push toward the construction of heavy industry.

The collapse of the world economy during the Depression years has obscured the crucial importance of political factors in the Great Debates of a decade before. Stalin's grandiose pronouncements on the triumph of his economic policies in both overcoming the stagnation of monopoly capitalism and laying the basis for a communist order of abundance took on a superficial plausibility to those in the West appalled by mass impoverishment and rising fascism in their own countries. Increasingly, planning, the creation of collectivist property relations in the countryside, and the turning of the terms of trade against rural producers were all justified in terms of their positive economic effects.

It is at this point Luxemburg's theory of primitive accumulation and Lenin's post-revolutionary analysis of the parasitic nature of monopoly capitalism could and were further used to legitimate the policies of many of the Third World states formed after the colonial era. Although most development theorists of the 1950s and 1960s did not share or agree with the Marxian theoretical tradition, arguments that favored promoting investments that would encourage unbalanced growth (Hirschman, 1958), which suggested that it would be possible to drain the agricultural sector of surplus labor without harming agrarian production (Lewis, 1954), which argued that dependence on the present international division of labor would doom Third World countries to perpetual agrarian status (Prebisch, 1959), or which noted more generally that state action was necessary to break an underdeveloped society out of processes which perpetually produce poverty (Myrdal, 1968), evoked some of the same perspectives discussed by early twentieth century theorists and activists.

Certainly, development economic theory did not simply reproduce Marxian arguments. The greater theoretical rigor and more thorough commitment to empirical investigation has gradually led to a much better understanding of development processes. Historical experience too has taught us more about the limits of statist development policies which engage in "primitive socialist accumulation" without taking account of the negative incentive effects on both the countryside and the state sector. Bolshevik defenders of NEP were sensitive to these issues but never discussed these problems with the degree of systematic abstraction and empirical rigor which might have permitted an effective synthesis between Preobrazhensky's and Bukharin's perspective.

Such a unification could have used the empirical methodology suggested by the young Lenin's investigation of the development of capitalism in Russia. His concern was to study the actual capitalist development process in order to determine how

Marxists could intervene in order to structure this process in a way favorable to the socialist movement. Now that the Stalinist project has collapsed and now that it is clear that neither Lenin's monopoly capitalist nor Luxemburg's primitive accumulation analysis adequately describes contemporary capitalist developments, we are thrust back to Lenin's original problematic. It is still one that is profoundly important to progressives attempting to counteract liberal capitalist advocates of structural adjustment. The struggle to find democratic and empowering political, social, and economic institutions that also promise a future of sustainable material abundance continues. Our return to the theoretical and practical issues facing the early twentieth century Marxists suggests we could learn much from a more serious study of the insights and failings of these brilliant revolutionary intellectuals.

# CHAPTER 6

## MARXISM AND EUROCENTRIC DIFFUSIONISM

### J. M. Blaut

### 1. Introduction

The grand old anthem of Marxism, "The Internationale," begins with these words: "Arise ye prisoners of starvation/Arise ye wretched of the earth." At the time the song was written, in 1888, Marxists knew very little about the faraway places where most of the wretched of the earth lived and starved. They held firmly to the world model bequeathed to them by Marx: Historical progress occurs naturally in the European part of the world; the rest of the world receives the fruits of this progress by diffusion. Socialist revolution will take place in the European world, and socialism will then spread out to the rest of the world and emancipate all of the wretched of the earth, everywhere.

Today we would label this view Eurocentric and diffusionist, and it certainly was that. But every European thinker of Marx's time accepted the Eurocentric-diffusionist model of the world's history and geography. And the evidence about the non–European world that was available to Marx consisted mostly of books and documents written by the agents and agencies of diffusionism: newspaper accounts, colonial office documents, books written by colonial officials and missionaries, and the like.[1] Marx, moreover, had no reason to question the traditional historical accounts about the determinative role of Europe in all of world history, given his classical German education and his intellectual surroundings. Summing up: Marx questioned all of the unfounded elitist doctrines that he encountered; but he did not, and could not, question such doctrines when they related to places and peoples unknown to him.

But though Marx could not have been expected to reject the Eurocentric-diffusionist model, the same excuse cannot be made for later Marxists. After the turn of the century, enough reliable information was circulating in Europe about the nature of non–European societies, and about anticolonial struggles (notably in India and the Dutch East Indies), to raise questions, if anyone chose to do so, about the naturalness and inevitability of European diffusions into the non–European world. Yet most Marxist thinkers refused to do so. In the writings of Bernstein, Bauer, Hilferding, Kautsky, and other major thinkers of the period, the European world was still seen as the arena of historical changes, past and future, and non–Europe as the recipient of diffusions from Europe. In this matter they held views not notably different from mainstream European thinkers.

## 2. Euro-Marxism

By the time of the First World War, a few Marxist thinkers had begun to question the Eurocentric-diffusionist model, or at least major parts of that model. Luxemburg argued that the survival of capitalism depended on wealth brought in from the non–European world; hence non–Europe had an important effect on Europe, as well as the other way around. (Europe, in this paper, refers to the continent itself and European-settled regions elsewhere, notably Anglo-America.) Lenin carried the argument considerably further. Unlike Luxemburg, he maintained that colonies and other dominated regions would carry out successful liberation struggles, and so would stop, and turn back, the diffusion process by which Europeans gained political control and economic dominance of the non–European world.[2]

Since the First world War, there have been in essence two Marxist schools of thought on the matter of Eurocentric diffusionism. One of these I will call Euro-Marxism because it proclaims the centrality of Europe in the past and present, the priority of Europe at all times in historical progress, and the naturalness and desirability of European influence on the non–European world. The opposing school, which can be called nondiffusionist or uniformitarian Marxism, broadly denies these propositions. The difference is not a matter of politics: there have always been communists and evolutionary socialists on both sides of the issue. One school questions the traditional European doctrine of Eurocentric diffusionism; the other upholds it. Most Marxist thinkers in the non–European world — now the Third World — tend to question and reject the doctrine; most Marxists in the European world today are, to one degree or another, Euro-Marxists. Marx himself was not a Euro-Marxist: to be one implies a full awareness of the alternative world model, and Marx did not have, could not have had, such an awareness.

## 3. Eurocentric Diffusionism[3]

At this point in the discussion we should pause and examine the doctrine of Eurocentric diffusionism as it has evolved during the past two centuries. Its origins go back to the sixteenth century, when Europeans began to formulate theories about themselves in relation to the non–Europeans whom they were conquering and exploiting. After the Napoleonic period, when colonialism was intensifying and when Europeans were acquiring significant knowledge about non–Europeans in the regions they had conquered or planned to conquer, the doctrine solidified into a theory, or more properly a world model. In the nineteenth century this model was built upon the following grounding propositions:

(1) Europe naturally develops and progresses.
(2) Non–Europe naturally remains stagnant, traditional.
(3) The main reason for Europe's progress is some intellectual or spiritual quality,

some sort of rationality, which leads to technological and social invention and innovation.

(4) The main reason for non–Europe's nonprogress is a lack of this rational quality.

(5) A secondary reason for Europe's superiority is its superior environment.

(6) The natural way that non–Europe develops is by accepting diffusions from Europe, consisting of new ideas and beliefs, commodities, settlers, and colonial domination.

(7) As partial repayment for these gifts, non–Europe naturally provides Europe with raw materials, plantation products, labor, and art objects.

Thus, two world sectors, Europe and non–Europe (or core and periphery), and interaction between them consisting of the diffusion outward of civilizing traits and the counterdiffusion of value.

This Eurocentric-diffusionist world model explained why Europeans were superior to all others and why it was natural and proper for them to conquer and exploit the non–Europeans: in short, it was a rationale for colonialism, and its hegemony in European thought was explainable by the importance of colonialism to Europeans (or at any rate to the European elites). It underlay most grand social theories of the period, theories about Europe's own nature and history as well as that of the rest of the world. World history was European history; to explain any fact of earlier European history, one looked back at prior European history, not at the outside world, since progressive diffusions went outward, not inward, and the non–European world was stagnant, uninventive, and ahistorical. (I call this "tunnel history.") All European thinkers of the nineteenth century apparently accepted one or another form of this world-model. Marx could not help doing so, since he had no evidence of the historicity and progressiveness of the non–European world.

This doctrine has not been abandoned in our own time but merely modified and softened. After World War II it assumed the form of modernization theory. European historical progress is still *sui generis*. Non–Europe is historical in the sense that parts of it at certain times have progressed, have advanced technologically and socially, but more slowly than Europe. All of the great stages in historical development still happened in Europe. Today, the only way that non–European regions can develop is by following the route taken previously by Europe, up to and including capitalism: by accepting modern European diffusions of capital, technology, social values; by integrating their economies with European corporations; and by accepting informal political control. The doctrine of Eurocentric diffusionism is now more important than ever because it must persuade non–Europeans, who now have political independence, that the one, the proper way to progress out of poverty is to accept European diffusions and domination.

## 4. Ancient Society

I will now describe some of the Eurocentric and diffusionist theories that are important today in Marxism and criticize them. Since this is a short essay, the descriptions and critiques will have to be brief and somewhat schematic. I have discussed some of these theories in other writings and will shamelessly cite these writings where it seems appropriate to do so. Focus will be on Euro-Marxist theories of history and Euro-Marxist theories about modern interactions between Europe and non–Europe.

One of the pillars of traditional Marxism is the notion that history has proceeded through a series of stages, each associated with a particular mode of production. Primitive communism gave way to class society. The first stage in the evolution of class society was slave society or the slave mode of production. Next came feudalism, the feudal mode of production. Next, capitalism, the capitalist mode of production. The future will see a socialized mode of production and the elimination of class society. Marx himself believed, as did other educated Europeans of the mid-nineteenth century, that Greece and Rome were the first true class societies, and were underlain by slave labor. Hence class society arose in Europe. And the origin of class society signalled the origin of evolutionary progress: other preclass or nonclass societies, and presumably the ancient barbaric civilizations, had no tendency to evolve toward modernity. Therefore autonomous social development was seen by Marx as a European innovation. This, of course, is one of the central propositions of Eurocentric diffusionism: autonomous development at the European center and lack of such development in the non-European periphery.

The belief that the Greeks somehow invented progress was widespread in European thought until roughly the mid-twentieth century. Today we know that other civilizations, contemporary with classical Greece, were also progressive and progressing, and we know that the elevation of Greece to the status of prime mover in history was, in part at least, a product of racism and anti-Semitism.[4] However, many Euro-Marxists either deny or ignore the new evidence and continue to defend Eurocentric theories on this matter, theories which were accepted by Marx but that modern scholarship has shown to be false. One of these proceeds from the idea that the slave mode of production was the inauguration of class society and class struggle, and then maintains that a slave mode of production only existed in ancient times in Greece and Rome. Another departs from the theory of the so-called Asiatic mode of production and the related theory of Oriental Despotism. A word now on each of the two.

Marxists can reject the theory that Graeco-Roman slavery inaugurated class struggle without abandoning the Marxian proposition that class struggle has been *the*, or even *a*, motor force in history. One might speak (as some Marxists do) of an ancient mode of production, and allow both slavery and wage labor (which was abundant in those times) to constitute its exploitative basis. But the idea of a Graeco-Roman slave mode of production as (so to speak) the starting motor of history is still widely held in Euro-Marxism. (See, for instance, Anderson, 1974b; Padgug, 1976; Manfred, 1974; de Ste Croix, 1981; Godelier, 1981; Milonakis, 1993–1994.) Yet we know that some combination of slave and wage labor was characteristic of many civilizations contemporaneous with classical Greek and Roman, including Han China and Mauryan India (see, e.g. Elvin, 1973; Habib, 1969). We know, also, that slavery was the most important form of nonpeasant labor only under very special circumstances: in both Greece and Rome, the main source of slave labor at all times was the capture of prisoners or the purchase of slaves captured by others

(Finley, 1981; Woods, 1988). This could happen only under conditions of military conquest or a very strong trading economy, both of which were short-lived in the Athenian Empire. It is hard to think of this as a historically consequential mode or system of production in the ancient world: the need to capture or purchase slaves implies that ancient slavery was never in long-term equilibrium; and it implies that ancient slave-based production would have to be explained in terms not of a theory of social evolution within a society but in terms of theories of conquest and external trade. It is also the case that the geographical area in which slave labor was the predominant form of exploitation was quite limited; perhaps slavery in the Athenian Empire had a parallel in highly developed regions of comparable size within the Han Empire. And finally, as Habib (1969) has argued, something like a slave mode of production existed in ancient India but it followed, rather than preceded, a basically feudal mode — inverting the classical Marxist sequence. In any event, the theory that slavery in Mediterranean Europe was the nursery-bed of progress is false and of course Eurocentric.

In Marx's day, the belief that Europe had been uniquely progressive throughout history was tied to the then widely accepted theory of Oriental Despotism. This theory stipulated that non–European civilizations never had known the idea and experience of freedom. These civilizations were innately despotic. The most common explanation was a combination of simple racism and a belief that only Christians can be truly free. Marx (and of course Engels) puzzled over the question why Asian civilizations had not progressed through the normal sequence of historical stages but had remained (as they thought) in an essentially preclass condition and so stagnated (see Blaut, 1993, for a discussion of this matter). They explained this, as did most thinkers of the time, in terms of the despotism that evidently had prevailed in Asia throughout history. But they were not racists, and they sought to explain this despotism in naturalistic terms. They suggested, somewhat tentatively, that the cause lay in the arid climate that (they thought) characterized Asia; thus, the need for irrigation (Marx and Engels, 1975: 75–80). Large irrigation systems would require despotic management for maintaining canals, for allocating water, and so on. These civilizations, then, were characterized by a distinctive Asian mode of production, with preclass peasant communities and a governing class that managed things despotically but did not exploit: it was not truly a ruling class. Hence no class struggle and little or no progress. But in fact most of Asia is not arid. Irrigation is not important in many of its regions, and, where it is important (as in rice-producing areas) the canal systems usually are local or small-scale affairs. In the case of the large-scale irrigation systems of western Asia, the ones Marx and Engels had in mind, the associated class society is as ancient as it is in Europe, and one can just as well argue that the ruling class forced the development of irrigation systems as the other way around. The theory of an Asiatic mode of production is simply bad historical geography. But it continues to be advanced by many Euro-Marxists (see, e.g., Godelier, 1969; Bailey and Llobera, 1981; LaCoste, 1969; Melotti, 1977; also see the 1957 book *Oriental Despotism* by the ex-Marxist Karl Wittfogel). This theory forms one of the basic foundations of Euro-Marxist history because it seems to support the Eurocentric-diffusionist argument that progress was natural only in Europe.

## 5. The Rise of Capitalism

For Marx, the slave or ancient mode of production gave way to the feudal mode of production. Marx firmly believed that the feudal mode of production was a strictly European phenomenon (Marx, 1972a). This is no longer tenable. It is known that several other regions (Japan, China, Turkey, etc.) have been at one time or another feudal societies. Serfdom, the manorial system, and indeed all of the attributes that Marxists consider to constitute the feudal mode of production (or the feudal economy — an alternative concept preferred by some Marxists) are found in many societies of Asia and Africa; some even in pre-Columbian Mesoamerica (Blaut, 1993). Amin (1985) and many others now use a broader concept, the tributary mode of production, which they consider to have been characteristic of many or most medieval societies; European feudalism was simply a regional variant of the tributary form. In spite of the newer evidence, and newer theory, many Eurocentric Marxists still maintain that the feudal mode of production was uniquely European (for Laclau, 1977, it later diffused, quite naturally, to the Americas). (Some of them accept the idea of a tributary mode of production but insist that there were two forms of this mode of production, a progressive European form, anchored in rent and exploitation, and a non–European and nonprogressive form, anchored in taxation (see Wickham, 1988). Euro-Marxists use this argument as an underpinning for the Euro-Marxist theory that, since capitalism could only have arisen out of feudalism, and since feudalism was unique to Europe, capitalism could not have arisen elsewhere. This extremely important theory must now claim our attention.

One of the central beliefs of Eurocentric diffusionism is what I have called tunnel history, the assumption that the facts of European history are to be explained in terms of prior facts of European history, with no real attention to causal forces entering Europe from elsewhere. Marx held to this assumption. Until recently, most Marxist historians tended to accept it also, at least with regard to the transition from feudalism to capitalism. It is fair to say that European Marxists did not know about the significance of colonialism, as a source of accumulation in Europe, as a force leading to internal social change in Europe, and as a conduit for the diffusion into Europe of technology and other factors of change, before the 1960s. Lenin and some of his contemporaries analyzed the significance of colonialism for modern capitalism, but it was only with the work of several non–Europeans, notably James (1936, 1970) and Williams (1944), that the significance of non–Europe in the earlier history of Europe began to be described. After World War II there was an acceleration of research by historians, Marxist and non-Marxist, European and non-European, into the history of Asia, Africa, and Latin America, and this brought with it new knowledge of the effects that these regions had on Europe after 1492 (Blaut, 1993). A very famous debate on the problem of the transition to capitalism took place in the 1950s and early 1960s (Hilton, 1976). Ironically, none of the participants were really aware at this time of the new evidence from outside of Europe, so the debate was mainly over the question whether the rise of capitalism resulted from primarily rural European forces or primarily urban and commercial European forces, although several participants (Hobsbawm, Sweezy, Dobb) commented that evidence was beginning to emerge about non-European feudalism and this would perhaps force a rethinking of the transition problem. None of this should be described as Euro-Marxism: it was a matter of lack of available information.

After the mid-1970s, however, so much evidence was available about non-Europe and its significance for the rise of capitalism that any tunnel-historical theory claiming that medieval European society was solely responsible for the rise of capitalism in Europe, and for the later industrial revolution in Europe, should be categorized as Euro-Marxism. Many such theories have been proffered. The most influential one was put forward by Robert Brenner (see Aston and Philpin, eds., 1985, a compilation of Brenner's writings on the subject and various comments by others; also see the critical discussion of Brenner's theory in Blaut, 1993, 1994). Brenner theorized about the transition from medieval feudalism to capitalism in some 200 pages of text without once mentioning non-Europe for times prior to the mid-seventeenth century, hence long after the rise of capitalism in his theory. He argued that peasants in England failed in their class struggle with feudal landlords and this led to the rise of a class of large-scale tenant farmers who rented land and hired landless peasants, becoming the first true capitalists. Capitalism thus arose in the English countryside (not in towns, not in other parts of Europe, not in non–Europe). A crucial aspect of Brenner's theory is the way in which he used it to denounce the views of those who were arguing against Euro-Marxism (notably Sweezy, Wallerstein, and Frank), arguing, that is, that the rise of capitalism was a world-scale process, not a strictly intra-European process. Brenner bluntly stated that the historical insignificance of non-Europe proves that Third-Worldism is wrong, and Europe, even today, is the center of social change (see Brenner, 1977; for a similar deduction see Godelier, 1969). Brenner's theory has been supported by a number of Euro-Marxists (see, e.g., Woods, 1988). Other tunnel-historical theories on this topic have been advanced by other Euro-Marxists, and have been criticized in their turn by Amin (1976, 1988) and others, including the writer (Blaut, 1989, 1993; Blaut et al. 1992).

Euro-Marxism offers historical theories dealing with dimensions of culture other than the economy, modes of production, and the like, and a word must be said about two of these bodies of theory: the idea of Europeans' unique rationality in history, and Eurocentric theories about nationalism and the national question. The first can be disposed of quite rapidly because it is much less characteristic of Euro-Marxism than it is of conservative historiography. In mainstream historical thought, considerable weight is given to the Weberian theory that Europeans possessed, throughout all or much of history, a unique rationality that led to greater inventiveness, innovativeness, progressiveness, etc., than was characteristic of other societies (see, e.g., Jones, 1981; Mann, 1986; Landes, 1998). This view cannot be found in Marx, and it is rare among Marxists today. Brenner advances one form of it, arguing that the birth of capitalism in the late Middle Ages somehow produced a new kind of mentality, one that would generate rapid and continuous technological progress (see Aston and Philpin, eds., 1985; Warren, 1980; see Blaut, 1994, for a critique). Brenner deduces this from Marx's argument that capitalism must always advance in technology (but Marx was thinking of modern industrial capitalism, not the late medieval rural economy). Other Euro-Marxists who believe that Europeans triumphed in history because they were more rational than non-Europeans include Melotti (1977) and Smith (1992).

## 6. The National Question

Marxist theoreticians have given a great deal of attention, for rather obvious reasons, to the problem of explaining the formation of nations and nation-states: the national question (Blaut, 1987). There is consensus among both Marxists and mainstream thinkers that the first modern nation-states were Britain and France, and their emergence had something to do with the political triumph of capitalism in the seventeenth and eighteenth centuries. Since the 1840s Marxists have been preoccupied with the problem of understanding, and deciding how and when to participate in, struggles to form new nation-states. As a result, a number of Marxist theories of nationalism have been formulated, some of them very similar to conservative theories, others very different. They can be classified into two sets: theories that view national movements as basically independent inventions, although usually associated with the (peaceful or violent) diffusion of capitalism, and theories that view nationalism itself as a European phenomenon that has diffused outward from its original home in northwestern Europe. The classical Marxist view, which mainly concerned the national question in Europe, was, broadly speaking, nondiffusionist or independent-inventionist (see, e.g., Engels, 1974). Marx and Engels argued that rising capitalism persuaded local bourgeoisies to struggle (sensibly in some case, not so in others) for a state of their own, and Marx and Engels also accepted a small bit of the Germanic or Hegelian doctrine that there is a natural tendency in ethnic groups to want to have a state of their own (again either sensibly or otherwise). The important and influential nondiffusionist theory on the national question was formulated by Lenin in the period 1914–23.[5] He argued that the great capitalist states oppress ethnic communities within the state (as in Russia), and in colonies, because this is an imperative for accumulation. Not only do local emerging bourgeoisies struggle against this oppression in order to rise, but workers and peasants sustain even greater oppression, as well as superexploitation (i.e., exploitation greater than that experienced by workers in the imperial centers). Hence, national movements arise quite naturally, and they are multiclass formations (not just bourgeois nationalism). In the case of colonies, they are progressive and — here a major departure from other Marxist theories of the period — they are likely to win their struggles, defeat colonialism, and create new states. This general theory was the first formulation of a center-periphery world model that envisions centripetal as well as centrifugal forces, back-and-forth struggle, between the two sectors. This world model underlies most modern Marxist and dependency theories about the Third World in relation to Europe.

Stalin put forward a fully diffusionist theory of nationalism in 1913; ironically, his point of departure was Lenin's earlier views, before Lenin had analyzed the dynamics of colonialism and imperialism. Stalin's 1913 essay, "Marxism and the National Question," has had immense influence on Marxism down to the present, mostly because its basic thrust is to argue that nationalism is essentially a bourgeois phenomenon, and national movements are not, in most cases, progressive and they will not, in general, succeed in forming new states, an argument that has almost always been used by those Marxists who reject nationalism in general or oppose some particular national movement (see Blaut, 1987). Stalin's theory starts with the axiom that national movements are simply an aspect of the rise of capitalism; they are progressive only when capitalism is commencing its rise in a particular region; they are not progressive — are either frivolous or reactionary — in all other circumstances. Capitalism has now fully risen, says Stalin; therefore, national movements are not progressive, although (putting forward the Bolshevik position) the right of peoples to struggle for independence must be recognized. This is pure Euro-Marxism. It sees capitalism as a wave diffusion spreading out from Western Europe across the world's landscapes, and nationalism as nothing more than a part of that diffusion; hence as bourgeois nationalism.

This basic theory has been elaborated into two quite distinct theories by modern Euro-Marxists. One body of thought is largely consistent with the dominant mainstream view of nationalism (see, e.g., Snyder, 1957; Kedourie, 1970; Hayes, 1960; Anderson, 1983). In this view, nationalism is a European idea, essentially the idea of freedom, and this idea diffuses out across the world along with European influence. (Colonialism, which of course is the opposite of freedom, is supposed somehow to instill in colonial peoples the idea of freedom. So colonial liberation movements supposedly do not arise from oppression or exploitation, but rather reflect the arrival by diffusion of an attractive European idea.) Although Marxists in general are reluctant to give the primary causal role in social change to an idea, to pure ideology, this Euro-Marxist theory of nationalism is an important exception. (See Bauer, 1907; Davis, 1978; Debray, 1977; Ehrenreich, 1983; Nairn, 1977. See Blaut, 1987, for a critique.) The second theory, by contrast, rests in the Marxian idea of class struggle, but it asserts (as Stalin did) that nationalism directly reflects the diffusion of capitalism, the struggle of the rising bourgeoisie. Hobsbawm (1962: 174), for instance, argues that there really was no significant nationalism outside of the European world in the first half of the 19th century because capitalism had not yet truly begun to rise in those regions. Later, the diffusion of capitalism led to the popping up of rising bourgeoisies and hence bourgeois nationalism in place after place. Today, says Hobsbawm, nationalism everywhere is passé, an irrational and generally silly survival of a process that was rational only while capitalism was rising (Hobsbawm, 1977b). Another important advocate of this Euro-Marxist theory is Nigel Harris (1986), who says, in effect: capitalism has fully risen and diffused its fruits across the world; hence, there no longer is an excuse for Third World nationalism; indeed, there no longer is a Third World. The all-nationalism-is-bourgeois theory is still very widely held among Euro-Marxists.

## 7. Colonialism

There is historical continuity in Euro-Marxist thought, from abstract theory about the role of Europe in past social evolution to another kind of abstract theory — and not-so-abstract politics — concerning the role of Europe in the present. We may recall Brenner's argument that, since capitalism arose as an intra–European phenomenon, today Europe, with its "historically developed class structures" (Brenner 1977: 91), remains the proper focus of attention. "[The] dynamic of capitalist development [is] in a self-expanding process of capital accumulation by way of innovation in the core" (Brenner, 1977: 29); those who now claim a major role for the periphery, the Third World — he calls this "Third-Worldist ideology" (Brenner, 1977: 92) — are advocating an empty kind of populism: the real dynamism is in the developed capitalist countries (including of course Japan). Godelier (1969: 58) argues along basically the same lines: the West displays "the purest forms of class struggle" and "alone has created the conditions for transcending . . . class organization." Similar views are held by Brewer (1980), Harris (1968, 1986), Warren (1980), and many other Euro-Marxists. The opposing, non-Eurocentric view of core-periphery interactions, in the present and in the past, has been presented by a number of scholars (both Marxist and non-Marxist), notably Amin (1976), Chilcote (1984), Frank (1984), James (1970), Said (1979), Wallerstein (1974), and Wolf (1982).

The Eurocentric Marxist theories of core-periphery connections, past and present, are similar to various versions of modernization theory, the form of modern Eurocentric diffusionism discussed previously. Both argue that capitalism rose and developed in Europe, without outside help, and that development for the Third World today consists in the diffusion of capitalism outward from Europe. Euro-Marxists differ from conservatives mainly in seeing capitalism as a prelude to socialism; a means, not an end. Some of the basic propositions common to many theories in both groups seem to be the following:

(1) European colonialism in the past was not of much significance for the development of Europe and European capitalism.

(2) Colonialism did not underdevelop the peripheral regions (leaving aside the sixteenth-century holocaust in the Americas); it transformed them in various ways, some very painful, but in general it led them (via colonial "tutelage") toward economic development and modernity.

(3) Decolonization was a positive transformation, in a political sense, but the basic relationship between the European core and the newly independent countries of the Third World is, and (for some Euro-Marxists) should be, a continued diffusion of capitalist processes, including modern ideas and institutions and modern technology, as well as an even closer economic linkage between the core and the periphery than prevailed in colonial times.

(4) These processes, collectively described as globalization, spread modern capitalism to the periphery and thus will erase the economic disparity between the two sectors. (For Nigel Harris, 1986, this signals "the end of the Third World.")

The belief that colonialism in the past was not significant for the development of Europe has been disputed by a number of Marxist and other historians. Galeano and others have argued that the American bullion obtained by Europeans in the sixteenth century had much to do with the initial rise of capitalism (see Galeano, 1972; Amin, 1992; Frank, 1992; 1998) and with the centration of capitalism in Europe (Blaut, 1993). A number of historians have argued that colonial processes helped to initiate and sustain the industrial revolution. C.L.R. James (1938, 1970) argued that the slaves of Saint Domingue in the eighteenth century were no less important than wage workers in Europe in the development of the Atlantic economy and the early industrial revolution. Eric Williams argued that slavery, the slave plantations, and the slave trade mobilized the initial capital for England's industrial revolution (Williams, 1944; also see Solow and Engerman, 1987). A number of historians have documented the technological diffusions from Asia into Europe during the colonial period (see in particular Needham 1954–1984). Frank (1998) argues that some sort of industrial revolution (or at any rate a continuation of earlier industrial development) would have been centered in modern Asia rather than Europe had it not been for several conjunctural factors. Lenin, as we saw, argued, early in the twentieth century, that colonialism sustains capitalism, and were it not for what he called colonial superprofits and superexploitation, which among other things improved the lot of European workers, a socialist revolution would already have broken out in Europe.

Euro-Marxists do not dispute the fact that colonialism had something to do with the development of capitalism in Europe but they minimize its significance. We saw that Euro-Marxists tend to explain the initial rise of Europe in terms of preexisting facts and forces within Europe, and this argument extends into the colonial period. For instance, Hobsbawm, in his book on the industrial revolution in Britain, very much underrates the significance of external factors. The industrial revolution

> cannot be explained primarily, or to any extent, in terms of outside factors . . . By the sixteenth century it was fairly obvious that, if industrial revolution occurred anywhere in the world, it would be somewhere within the European economy (Hobsbawm, 1968: 35–36; also see Hobsbawm, 1962, 1975, and Warren, 1980.)

On the question whether colonialism underdeveloped the colonial world, that is, drove colonies backward away from development, most Marxists, including some Euro-Marxists, argue that colonialism was, indeed, retrogressive and decolonization was progressive. But some Euro-Marxists argue the contrary position. They depart from Marx's view that capitalism, although it corrodes local social and economic structures in colonial societies, nevertheless frees them from ancient fetters and so prepares them for socialism. A number of Euro-Marxists (including Brenner, quoted above) maintain that progress toward socialism can only come where, and when, the technological potentials of capitalism have been exhausted; Europe being the most advanced region, Europe must be the center of present and future social evolution. Given this view of the colonial process, a number of Euro-Marxists (e.g., Warren, 1980; Hobsbawm, 1977, 1990) have questioned whether colonialism was really, on balance, a bad thing for the colonial peoples. In earlier times some Marxists actually applauded colonialism (see Bernstein, 1909). In a word: Euro-Marxists tend either to support or to have mixed feelings about colonialism, the most catastrophic diffusion process of modern times. The opposite view is taken by most European Marxist scholars and nearly all non-European scholars. Broadly, Africa and Asia were not stagnant prior to colonialism, and most areas were not backward and traditional. On the eve of colonialism, in 1500, some non-European regions were as developed as Europe (Blaut, 1993; Frank, 1998). Colonialism truncated development in these regions; it did not bring development as a gift from the colonizers.

## 8. Imperialism

Marxist theorists, understandably, focus most of their attention on the present-day world, the world in which colonialism has almost disappeared.[6] Euro-Marxists merely extend their Eurocentric-diffusionist world model down to the present. One cannot bifurcate modern Marxist thinking into purely diffusionist and completely nondiffusionist schools: there are many intermediate views. For brevity's sake I will contrast the two pure or polar theories: globalization on the one side, imperialism on the other.

Globalization theories tend to depict the landscapes of the Third World as basically or partly precapitalist during and after the colonial period. In recent times, capitalism has overspread these regions, has become global, and in doing so has brought beneficial changes to the Third World. The Industrial Revolution is diffusing outward over the world: Third World countries are becoming industrialized, hence modernized. And living conditions of Third World people are improving: for some Euro-Marxists the gap is closing and a fully globalized world, with no significant disparities between rich and poor countries, is on the horizon (see Warren, 1980; Harris, 1986; Willoughby, 1995). Needless to say, this view is close to that of mainstream scholars, although it has strong roots in early Euro-Marxism (notably in Kautsky's theory of ultraimperialism). There is considerable evidence against it. Genuine industrialization is emerging in very few regions, and these mainly are regions that had a considerable amount of heavy industry in earlier times. Brazil, India, and Mexico are prominent examples. Mexico is a unique case under the impact of NAFTA. Brazil and India have, in quantitative terms, a great deal of industry and a very large labor force engaged in manufacture, but in proportion to their (huge) size they may not be any more industrialized than the average Third World country. In other regions, we find a kind of industry that is really marginal to the domestic economy: branch plants of core-area corporations; assembly plants for mainly core-area consumers, typically using mainly core-area raw materials; and the like. This is not integral industrialization, and not a diffusion of the industrial revolution. And the supposed improvement in living standards is largely illusory. Medical advances have indeed diffused and people are living longer. But one may question whether real incomes have increased in the Third World (statistics to that effect being very questionable); in any case, any such increase masks a process of differentiation, with the rich getting richer and the poor getting poorer.

The Marxist theory of imperialism postulates a very different world dynamic. Lenin (along with Luxemburg and Bukharin) introduced the basic postulate: the effect of capitalism on colonial and semicolonial regions — now the Third World — is destructive and parasitic. It does not lead to development: for Lenin, it leads to immiseration and to anticolonial and anticapitalist revolution.[7] This view, it is safe to say, underlies most radical anticolonial thought, Marxist and non–Marxist: it is immensely important in the history of political ideas. The question to be asked, however, is whether imperialism, as envisioned by Lenin, is still in existence and still the dominant force in relations between the Third World and the European world. Some Marxists and many other third World radical scholars argue that today, as in the past, the effect of European capitalism on Third World regions is either corrosive and negative or, at best, the cause of a mixture of development and under-development, positive in some regions, negative in others. These scholars argue that capitalism became global quite some time ago, and its effect on most of the formerly colonized regions is still, qualitatively, the same as it was before decolonization, although there are prominent exceptions (such as some oil-rich countries). Globalization, they argue, is neocolonialism, and its effect will be, as in former times, increasing immiseration and resistance. There is evidence favoring both theories. However, the preponderance of evidence seems (to me) to favor the theory of imperialism, and the globalization theory is so firmly seated in Eurocentric diffusionism that one might question it on these grounds alone.

Many scholars and activists have rejected Marxist theory because of its Eurocentrism. I have tried to show in this essay that the Eurocentrism in Marxist theory can be identified, analyzed, and eliminated. Freed of Eurocentrism, the theory will be more powerful and more useful.

*140    J. M. Blaut*

## Notes

¹ Marx also, of course, read a number of books by European scholars and travelers, but these, again, expressed the diffusionist and colonialist view. Shortly before his death, Marx began to read systematically about the non–European world: see Marx's "Ethnological Notebooks," edited by L. Krader (Marx 1972a). Engels's 1884 book, *The Origin of the Family, Private Property and the State*, moves away from Eurocentrism in significant ways. Wherever I mention Marx in this paper, the reader should infer that I mean Marx and Engels, except where this is clearly unwarranted in the context. Here I follow a convention that is somewhat unfair to Friedrich Engels.

² See in particular Luxemburg 1908–1909, 1913; Lenin, 1915a, 1916a, 1916b, 1916c, 1921a, 1921b (a series of short articles that, together, give the outline of his model).

³ The discussion in this section is a summary of chapter 1 in Blaut (1993).

⁴ See Bernal (1987), Amin (1989), Whitman (1984).

⁵ See Lenin 1915a, 1915b, 1916c, 1916d, 1921b.

⁶ A few classical colonies of course remain, the most important one being Puerto Rico.

⁷ Interestingly, Euro-Marxists interpret Lenin's theory in a very different way, as postulating, in essence, the inexorable diffusion of capitalism across the world. To support this view they cite Lenin's early works, in which he did indeed hold diffusionist views that he later abandoned. Also, they emphasize the argument of Lenin's pamphlet, *Imperialism: The Highest Stage of Capitalism* (1916a), without noticing that this pamphlet, because of censorship, avoided discussion of political and social aspects of imperialism — which, for Lenin, were the crucial questions — and discussed mainly the economics of capitalist expansion. All of this gives us a very distorted view of Lenin's theory of imperialism, making it appear to be basically a restatement of the economic analysis of Hilferding and Kautsky, instead of a fundamentally new theory of the relations between core and periphery. I discuss this matter in "Evaluating Imperialism" (Blaut 1997).

# CHAPTER 7

## DEPENDENCY AND IMPERIALISM IN LATIN AMERICA: NEW HORIZONS

## Ronaldo Munck

The Marxist discourse(s) on imperialism were interrupted, possibly even diverted from their course, by the Latin American dependency problematic of the 1970s. This was probably one of the most significant interventions of a Third World discourse in a Western paradigm in the whole post-colonial era. It is now commonplace to assert that the dependency approach reached an impasse in the 1980s. It is also seen as uncontroversial to state that the debates on the nature of imperialism have been replaced by the brave new world of globalization, whether seen as a panacea or as a new demonization. This article seeks some clarification in these processes and some rethinking of what dependency and imperialism (particularly in Latin America) might mean in these new times. This, I believe, should be neither a glib (re)assertion of superseded orthodoxies, or a thoughtless embrace of the latest approach. Rather, much as Jaques Derrida sees himself writing in a "certain spirit of Marxism" (Derrida, 1994), I would see this endeavor in keeping with a certain spirit of the dependency approach.

### Entrance

The first wave of Marxist theorizing on imperialism — as a system of uneven development between nation states — occurred in the period leading up to the First World War. Imperialism signified on the whole the aggressive expansion of Europe into Africa and Asia, the division of the world by the great powers, and the rise of interimperialist rivalries. For Lenin, imperialism was an integral part of late capitalism and not a mere policy. However, while he saw it leading inevitably to global conflict, he on the whole, conceived of capitalism as developing the forces of production everywhere. Rosa Luxemburg, while more explicitly concerned with the social impact of capitalism on the non–Western countries and societies also saw it as thoroughly expansionist. For Luxemburg, contra Lenin, imperialism was not a particular epoch of capitalism, nor was it tied to the development of monopoly or finance capital. She saw imperialism as part of the great drive to expansion, which was at the heart of the capitalist system. So, while Lenin was eventually to accept the importance and validity of nationalist revolt against imperialism, Luxemburg consistently saw nationalist responses as innappropriate. Neither, ultimately, had much to say to about what was then considered the undeveloped world.

The second wave of imperialism theory took place in the wake of the Second World War. From a certain interpretation of Lenin's theory — but firmly against Luxemburg's and other Marxist interpretations — these theories began to focus on the unequal relations between the advanced industrial societies as a whole and what was now emerging as the Third World. Imperialism now almost universally became seen as a block on the development of the productive forces — i.e., industrialization — in the non–West. The debates ranged over the precise nature of unequal exchange between nations, the methods of surplus extraction, and the role of the multinational corporations. They all conceived a growing polarization between the advanced pole or center of the world economy and the underdeveloped periphery. The language of nationalism, socialism, and antiimperialist solidarity, flowed naturally from this analysis. Due to the emergence of the NICs (Newly Industrializing Countries) in the 1970s, the discourse began to lose its purchase in analytical terms. The end result of national liberation in Algeria, Vietnam, and even Cuba, meant that this vocabulary and political orientation also began to lose its attractiveness in the broad milieu influenced by Western Marxism. The issue of democracy was coming to the fore.

The dependency approach to uneven development between nation-states emerged in Latin America during the 1960s, at least in part responding to the perceived Eurocentrism of the Marxist theories of imperialism. Lenin, Luxemburg, and the other classical Marxist theorists of imperialism seemed interested in the phenomena only insofar as it affected their own countries or interimperialist rivalries. Now attention was to be focused on the countries conquered, exploited, and colonized by the West. This was a view from below, a postcolonial move, a nativist reaction even. It rejected the notion that Latin American societies were undeveloped — waiting for capitalist development to modernize them — in favor of a conception of *under*development, actively caused by the process of development in the advanced industrial societies. Underdevelopment in the non–West (the South by the 1970s) was simply the other side of the coin of development in the West. The Cuban Revolution was a powerful radicalizing influence on the dependency discourse because it appeared to question the very possibility of sustained national development under capitalism. So, not only did imperialism constrain the development of the productive forces but, ultimately, made development impossible. Development could only be brought about with the overthrow of capitalism and imperialism.

Whereas Marxism was a modernization theory in the sense that it saw capitalism developing the forces of production, dependency was strongly stagnationist (although some writers did, of course, recognize the possibility of dependent development). The diffusion of capital does not lead to development from this perspective but rather the stagnation and decapitalisation of rural areas. The national industrial bourgeoisie is not the dynamic *bourgeoisie conquerante* of the Communist Manifesto but a weak partner of imperialism at best, and one subordinated to agrarian interests. Capital and technology from the West does not lead to development but can only deepen underdevelopment. It is not more capital that is required but rather a break with international capitalism is a prerequisite to development. The international integration of the West, through the development of imperialism under U.S. hegemony in the postwar period, was seen to lead to an increase in national disintegration in the Third World. Dependent capitalist development was, in its essence, a distorted development, its perverse pattern of growth making impossible an organic development towards a reformist or democratic capitalism. The choice Latin America (as elsewhere in the Third World) was, thus, not between variants of capitalism but, rather, between the stark alternatives of fascism or socialism. Quite simply, if socialism could not prevail the long night of fascism would descend on the continent. In recent decades most radical analyses see, on the other hand, that the choice is between variants of capitalism (U.S., Japanese, German, and Scandinavian models, for example).

**Deconstructing Dependency**

There are now reliable accounts of the rise, fall, and possible revival of the dependency approach (see, in particular, Kay, 1989) so that we can afford to focus on certain salient theoretical aspects here. If we treat dependency as a discourse, it is very significant to examine how it was taken up in various milieus. Due to the perceived vagueness of the concept, a number of writers in the United States sought to operationalize it, basically make it measurable. Various criteria of dependency were isolated and measured against a cross-cultural matrix through the full panoply of quantitative methods. The results supposedly would indicate degrees of dependency, conceived as a simply linear continuum between dependency and independence passing through interdependence. Fernando Henrique Cardoso (1977) early on rejected this ahistorical, formalistic consumption of the dependency approach in the United States Measuring dependency was never the issue in Latin America; rather the dependency approach was seen as a critical historical-structural focus on the particular nature of class conflicts and alliances in those nation states dominated by imperialism. Within that problematic there were, of course, a whole range of political positions on the way forward. Another anomaly in the cultural reception of dependency approach has been the inordinate space given in the English-speaking world to André Gunder Frank. This is not to detract from the role of Frank as iconoclastic gadfly, consummate synthesizer, and someone not afraid to move on to new problematics. However, his role has led to a distortion of the understanding of the dependency perspective outside Latin America. Many of the criticisms leveled at dependency theory have, in fact, been criticisms of Gunder Frank, which did not in the least apply to Latin American writers, such as F. H. Cardoso (see Palma, 1978). A postcolonial analysis of this process would see this as yet another (mis)appropriation of the periphery by the center. Another effect of the Frank pehnomenon has been an excessive personalization of the dependency debate. Whether Gunder Frank was right or wrong, or changed his mind or did not, seems more important than the issues at hand sometimes. This personalism has even had its effect in Latin America, with a rather irrelevant debate as to who the real founder of the dependency approach really was (see Dos Santos, 1996, 1998). These are not really very relevant political issues.

There was, of course, no unified political belonging to the dependency approach, being used as it was by generals and guerillas, nationalists and socialists. It is a fluid, labile, concept that can be readily appropriated by different political ideologies. It can mean quite different things to different people and in different contexts. This is not, however, surprising or necessarily a problem, if we think of how democracy, socialism, or feminism also have very different meanings and interpellations. The typology I would have in mind would distinguish between a reformist, a radical, and a methodological approach to dependency. The reformist approach is best exemplified by economists such as Celso Furtado and Osvaldo Sunkel who realized the limitations of the ECLA (Economic Commission for Latin America) approach in the mid-1960s, given its reliance on foreign capital inflows. The radical dependency writers such as Theotonio Dos Santos and Ruy Mauro Marini not only sought to uncover the laws of dependent capitalism (practically seen as a new mode of production) but also posited an ineluctable choice between barbarism and socialism. As Caputo and Pizarro put it: "it is impossible to develop our countries within the capitalist system" (Caputo and Pizarro, 1974: 51). Such was the mood of the times (shared by Munck, 1984).

The third variant, which seeks to develop a methodology to understand the various situations, of dependency is best associated with Fernando Henrique Cardoso. It rejects the formalism of both the empirical measurers of dependency and those who would construct an overarching theory of dependent development applicable to all situations. The approach is historical and dialectical, recognizing that its object of study is simply the particular routes of capital accumulation and class struggle in the periphery. For Cardoso (and Faletto): "Historical-structural analysis illuminates the basic trends through which capital expansion occurs and finds its limits as a socio-political process" (Cardoso and Faletto, 1979). What is particularly interesting about Cardoso's role in the genealogy of the dependency approach is that it has evolved but has maintained a continuity since the mid-1960s. Not only do we have his more recent writings (Cardoso, 1993), which seek to redefine dependency in the era of globalization, but we have his current role as President of Brazil, where we can see a consistency in relation to his writings, insofar as it exemplifies his belief in the considerable room for social and political action in dependent societies. This consistency is recognized even by those who are hostile to what they see as Cardoso's reformist social democratic project (see, for example, Cammack, 1997).

If we now begin to deconstruct dependency theory (taken as a broad paradigm over and above its particular proponents), certain aspects become clear. In deconstruction, one seeks to reveal the contradictions and the assumptions of a discourse. Unlike the traditional Marxist critique, it does not do so from the perspective of another presumed correct discourse or vantage point. The litany of dependency's assumed sins is a long one. Kay (1989: 175) lists, among others, economism, utopianism, idealism, structuralism, non-Marxism, eclecticism, nationalism, populism, globalism, determinism, and the list continues. Some variants at some time probably shared some of these characteristics but this shotgun approach to critique is bound to hit its target at some time. It is probably true to say that according to the positivist hypothetical — deductive methodology (O'Brien, 1975: 11), which would entail measurable evidence to test its rigorous hypothesis, dependency would not make the grade. Nor would it substitute for an adequate Marxist (or other) theory of imperialism, which never seemed quite to materialize. Dependency remains however as a challenge, both to the complacent apologists for global neoliberalism who believe we live in the best of all possible worlds, and to those Marxists and other radicals who were once enamoured with Third Worldism but have since found more fashionable theoretical or political pursuits elsewhere.

It is probably still safe to say that the dependency approach, on the whole, was economistic (see Castañeda and Hett, 1981). Not that social or cultural aspects were not dealt with, but that they were largely seen as derivative of economic processes. It was not unique to dependency theory insofar as the orthodox (if disputed) Marxist notion of determination in the last instance by the was still then prevalent. This economism was allied with a certain mechanistic analysis, characteristic of functionalism, in which things were the way they were due to inexorable laws. The question of political agency did not loom large in most dependency analyses and when it did, in political practice, it was usually characterized by extreme voluntarism. Finally, it can be said, without fear of contradiction, that most dependency variants were a form of economic nationalism. It seemed, sometimes, that the problem with capitalism was that it was foreign (the evil multinationals) and that a national development would be inherently more democratic. Again, this is hardly surprising given the postcolonial situation in which it arose and the nationalist tinge of Marxism in the Third World at that time. To reassert a metropolitan Marxism oblivious, if not hostile, to the national question (see Warren, 1980) was hardly an adequate response.

Another area where the dependency approach was quite weak was in terms of presenting a viable development alternative. The undoing of dependency was too often presented in terms of delinking, from the world economy, a form of autarchy, which could only result in the catastrophe of Cambodia. There was, of course, more nuanced work on dependency reversal in terms of the need for more self-reliance and the quests for another development (see Muñoz, ed., 1981). In this area of enquiry, the dependency approach was a precursor to more recent work on alternative development models and what has become known as post-development (see, Rahnema and Bawtree, eds., 1997). What is probably most remarkable in going back over the debates and the whole discursive terrain of the 1970s was the extent to which socialism (not too well defined, although Cuba was clearly the referent) was simply assumed to be the answer to the problems of dependency. Socialism was the facile, if attractive, solution to the failures of national development strategies in Latin America. So, not only did socialism become simply a national necessity and not a strategy for social transformation, but those imbued with this spirit (which did not include, of course, Cardoso) seemed oblivious to what was going on in terms of dynamic, if dependent, capitalist developments.

Standing back from the particular standpoints, the dependency approaches all tended to adopt a totalizing approach, in typical modernist fashion. The holistic *enfoque totalizador* (totalizing perspective) takes as its object of analysis the totality and assumes the overdetermination of the parts. As Salomón Kalmanovitz pointed out, this type of undifferentiated level of analysis tends to erase or elide the internal movement of the parts and can obscure the multiple relations between these and the totality (Kalmanovitz, 1983: 16). The postmodern turn in critical enquiry since the 1980s has made us even more wary of a totalizing perspective, which both assumes a totality (society, imperialism, etc.) and self-righteously rejects all other perspectives. It now seems clearer that no one theoretical perspective can (even should) account for all forms of social relations and political practice in a whole society. The totalizing ambitions of dependency theory, which it shared with the Marxism at the core of many of its variants, (including Cardoso's), are now more likely to be seen as arrogant, misguided, and exclusionary because of what it inevitably did not include or even see. This organic unity of the totalizing persective is not necessarily superseded by a celebration of diversity and fragmentation, so the problem remains an open one.

If we were to apply Jacques Derrida's concept of logocentrism to development theory we would see how "even the most radically critical discourse easily slips into the form, the logic, and the implicit postulations of precisely what it seeks to contest" (Manzo, 1991: 81). Logocentric thought claims legitimacy by reference to external, universally truthful propositions and is grounded in a self-constituting, self-referential, ultimately circular logic. Dependency theory certainly seems to fit this picture and that is one reason why it never really broke out of the development paradigm. What dependency did, on the whole, was simply reverse the binary oppositions with which mainstream development theory operated. Where one said increased integration with the world economy, the other said delinking. Modernization and dependency theories operated very much as binary oppositions themselves, inextricably bound up with one another's assumptions, sharing the same discursive terrain. After all, the two theoretical perspectives shared the same aspiration of development as a rational Western model of progress, and shared the national terrain and state intervention as appropriate tools. This is probably the main reason for an impasse in development theory, which was equally an impasse for the Enlightenment model and the modernist project.

It is now commonplace to detect an impasse in development theory in the 1980s (see Booth, 1985, and, for a critique, Munck, 1999). To a large extent this was an impasse self-constructed by erstwhile critics of the mainstream development model who wished to return to the fold. The widely perceived crisis of Marxism in the late 1970s and early 1980s led many to abandon the project of constructing an alternative development theory. Yet there was also the very real failure to produce a synthesis between dependency and Marxism (see Chilcote, ed., 1981). There was no resolution of the debate between proponents of the dependency approach and the more orthodox modes of production approach. Dependency remained as a challenge to historical materialism (see Larrain, 1989) but one overtaken by the almost total collapse of Marxism in the 1990s. Ultimately, the dependency approach cannot be understood outside the context in which it emerged. Apart from its relation to Marxism we need to mention, finally, how it was bound up with a particular phase of capital accumulation in Latin America, when the old national capitalisms were entering a period of crisis and many social groups (including enlightened establishment elements such as ECLA) were seeking a reorientation. Neoliberalism was, of course, ultimately to fulfill the role of transcending this impasse, outflanking by the right, reformist and revolutionary positions alike, in fact donning the self-righteous mantle of the latter.

### Globalization or the New Imperialism?

In the era of globalization, the discourse of imperialism has faded from view, but we could argue that globalization is simply the latest variant of imperialism. As Bob Sutcliffe puts it:

> Globalization in this account is simply seen as an increase in the power of the countries of the North over those of the South through the penetration of the multinational corporations and debt dependency supervised by the IMF and the imposition of neoliberal policies through the International Trade Organisation and the World Bank' (Sutcliffe, 1999: 147).

Globalization is thus represented as a culmination of trends already diagnosed by Marx, as capital permeates every corner of the world economy. It is even possible to compare the current phase of the world economy with the internationalization that occurred around the turn of the last century. Paul Hirst and Graham Thompson (1996) have articulated this revisionist case most clearly, seeking to relativize the role of the transnational corporations and the crippling political effect of the idea that there is no alternative to globalization. However, their quantitative analysis of internationalization risks obscuring the very real qualititative changes that have occurred over the last two decades. The global reaches of the nineteenth century colonial empires are not the same as the current international economic order with its "dense networks of regional and global economic relations which stretch beyond the control of any single state" (Held, 1995: 20). The somewhat reductionist and economistic perspective of the revisionists is politically conservative in that it tells opposition forces to global neoliberalism that business as usual will suffice as a strategy. Perhaps globalization is more than just more of the same though.

Indeed, there is now a flourishing literature on globalization as something completely new, already establishing an academic niche market for itself. The conceptual inflation (and consequent devaluation) of the term globalization now rivals that of dependency. Not only is globalization being conceived of as a brave new world — whether from a Panglossian or a demonization standpoint — but its guiding principles are becoming accepted as the new common sense for the era we are entering. Globalization is seen as obvious, inexorable, and, basically out there. Yet this amorphous and labile term can probably conceal more than it reveals. Globalization is, *par excellence*, a totalizing notion and it is imbued with a deep teleology insofar as its destination seems clear. One critical study group on globalization has argued persuasively that it is flawed due to its technological determinism (information technology cannot make a new society), its essentialism (reducing complex socially constructed events to one issue such as post-Fordism, for example), its instrumentalism (conflating the identity of globalization and the reality of global trends) and its return to the old-fashioned and discredited notion of convergence (Amoore et al., 1997: 183–4). Globalization, in conflating epoch and epistemology, seems a poor guide for critical analysis of the world around us.

We do not really need to become either propagandists for globalization or demonize it, a binary opposition if ever there was one. With care and suitable provisos, the new literature on globalization can provide us with a better understanding of the current phase of imperialism. We can usefully follow Ash Amin in conceptualizing globalization "in relational terms as the interdependence and intermingling of global, distant and local logics, resulting in the greater hybridization and perforation of social, economic and political life" (A. Amin, 1997: 133). In this way we can overcome one of the inherent simplifications in the globalization worldview, which is to conceive of the global as dynamic and fluid, pit against the local as embedded, static and place bound. It points us, rather, in the direction of hybridity, open, fluid, and multipolar solutions to the old/new social issues arising in the era of globalization. It is also worth developing the notion that while globalization disempowers it may also be creating the conditions for increased democratization, pluralism, and empowerment of opposition forces. If imperialism in its classic guises called forth anticolonialism, we are perhaps only just beginning to see some of the myriad forms of resistance to globalization that might emerge.

We should probably start from the truism that the world is more complex now than when either the first or the second wave of debate on imperialism took place. Manuel Castells has recently completed a three-volume study of what he calls the information society (Castells, 1996, 1997, 1998). Certainly as ambitious as Marx's three volumes of *Capital*, it remains to be seen whether it will be as influential as its back cover endorsements claim. What it does demonstrate is the enduring power of materialist (if not Marxist) analysis of the world around us and that we need not take refuge in the dictum that "all that is solid melts into air." We do not need to buy in to the whole analysis carried out by Castells (contestable in a range of issues but, particularly, from my point of view in its writing off of the labor movement, on which see Munck, forthcoming) to accept as a starting point in our critical analysis, his argument that a new world is taking shape in this end of millenium (Castells, 1998: 336). He traces this new great transformation to the interrelated processes of the information technology revolution, the economic crisis of both state socialism and capitalism, and the rise of the new social movements of feminism, ecology, and human rights. The new network society based on the restructuring following these processes is based on a space of flows and a timeless time where the future is an open one. There are already significant studies of how this new great transformation is affecting Latin America (see Korzeniewicz and Smith, eds., 1997), which seem to be renewing the critical intent of dependency theory while being more fluid and less necessitarian.

If the world is more complex, it is also more brutal for those living outside the golden circle of the West, the so-called Fourth World. Cardoso (1993) has persuasively called this the new dependency. The new spirit of globalism is not ushering in democratic development for all. Taking Latin America as a whole, we find that while the gap in incomes in relation to the West remained fairly steady until the late 1970s, at 36 percent of its level, this had dropped to 25 percent by 1995. Only Chile comes near the Asian tigers (now not so healthy) in terms of closing the gap with the West. Of course, there are those countries that simply do not get on to the globalization bandwagon at all. We are witnessing, according to Cardoso, a far crueler phenomenon than the associated-dependent development he wrote about in the late 1970s and early 1980s: "either the South (or a portion of it) enters the democratic-technological-scientific race, invests heavily in R & D, and endures the 'information economy' metamorphosis, or it becomes unimportant, unexploited, and unexploitable" (Cardoso, 1993: 156). The nationalist response of the dependency era is no longer a viable one. If there is one thing worse than exploitation it is not being exploited at all.

What a new theory of imperialism would definitely need to include, finally, is a better understanding of the cultural dimension. Contemporary debates on development seem to be at their most critical around issues of culture because neither modernization or globalization can be conceived of any more as simple unreflexive processes. Culture, in this context, relates back to the definition by Raymond Williams of it as "the signifying system through which necessarily . . . a social order is communicated, reproduced, experienced, and explored" (Williams, 1981: 13). Culture, in this sense, is not some level in society separate from economics or politics, for example, but refers to a way of life, how we constitute our subjectivities, and how we give meaning to the world around us. There is now significant and overdue work, integrating culture into the story of imperialism (Said, 1994) and an even more flourishing interest in culture and globalization (Tomlinson, 1997). The cultural implications of globalization are seen to be more complex than the rather more negative reviews coming but of the political economy perspective. It would seem that we are not witnessing a simple unidirectional Westernization of the world as the old cultural imperialism, implicitly believed. Europe is being provincialized from a postcolonial perspective, and Islamism is taking up the mantle of the old anticolonial movements. Cultural studies, and the new cultural politics in particular, is helping us regain a critical perspective on how reality is a social construction and not a natural given. One particular area where the study of imperialism has revived is in relation to its ideology, which shows the new imperialism to be as racist and irrationalist as it was a century ago (see Furedi, 1994).

**Postdependency?**

Gunder Frank once wrote an article entitled "Dependence is dead, long live dependence and the class struggle" (Frank, 1977). We could, indeed, make the case that dependency is alive and well in Latin America today. The Washington consensus underlying the neoliberal revolution in Latin America over the last decade or so has as an article of faith that convergence between the advanced industrial societies and the developing, countries will ensue (see Edwards, 1995). However, the 1997 International Monetary Fund report on the opportunities and challenges of globalization was frank: "On average there has been no convergence of *per capita* income levels between the two groups of countries" (IMF, 1997: 72). There has in fact been, according to the IMF, a "sharp decline in upward mobility" (IMF, 1997: 77) of Third World countries within the international economic system and a polarization between high- and low-income groups of countries. Thus, while in 1965, 52 of the 102 non-oil producing Third World countries for which data was available, were in the lowest-income quintile, this figure had risen to 84 countries in 1995. While the IMF finds this lack of cross-country income convergence surprising (IMF, 1997: 78), it is entirely consistent with the basic tenets of dependency theory.

Another major issue for Latin American economic structuralism and dependency was the terms of trade between advanced and developing countries. The 1997 Human Development Report found in this regard that since the early 1970s a cumulative decline of 50 percent in their terms of trade (UNDP, 1997: 84). Commodity prices had dropped by 45 percent between 1980 and 1990 alone, just when globalization was getting into its stride. Nor was the much-vaunted industrialization of some Third World countries much good, as developing countries terms of trade for manufactured goods fell by 35 percent between 1970 and 1990. The dependency approach always also focused on the uneven development within the Third World and the polarization of incomes internally. Now UNCTAD's 1997 report on globalization, distribution, and growth confirms that in Latin America, average *per capita* incomes have fallen from over one-third of the Northern level in the late 1970s to one quarter today (UNCTAD, 1997: 1). It was not only the debt crisis of the early 1980s and the ensuing economic slowdown which led to a worsening of income distribution in Latin America, as this pattern has subsisted in the subsequent recovery and even economic miracles of some countries, such as Argentina.

While the pressing social issues addressed by dependency still exist, have indeed worsened, I would argue that we need to move to a postdependency approach. This is in part due to the inherent contradictions it always had, which cannot be simply patched over, although Paul James does make a coherent attempt to develop a post dependency approach in this vein (James, 1997). My own feeling is that we need to go further than patching up old paradigms. Not only has the world changed significantly due to globalization, but critical approaches for its understanding have been revolutionized by poststructuralism and poststructuralism. I would argue that we are now clearly in a time of paradigmatic transition in relation to modernity in general and development in particular. Boaventura de Sousa Santos boldly, yet correctly in my view, takes it as a given that "the paradigm of modernity has exhausted all its possibilities of renovation" (Sousa Santos, 1995: ix). Radical critique of dominant paradigms — and this applies to globalization as the new imperialism — will necessarily be from the stance of the postmodern, without this implying taking on all the excesses committed in the name of postmodernism. To a complacent, conservative postmodernism, which revels in the Northern view of the network or spectacle society, we can plausibly counterpose a radical, contestatory, and emancipatory postmodernism.

Basic to the postmodern critique of modernist social theory is the undermining of the universalist pretensions of the Enlightenment. The notion that the whole world could be analyzed according to objective universal criteria of truth, justice, and reason looks particularly shallow from a Third World perspective. It is quite symptomatic, I believe, that when Habermas was asked whether his universal model of discursive rationality could be of use in the Third World and whether Third World struggles could be of use in the West, be replied: "I am tempted to say no in both cases. I am aware of the fact that this is a Eurocentric limited view. I would rather pass on the question" (Habermas, 1985: 104). The postmodern social theorists also tended to pass on the question but they have since been taken up vigorously by Third World theorists themselves. A key postmodernist theme is Lyotard's proclamation that this movement/theory means, essentially, "an incredulity towards metanarratives" (Lyotard, 1984: xxiv). And there is no clearer metanarrative than the theory/discourse/ideology of development. It also follows that the Enlightenment notions of truth and objectivity mask the underlying power relations. A claim to truth is also a claim to power. Nor does anyone have a legitimate right to speak for others. Methodologically, the main implication is that "there is no single, privileged or unique paradigmatic way to think the unthought" (Hoy, 1996: 130). So, the search for the master-key to the secrets of development, and the expertise of the development expert, must be viewed with some scepticism.

Michel Foucault has had an influence on development on Third World studies, to some extent compensating for this own lack of attention to the subject. Arturo Escobar, for example, has written an imaginative Foucaultian deconstruction of the development discourse. A fundamental insight, pursuing Foucault's analysis of power, knowledge, and discourse is around

> the extension to the Third World of Western disciplinary and nor-
> malizing mechanisms . . . and the production of discourses by
> Western countries about the Third World as a means of effecting
> domination over it (Escobar, 1984–5: 377).

Development discourse from this perspective is about disciplining difference, establishing what the norm is, and what deviance is, indeed, creating underdevelopment as Other to the West's development. Western forms of rationality and the imbrication of power and knowledge in the development discourse/industry/practices, have sought to normalize the Third World and its peoples.

Perhaps the most exciting and far-reaching interaction between theory and practice has been between feminism, postmodernism, and development (see Marchand and Parpart, eds., 1995). Western feminism had for some time been coming to terms with the vexed question of difference and the Third World Other. Chandra Mohanty, amongst others, had firmly rejected the image of Third World women as uniformly poor and powerless in contrast to the modern ideal of Western woman (Mohanty, 1988). The critique of essentialism in feminist theory represented a genuine methodological breakthrough in relation to both liberal and Marxist feminisms. For essentialism, a group's characteristics are given, they are innate and do not vary historically or across cultures. Against the use of essentialist or universalist categories, postmodernism and some femimisms argue that categories such as *woman* (or *patriarchy* or *Third World* for that matter) must be understood historically and in culturally specific terms. When postmodern feminism began to engage with the issue of development, Jane Parpart notes how it focused on "the connection between knowledge, language and power and seeks to understand local knowledge (s) both as sites of resistance and power" (Parpart, 1996: 264). We now accept much more readily that there are multiple, unstable, and re-constructing identities involved in the development process.

It is also clear that the social movements, old and new, across the continent are a response to the failure of development to address the needs of the poor. These social movements seem to express not only a political struggle for power or resources but also a cultural struggle for identity. They also play a not inconsiderable role in demystifying development, a process that in recent decades in Latin America has spelt exclusion for most. The region's social movements, as Sonia Alvarez and Arturo Escobar argue, "represent a tangible hope for imagining and bringing about different means of organizing societies in ways more conductive to genuine improvements in living conditions — both cultural and material" (Alvarez and Escobar, 1992: 329). It is from such movements that a genuine alternative development strategy based on empowerment might materialize. In the most recent debates on the new social movements in Latin America, there is a growing emphasis on a cultural politics that is neither culturalist or political reductionist. It is not just the social movements concerned with identity (indigenous or sexual, for example) that have a cultural dimension in this new sense, but also the old social movements, such as labor and urban movements. As Sonia Alvarez and her coauthors put it: "For all social movements . . . collective identities and strategies are inevitably bound up with culture" (Alvarez, Dagnino, and Escobar, 1998: 6). The way social meaning is constructed is a cultural process, and all social struggles are about perceptions and interpretation. Culture is political, and politics are cultural.

The specific Latin American postcolonial situation has thrown up particularly vibrant and novel challenges to development orthodoxy. The new utopian postdevelopment scenarios have come out of the social movements and the postdictatorship and reinvigorated civil society more generally. As Fernando Calderón notes, in a broad synthesis of the literature on social movements, democracy and development, there is considerable

> evidence of a profound transformation of the social logic . . . a new form of doing politics and a new form of sociality . . . a new form of relating the political and the social, the public and the private (Calderón, 1986: 300).

The social movements are symptoms of a crisis of development but they have also, at least in part, led to a new postdevelopment mood in a radical postmodern tradition. A new social order and a new model of development will not emerge overnight but their seeds seem present in the complex reality of Latin America today.

In conclusion, if the limitations of modernism cannot be overcome by the binary opposite countermodernism, perhaps postmodernism will offer a new horizon of possibilities. Certainly this is not a naive chronological conception of postmodernism, which believes that it comes after modernism, or implies that the agenda of modernism has been fulfilled in regions such as Latin America. Certainly Latin American societies remain trapped in the failures of modern development and even some leftover problems of premodernity. Yet the *hybrid cultures* of Latin America are also postmodern *avant la lettre*. In Latin America, there has always been a creative rendering of theories and concepts developed in the

West/North. This syncretism, as Fernando Calderón and coauthors explain, points to a process involving

> the creative metamporphosis of old forms into new ones, the transposition of universal theories and concepts into locally relevant forms of understanding, and the rendering of a historical frameworks into concrete forms of explanation (Calderón, Piscitelli and Reyna, 1992: 35).

This is the type of task we need to embark on to imagine a postdevelopment era.

**Exit and Beyond**

In the current debates on imperialism, as in critical social science generally, we can detect a cultural turn. Yet this does not mean that political economy no longer matters. What it calls for is a critique of political economy from a poststructuralist perspective. One of the most noticeable things about most radical political economy is how capitalocentric it is. Radical political economy seems to have constructed a model of capitalism as all-powerfull, all-seeing, infinitely expansive and, somehow, self-reproducing. It seems hard to break out of this shell, conceive of an alternative in the here and now that could generate a transformative strategy. Capitalist hegemony seems to be assumed, and an alternative is unimaginable. J. K. Gibson-Graham (1996) have begun an imaginative deconstruction of these debilitating structures, seeking to problematize capitalism as an economic and social descriptor and helping us to demystify the current infatuation with globalization. Their discursivist and pluralist vision of contemporary capitalism is potentially destabilizing of capitalism's hegemony. It is not quite like the old Maoist slogan (long since forgotten) that capitalism is a paper tiger but that its identity and relations are only ever partially fixed and always open to subversion. Latin America, from a position of hybridity, is well placed to rethink capitalism and build contestatory social and cultural practices. There is at least the potential to create a space of economic difference wherever non-capitalist relations prevail or where they might have cultural resonance.

If we take a broad perspective, we can see the 1960s debates on dependency in Latin America as tied up with the search for identity. It was about establishing the essential difference of Latin America. Whereas in the 1960s the issue centred around the nature of society and how to change it, in the 1990s we see a return to the quest for cultural identity. It is no coincidence that this rethinking is occurring at a time when the project of the Enlightenment seems to be running its course. A crisis in European rationality has opened up again the search for an absent identity in Latin America. This is no mere culturalism, a distraction from the project of constructing an alternative rationality. Indeed, the cultural element is central to the development and dependency debate. Aníbal Quijano, a key figure in the earlier dependency debates, now focuses on how "Latin America . . . is beginning to constitute itself through new social practices of reciprocity, solidarity, equity, and democracy, in institutions that are formed outside or against the state and private capital." (Quijano, 1995: 216). It is in these spaces that alternatives to the IMF globalization project are being constructed in practice. This is no simplistic binary opposition to the dominant project, which could only fail. It is certainly in the same spirit as the dependency debates.

Dependency saw only one enemy: U.S. imperialism. In the postmodern era in hybrid social formations, under globalization there is no one enemy. While the inequality between North and South, described by dependency theory, persists and even deepens, the nature of the assymetry is now more complex. García Canclini argues that the new cultural reorganization of power means that we need to analyze "what political consequences follow when we move from a critical and bipolar conception [of sociopolitical relations] to one which is decentred and multidetermined" (García Canclini, 1995: 323). What we seem to be witnessing in Latin American politics is a paradigmatic shift where the old has not quite died (will it ever?) and the new is only just beginning, to misquote Gramsci. The mixed-up but intertwined temporalities, NAFTA (North American Free Trade Association) as regional project of globalization, and the Zapatistas as postmodern or informational guerillas, may not be just a result of structural heterogeneity and hybridity. It may make more sense to conceive of these symbolic processes as symptoms of a transitional political period. Following Sousa Santos, I would argue that "ours is a paradigmatic epistemological and, though less visibly or more embryonically, sociocultural transition as well" (Sousa Santos, 1995: 445).

The reason Derrida (against the fashion) continues to "take inspiration from a certain spirit of Marxism" (Derrida, 1994: 88) is to keep faith with the notion of *radical* critique, a procedure always willing to undertake its own self-critique. That is why the spirit of dependency is also relevant today and why it is possible for this Latin American tradition of critical theory to renew its creativity (De la Peña, 1994) as other once dominant paradigms begin to crumble. Nestor García Canclini, who has done so much to overcome false oppositions between a political economy approach and a cultural one in his analysis of the hybrid cultures of Latin America, says in the last sentence of his classic book that we need to find ways to be radical without being fundamentalist (Garcia Canclini, 1995: 348). I agree.

# *PART III*

---

## GLOBALISM OR IMPERIALISM?

# CHAPTER 8

## CAPITALISM, IMPERIALISM, GLOBALIZATION*

## Samir Amin

The dominant discourses have imposed for the last twenty years the use of the term *globalization*[1] to designate in general terms the phenomenon of world scale interdependencies of contemporary societies. The term is never related to the expansionist logic of capitalism or to the imperialist dimensions of its deployment. This absence of precision lets us understand that we are confronted with an inevitable condition, independent from the nature of social systems: globalization will impose itself equally on all countries, no matter what their fundamental choice — capitalism or socialism — and it will thus act like a natural law produced by the shrinking of the global space.

I will show that we are dealing with an ideological discourse used to legitimize the strategies of the imperialist capital that dominates the present phase, and that, as a result, the same objective conditions of globalization, rather than appearing without any possible alternative, can be considered within different political perspectives than the one presented to us. The content and social effects of the processes of globalization will themselves differ. The form of globalization depends, thus, like everything else, on the class struggle.

Moreover, globalization is not a new phenomenon, and the interaction between societies is without any doubt as old as the history of humanity (Arrighi, 1994; Bairoch, 1994; Braudel, 1979; Frank, 1978b; Szentes, 1985; Wallerstein, 1989). Since at least two thousand years ago, the silk routes have promoted the exchange not only of goods but also of technical and scientific knowledge, and religious beliefs that have shaped — at least in part — the evolution of all the regions of the ancient world, Asiatic, African and European. The mechanisms and extent of those interactions were nevertheless very different from what they have become in modern times under capitalism. Globalization cannot be separated from the logic of the systems that underlie its development. The social systems antecedent to capitalism, which I have defined elsewhere as tributary systems, were founded on the logic of

---

* Translation by Francesca Castaldi, a doctoral student at the University of California, Riverside, who is completing her dissertation on dance forms and their societal significance in Senegal.

submission of economic life to the imperatives of the reproduction of the political-ideological order, as opposed to capitalism, which has inverted the relationship (in the ancient systems, power is a source of wealth, while under capitalism wealth constitutes power — I have written about this elsewhere). The characterization of this contrast between the ancient and modern social systems implies a major difference between the mechanisms and the effects of globalization in the ancient times, and globalization under capitalism.

Globalization in ancient times offered some real chances for the less advanced regions to catch up with the more advanced ones (Amin, 1996a). This possibility was realized or not according to particular cases, but it depended only upon the internal determinants of the societies in question, in particular upon the reactions of their political, ideological, and cultural systems to the challenges represented by the most advanced regions. We find the most remarkable example of success of this kind in the history of Europe, a region peripheral and late — up to the Middle Ages — in its development when compared to the centers of the tributary system (China, India, and the Islamic World). Yet, Europe made up for its lateness in a very short time — between 1200 and 1500 — and since the Renaissance asserted itself as a center of a new kind, potentially more powerful and the agent of more influential evolutions than its predecessors. I have attributed this advantage to the greater flexibility of the European feudal system, precisely because it was a form peripheral to the tributary mode.

In contrast, globalization during modern times, associated to capitalism, is by its very nature polarizing (Amin, 1996b). By that I mean to say that the logic of global capitalist expansion produces in itself a growing inequality between the members of the system. In other words, this kind of globalization does not offer the possibility of catching up, which depends on the internal conditions specific to the members of the system. Rather, the catching up from late development implies always the activation of voluntarist politics that come into conflict with the unilateral logic of capitalist expansion. These politics, then, can be qualified as antisystemic politics of *delinking*. This last term, as I propose it, is not synonymous with *autarchy* and to absurd attempts to "move out of history." Delinking means submitting one's own relationships with the exterior to the primary requirements of one's own internal development. This concept is thus the antonym of the concept that calls for adjustment to the dominant global tendencies because such unilateral adjustment necessarily ends up increasing the peripheralization of the weakest members of the system. Delinking means becoming an active agent that shapes the globalization process forcing it to adjust to the requirements of one's own development.

The demonstration of this thesis rests on the distinction that I intend to make between the general mechanisms typical of the capitalist system through which the law of value is expressed, and the globalized form of that law. Within capitalism, the economy is emancipated from its submission to politics and becomes the direct dominant instance that determines the reproduction and the evolution of society. Therefore, we argue that the logic of capitalist globalization is precisely that of deploying the economic dimension on a world scale, submitting the political and ideological instances to its exigencies. Now, the globalized law of value that orders those processes cannot be reduced to the law of value as it operates on an abstract level in relation to the concept of the capitalist mode of production. The law of value, analyzed at this level, assumes the integration of the markets in all of their dimensions, which is to say, as markets of products, of capital, and of labor. On the other hand, the globalized law of value is expressed within the globalization of markets operating only in the first two dimensions: the markets of goods and capital tend to be globalized, while the labor market remains segmented. This contrast expresses the articulation, typical of the modern world, and of an economy more and more globalized on one hand, and on the other of the persistence of distinct political societies (be they independent states or not). This contrast in itself generates the polarization of the world: the segmentation of the labor market implies by necessity the worsening of inequalities in the world economy. Capitalist globalization is by its very nature polarizing.

The polarization specific to the capitalist world has taken on forms associated to the principal characteristics of the successive expansionist phases of capitalism that are expressed in forms appropriate to the globalized law of value. Those have been produced by the articulation of the law of the truncated market (caused by the persistence of the segmentation of the labor market) on one side, and on the other, by the politics of the dominant states that have as their objective the organization of those truncated markets in appropriate forms. To separate politics from economics does not make sense: it is not possible to have capitalism without capitalist states, other than in the imagination of the ideologues of bourgeois economics. These appropriate political forms articulate the internal modes of social domination specific to the societies of the system and their mode of insertion within the global system, as dominant formations (central) or dominated (peripheral).

During the mercantilist phase (1500–1800) that preceded the Industrial Revolution, and that we can consider as a transition from feudalism to developed capitalism, we find then the conjunction of appropriate political forms — the absolutist monarchy of the ancient regime, founded on the social compromise feudalism/mercantile bourgeoisie — with political processes that establish the first form of polarization: the military and naval protection of the great commercial monopolies, the conquest of the Americas, which were shaped into the peripheries of the system of the time (specialized to produce in ways particularly favorable to the accumulation of merchant capital), and the Atlantic slave trade associated to it (Braudel, 1979; Frank, 1978; Wallerstein, 1989).

From the Industrial Revolution up to the period right after the end of the Second World War (1800–1950) we see a second phase of capitalist globalization founded on the contrast between the industrialized centers and the peripheries that have been denied industrialization (Arrighi, 1994; Bairoch, 1994). This contrast, which defined a new type of the globalized law of value, is not the natural product of comparative advantages invoked by bourgeois economics. Rather, it is systematically produced by means pertaining both to the economic dimension (the "free trade" imposed to the partners of the new developing nations) and the political dimension (the alliances with the traditional dominant classes of the new peripheries, their insertion within comprador systems, military interventions, and, at last, colonial conquest). These forms of globalization are articulated under political systems typical of the industrial centers, issued forth in some cases by the bourgeois revolutions (England, France, and United States), in other cases by national unifications that take their place in the constitution of the appropriate national markets (Germany,

Italy), and yet in other instances by "enlightened despotic" modernizations (Russia, Austria-Hungary, and Japan). The variety of social hegemonic alliances characterized above should not let us forget their common denominator: all of these forms aim to isolate the working class. They determine simultaneously the forms and the limits of the bourgeois democracies of the time.

This complex system underwent a strong evolution characterized among other things by the domination of monopolies within the industrial and financial economies of the centers — beginning with the end of the nineteenth century — and beginning with 1917, by the separation of the USSR. Globalization is then characterized by the increase of intercenter conflicts (interimperialist) and by the acceleration of the colonization of the peripheries, one of the major stakes in the deepening of competition (Amin, 1993a; Foster, 1986). In conjunction with this evolution, new political forms took shape that associated to the system, at least partially, the political representatives of the working class of the center, even if those systems of social-imperialism were still in embryonic form at the time. Until the New Deal of Roosevelt and the French Popular Front — at the end of the 1930s — the hegemonic blocs were always antilabor. The Second World War changed dramatically the conditions that had directed the polarizing capitalist expansion during one and a half centuries of modern history. The defeat of fascism modified deeply the social relations of force in favor of the working classes (which came to acquire positions within the centers that they had never before occupied) in the capitalist system, in favor of the people in the peripheries (where the liberation movements returned political independence to their nations), in favor of the soviet model of actually existing socialism (which appeared as the most successful strategy for the project of delinking and of catching up). At the same time the affirmation of the dominance of the United States over all the other capitalist centers modified the conditions of interimperialist competition.

I have proposed elsewhere a reading of the half century following the World War II (1945–1990) founded on this new articulation of the sociopolitical systems of the three groups that constitute the world on one side, and on the other of the forms of globalization that go along with it (Amin, 1993a). On the level of the internal organization of the societies in questions, we can thus point to (1) the great capital-labor compromise that characterizes the ancient centers (the Welfare State, Keynesian policies etc.), (2) the national, populist, and modernizing models of the third world, (3) the Soviet model of socialism (I prefer to call it "capitalism without capitalists"). The globalization specific to this third great phase of modern history is therefore negotiated (by the United States), framed and controlled by the compromises that those negotiations guarantee. These conditions are not directed unilaterally by capital of the dominant centers as they were during the preceding phases. That is because this phase is dominated by the discourses of development (which is to say of catching up) and by practices of more or less radical antisystemic delinking, which are in conflict with the unilateral logics of capitalist deployment.

This phase is now closed by the erosion and the collapse of the three models that were at its foundation (the retreat of the welfare state in the West, the disappearance of the Soviet models, the recompradorization of the Southern peripheries) and by the return of relationships of force that are favorable to dominant capital. I will come back later to the new forms of alternative globalization that are taking shape within those conditions and the conflicts that result from them.

In the previous analysis, the emphasis placed on the polarization intrinsic to the global expansion of capitalism is essential. Now, this permanent feature of the capitalist globalization is simply denied by the dominant bourgeois ideology, which continues to state that globalization offers an opportunity that societies can seize or not according to reasons that pertain to those very societies. But what is worst, according to me, is that socialist thought (including historical Marxism) has shared, at least in part, the illusion of a possible catching up within the capitalist framework.

The theory of capitalist globalization that I have proposed, and that I have sketched in large strokes in the previous pages, makes globalization synonymous with imperialism. Imperialism is therefore not a phase — be it the supreme phase — of capitalism; it is its permanent feature.

The discourses of the dominant ideology of the recent phases of capitalism, subjected to the exigencies of social relationship specific to those subsequent phases, formulate concepts of globalization that are specific to them. The term *globalization* is here a substitute for *imperialism*, which is banned from those discourses.

From 1880 to 1945 this discourse is liberal, national, and imperialist (in the Leninist sense of the term). Liberal in the sense that it is founded on the affirmation of principles of autoregulating markets, even if, in fact, state policies frame their functioning so as to place them at the service of the dominant social alliances (protecting the agriculture of small peasants to assure themselves their electoral support against the working class, for example). National in the sense that the reproduction of the autocentric national market is central to state policies, in their internal and external dimensions. Imperialist in the sense that, at the time in which monopolies became dominant, these policies accentuate international competition which they transform into violent interstate conflicts. But, if the dominant discourse admits without difficulty to the first two features, which it legitimizes by associating them to the exercise of parliamentary democracy, it does not admit its imperialist character, which it never addresses. Furthermore, the very term *globalization* is unknown, even confused with *antipatriotic cosmopolitanism* and its opprobrium. Rather, this discourse promotes a chauvinistic nationalism that has the function of coalescing the majority, if not the totality, of citizens behind the state of the monopolies. Thus, the globalization that dominates remains defined by colonization and contempt for non–European people. But one does not speak about that hardly at all, it goes without saying. The brake inaugurated by 1917, with the declaration of a socialist social objective, is not accepted: it is nothing other than a savage and irrational aberration.

In the period following World War II the dominant discourse changes; I qualify it as social and national and operating within a controlled globalization (Amin, 1993a). By social I mean to say that it is founded precisely on historical social compromises that integrate (or propose the integration — and succeed for the most part) the working classes of the center, the popular classes of the East, and of the South. *Social* is not synonymous with *socialist*, even if this qualification has been used here and there to serve the social projects in question. National in the sense that the compromises are defined within the framework of the political states and are elaborated within systematic politics of public national powers. The term *globalization* enters those discourses, even if it is reserved only to the free world excluding communist countries, which are proclaimed totalitarian. This globalization is legitimized by almost natural considerations similar to those that we find in contemporary discourse: the contraction of the planet. Nevertheless, its imperialist dimension is detached from the previous colonial form, defeated by the victory of the liberation movements of the people of the peripheries. The imperialist conflict is similarly erased as the alignment behind the United States — which has become a kind of superimperialism — is accepted and even exalted in the name of the common defense against communism. Even the European construction does not question this global hierarchy; it accepts to function under NATO.

The global capitalism of the period after the war is singular in a double sense. First, because it functions according to social relationships, which give to labor a place that does not reveal the logic specific to capitalism, but that on the contrary expresses a compromise between that logic and the antisystemic popular and national logics. The increase in wages, which parallels the increase in productivity, full employment, social security, the management of industrialization by the state, the redistribution of income, not counting the great agrarian reforms or collectivizations, do not proceed from the logic of maximization of profit that governs the capitalist world but express the ambitions of the popular and national societal projects. This compromise between conflicting societal logics forces capital to adjust to the demands of workers and citizens. It is this pressure that has paradoxically allowed the strong and unequaled growth on a global scale that characterizes this period. This model is thus situated at the antipodes of the model proposed and imposed nowadays, which is founded on the exclusive logic of capital and the pretention that it is up to workers and to populations to adjust to it, which, in turn, traps the economy in stagnation. As a logical complement to these social compromises, the globalization that accompanies it is controlled by the states, which are its guarantors. The period is then one of reduction of the polarizing effects of the unilateral logic of capitalist expansion, a reduction that is expressed in the strong rhythms of industrialization of the countries of the East and the South.

The societal models that imposed the compromises in question have attained their historical limit because of their very success. Having exhausted without having created the conditions that would permit the popular and democratic forces to go further, the themes on which their legitimacy was founded (the welfare state and endless material progress, the construction of socialism, the affirmation of modernized Third World nations) appeared as illusions (Amin, 1989b). The conditions were then put into place to allow for a massive offensive of capital, which worked to impose its unilateral logic. After the OECD countries refused the New Economic World Order project proposed by Third World countries in 1975, (a project of rejuvenation of the controlled globalization, which would have allowed for the pursuit of general growth), the recompradorization of the Third World becomes commonplace. It manifest itself in the programs of so-called "structural adjustment," in reality programs to dismantle the gains of the populist nationalism of the preceding decades. After Thatcher and Reagan declared their will to dismantle the welfare state beginning with 1980, followed soon after by all the governments of the OECD countries, neoliberalism became the dominant ideology. Finally, the collapse of the Soviet systems of Eastern Europe and the USSR and the end of the 1980s opens up onto the reconquest of these societies by a savage capitalism that from now on has the wind astern.

The unilateral logic of capital, reestablished, is expressed by policies that are employed everywhere in the same way: high interest rates, the reduction of public social expenditures, the dismantling of the policies of full employment, and the systematic pursuit of the reestablishment of unemployment, the reduction of taxation to the benefit of the rich, deregulations, privatizations, etc. The ensemble of these measures brings forth the return of the antiworkers and antipopular hegemonic blocs. This logic functions to the exclusive benefit of the dominant capital and particularly of its most powerful segments — which are also the most globalized — financial capital. "Financialization" constitutes therefore one of the major characteristics of the present system, both in its national dimensions and in its global dimension. Within this latter dimension, the exclusive logic of capital is expressed through the removal of the control over the transfers of capitals of any kind, be they destined for productive or for speculative investment, and through the adoption of a principle of free and fluctuating exchanges (Amin, 1995; 1993b; Beard, 1989; Chesnias, 1994; Kreye, Frobel, Henrichs, 1980; Pastré, 1992).

The reestablishment of the unilateral law of capital does not inaugurate a new phase of expansion. On the contrary, it results in a stagnationist spiral, because the search for maximum profit, if it does not come up against powerful social obstacles, it entails almost fatally the worsening of inequalities in the distribution of income (it is Marx's law of pauperization). This is in fact manifest among all of the members of the present system of the West, the East, and the South, as it is equally manifest on the international level. This inequality produces in turn the crisis, that is to say, a growing surplus of capital that does not find an outlet in the expansion of the productive system. The powers in place are then exclusively worried about the management of this crisis, incapable as they are to find a solution to it. Then, behind the globalized neoliberal discourses are hidden policies that are perfectly consistent with the management of the crisis whose exclusive objective is to create financial outlets for the surplus of capital, so as to avoid that which capital fears the most: massive devalorization. Financialization is the expression of this management at the national level, as well as at the international level. The high interest rates, the fluctuating and free exchanges, speculative transfers, privatizations, but also the deficit in the balance of payments of the United States, the external debt of the countries of the South and of the East, fulfill those functions.

The discourse of globalization must be understood within this framework of crisis-management. To its economic dimensions, we must add the complementary political strategies, that I will qualify equally as means for the management of the crisis. The central objective of these policies is that of dismantling the capacities of resistance that the states could display so as to make impossible the constitution of effective popular social forces. Ethnicism is mobilized for this purpose, to legitimize the explosion of states: as much Slovenias and Tchechenias as possible, this is the objective pursued here with so much cynicism, hidden behind a supposedly democratic discourse of recognition of the "rights of people"! Other means are equally mobilized, ranging from the encouragement of religious fundamentalisms to the multiple manipulations of public opinion. We see that in reality the interventions in favor of democracy and human rights are strictly subjugated to the strategic objectives of imperialist powers. Double standard is then the rule. In a general manner, these politics empty of all substance the democratic aspirations of peoples and prepare the management of chaos through what I call "low intensity democracy," parallel to interventions — including also so-called low intensity military interventions — that encourage civil wars.

Neither the reactionary utopia of an unbridled globalization and of a widespread neoliberalism nor the practices of the political management of chaos (and not of a new global order, no matter what kind) that such utopia implies are possible. To attenuate its destructive effects and to limit the danger of violent explosions, the systems of powers try then to put a minimum of order into the chaos. The regulations conceived within this framework pursue this objective by attaching the different regions of the periphery each to the three dominant centers: the North American Free Trade Agreement (NAFTA) already subjugates Mexico (and in perspective the whole of Latin America) to the U.S. wagon, and the association of the African, Carribbean, and Pacific countries within the European Union (EU-ACP association) subjugates African countries to Europe, the Association of South East Asian Nations (ASEAN) can facilitate the establishment of an area of Japanese domination in South and East Asia (Amin, forthcoming; Yachin and Amin, 1988). European unification is itself affected by the turbulence of this neoimperialist reorganization associated to the use of the neoliberal utopia. The submission of the European project to neoliberal principles, expressed in the Maestricht treaty by the priority given to the creation of a common currency (the euro), the management of which is founded precisely on neoliberal principles to the detriment of the advancement of a common progressive political and social project, renders already fragile the European project itself, and will make it even more fragile as social movements which protest and reject the evolving neoliberal politics will develop.

The contradictions of the present-day system of globalization are then enormous and destined to worsen, because of the resistance of peoples — in the centers and in the peripheries — and because of the deepening of divergencies within the dominant imperialist bloc, which the development of those resistances cannot but reinforce.

The greatest of these contradictions is expressed by the striking contrast that opposes the two new halves of the global system. We see in fact that the American continent in its entirety, Western Europe, and its African annex, the countries of Easter Europe and the USSR, the Middle East, and Japan are all struck by the crisis associated to the establishment of the globalized neoliberal project. On the contrary East Asia — China, Korea, Taiwan, South-Eastern Asia — had largely escaped it until the very recent crisis that started to strike them in 1998, precisely because the powers that govern it refused to be subjugated by the imperatives of unbridled globalization that has imposed itself elsewhere. India is halfway between this new West and East. This Asiatic option — a discussion of its historical origins would take us astray from our subject — is at the root of the success of the region, where economic growth was accelerating at the very moment in which it was stagnating in the

rest of the world. The strategy of the United States aims now at braking this autonomy that East Asia had achieved in relation to the global system and mobilizes to
that effect the conditions created by the current crisis. It applies itself, then, toward
the goal of dismantling China, around which the ensemble of the East Asiatic region
could progressively crystallize. Here it counts on the dependency of Japan, which
needs the support of Washington not only to confront China, but also Korea and
even Southeast Asia, and to this end it proposes to substitute an Asian-Pacific region
(Asian Pacific Economic Cooperation-*APEC*) to the informal East-Asiatic
regionalization at work.

Europe constitutes a second region to suffer from predictable turbulences. The
future of the project of the European Union is in reality threatened, because of the
neoliberal stubbornness of the governing classes and because of the predictable
growing protest of the popular classes (Toulemon, 1994). But this project is equally
threatened by the chaos in the East. This is because the short term logic of neoliberalism has led to the choice of Latin-Americanization of East Europe and of the
countries of the ex-USSR. Now this peripheralization, that will work most probably to the benefit of Germany, weights in favor of a global evolution, which favors
a German Europe. Within the short run, this option favors the persistence of the
American hegemony on a world scale, as Germany is choosing, like Japan, to remain
within Washington's wake. But in the longer run, it risks reawakening the dormant
intra European rivalries.

In the other regions of the world, the game is not yet played out. In Latin
America, NAFTA has coincided, not haphazardly, with the revolt of Chiapas in
Mexico. And the project of extension of the model offered by NAFTA to the totality of the continent its already coming up against the questioning, in the Southern
capitals of the continent, of the option, which favors unbridled globalization.
Although the project of Mercosur (Brazil-Argentine-Uruguay, open to Chile,
Paraguay and Bolivia) was originally conceived within a neoliberal optic that was
not contested, we cannot be sure that it would not evolve in the direction of an
autonomization — even if relative — of the region vis-a-vis NAFTA.

Up to this day, then, the management of the contradictions of globalization has
provided a new opportunity to the maintenance of American hegemony. "Less
State" means less state everywhere, with the exclusion of the United States, which,
thanks to the double monopoly of the dollar and of the power of military intervention, supported Germany and Japan, playing the shining seconds, maintains its
hegemonic position on the global scale, facing East Asia, which Washington tries to
deprive of the possible alliance with Europe and Russia.

The future of the global system remains, then, mostly unknown, like the forms of
globalization within which the relationship of force will be expressed, and the logics
which will govern its eventual stability. This incertitude allows — for those who want
it — to indulge in the gratuitous game of scenarios since everything can be imagined. I will propose in contrast to conclude the analysis of globalization here proposed with the examination, on one side, of the tendencies of evolution, which are
coherent with the internal logic of capitalism, and in counterpoint, of the strategic
and antisystemic objectives that the popular struggles may take under the conditions of the contemporary world.

I have suggested elsewhere that the tendencies of contemporary capitalism are articulated around the strengthening of what I have called the "five monopolies" that shape the polarizing globalization of contemporary imperialism: (1) the monopoly of new technologies, (2) the monopoly of control over the financial flows on a global scale, (3) the control over the access to the natural resources of the planet, (4) the control over means of communication and the media, (5) the monopoly of the weapons of mass destruction (Amin, 1996a; 1996b; 1993b; Casanova, 1994). The working of those monopolies is actualized through the conjunct action, complementary but sometimes conflicting, of the dominant capital of the industrial and financial multinationals and the states that serve them, (thus the importance of monopolies of a non-economic nature here mentioned). Taken together, these monopolies define new forms of the globalized law of value, allowing centralization to the benefit of that dominant capital of profits and superprofits gained from the exploitation of workers, a differential exploitation founded on the segmentation of the labor market. This new stage of the development of the globalized law of value does not then allow the catching up through industrialization of the dynamic peripheries, but establishes a new unequal international division of labor in which the activities of production localized in the peripheries, made subaltern, function like subcollectors of dominant capital (a system that reminds us of the "putting out" of primitive capitalism).

It is not hard to imagine the picture of a future globalization coherent with the domination of this form of the law of value. The traditional dominant centers will keep their advantage, reproducing the hierarchies already visible: the United States will keep its global hegemony (because of its dominant position in research and development, the monopoly of the dollar and that of the military management of the system), followed by Japan for its contribution to research and development, Great Britain as a financial associate, Germany for its control of Europe. The active peripheries of East Asia, of Eastern Europe, and of Russia, India, Latin America will constitute the principal peripheral areas of the system; while Africa and the Arab and Islamic World, marginalized, will be abandoned to convulsions that will threaten no other than themselves. In the centers themselves, the accent placed on the activities tied to the five monopolies here mentioned will imply the management of a society "at two speeds" as we already say, based on marginalization, poverty, small jobs, and unemployment of important fractions for the population.

This globalization — that is the one that its delineating behind the options now in progress and that neoliberalism tends to legitimize presenting it as a "transition toward universal happiness"! — is certainly not fatal. To the contrary, the fragility of the model is obvious. Its stability assumes that peoples will accept indefinitely the inhuman conditions that are reserved to them, or that their revolts will remain sporadic, one isolated from the others, fed by illusions (ethnic, religious) and will incur into impasse. Clearly, the political management of the system by the conjunction of media mobilization and of military means will be used to preserve this situation, which dominates the scene today.

In counterpoint, then, the strategies for an efficacious answer to the defeat of this imperialist globalization will have to have as their objective the weakening of the power of the five monopolies in question, and the options of delinking must be renewed and redefined within this perspective. Without entering into a detailed discussion of these strategies, that cannot be anything but concrete and founded on the effective mobilization of the political and social popular forces, operating within the conditions proper to each country, we can enumerate the great principles around which the fronts of popular and antisystemic struggle should organize.

The primary requirement is to form popular and democratic fronts that are anti-monopolies/antiimperialist/anticompradors. Without them no change is possible. The reversal of the relationships of force in favor of the working and popular classes is the most important condition for setting back the strategies of the dominant capital. Those fronts will have to define not only realistic targets for their economic and social objectives and the ways in which those are to be attained, but also they will have to consider the need to question the hierarchies within the global system. This means that the importance of their national dimensions should not be overlooked. We are dealing here with a progressive concept of the nation and of nationalism, far from all obscurantist, ethnicist, religious fundamentalist, and chauvinist formulations that are currently in the forefront of the stage, and that are encouraged by the strategies of capital. This progressive nationalism does not exclude regional cooperation; on the contrary it will need to promote the constitution of large regions, which are a necessary condition for an effective fight against the five monopolies mentioned. But we are dealing here with models of regionalization, which are very different from those advocated by the dominant powers, which conceive of them as transmission belts for the transition to the imperialist globalization. Integration at the level of Latin America, of Africa, of the Arab world, of South and East Asia, next to the countries-continents (China and India), but also of Europe (from the Atlantic to Vladivostok) founded on social alliances, popular and democratic, imposing on capital to adjust to their requirements, constitute what I call the project of an authentic policentric world, another modality of globalization. Within this framework we can imagine technical modalities for the organization of intra-and interregional dependencies, for what concerns both the markets of capital (where the objective will be to incite them to invest in the expansion of the productive systems) and the monetary systems or the commercial agreements. The ensemble of these programs will give all of their strength to the ambitions of democratization both at the level of national societies, and at the level of the global organization. For this reason I place them within the perspective of the long transition from global capitalism to global socialism, as a step along such transition.

*Note*

---

[1] *Mondialization* in French.

*Acronyms given in French*

---

**ACP-CEE. CEE**: Commission Economic pour l'Europe

**ALENA:** *NAFTA*

**APEC:** *APEC*: Asian Pacific Economic Cooperation

**ASEAN:** *ASEAN*: Association of East-Asian Nations

*EEC*: European Economic Community

**OCDE**: Organisation de Cooperation et de Developpment Economic

*OECD*: Organization for Economic Cooperation and Development.

**OTAN**: *NATO*

# CHAPTER 9

## ON THE PITFALLS OF BOURGEOIS INTERNATIONALISM

## Prabhat Patnaik

In a recent interview John Kenneth Galbraith has said that the internationalization of economic, social, and political life has been one of the beneficent influences of the last 50 years (*The Hindu*, October 2, 1996). He laments that national sovereignty should protect internal disasters and internal conflicts and argues the need on grounds of humaneness for an international force, a sort of international policeman, that would prevent internal slaughter.

I choose Galbraith because he is among the best in this genre of thinkers. The genuine humaneness behind his observations can scarcely be questioned. He is sufficiently sensitive to national aspirations to ask for a "compromise between intelligent and historically-motivated internationalism and national pride and sovereignty" rather than an outright supersession of the latter. And he is sufficiently perceptive to dangers of domination to suggest that the role of the international policeman should be given to the United Nations rather than to the United States.

While others in this genre may be less sensitive than Galbraith, there can be little doubt that the genre itself is profoundly influential at the moment. I call this genre, namely the advocacy of internationalism in a capitalist world, *bourgeois internationalism*. This has to be distinguished from *proletarian internationalism*, which revolutionary socialists have always talked about. Bourgeois internationalism as an ideology has at least four important components: first, a belief in the possibility of a humane capitalist order pervading the entire world, not only the northern segment but also the south; second, a belief in the possibility of progress under this order, not only in the north but also in the south; third, a belief in the proposition that "internal disasters and internal conflicts" in the Third World have nothing to do with capitalism but are instead the product of autonomous and internal forces in these societies having their roots in the precapitalist milieu characteristic of these societies; and fourth, a belief in the "nonessentiality" of conflict between different countries and regions of the world even in conditions of capitalism. To put it in a nutshell, underlying bourgeois internationalism is a view of capitalism as a potentially progressive and humane force based on a harmony rather than a conflict of national interests.

The dichotomy where absorption into metropolitan capitalism is seen as progressive in contrast to the backward, reactionary, and inhumane internal precapitalist structures, which underlies Galbraith's view, is reminiscent of the dual economy models of development economics, which drew a distinction between the modern and the traditional sectors. The problem of development according to this view consisted in the fact that the modern sector was too small relative to the traditional; this problem could be overcome if fetters upon the growth of the modern sector were removed, in which case it would keep expanding until the entire economy was transformed and modernised. In a similar fashion the bourgeois internationalist view holds that there is a progressive and humane international current in contrast to the backward and reactionary domestic one; once a country opens its doors to the former it would be on the path to development; at the very least a necessary condition for building a socially, politically, and economically progressive society is to open one's doors to the former.

One can scarcely doubt that this perception will be shared by many in Third World societies, too. I have often come across in columns of newspapers and newsmagazines the view that globalization as a modernizing force represents an antidote to communalism in India. Indeed adherents of this view can be found even in left circles. This is not as surprising as may appear at first sight since an uncritical belief in the progressive, indeed revolutionary, role of capitalism, wherever it makes its appearance, continues to characterize many left-wing groups even to this day, more than six decades after the path-breaking theses on the colonial question adopted at the Sixth Congress of the Comintern.

I strongly disagree with this perception and shall devote the rest of this paper to a critique of it. At the outset however I would like to demarcate my critique from other possible ones. An analogy with the dual economy models will be useful here. These models can be critiqued in diverse ways: through a rejection on ethical grounds of the concept of modernization, through a denial of the so-called backwardness of the backward sector, through an underlining of the complexity of life, which is inadequately captured by postulating merely two sectors, through doubts about the ability of the modern sector to pull the backward sector with it instead of being dragged back by it, and so on. In addition to these, however, there is a critique that sees the dichotomy between the two sectors as unreal, which sees the two as being dialectically related, as constituting one interlinked whole, and that therefore rejects the perception of the dual economy models as being fundamentally flawed. My critique of the bourgeois internationalist view is along these latter lines. It is fundamentally flawed because the so-called progressive capitalism and reactionary internal structures constitute one integrated whole. Globalization is not an antidote to communalism because globalization and communalism are dialectically related. The internal conflicts and internal disasters that Galbraith feels so concerned about cannot be overcome by his brand of internationalism because this internationalism is itself one of the components of the brew that produces these conflicts and disasters. Let me elaborate on this.

Capitalism from its very inception has been founded upon external conquest. It is unfortunate that in the main body of the work that Marx could complete in his lifetime, the *theoretical* analysis of capitalism was undertaken as if it constituted a closed system. This fact tended to perpetuate a belief in some left circles that its external conquests and domination, though empirically an important historical legacy, were some kind of an inessential appendage, i.e., not a part of the *essence* of its working. (This was to find an echo in Schumpeter's writings later.) No doubt Marx himself wrote extensively on colonialism but these were written separately from the main theoretical body of his work; and he never lived to integrate the two. When Lenin extended Marx's analysis by incorporating monopoly, finance capital, and imperialism into the theoretical corpus, his emphasis was on capturing the conjuncture rather than systematically reworking the analysis of capitalism as an open system that subjugates other noncapitalist systems. The general crisis of capitalism, marking the period of transition to socialism, had come on the agenda and his energies were urgently needed for a concrete analysis of the prevailing conjuncture for the purpose of immediate revolutionary intervention. (The Sixth Congress of the Comintern, as noted earlier, provided a vital lead in unraveling the dialectics of capitalism and underdevelopment, but its document was designed for action, not as a theoretical opus).

Within the Marxist tradition, Rosa Luxemburg did attempt to incorporate capitalism's subjugation of sectors external to it into the essence of its working. But there was a basic ambiguity about her analysis that was rooted in the fact that she was engaged in a bitter controversy with the revisionists led by Eduard Bernstein. If capitalization of surplus value occurs, as she argued, through an interaction with the precapitalist sector, then this does not mean that in the process of this interaction the precapitalist sector is assimilated into the capitalist sector itself. In other words this interaction may very well mean that a subjugated, pauperized precapitalist sector continues to linger on, rather than the world becoming over time more and more exlcusively capitalist. And yet in Luxemburg while there is recognition of the former possibility in places, the overall view coincides with the latter perception. The reason lies perhaps in the theory of collapse, which she advocated against Bernstein, who had pooh-poohed such a notion, as part of the reestablishment of the revolutionary cause: if a system's inner working was propelling it towards a breakdown, then its historical transitoriness as underscored by the revolutionary tradition would have stood vindicated. And she argued the theory of collapse as follows: if capitalism needs precapitalist sectors, and if such sectors keep disappearing through their assimilation into capitalism, then a time would come when the world would be exclusively capitalist and hence no further possibility for accumulation would remain; the system would have reached the point of collapse.

Today when capitalism has shown far greater reserves of strength than was imagined earlier, it is essential not only to rework the analysis of its functioning, taking cognisance of its being an open system, but also to carry this analysis much beyond Luxemburg. There are at least two spheres in which this has to be done.

First, capitalism's (and here we necessarily mean metropolitan capitalism's) need for outlying precapitalist and semicapitalist regions must be seen to arise not only for obtaining markets, raw materials, labor-power, and spheres of lucrative investment, i.e., not only because it needs a global reach, but also because it needs labor reserves located at a respectable distance enabling it to achieve economic and social stability. (This proposition is argued at length in Patnaik, 1997). Marx had argued that a reserve army of labor was essential for the functioning of capitalism. As a matter of fact even if the domestic reserve army is reduced giving the system a respectably high employment rate, which it parades as success, a reserve army in the outlying regions is essential for its survival. Universal near-full employment is impossible under capitalism. This (together with the fact that the development of the backward regions would put enormous pressures on the available supplies of nonrenewable resources) entails that there are fundamental conflicts of interest between the advanced and the backward economies. International harmonism under capitalism is as vacuous as class-harmonism.

Secondly, as saying this itself presupposes, the outlying regions continue to remain outlying regions. If there is a conflict of interest between capitalism at the core and the outlying regions then this arises precisely because the two remain distinct, though interrelated, entities. If the dualism of the dual-economy models precluded a perception of their interrelatedness, Luxemburg's monism, which sees the world as becoming more and more exclusively capitalist, precludes a perception of the distinctness of the two entities.

The conflict between the two entities is resolved to the satisfaction of the core through a combination of force (often as a last resort), of ideological hegemony, of manipulation, and of inflicting ideological and political paralysis. Often ideological and political paralysis gets spontaneously engendered by the fact of subjugation to the core itself. The mediations of this subjugation will be examined later, but the point to note is that it is this subjugation, which either directly stimulates or prepares the soil for the so-called internal conflicts and internal disasters, which Galbraith talks about. And they constitute not just accompaniments of this subjugation but vital processes making the continuation of this subjugation possible.

I should make one point clear here. My argument does not amount merely to stating that the current internal disasters and internal conflicts are a legacy of colonialism, that it is merely the historical experience of subjugation that has a left a residue even today in terms of conflicts and disasters; nor am I merely making the point that since subjugation continues, these disasters and conflicts, which accompany subjugation, continue despite the fact of formal decolonization. There is force in both these propositions but I am in fact making a much stronger point, namely that the form and contours of this subjugation change through time, that the fact of the *recent* internationalization of economic, social, and cultural life that Galbraith talks about in such glowing terms and that represents in my view a new form of subjugation has given rise to a *new spate* of disasters and conflicts. Let me take up two examples of such recent disasters to illustrate my point that they are linked to the process of globalization currently underway; the first relates to the food question while the second relates to ethnic or communal conflicts.

Almost everyone who talks of internal disasters in the Third World today would cite the African famines as a major example of such a disaster. And social scientists almost unanimously have attributed the African famines to a variety of internal causes ranging from high population growth to the inefficiency of African agriculture, to the prevalence of drought, to the absence of infrastructure, etc. There may of course be some justification behind citing each of these factors but in citing them a decisive element is missed out, namely the integration of Africa as an agricultural exporter to the advanced capitalist countries. Such integration, to be sure, was always there but it has also been greatly strengthened under the *diktat* of the IMF and the World Bank in recent years.

The circumstances under which Africa came under thraldom to the Bretton Woods institutions are worth exploring. While the effect of the oil-price hike on the balance of payments of the African countries was itself not very significant, in the wake of this hike world manufactured goods prices, which are administered by corporations belonging to the advanced capitalist countries went up. This meant a terms of trade shift against the underdeveloped primary commodity producing economies, among whom the African economies are to be counted. African economies therefore witnessed an adverse terms of trade shift not so much because of the oil-price hike, as due to the strategy of metropolitan capital in the wake of this hike (Patnaik, 1986). Because of this adverse terms of trade shift, however, they became indebted to the Bretton Woods institutions, and under their cover, to commercial lenders. Thus Africa's coming under the Bretton Woods *diktat* was itself for reasons external to it; it was a consequence of the strategic behavior of metropolitan capital. To say this of course is not to exonerate the African bourgeoisie, its corruption as well as its profligacy. But given the background of this corruption and profligacy, and the penchant of this bourgeoisie for linking itself with the metropolis, the fact still remains that the immediate provocation for turning to the Bretton Woods institutions was the externally imposed adverse terms of trade shift.

Paradoxically, therefore, it was the squeeze of metropolitan capital itself that forced Africa to subjugate herself to the Bretton Woods institutions and through them to metropolian capital. Paradoxically too this subjugation which came in the wake of the oil-price hike was not confined to the nonoil countries: it incorporated within its ambit the oil-producers too through what has now come to be referred to as the oil-induced debt-trap. The oil-producers, who saw an increase in their revenues initially, launched all kinds of ambitious projects. As the terms of trade, which had initially shifted in their favor, moved against them through the administered increase in manufactured goods prices, they sought to maintain their expenditures by borrowing, in the confident belief that being oil-producers they would never have problems paying back. As a matter of fact however, the adverse terms of trade movement against them after the first two oil-shocks was never reversed; there was no third oil-shock. And they too sank into a debt-trap entailing submission before the Bretton Woods institutions.

One consequence of this subjugation was the promotion of agriexports at the expense of food-crop production. U. Patnaik (1996) has provided some estimates of food-crop output and its growth rate for African countries during the eighties. She includes cereals (wheat, maize, barley, and millets), tubers (potatoes, cassava, and yams), and plantains (bananas and plantains) under food crops for Africa, and aggregates them by using the convention that 5 kg. of tubers or plantains equal 1 kg. of cereals. (She also gives Indian and Chinese figures for comparison, but the term *food crop* is interpreted differently in the latter two: for India it covers only cereals and pulses but not potatoes, while for China it covers cereals, soybeans and potatoes). Already in 1980 the 46 countries of sub-Saharan Africa had a low level of per capita food-crop production, about 138.5 kg. gross (or, even if we correct for possible underestimation by revising the figure upwards by as much as 20 percent, then not more than 166 kg.), which was lower than India (190 kg.) or China (285 kg.). What has happened during the eighties, however, is a deterioration in per capita food-crop output in sub-Saharan Africa. For the entire sub-Saharan region the decline in per capita food-crop output between 1980 and 1987–89 (three-year average) was 11.5 percent. For the six most populous countries of the region the corresponding decline was of the order of 20 percent.

It may be argued that this *per se* is of little consequence. Agriexports, even if squeezed out at the expense of food-crop production via a shift of acreage, can nevertheless finance food imports that more than offset the decline in domestic output, so that per capita availability improves, relative to what it otherwise would have been. The African case however belies any such expectations. Between 1980 and 1990, cereal imports net of food aid in cereals declined in absolute terms in every single one of the six most populous countries in sub-Saharan Africa (Table 1).

One can draw at least two logical inferences from this decline in the absolute magnitude of imports net of aid: first, wherever one observes a decline in per capita food production, owing to a shift of acreage to agriexports, together with a decline in per capita food availability, the latter must be attributed in a proximate sense to

**Table 1. Selected Food Statistics**

| COUNTRY | CEREAL IMPORTS (000 T.) | | FOOD AID (CEREALS) (000 T.) | | CHANGE IN IMPORTS net of food aid (000 T.) | % CHANGE PER HEAD CALORIES |
|---|---|---|---|---|---|---|
| | 1 | 2 | 3 | 4 | 5 | 6 |
| | 1980 | 1990 | 1979–80 | 1989–90 | 1980–90 | 1979–81 to 1989–91 |
| Tanzania | 399 | 73 | 89 | 22 | −259 | −2.17 |
| Ethiopia | 397 | 687 | 111 | 538 | −137 | −9.92 |
| Uganda | 52 | 7 | 17 | 35 | −63 | −6.0 |
| Nigeria | 1828 | 502 | — | — | −1326 | 15.45 |
| Kenya | 387 | 188 | 86 | 62 | −175 | −9.86 |
| Zaire | 538 | 336 | 77 | 107 | −232 | 1.54 |

Source: For columns 1 to 4, various issues of the World Bank's *World Development Report*; for column 6 FAO's *Food Balance Sheets: 1992–4 Average*, Rome 1996.

Note: Column 5 = (2 − 4) − (1 − 3). Since import figures refer to calendar years while food aid figures refer to crop years (July–June), their comparison can give only an approximate picture. Since aid data are from the donors, July–June is compared with the following January–December to take care of lags in aid arrival.

the processes that brought about the former. Secondly, even where there is no decline in per capita food availability, if there is an acreage shift to agriexports, then the reason for availability not being higher than what it was must lie in this acreage shift.

The conclusion derived from the case of six countries is likely to be valid for sub-Saharan Africa as a whole, namely, wherever there have been acreage shifts to agriexports (and the phenomenon appears rather widespread), such shifts constitute the proximate explanation for the observed behaviour of food availabbility.

To be sure there are several long-term problems associated with African agriculture. There is also the undeniable fact that given Africa's high rate of population growth, around three percent per annum, improving her per capita food availability is a daunting task anyway. But the fact that there has been a shift from food-crop production for the domestic market to agriexport production for the international market, over roughly the same period when imports have actually declined, suggests that the *immediate, binding* constraint on domestic food availability in Africa is to be located in globalization rather than in any of the other, long-term factors usually mentioned. Globalization has therefore laid the groundwork for acute food scarcity periodically bursting into famines.

Why has this happened? Why has globalization not led to an increase in food availability, despite shrinking food production per capita, the way traditional economic theory visualizes? The reason is the following: since all Third World economies under thraldom to the Bretton Woods institutions are being simultaneously asked to enlarge exports of primary commodities, the terms of trade have remained subdued for such commodities. Consequently the magnitude of free foreign exchange left after meeting debt-service obligations and liberalized manufactured goods imports has been too small to permit the maintenance of, let alone an increase in, the level of per capita food-grain imports. And this is why even in years when there have been record world food stocks, African countries have experienced famines: on the one hand they have lost domestic self-sufficiency; and on the other hand the foreign exchange available in their hands has been too small.

This predicament however has been a part of the very process of globalization lauded by Galbraith and others. If Africa today appears to be a basket case, which cannot do without humanitarian aid, and whole invading armies to ensure that this aid reaches the starving, it should be remembered that the process of its being reduced to a basket case has been presided over by the very powers that come with humanitarian did and invading armies to boot!

Though I have talked so far only of Africa, what is true of Africa is true of other Third World countries as well. Globalization, which opens up their economies to world market forces, necessarily undermines their food security and makes them vulnerable to famine-like conditions. To be sure this is not the sole effect of globalization on Third World economies. One can in fact discern three separate economic implications of globalization: first, ensuring cheap supplies of primary products from the Third World by undermining their domestic self-sufficiency and making them export-oriented; second, opening up their economies to the free movement of finance capital, which has come to acquire so important a position in the advanced capitalist economies; and third, making their markets available for exports of manufactures and services from the advanced capitalist economies. The net effect of these three processes is to perpetuate stagnation, to worsen income distribution within the Third World and to reduce Third World economies to the same status, which they enjoyed during the colonial era, from which they had attempted to break out through their long struggle for decolonization. An important component of colonial status, as is well-known, is vulnerability to famines, which is what we have been talking about till now.

I now come to the other example of internal disaster, namely internecine conflicts within the Third World along communal or ethnic lines. The exacerbation of these conflicts too is not unrelated to the process of globalization. In general terms one can put the matter as follows. The welding together of diverse groups into a nation-in-the-making was one of the consequences of the struggle for decolonization. With the setback to this struggle, which the process of globalization under capitalism entails, it is hardly surprising that particular group consciousnesses begin to come to the forefront. Not that these particular consciousnesses had ever been obliterated; they had only been covered by an overarching national consciousness. But with a recession in this overarching national consciousness which is inevitable if the country is to be absorbed into the globalization process, these particular consciousnesses emerge to prominence. Putting it differently, the espousal of bourgeois internationalism is accompanied paradoxically by a strengthening of particular *subnational* consciousnesses.

But it is not just in general terms that globalization exacerbates internal contradictions and conflicts. It also makes very specific contributions. One can distinguish four different cases here. First, sometimes certain fundamentalist forces are directly supported and encouraged by one or the other of the capitalist powers for purely material reasons. Their fundamentalism gives them a degree of social support, which is utilized by the capitalist power in question for its own gain. And obviously supporting these forces and enabling them to come to power entails an exacerbation of internal conflicts. An obvious recent example of this is the *Taliban* being supported by the United States for greater control over Central Asian oil, at any rate until 1997 (Mackenzie, 1998).

Second, in so far as globalization means a worsening of the lot of the common people while a section of the domestic rich not only becomes richer but gets closely identified with the West and also indulges in lavish consumerism, an antiimperialist and antielite feeling necessarily develops among the people; in certain circumstances this feeling takes a fundamentalist color, especially where there has been a previous history of suppression of progressive and democratic movements. The classic case of this of course is Iran where the installation of the Shah and the suppression of the left and democratic movement by the United States had the ironic sequel of a fundamentalist movement exploiting popular discontent through a populist anticonsumerist rhetoric to capture power. Fundamentalism of this kind, though reactionary, authoritarian, ruthless, and repugnant, represents nonetheless a distorted version of antiimperialism.

Third, there may be yet another kind of fundamentalism, which is opportunistic to the core in the sense that it takes advantage of popular distress not for an antiimperialist platform, however distorted, but for singling out some minority group as the source of distress. Since this kind of singling out does no harm to the interests of imperialism, but on the contrary deflects attention from an antiimperialist struggle, the latter tends to be well-disposed towards such fundamentalism. This does not of course mean that imperialism necessarily supports *the quest for power* on the part of such forces. But it approves of them as a *dog on a leash*, a term used by M. Kalecki (1972). Such comprador fundamentalist forces (among whom of course there may be divisions with some sections opposing some aspects of imperialist penetration) attempt to come to power by appeasing imperialism and the domestic elite that supports globalization, but by mobilizing support through pogroms and riots against some hapless minority. The obvious example that comes to mind in this context is the wave of Hindu fundamentalism that has carried a communal party like the BJP to power in India. The important thing to note is that this too, like antiimperialist fundamentalism, gets strengthened by the globalization process and the attendant worsening of the condition of the people through unemployment, wage-cuts, subsidy-cuts, etc.

Finally, globalization tends to promote secessionist movements, which may also take a fundamentalist color (e.g., Sikh secessionism) but which in any case generate internal conflict. Such secessionism arises at both ends of the spectrum (Patnaik, 1995). The advanced regions within the Third World economy develop a secessionist tendency since, economic progress becoming dependent on the inflow of direct foreign investment in a globalized setting, they think they have a better chance of attracting such investment from multinational corporations if they are unencumbered by the company of the backward regions. The first state to secede from the former Soviet Union, it must be remembered, was Lithuania, which was the richest, and the first to do so from the former Yugoslavia was Slovenia, also the richest. Though neither the Soviet Union nor Yugoslavia were Third World economies, the examples nevertheless are instructive. On the other hand, the backward regions develop a secessionist tendency since they feel they are getting a raw deal, which accounts for the perpetuation of their backwardness.

All this is hardly surprising: globalization necessarily involves a fracturing of the economic integrity of the nation with each region competing against others in attracting direct foreign investment, and with each region's commodities commanding a price determined not by national-level decisions but by the world market. Secessionism is simply the outcome of this fracturing.

Thus, it is the recession of antiimperialist nationalism, which globalization and bourgeois internationalism are based on, that brings to the fore a whole variety of ethnic and fundamentalist consciousnesses. The economic hardships created by globalization breed conflicts based on such consciousnesses. What appear as internal conflicts therefore are the other side of the coin to globalization and bourgeois internationalism. The two, far from being counterposed to one another, are in fact dialectically related.

So far we have talked of conflicts which, though nourished by the material conditions created by globalization, are located essentially in the realm of consciousness. But globalization also breeds yet another set of conflicts, namely elemental conflicts between people over available resources, caused by the desperate need for survival in the face of growing immiserisation. Again the classic examples come from Africa. The sites of the worst recent conflicts in Africa, namely Central Africa (Rwanda, Burundi, and Zaire) and the Sahel region, are among those where material living standards have dropped most significantly and where declines in alternative employment opportunities have made the struggle over land and other resources so much more intense. Thus the so-called tribal and ethnic struggles in these regions are also desperate fights to ensure minimal livelihoods and economic survival. According to some the conflict in Algeria too would fall into this category.

Once we bear in mind the difference in the positions of the advanced and the backward economies we can appreciate why the same terms have very different implications in the two contexts. Take for instance nationalism. Galbraith sees the Second World War as an extreme manifestation of nationalism. For him and for people of his generation the horrors of that event invest the term nationalism with an undesirable connotation. For them bourgeois internationalism appears a positive development as something that ensures that such horrors would not be repeated. But nationalism of the imperialist powers and nationalism of the oppressed colonial people are not the same thing. To take nationalism as an undifferentiated category and to decry it, no matter what the context, on the grounds that it underlay the horrors of the Second World War is not only wrong but also dangerous (no matter how well-meaning and innocent it may be) because it connives with imperialist oppression. And this holds true even for a whole range of radical tendencies that pooh-pooh Third World nationalism because they are opposed to *all* nationalism.

If we do away with undifferentiated concepts and look at the matter instead from an antiimperialist perspective, then the Second World War would appear not as a mere manifestation of nationalism but as a manifestation, *inter alia*, of interimperialist rivalry. Indeed the entire period from the turn of the century can be characterized as one of interimperialist rivalry. This rivalry not only produced the Great Depression and two World Wars (though the Second World War was four different wars rolled into one, of which the war between fascism and socialism became the most prominent and decisive) but also allowed space for Third World nationalism and the struggle for decolonisation. By contrast the more recent period has been marked by a degree of common purpose among capitalist powers. How this relative unity has come about need not detain us here: one contributing factor has no doubt been the emergence of internationally mobile finance capital, which has precluded the cordoning off of national spaces among the advanced capitalist countries. But the implication of this unity has been a common front against the Third World as a result of which the space for Third World nationalism, already in crisis owing to its promise being subverted by the urge for primitive accumulation among the bourgeoisie, has become severely restricted. The collapse of the Soviet Union has also no doubt been a crucial factor behind the restriction of this space but this collapse itself is not unrelated to the relatively greater unity among the capitalist powers. (A fuller discussion of the contradictions and possibilities of economic nationalism in the Indian context can be found in P. Patnaik and C. P. Chandrashekhar, 1998).

The internationalization of social, political, and economic life mentioned by Galbraith, therefore, is a process that has two quite distinct components: a process of relative unity as opposed to interimperialist rivalry among the advanced capitalist countries; and second, a process of common purpose *against* the Third World on the part of the united capitalist powers, which denies space to Third World nationalism, which breaks down their quest for economic self-reliance and which coerces them into accepting a global order dominated by these powers. The fact that the advanced countries managed to settle their differences and erect the WTO, whose detrimental effects on food security and self-reliance within the Third World have been much discussed (see for example Dasgupta, 1998), only supports the argument I am advancing. These two components are of course interlinked. And while it would be absolutely perverse for anybody desirous of Third World liberation to wish to see a revival of interimperialist rivalry to a point where the horrors of war among them are repeated, to pretend that these two components together constitute a progressive advance in the direction of internationalism is patently untenable.

Socialists have always stood for internationalism. But to believe that the current globalization is a move in the direction of that internationalism, that it represents willy-nilly a sort of halfway house towards that goal is grossly erroneous. What is more, in so far as this globalization, together with its ideology of bourgeois internationalism, represents imperialist domination, the progressive forces have to fight for a democratic *national* agenda in the Third World *in opposition to* this bourgeois internationalism. To be sure, in a world where the Soviet Union has collapsed and where interimperialist rivalries are muted, fighting for such an agenda is no easy task. But the current setback to the forces of socialism and the current common front presented by the capitalist powers would not last long; and the fight, being for a just cause, has to be joined no matter what the conditions.

# CHAPTER 10

## GLOBALIZATION: A CRITICAL ANALYSIS

## James Petras

### Introduction

The term *globalization* has been used in a multiplicity of senses. Concepts like the global interdependence of nations, the growth of a world system, accumulation on a world-scale, the global village, and many others are rooted in the more general notion that the accumulation of capital, trade, and investment is no longer confined to the nation-state. In its most general sense, *globalization* refers to the cross-national flows of goods, investment, production, and technology. For many of the advocates of the globalization thesis these flows, both their scope and depth, have created a new world order, with its own institutions and configurations of power that have replaced the previous structures associated with the nation-state (Reich, 1992; Oman, 1997; Luard, 1990; Waters, 1995).

The globalist theories have been engaged in a debate with critics over the meaning and significance of the changes in the capitalist political economy (Tabb, 1997; Magdoff, 1992; Krugman, 1996; Edelstein, 1982; Zevin, 1992; Weiss, 1997; Rodrik, 1997). The center of the debate revolves around whether the present stage of capitalism represents a new epoch or is basically a continuation of the past, or an amalgam of new developments that can be understood through discussion of whether the term *globalization* itself is a useful term in understanding the organization and nature of the movements of capital, goods, and technology. Counterpoised to the concept of globalization is the notion of imperialism, which attempts to contextualize the flows, locating it in a setting of unequal power, between conflicting states, classes, and markets.

This essay is an effort to rethink the concept of globalization, both at the theoretical and practical level. The fact that capitalism today has spread to practically every geographical region of the world, subsumed all economies under its sway, and exploits labor everywhere for private accumulation, raises several specific analytical questions, which will be addressed in this essay.

First from the perspective of conceptual and historical analysis: what are the origins of the transnational flows of capital, goods, and technology (CGT)? Is globalization a phenomena of late or early capitalism? If the latter, how is it similar or different from the later expression? What are the interstate relations that allowed for transnational flows of CGT? Who were the social agents and what were the objectives of the flows?

If what is described as globalization existed earlier, why is it attributed novelty today? If there is not a linear process leading to globalization is it more appropriate to examine cyclical tendencies toward outward flows (world market) and inward flows (internal to the nation-state) of CGT? If the direction of flows is variable, what are the underlying socio-economic and political institutions and classes that are determinant? At the more general theoretical level, if the CGT flows vary over time and place, subject to the influence of different political actors, what does that tell us about a major thesis of globalist theorists, specifically the argument that globalization is inevitable and the counterthesis of its critics who argue that it is contingent?

We will proceed to critically analyze several of the basic premises of globalization theorists: the claim of inevitability, the notion that it represents a novel development, its denial of alternatives, and the divergence between its grand claims and meager explanatory power: the claim of being the filet mignon of social theory and the results, which approximate a baloney sandwich, Hence the introduction of the concept of globaloney as a way of highlighting the contrast between globalist rhetoric and contemporary realities. In the following section we will turn to analyzing the political, economic, technological bases for the increasing transnational flows of CGT by focusing on the inner dynamics of the capital/labor relations and state power. The hypothesis explored here argues that historic changes in political and class power in the context of a severe crisis of accumulation led to the creation of conditions favorable to increased flows in previously closed areas. Technological innovations were first consequence and then causes of these increasing flows.

The political changes that facilitated external flows also had a profound impact on the distributional consequences. The hypothesis here is that the growing power of capital over labor that liberated capital to move also led to massive reconcentration of wealth. The hypothesis here is that one of the key elements in understanding the globalist theory is its use as an ideology to justify growing social inequalities, greater social polarization and the increasing transfer of state resources to capital. If indeed globalization theory has little intellectual merit, it is argued it does serve an essential political purpose, as an ideological rationalization for growing class inequalities.

The last section of the paper focuses on the resistance, opposition, and alternatives to the new world order. If the previous analysis of the CGT transnational flows is correct in pointing to class and state relations as the decisive nexus, then it follows changes in class relations and power that reverse current capital/labor relations can create the basis for alternatives to globalization. The final section of the paper examines a key element in globalist ideology: privatization and its limits and surveys the state of resistance. The essay concludes with the positing of alternatives that call into question globalist dogma.

**Conceptual and Historical Analysis**

Historically the international flows of CGT have taken place via three routes. In the first instance through imperialist and colonial conquest; second, via trade and investment between advanced capitalist countries; and third, via exchanges between Third World countries. Each of these routes embodies different relations and has had different consequences. The imperial-colonial flows of capital led to unequal accumulation and a division of labor in which economic diversification and industrialization in the imperial center was accompanied by specialization and vulnerability to raw material fluctuations in the colonized regions. The second route of international flows between advanced imperial centers was mutually compatible as foreign capital was regulated to complement endogenous capitalist development. The third route to globalization, exchanges between Third World countries, was limited by the intrusion of imperial powers and the articulation of Third World economies with their imperial centers. The main periods of intra-Third World exchanges occurs before they are colonized and in the postcolonial industrializing phase.

The theoretical point is the long history, diversity of sources, and differential relations and consequences accompanying the expansion of international flows of CGT. The historical fact is that the United States, Africa, Asia, and Latin America have a long history of several centuries of ties to overseas markets, exchanges, and investments. Moreover, in the case of North America and Latin America, capitalism was born globalized in the sense that most of its early growth was based on overseas exchanges and investments. From the fifteenth to the nineteenth century Latin America's external trade and investment had greater significance than in the twentieth century. Similarly, one-third of English capital formation in the seventeenth century was based on the international slave trade. Born globalized, it is only in the middle of the nineteenth century that the internal market began to gain in importance, thanks to the growth of wage labor, local manufactures and, most significantly, a state that altered the balance of class forces between the domestic and overseas oriented investors and producers.

The significance of the historical shift from globalism to domestic development was based on the emergence of middle classes determined to play a central role in the political economy over and against financiers, staple and grain producing agroexporters. The transition was not smooth: in the United States, the Civil War that subordinated the globalizing plantation owners to the western farmers and eastern industrialists, cost two million lives. In Latin America, civil wars and overseas intervention raged throughout the nineteenth century as globalizers and domestic producers battled over the direction of the economy. In Asia, major wars (the Opium War, Perry's expedition to Japan, etc.) were waged to globalize Asia, while emerging domestic producers resisted under the leadership of traditional elites. The point is that globalization in its old imperial form based on European traders, manufacturers, and local agricultural and mining elites was seen as a major obstacle to development by the modern emerging producers. The fact that the immediate enemies of globalization were decrepit emperors (China) or corrupt dictators (Latin America) should not obscure the fact clearly illustrated in the United

States, that globalization as it had emerged from the fifteenth to the nineteenth century had become a serious obstacle to the development of a modern economy.

Sociologically speaking, the objects and subjects of globalization up to the twentieth century were distinct social groups. While capital and goods expanded across national boundaries, it was centered in specific nation-states. The results of expansion provided unequal benefits between classes in both the capital exporting and receiving countries. Today this tendency is even more marked, even as countries that previously were mere objects of CGT have become themselves exporters. The crucial difference today is the presence of transnational capitalists from the former colonial countries engaged in capital export and establishing regional dominance.

The cases of China, Hong Kong, Taiwan, South Korea, Chile, Mexico, Saudi Arabia are only a few of the instances. The point, however, remains that the multiplication of new centers of accumulation and the addition of new billionaires from the ex-colonial countries does not change the qualitative class and national relations: much of Latin America, Africa, and Asia continues to specialize in primary goods exports, labor power with high rates of exploitation and substantial imbalances in payments for rents (royalties) and services (insurance and interest). The point is that the expansion of flows of CGT via unequal relations in the contemporary period is a continuation of the imperialist relations of the past. The subjects of globalization, the principal traders, investors, and renters of services, have different and antagonistic interests to the objects of their policies, the workers, peasants, and national producers in the targeted countries. What is described as globalization is thus essentially a continuation of the past based on the deepening and extension of exploitative class relations into areas previously outside of capitalist production. The current globalist claims of novelty and the assertion that we are entering a new stage of the world economy is largely based on the assertion that accretions and expansion of capitalist relation are sufficient to defining the new period. Globalist ideologues forget that in the past economic activities were more rooted in international exchanges and production and that current expansion based on international flows is of recent vintage and still not the predominant engine of capitalist reproduction. Moreover, the shifts in the axes of capitalist expansion from domestic production and exchange (enlarging the home market) to the world market has always been contingent on the political and socio-economic composition of the state, which orients economic policy.

It is useful to compare and contrast the concept of globalizaton to imperialism to highlight the analytical weaknesses of the former and the strengths of the latter, There are several dimensions to consider the explanatory power of the respective concepts: measures of power, specificity of agency, understanding of regional, national and class inequalities, directional flows of income, investment, payments (royalties, interest, profits, rents).

The concept of globalization argues for the interdependence of nations, the shared nature of their economies, the mutuality of their interests, the shared benefits of their exchanges. Imperialism emphasizes the domination and exploitation by imperial states and multinational corporations and banks of less developed states and laboring classes. In today's world it is clear that the imperial countries are hardly dependent on most of the Third World countries they trade with, they have diverse suppliers; the economic units operating are owned and operated in large part by stockholders in the imperial countries; the profits, royalties, interest payments flow upward and outward in an asymmetrical fashion. In the international financial agencies and other world bodies, the imperial countries wield disproportionate or decisive influence. On the other hand, the dominated countries are low-wage areas, interest and profit exporters (not importers), virtual captives of the IFIs, and highly dependent on limited overseas markets and export products. Hence the imperial concept fits the realities much better than the assumptions that underlie the notion of globalization.

With regard to the specificity of the social agency, the mainspring of transnational flows of CGT, the concept of globalization relies heavily on diffuse notions of technological change accompanied by information flows and the abstract notion of market forces (Sassen, 1997; Castells, 1993). In contrast, the concept of imperialism sees the multinational corporations and banks, the imperial states as the driving force of the international flows of CGT. A survey of the major events, world trade treaties, regional integration schemes quickly dispels any technological determinant explanations: it is the heads of the imperial states that establish the shell or framework for global exchanges. Within that shell the major transactions and organizational forms of capital movements are found in the multinational corporation (MNC), supported by the IFIs (whose personnel is appointed by the imperial states in line with MNC interests). Technological innovations operate within the parameters furthering this configuration of power. The concept of imperialism thus gives us a more precise idea of the social agencies of worldwide movements of CGT than the notion of globalization.

Data covering long- and short-term large-scale flows of incomes both at world, national, and class levels consistently show an increase of inequalities between imperial states and dominated states, investors and workers, agro-exporters, and peasants. The assumptions of the theory of imperialism are compatible with this outcome; the assumptions of globalization theory have proven unilluminating in this regard also. Moreover, there is a robust relation between the growth of international flows of CGT and the increase of inequalities between states and within states between CEOs and workers. The best face that globalization can put on the matter is to shift from arguing for greater general prosperity to justifying the inequalities in terms of unequal rewards for differential contributions. Here the argument revolves around emphasizing the contribution of capital and devaluating the role of labor, in a rather self-serving and tautological fashion. Even here the imperialist concept with its focus on value creation of labor and the value appropriation by capital is more to the point: it sheds light on the different locus of exploitation (labor, dominated countries) and accumulation (capital imperial firms/states).

The structure of the international flows of income, investment, royalty payments does not correspond to any notion of interdependent world, premised by globalist theorists. In contrast, the singular concentration and unidirectional flow toward the imperial based corporations is readily understood within the conceptual framework of imperial theory.

The same is true regarding military policy and intelligence operations. The flow of intervention is unidirectional, from the imperial centers to the dominated countries. There is not mutual penetration of military commands, but the extension of military missions from the imperial center to the dominated countries. In legal terms only the imperial countries raise claims of extraterritoriality (the supremacy of their laws over the laws of other sovereign nations) — the dominated countries are the targets.

These empirical measures allow us to argue for the greater scientific utility of the concept of imperialism over globalization. Both as explanation and organizing principle of the major structural relations in the world political economy the notion of imperialism has become more not less relevant.

The struggle in the world today is not only between different conceptual, historical, or analytical frameworks but also by living forces. As important as the issue of theoretical clarification is, it is crucial to look at the political actors engaged in the struggles.

### Advocates, Adversaries and Ambivalents of "Globalization"

Though there are a variety of types of international exchanges that are not embedded directly in imperial relations (exchanges between imperial states, exchanges between dominated countries, exchanges regulated by regimes of popular accumulation), we will focus on the imperialist component of global flows of CGT.

There are essential three classes in the world political economy: the advocates and beneficiaries of globalization, the adversaries and exploited classes, and states and the ambivalents who experience both exploitation and benefits and who waver in their response. The proponents of globalization, both now and in the past, are always the ascending countries and states within the world economy. In this logic the principal supporter is the hegemonic state. Obviously their superior competitive position gives them little to fear and much to gain from opening the economy. Nevertheless, two caveats are in order: not all classes in the ascending nation-state are beneficiaries — mainly the large-scale dominant enterprises. Secondly, while proclaiming the universality of global principles (free trade, free markets, and free remittances), the ascending power frequently restricts entry to protect political allies of the regime (in backward sectors of the economy) and establish privileged trading zones to exclude competitors.

While ascending states and their dominant economic enterprises are the main proponents of globalization, their political and economic counterparts in the dominated countries are also staunch advocates. Here the internal divisions are crucial as are the structural effects. Agrobusiness and financial classes, importers, mineral exporters, big manufacturers, or sweatshop owners subcontracted for export markets are all strong advocates for globalization.

Hence globalization is both an imperial and a class phenomenon. The assymetrical income flows affects the growth of the internal market as a whole but favors the rapid growth of export enclaves and the enrichment of local classes in the global circuit.

The third group, a subordinate element to the first two, supporting globalization, are the high-level state functionaries (self-styled technocrats), academics, and publicists linked to the international circuits. In the imperial countries they manufacture the theories and concepts justifying and prescribing globalist programs, strategies, and tactics. A long list of globalist advocates in the dominated countries were trained by academic mentors in prestigious universities of the imperial countries. Frequently the academics shape the economic programs of the dominated countries to maximize the global interests of multinationals and receive lucrative consultation fees. Their former students in government shape policies, engage in corrupt business practices, and accumulate private fortunes through the privatization policies.

The fourth class promoting globalization are the commercial classes: the importers and exporters of goods. They are advocates of free trade as well as beneficiaries, up to a point. The point of differentiation is when large-scale, foreign-owned commercial traders displace local commercial groups. Otherwise, this sector, particularly where it does not have ties to local producers, is a staunch advocate of globalist principles of free trade.

Together this bloc is a formidable configuration as long as it retains state power. Its principal power base is its structural position — at the nodule of trade, finance, and investment transactions — and the amount of money at its disposition to finance political campaigns and social organizations. Yet money as a singularly important resource is not the only resource: social power and mass organization is a potential crucial counterweight.

The adversaries of globalization make up in numbers what they lack in financial power. The major adversaries of globalization in the dominated countries have been the peasant movements, particularly in Latin America and parts of Asia and to a lesser degree in Africa. The free-trade policies have led to the devastation of local producers, unable to compete with cheap grain imports. The subsidies to agroexport producers have stimulated the expansion of land ownership, concentration of credits and technical assistance at the expense of small producers. The introduction by corporate agroproducers of technology on extensive holdings has displaced local peasants and created a mass of displaced producers. The imperial state's eradication of nontraditional crops (coca, poppies, etc.) has undermined world market niches for small farmers. As a result there is a growing mass of radicalized peasants and landless rural workers in key countries such as Brazil and Mexico, India, the Philippines, Ecuador, Paraguay, Bolivia, as well as elsewhere.

The second major adversary class confronting globalism are the workers in both the imperial and dominated classes. Workers in France, Germany, South Korea, Brazil, Argentina, South Africa, as well as numerous other countries have engaged in general strikes against globalization policies. In the imperial countries against the threats of plant relocations, the cuts in pensions, health plans, vacations, and most important the massive growth of job insecurity. In the dominated countries workers have mobilized against low wages, despotic work conditions, autocratic managerial rule, long work days, and declining social benefits.

The third class of adversaries is the bulk of the public employees affected by huge cuts in budgets, privatizations, and the massive loss of purchasing power. One again the opposition of this class is found in both the imperial and dominated countries.

The fourth class is small business, particularly provincial classes affected by state cutbacks of public subsidies, deindustrialization, privatization of minerals and transport, which has impoverished the interior of the country and concentrated wealth in a few enclaves in the central cities. The flood of cheap imports has driven many local producers bankrupt and provoked widespread civic protests based on multi-sectoral alliances, which confront the central government. Experiences of this sort have occurred widely in Argentina, Bolivia, Colombia, Ecuador, South Korea, India, and Peru, at least prior to the Fujimori dictatorship.

In the past one would have included noncompetitive or newly industrializing nations as part of the adversarial alliance against globalism. However, that is a difficult position to maintain since the governing and ruling classes of these countries have become beneficiaries of the global circuits and define policy in accordance with imperial imperatives of free trade, free markets and free flows of capital.

There is a third category of classes that are ambivalent toward globalism: those who both win and lose from specific policies. For example, industries who have difficulty competing in the global market and yet benefit from the reduction of social payments and declining wage levels. Manufacturers who are bankrupted by overseas competition and convert to importing and other commercial activity. Low-paid wage workers who are consumers of imported cheap consumer goods. Families of peasant migrants who lose family members and see the prices of their produce decimated by imports but depend on overseas remittances, freely reconverted. What is decisive in the swing of these sectors is political intervention, organization, and struggle. When the globalist classes are in command, the ambivalent classes adapt to, rather than resist, globalist encroachments. If and when the adverse classes are in ascendancy, the ambivalents join in civic strikes, increase demands for state protection, and look toward state regulation of sweatshops and assembly plants.

The division among advocates, adversaries, and ambivalents of globalization today cuts across classes, even as the major beneficiaries are found in the imperial classes, and the exploited in the dominated countries. The point, however, is the international network that link competing advocates and exploited adversaries are unevenly developed. The advocates have their own international forums and organizations and act in common. The exploited adversaries are still fragmented within countries and between countries. There is a gap between the structural affinities of the adversaries and their subjective dispersion. The key point, however, is *the central control by the advocates and beneficiaries of the nation-state and their capacity to wield it as a formidable weapon in creating conditions for global expansion.* The weakness of the adversaries is in part organizational — opposition built around sectoral demands without strong international ties and ideological commitments. In the latter case, the adversaries have been sidetracked from the struggle for state power by the diffusion of the rhetoric of civil society and the notion that the nation-state is an anachronism. Approaches that fail to recognize the continuing power of the nation-state to shape the universe in which the classes operating in the world economy function.

The configuration of advocates, adversaries, and ambivalents is intimately tied to the distributive outcomes of globalist politics. There has been a geographical reconfiguration of wealth. The MNC and MNB in the imperial countries (North America, West Europe, and Japan), Hong Kong, Saudi Arabia, Taiwan, and Korea concentrate the vast majority of the world's assets and wealth along with enclaves of wealth in the dominated countries among the billionaire directors of the new conglomerates emerging from the privatization programs.

The key regions of impoverishment in the dominated countries are the urban suburbs, rural, and provincial towns as well as older mining and seaport regions. In the imperial countries former industrial and agricultural regions have been battered, particularly areas of militant unionism.

Within the working class, children, women, and ethnic minorities have been paid below the general wage rates and have virtually no protective coverage. Their main defense is employment turnover, as is the case of mainland Chinese working in coastal factories owned by diaspora millionaires. Migrant workers, the unregulated sector (so-called informal sector) and young people in temporary employment are tyrannized at the workplace by the absolute power of hiring and firing by global capital and its threat to relocate. The downwardly mobile public employees, teachers, and health workers, have been in the center of social struggles throughout Latin America and parts of Europe and Asia as wage and salary levels decline.

While the mass of old and new workers experience relative or absolute decline in living standards, a new class of billionaires emerge in finance, sweatshops, mass entertainment, and in drugs, porno, and contraband activities. The latter is particularly strong in the former U.S.S.R. and East Europe.

Positions toward globalization are clearly defined by structural position and distributive consequences: the ideology and its universal appeals are grounded in mystifying its profound class roots and class inequalities. The appeal to universalism and to abstract internationalism is contradicted by its powerful continuing ties to the nation-state and ruling classes rooted in those states.

**Cyclical Nature of Globalization**

The development of capitalism has been accompanied by shifts in its nature and by the particular sectors of capitalists who have directed the state. The capitalist state in turn has been at times influenced by the demands of the labor movement, left parties as well as by economic processes (crises, depressions, inflation, crashes, etc.) and technological breakthroughs. These changes have had a powerful effect on shaping the direction of capitalist investment inwardly or outwardly and the proportions of each.

Over the past five centuries capitalist expansion has alternated between dependence on global flows and the deepening of the internal market. The early colonial conquest led by mercantile capitalists, trading companies, slave merchants was the driving force of early globalization (fifteenth century to the eighteenth), the growth of protectionism and national industry (from the latter eighteenth to the mid-nineteenth century) stimulated the growth of domestic industries and the relative decline of global flows as centerpieces of accumulation. In Asia, Africa, and Latin America precolonial productive systems (some, as in India, textiles with marked capitalist features) were basically oriented toward domestic markets and/or long distance non–European trade (Africa and Asia). Colonization set the stage for the emergence of settler colonists who displaced indigenous ruling economic elites and reoriented the economies toward the world (European and later North American) market. In the nineteenth century national independence movements in Latin America led by the indigenous export elites (mine owners, landowners, merchants) deepened the process of globalization. Latin America's integration into the world market become more pronounced, except for cases like Paraguay which attempted to initiate industrial-protectionist policies similar to the Euro-American approach.

Beginning in the late nineteenth century the last great push (prior to the present) toward externally generated growth began with the notable exception of Germany and the United States. The latter combined heavy protection of emerging industries with selective imperial outward expansion. Globalization involved laissez faire economic policies far in advance of what is practiced today: travel without passports, absence of labor, and environmental legislation, no currency controls, limited powers to Central Banks (if they even existed), (Krugman, 1996; Edelstein, 1982; Hoogvelt, 1997; Zevin, 1992). This period ended with (some might argue, led to) World War I. There was a brief revival during the 1920s, and then definitively closed (or so it seemed for over a half century) with the World Depression of 1929. The reemergence of globalization or the international flows of CGT between 1945 and 1997 has been gradual, only accelerating since the end of the 1980s. Even today global trade does not account for the major part of the goods and services that go into the GNP even as it has been growing rapidly in recent years.

In the Third World the laissez faire policies accompanying global integration were weakened by World War I, as new manufacturers and middle class producers emerged demanding greater protection and development of the internal market.

As the internal market gained relative importance, a process of class differentiation took place between national producers and the allied popular classes (laborers, peons, peasants, etc.) on the one hand and the export globalist classes on the other (merchants, traders, large landowners, mine owners). The crash of 1929 sealed the fate of the globalist strategies, even as it did not definitively displace the export classes. From the early 1930s to the 1970s Latin America's GNP was increasingly based on production for the domestic markets, even as local producers continued to depend on export elites to generate foreign exchange to finance capital imports. The reversion of this pattern and the return to globalist dependence on external flows of CGT began in the 1970s, but it has been a prolonged, highly unsuccessful effort to create a new source of dynamic growth. The Latin country with the highest resource endowment (minerals, timber, maritime, fruit) that fits in with world market conditions, Chile, has been the most successful in making the transition. It is also the country that has the highest rate of exploitation of its nonrenewable resources and thus has the least sustainable development. Most other countries that depend relatively less on resource exploitation have had only limited capacity to sustain reasonable rates of growth across economic sectors and classes and over time.

In Asia, North America, and Europe the push toward dependence on external flows of CGT has been uneven: while growing across the board, it has also been selective (that is, combined with protectionism), integrative (exchanges between advanced capitalist countries predominate), and still based on the nation-state for substance, support, and promotion.

The globalist claims of an economy deeply tied to international exchange is thus a slowly emerging, cyclical process that is still deeply implicated in the national economies and highly dependent on the nation-state for its projections abroad (Barly, 1994; Mann, 1997; Petras and Morley, 1995). The principal actors, the multinational corporations in their majority, still receive the bulk of their profits from the domestic market, even as the percentage from overseas earnings increases. The subsidies for technological innovations, plant construction, export promotion, labor control, tax write-offs, which are essential components of multinational corporate growth strategies are still formulated within the nation-state.

What accounts for past and present outward cycles of capitalist expansion? Essentially we can identify three general, interrelated sources: changes in the world political economy such as wars, crises, opening of new markets; the ascendance of export classes to political and economic power; the changing composition of the state and the reallocation of resources to furthering the outward expansion economic strategy.

Far from being a linear process, historically the international flows of CGT has been a process interrupted and ruptured for extended periods of time. In historical time, at least over the past century, it has been the exception rather than the rule as capitalist rivalries have incited nationalist protectionist measures, wars have statified the economy and social opposition has channelled resources internally.

The current wave of globalization is very recent, is meeting stiff resistance in Latin America, Europe, and Asia and has a problematical basis of social support, even as its legitimacy as an economic program is increasingly being called into question. What is unquestionable is that the tendencies toward increasing dependence on external flows is increasing, the power and willingness of states to proceed and deepen the process is growing. Under present circumstances the economic linkages between markets and multinational corporations has had a wrenching effect on workers, employees, farmers, and peasants. A break with globalist state strategies will also involve a period of socioeconomic dislocation and a particularly high cost for financial corporations, multinational executives and their supporting classes. The point, however, is that the breakdown of communism, the defeats of the revolutionary left, the subsequent decline of the labor and social movements provided optimal terrain for the imposition of globalist policies.

The political nature of the high profits is evident in the stagnant economic growth pattern that accompany globalization. Japan, Germany, and the United States during the present globalist period have shown meagre growth results. The so-called technological revolution has been of little or no significance in stimulating overall growth. In fact, the more technologically backward countries, China, India, Chile, and Turkey, have shown the most growth, based largely on intensive/extensive labor exploitation, the extraction of raw materials, and the production of cheap manufacturing goods. The process of internationalization of capital is thus based on exploiting new frontiers and locating sites for high profits — not developing and deepening the forces of production. The international movement of CGT is thus creating more capitalism, more wage workers, more exports/imports, but overall has failed to overcome the tendencies toward stagnation.

If the external opportunities do not lead to dynamic growth, what accounts for the ascendancy of the export classes? The answer must be found in the shift in the political and social power within the nation-states and their extension outward from the imperial center to the rest of the world. The basic fact of the matter is that the capitalist class in the West has to a greater or lesser degree inflicted severe defeats on the working class in every sphere of life: in terms of state control, social policy, ideology; at the factory level in terms of work rules, wages, bargaining power, employment; at the personal level in terms of vulnerability, consciousness, fear.

Beginning in the early 1970s and accelerating through the 1990s, the capitalist class has taken advantage of a highly bureaucratized trade union movement divorced form the rank and file and highly dependent on state favors to roll back labor's bargaining power. While capitalists have developed close ties to the political parties of the state and thus wield effective power over their politicians, labor bureaucrats continued to depend on essentially the same capitalist parties to further their interests. While capitalists have developed a forthright, coherent capitalist strategy that bars any concessions on welfare issues, labor bureaucrats have remained tied to an earlier concept of social contracts and the welfare state, unable and unwilling to develop an anticapitalist strategy or consider a and socialist alternative. While capitalists have taken hold over the state, labor remains a pressure group, an outsider, linked to sectoral struggles and narrow wage issues. While capitalists dominate the mass media, labor lacks any alternative media; while capitalists launch wave after wave of antilabor legislation, intensifying the class struggle from above, labor turns toward service activity as its members decrease.

The centrality of class struggle in defining globalist policy is evident if we compare where it has gone the furthest: England and the United States, where strikes are few and often lost, and France and Germany where trade unions wield the strike weapon and workers still retain a large state sector, social programs, and national industries. In the Third World, the transition toward the globalist model has proceeded furthest under conditions where labor was most severely repressed by the state — Mexico, Chile, and Argentina.

The *reverse* pattern is also evident in past experiences. From the early 1930s to the mid-1970s, the advance of the middle and working classes undermined the power of the export classes and made the growth of the domestic market the center of economic policy. The creation of a welfare state and the proliferation of public enterprises was a product of the collapse of the export model and the crisis and displacement of the classes which supported it. The growth of noncapitalist countries in Europe, Asia, Eastern Europe, Latin America, and the growth of nationalist regimes in Africa forced the West European and U.S. capitalist class to compete for the allegiance of the working class by offering wage and welfare concessions. Export capitalists were harnessed to internal demand. Globalism was tempered by worker and peasant militancy and the specter of Communism made social welfare a necessity for capitalist survival.

Working class defeats in Brazil 1964, Indonesia 1966, and throughout Latin America in the 1970s, China's counterrevolution from within in the late 1970s, the U.S.S.R.'s collapse, and the conversion of European Social Democrats to neoliberals and U.S. liberals to Free Market conservatives were political events that transformed state policy from a force mediating between globalism and welfare into a straightout instrument for international flows of CGT (Petras and Vieux, 1996).

The change of class power and the recomposition of the state are the basic conditions underpinning the growth of international flows and the emergence of globalism as an ideology to legitimate power.

## Globalism: Past and Present

Is contemporary globalism different from the past? The answer depends on what we are looking at. In the past during periods when export classes predominated, globalism was much more significant than in contemporary times in terms of its impact on growth. This was particularly true for the imperialist centers and the newly colonized countries between the sixteenth and nineteenth centuries. Nevertheless, there were entire regions and countries in which the capitalist mode of production was only incipient or nonexistent, particularly in rural areas of the Third World and even in parts of Europe. Today there is nary a country or region that has not been incorporated into the capitalist mode of production. Today's market exchanges, unlike those in many parts of the world in previous centuries, take place within the capitalist system.

Secondly, for a greater part of the twentieth century substantial regions of the world were organized in a noncapitalist system, a form of collectivism, which did not operate within the capitalist mode of production. In the last decade these areas have been incorporated and subordinated to the logic of capitalist accumulation, even as in the case of most of the U.S.S.R., the would-be capitalists resemble sixteenth century English pirates, plunderers, and slave runners engaged in accumulating wealth through noneconomic means.

The significant continuities are found in the point of origin of globalization, centered in the advanced imperial countries (though the particular countries have changed), and the unequal effects that it has on the classes and nation-states in the imperial relation. Today, as in the past, major trade takes place via the giant firms in the major European, Asian, and North American economies. Today, as in the past, the greater part of the profits are appropriated by the ruling classes linked through investments, trade, rents, and interest payments. In the past as well as today, the nation-state is the principal political instrument for organizing the global expansion: trade treaties, subsidies, labor controls, military intervention, ideological promotion (free trade doctrines) are all essential functions performed by the governing elite of the nation-state. Then, as now, the nation-state is unable to control speculative booms and busts, the tendencies toward overproduction and stagnation crises inherent in the capitalist mode of production.

The apparent novelty of contemporary globalism is found in the fact that it is coming out of a prolonged period of inward oriented growth under a coalition of class forces that elaborated an ideology (Keyesianism, communism, corporatism) and policies in which external exchanges and investments were subordinated to the growth of protected industries and the enlargement of the domestic market. If one took a longer view of economic history, predating the ascendancy of inward directed development, one would find substantial structural similarities to the current pattern of globalism.

What is different from the past is the fact that the earlier period of outward development went into a deep crisis and collapsed in wars and depression. The current variant has yet to enter into its final phase — though there are telling symptoms that suggest that this feature of the past will recur. For example, both in the present and past, speculative activity outran productive investments; collapse was proceeded by period of prolonged stagnation, a pattern evident in the United States, Japan, and Western Europe. With inequalities heightening and social discontent deepening, it is probable that globalism is, in the words of one investment banker, "coming to the limits of political acceptance of these approaches" (*New York Times*, June 20, 1997, p. A-10).

As was mentioned earlier, the major difference today is that capitalism has spread everywhere and is the only economic system at the moment. This means that the direct adversaries of capitalism are not other states or regions resisting capitalist encroachment but classes (working class, peasants, etc.) located within the system. The opposition is not from pre- or postcapitalist elites or excluded classes, but from those incorporated and exploited, those who create value.

The second new feature of globalism is the greater volume of capital movements (Howells and Wood, 1993; Cerny, 1999; Daniels and Lever, 1996). The transfers of wealth across national boundaries, particularly financial movements, far exceeds past movements. This is made possible by large-scale organizational networks that have been implanted, as well as by the new electronic technologies. These movements, however large, operate through many of the older networks that predate the current boom in globalist expansion. The various ethnic diaspora networks (Chinese, Indian, Middle Eastern, Jewish, etc.) and the extended family conglomerates (particularly effective are the Asian Chinese diaspora) influence the modern channels of banking and investment. In Western Europe and North America preexisting family/class networks have deepened their influence through the electronic innovations. Hence while volume of flows increases, the decisive decision-making units are embedded in national multinational corporations.

The transmission and accumulation of information is more rapid and of greater quantity under contemporary globalism, but it does not seem to have made much of a difference in terms of breaking open a new period of robust growth. Even Japan and South Korea, the foremost leaders in the new technology-induced development during the 1970s and 1980s are bogged in deep crises. The United States, despite the self-laudatory posture adopted by Clinton, wallows at a level of growth that barely keeps up with population increase. The technologies are different from the past, but that in itself has not led to either a new class structure or provided a new economic dynamic or state structure. The new technologies are embedded in preexisting classes, nation-states and the larger constraints and imperatives of the capitalist system. The notion of information as the new capital is, of course, nonsense as is the idea that the mass of new information and the glorified clerks feeding and processing information are the new captains of the economy.

The crucial point of information accumulation and communication is the analysis and use of it as well as the conceptual framework that formulate the questions which orient the information analysts. These are not autonomous actors, but individuals/classes embedded in structures of power — configuration that turn information, in some cases, to capital gains and other times into losses. But it is obvious that while information is an important element in earning profits, it does so because there are *capitalists* who employ information collectors to do the menial work of punching out charts, tables and graphs, summarizing data, and putting it on line in succinct and usable form.

The velocity of movement of capital allows for shifts in capital location as well as rapid accumulation but this simply accelerates the already existing volatility without adding anything to capital stock. Velocity is not directly related to the growth of productive forces. It largely operates in a parallel sphere. The paper economy is only tenuously related to how the real economy functions. This does not mean that it could not have a major impact on the real economy, for example, if there was a major crash in the financial markets or the stock exchange. This type of globalism, while novel in its volume and velocity, has not significantly changed the structure and operation of the *real* global economy in a qualitative way. At most, it has increased the autonomy of capital movements by giving individual agents greater access to more locations for money transfers. But even that is a *relative* autonomy because governments have *chosen* not to regulate this area, not because of the greater volume (trillions per day) or ease of movement (touch of the computer) but because the nation-states that most benefit (the United States, West Europe, Japan) have deregulated. Precisely because the high-speed computers can process billions of items a second and precisely because of the greater economic integration of capital and states, it is potentially possible to set forth new sets of regulations.

Finally, contemporary globalization has deepened and extended the international division of labor: cars are made of parts from factories located in distant nation-states. Information collection, processing and analysis is outsourced to labor in different regions. The process of exporting labor intensive industrial work to the Third World and retaining a mass of low-paid service workers and an elite of high-paid executives in the imperial centers has advanced. But this is a continuation of the past international division of labor between mining and agricultural workers in the Third World and manufacturing and service workers in the imperial countries. What has changed is the inclusion of manufacturing activities in the former Third World. This means greater proletarianization (the number of wage workers) in some settings. The key problem with the new international division of labor theorists is the fact that *most of industrial output*, both in the Third World and the imperial countries, *is for domestic consumption* and is produced by domestic owners. There are, of course, a few countries in which foreign exports and investors predominate, particularly in durable consumer goods, cultural services and financial sectors.

Returning to the initial question of this section: Is contemporary globalization different from the past? The answer is yes in quantitative terms, no im terms of the structures and units of analysis that define the process. Moreover, the main difference between past and present — the fact that the former had an end point (crises and collapse) and the latter is still fairly robust — itself is a problematical issue.

## Globalization: Inevitability and Contingency

One of the central tenets of globalization theorists is the idea that it is inevitable: that technological economic and political development converge to exclude any other form of economic growth except that which is based on the transnational flows of CGT (Oman, 1996). The claim, more normative than scientific, is that globalization is the highest and last stage in history in which all countries and economies are linked together through the capitalist market. One early and rather primitive version spoke of the end of history in which the markets, democracy and prosperity had put to an end to conflicts, authoritarian regimes and the reign of necessity.

The notion of the inevitability of particular political-economic processes has a long and ignoble history of inevitable refutation. What looks to observers, absorbed by conjunctural successes, as a predetermined outcome for all future generations is usually based on a tunnel vision of history in which all events are destined to a particular contemporary outcome. The tautological argumentation is evident in their review of history: what happened had to happen; what is happening is a product of a singular set of events; that which exists has a singular difference with all past history in that it lacks the points of conflict or contradictory processes of the past. This view of the singularity of present history is only the last of a series of egregious misconceptions. The view of history as a linear process of determined events is, of course, false: divergent outcomes from generally similar circumstances have been the norm.

For example, similar economic processes and colonial experiences (structural similarities) have had widely divergent outcomes. China in the 1920s was similarly underdeveloped as in the 1940s: in the former case the counterrevolution succeeded, in the latter period the revolution was victorious. Similarly, post-World War post-colonial outcomes varied because of contingent factors: political intervention, consciousness, organizational capacities, leadership, strategies, etc.

The emergence of globalization in the past was determined by a plethora of structural and historical circumstances, and the emerging antagonistic class and state relations engendered by the earlier cycles of globalization led to political ruptures and the relative demise of globalization — indeed in some cases of the very capitalist system. In each period of global expansion, globalist theorists emerge to glorify, legitimize, and gratify the leading classes of the global project, in the language of Pax Britannica, the American Century, etc.

The more reflective globalist theorists, at least take cognizance of the demise of globalist expansion in the past, and try to develop a different line of inquiry, conceding the imperfections of the past, but marking out the singularity of the present global world order (Krugman, 1996).

By ignoring past contradictions and how they play themselves out in the present, globalist ideologues fall back on a kind of technological determinism. By making blanket claims about the magical qualities of the new computer/electronic systems they hope to convince or delude the populace into believing that the new global system is a product of and guided by Science, technology and Reason that has erased or undermined class and antiimperialist conflicts. The emergence of contrary phenomena — that is major class conflicts and antiimperialist struggles are relegated to a residual category labeled *anachronistic phenomena* or described as the last gasps of outmoded groups and ideologists.

But labeling is not explanation; nor is residual categorizing an adequate approach to dealing with burgeoning movements that are centered in the vortex of the globalist imperative. The linkages between the new rural and provincial social movements in Latin America and Africa (The Democratic Republic of the Congo ex-Zaire) with urban struggles, the growing explosiveness of the new generation of the working classes in France, South Korea, and Germany speaks to the profound cleavages inherent in domestic exploitation to maximize global market shares.

To deal with the notion of inevitability on a less philosophical and more analytical level it is important to examine the origins, dynamics, and future perspectives of the current version of globalization.

In the first instance, the technologies that are cited as determinant existed prior to the current big push toward globalization. The addition or application of technologies has not had a major impact in increasing global growth, which as we have mentioned earlier has been largely stagnant. Technology and innovation has been incorporated toward furthering global processes shaped by more basic decisions in the political and socio-economic sphere. The origins of globalism are largely based on political changes and associated with the ascendancy of a particular variant of capitalism dubbed neoliberalism or free market.

The early starters were found in Chile, exclusively a product of the military coup d'etat and subsequently implemented by the Reagan and Thatcher regimes. This is not to say that multinationals and financial capital was not operating in the world market prior to these political regimes. It is to say that the globalizers had to share power and resources with local capital, the trade unions and other popular political forces. Hence forward the compromise between internal market development via the welfare state and the transnational flow of CGT was ruptured — by political force, either military dictatorship or by executive degree by minoritarian electoral regimes (which also applied force on a selective basis).

The origins of globalization as the economic strategy within the capitalist system was thus the consequence of an ideological project backed by state power and not the natural unfolding of the market. The fact that in the period preceding globalism the major technological breakthrough took place in a variety of nonglobalist settings argues against the ideological gloss that technoglobalists introduce into their polemics.

Contingency, not inevitability, is present in the origins, perpetuation and future destiny of globalist projects. Otherwise we cannot explain the constant and many times irrational and frantic efforts of the G-7 to prop up falling regimes (Mexico), make capitalism irreversible by accelerating economic reforms that massively destroy production and impoverish millions in the ex-U.S.S.R. and extending NATO affiliation to Eastern Europe. Surely the practitioners of globalism, if not the ideologues, are aware of the conditional sustenance of their project, the precariousness of its sustainability and the political limits of its continuation over time. Since globalization theory has a strong ideological component, it is important to confront it on those terms.

### Globalization as Globaloney: Rhetoric and Reality

One of the major characteristics of vulnerable social systems is the exaggerated claims made on its behalf. The belief being that sheer assertion of invincibility or inevitability will compensate for structural weaknesses. The whole ideological edifice constructed around the globalist perspective of the export capitalists and financiers is a cogent example. The notion that ideological dominance and sheer willing a reality will in fact sustain an otherwise fragile political economic enterprise reflects the simple minded psychologizing that substitutes for substantive programmatic politics among globalist politicians.

The term *globaloney*, first coined by Bob Fitch, most precisely captures the vacuous, tendentious, and tautological arguments put forth by globalist theorists.

In the first instance the globalist posits a general progression toward globalization which draws all nations and peoples into a common set of market relations. One does not know what to make of that statement when absolute majorities consciously reject the policies proposed to further the globalist project. I am referring to NAFTA, Mastricht, the free trade doctrines proposed in North America, Europe, and Asia. One senses that the *absence* of general support is a catalyst for making even more exaggerated affirmations: from the best to the only policy, from an advance in the economy to the culmination of human history. These unfounded claims, in particular, the notion of inevitability in the face of fragile social support is one of the major elements analyzed by the concept of globaloney.

The notion of inevitability as it is framed by globalists has the same kind of messianic message that patent medicine makers attributed to their products and itinerant preachers vowed would effect non-believers: if it isn't here it's coming; if it's not visible it's over the horizon, if you're still hurting, prosperity and wellness are around the corner. There is a bit of charlatanism in all this that is designed to beguile the innocent or to attract those who have lost faith in other inevitabilities and have a need to recur to the new faith.

Beyond the globaloney is the hard fact that the great majority of nations, and within them the immense majority of humanity, is against globalist practices. That is why globalist politicians when they are campaigning disguise their beliefs, and present themselves as critics of globalism — all the better to practice it after they take power. Clinton, Menem, Cardoso, Fujimori, Chirac, Prodi, Caldera[1] all ran for office originally as critics of free marketeering, the essential element in globalist ideology. Today in Europe, Asia, and Latin America massive opposition to globalist policies is plainly visible. As *The New York Times* headline put it, "U.S., Lauding Its Economy, Finds No summit Followers." If there are no sheep at the summit, it's because there are no donkeys in the streets. One of the key economic advisors to the South Korean president tersely remarked about Clinton's advocacy of globaloney for the rest of the world, "South Koreans would not stand for that kind of economic instability."

The second feature of globaloney is the assertion that it is the wave of the future. Here the ideologues paint a futuristic world of high-powered technology operating through global markets to produce quality goods and deliver advanced services that are consumed by growing multitudes. The global reality is very distant from the claims of globaloney: social conditions on the eve of the twenty-first century are reverting to the nineteenth century (Petras and Morley, 1995). Health care is becoming more precarious and more dependent on income levels. In the United States over 60 million have no or inadequate health care and over ten million children are not covered. Job insecurity increases as managers assume absolute power to hire, fire, and subcontract part-time and temporary work in a fashion dominant in the times of Charles Dickens. Impoverished families are forced to work at below subsistence minimum wage jobs or go hungry. More workers work longer hours today than they did 30 years ago. Retirement age is reaching nearly 70 years old. Pension plans are no longer provided by employers. Prison labor is employed by private employers for private gain. The number of children in orphanages is growing, as is the number of children living in poverty. Inequalities approach or surpass nineteenth century levels. A more appropriate sea metaphor (than the "wave of the future") for globalism is an undertow pulling working people back into an ignominious past. The future for most of the young generation looks insecure and fearful both in Europe and North America. For good reason: it will be the first generation since World War II that will be downwardly mobile. To argue that globalism is the wave of the future is to promise the upcoming generations a prolonged work life under declining wages without any job security or social assistance. To deny this reality and project a rosy future is the essence of globaloney.

The wave of the future ideology is tied to a specific group of capitalists operating at the center of globalism — the investment bankers and brokers. They moved to the forefront of the United States's richest companies. Goldman Sachs' group, Wall Street's biggest private partnership, will probably earn close to three billion in 1997. In 1975 brokerage and investment banking firms earned $4.8 billion; by 1994 annual profits had grown to $69.5 billion. In comparison, the biggest and most successful high-tech firm, Microsoft's, after-tax profits were $2.2 billion. Clearly *globalism is the wave of the future for speculators and financiers*, but it would be the height of impertinence to confuse this with the rest of humanity. The deliberate obfuscation of specific class differences in referring to advances of profits for some and the reversal of living conditions of the many is part of the polemical style of the practitioners of globaloney.

The last refuge for scoundrels, after all their arguments have been exposed and refuted, is to throw up their hands and cry, "There is no alternative," a rather self-serving rationalization for the failures of globalization. At its root this argument is a confession of failure, a denial of resistance and an attempt to demoralize adversaries. This stratagem is usually based on a simple dichotomy of failed communism and ongoing globalism, thus compressing complex experiences in boxes that exclude the rich mosaic of past and present alternatives. The argument is mainly based on a triumphalist posture. It is based on a superficial survey of the world today, highlighting the penetration of globalist ideology in previously hostile areas. The problem is that this visionary approach deals with epiphenoma and a relative short period of time. The analysis lacks depth in avoiding the internal conflicts engendered, the instability and volatility of unregulated speculation, and the lack of a center of economic dynamic. While profits grow, it is based on lowering labor costs not increasing living standards; while stock markets go up, the forces of production stagnate; while new technologies multiply, their impact on the real economy is over-shadowed by the gains of speculators.

Essentially there are three lines of criticism that confront globalists.

1. Global expansion is rooted in history and shaped by particular political, social, and cultural determinants. Globalists attribute inevitably to a particular conjunctural correlation of forces that are subject to reversal.

2. The socio-economic interests embedded in the globalist project are minorities, both in the imperial countries and among their collaborators in the global networks. It is a mockery of social analysis to confuse how this minority defines and pursues its interests with the needs, interests, and future of humanity. Moreover, it is the height of obtuseness to overlook the differential effect that globalism has on different classes, races, generations, and gender.

3. To attribute behavioral attributes and political commands to abstract entities such as the market is an abdication of the responsibilities of an intellectual to identify the institutions and decision-makers who are market makers and not merely market takers. Moreover, the attempt to reduce markets to one market owned and operated by a specific configuration of class forces and under tutelage by a particular state formation is the ultimate exercise in abstract reductionism. It makes sense to argue that the classes which predominate dictate contemporary forms of market exchanges. But in saying that one should acknowledge there are other real or potential markets, past and present, in which other actors will and can play a role and which can condition exchanges to provide outcomes very different from those resulting from today's market.

To approach the market in an analytical way, as opposed to the abstract reductionist approach of the globalists, means in the first instance to examine the class distributionist effects of market exchanges. The debate between globalists and their adversaries is, in part, about method: those who pursue a systematic analysis of exchanges and those who deduce outcomes from abstract impersonal forces to which they attribute human qualities (the reference to market imperatives).

The ideological confrontation with globalism and its relegation to the status of globaloney is only part of the debate. Equally pertinent is the debate over the dynamics of globalization.

**Dynamics of Globalization: Politics, Economy, and Technology**

The big push (BP) toward globalization was political and economic. Politically the BP was result of a dramatic changes in political power away from leftist, populist, and nationalist regimes toward globalist governments. In social terms, the BP resulted from the defeat and retreat of trade unions, the declining influence of the working class, lower middle class, and peasantry. The ascendancy of the social classes engaged in the international networks of CGT, but particularly the financial sector, set the stage for the globalist counterrevolution. What began in certain Third World (Chile, Mexico) and imperial centers (USA and England) spread throughout the world in an uneven fashion.

Globalists did not merely react to failures or crises of leftist regimes, they vigorously intervened to bring about the outcome that they predicted (Petras and Morley

1980). This active role was massive in scope and involved both direct military intervention, ideological, and cultural saturation as well as arms races and political alliances with the Vatican and philanthropic foundations. For example, in Latin America globalist classes emerged out of the violent military regimes that leveled opposition — with hundreds of thousands of victims. In Africa millions were killed in surrogate wars that destroyed the possibility of independent development in Angola, Mozambique, and elsewhere. The Reagan regime sponsored an arms race, which was deliberately directed toward bankrupting the Soviets who willingly cooperated. In Eastern Europe, particularly in Poland, the Vatican played a decisive propaganda and material role in pouring millions of CIA funds into the Solidarity organization. In Eastern Europe, billionaire speculator George Soros poured millions to cultivate Czech, Hungarian, and Polish intellectuals, who later became ardent procapitalists, pro-NATO politicos.

The internal crises of these regions played into this proactive globalist campaign by neutralizing potential popular opposition. The net effect of the initial undisputed ascendancy of the new globalist classes was the weakening of public control and limitations on capitalist exploitation of resources, markets and labor and the handing over of important levers of accumulation in the mineral, financial and manufacturing fields to private investors. The powerful role of the nation-state in holding down wages and slashing social programs, liberated immense funds for private enrichment by the globalist classes. The nation-state, far from weakening with globalization, became an essential political support in spreading the message. Imperial regimes, influential in the IMF and World Bank, conditioned loans and credits on so-called economic reforms, thus imposing a uniform globalist policy. The unpopular structural adjustment policies (SAP) deepened the power of globalist classes and extended their sway over the national patrimony through privatization and deregulation. The nation-state and its imperial policies were essential elements in the Big Push toward globalization.

Finally, the nation-state's political intervention in bailing out troubled overseas investor (Japanese and U.S. banks), speculators (Mexico 1994), and multinational corporations (Lockheed, Fiat) suggests the continuing role of politics in sustaining the crisis prone globalist perspective.

The Big Push from the political side was the counterpoint of a confluence of economic developments that engineered the dynamics of globalization. Essentially, four factors preceded and contributed to the BP: an overaccumulation crisis; a profit squeeze resulting from labor/capital relations; the intensification of international capitalist competition; the massive growth of financial markets as a result of deregulation.

These economic processes of course cannot be separated from the class relations and political configuration of which they form an integral part.

The overaccumulation crisis refers to the massive growth of profits with the shrinking space for investment at acceptable rates of profit. Put another way, the more capital grew within the bounds of the nation-state the smaller the rate of profit as more capital pursued smaller market shares. The radical solution of course would have been to change the class structure to increase demand, but that would have exacerbated the problem of the declining rate of profit. The reactionary solution, the one pursued, was to break down the internal constraints on external movements — to go abroad to overseas markets and in the process over the long haul to force down domestic costs. Globalist classes look at the mass of local producers in part as a cost not a market. Globalization was in the first instance a solution to the over-accumulation crisis in terms acceptable to the investor class.

The second and related economic determinant of globalization were the constraints imposed by labor-capital relations. The profit squeeze was rooted in the immobility of capital: in face to face relations, with the welfare state as a mediator, labor was able, for almost a quarter of a century to extract economic concessions whose cumulative costs became an unacceptable burden to capital. By reproducing the wage/capital relations through overseas investments abroad at sites of production with lower costs, the capitalist class created a global labor market that boosted profit margins, and put downward pressure on the local labor market. Hence globalization ruptured the post-World War II capital-labor equilibrium in its favor.

The movement of capital abroad was stimulated by the growth of international competition. The powerful export push from Asia and Europe forced the United States to invest overseas to open production sites closer to markets, to scale protective barriers and to learn about local markets. Similar patterns were followed by the Europeans and Japanese who opened production sites to ply the U.S. market. Integral to this process of competition was the constant intervention of the nation-state on behalf of their multinationals: demands for equal treatment, taxation, uniform labor laws (Bailey et al., 1994). The growth of multipolar regional economic blocs was paralleled by the intrabloc alliances by states and multinational corporations, which gave superficial observers the idea that the nation-state was becoming anachronistic, weak, or a peripheral actor. As is evident in the Mastricht meetings, the GATT gatherings, G-7 summits, etc., the nation-states hammer out the rules of the game for global expansion and competition.

Finally, and perhaps most important, the dynamic of globalization is in great part fueled by the massive growth of financial markets. I say *most important* because it is this sector that shows the greatest volume increase in flows of capital and the one that has had the least effect in stimulating world growth of productive forces. The paradox of massive globalization and puny growth of the major global actors is explained by the dissociation between massive financial flows and the real economy.

The deregulation of financial markets, the massive introduction and subordination of high technology communications and information systems to financial imperatives is probably the most salient element of globalization. The financial character of a good part of what passes for globalization does not deny the large-scale movements of goods and investments in minerals and manufactures. What it does say is that widespread financial betting far surpasses the real assets of the firm's shares bought and sold on the stock markets of the world. If one adds all the other speculative devices (derivatives, currencies, futures, junk bonds) that are traded via financial channels we get a true sense of what is the motor force of globalization. Hardly dynamic, hardly likely to benefit the masses, hardly likely to produce productivity gains that are socially useful, it is no wonder that globalists refer to countries (peoples and economies) as emerging markets. They see them through the tunnel vision of the financial investment and brokerage houses and what they see are short-term windfalls (interest differentials), selloffs (privatization), and sites for low-cost production (maquiladores). The key element in all this was a shift in the social composition of the regulatory regime and a new set of rules governing financial flows. The centerpiece of the new regulatory regime was precisely the undisputed reign of globalist policy-makers divorced from labor and tightly meshed with the leading financial globalist actors.

Where does the much vaunted technological revolution fit into the picture of the primacy of political and economic determinants of globalization? Contrary to globalist ideologues, it has an important but secondary role. The *innovations* themselves are *based* on *state* sponsored or subsidized research, later transferred to the private sector. The *application* of the technology is largely *determined by preexisting economic forces*. Even the most resourceful, new high tech entrepreneurs must sell to the fastest growing economic sectors, namely those firms already embedded in globalist networks. The addition of speed of transmission, the accessing of a greater quantity of information does not add significantly to the contours of the global economy. What is essential is the ruling concepts that govern the basic institutions interchanging information and, of course, moving CGT. The ruling concepts are capital accumulation, high rates of return, greater market shares, lower labor costs. High tech is the handmaiden of globalist financial engineering: rejiggering flows to accommodate short-term decisions based on immediate financial reports. The emphasis on *quantity* of data and the *rapidity* of processing, reflects the need to make rapid investment decisions on short-term shifts in the paper or real economy. Hence, high technology is reinforcing the most volatile and unproductive of economic activities, paper exchanges in the financial field.

It would be an exaggeration to deny the other multiple uses of high tech in reordering labor, consumer patterns, personal communication, etc. But the multiplicity of uses is precisely the point: at the institutional level its use is more *adaptive* to *existing* global classes rather than innovative in breaking down domination, exploitation, and stagnation. The social contradictions engendered by globalism are exacerbated by high tech applied from the institutional sites of power. And high tech does not have any internal corrective measure to ensure any other outcome.

The dynamic of globalization can be analyzed not only in its origins and expansion but in its distributive consequences. For what results from globalism can have serious consequences on its future.

**Distributive Consequences of Globalization**

The *distributive consequences of globalization cannot be separated from the patterns of ownership and control of the institutions, the class structure and state*. It is not possible to talk of equity or market socialism by looking at or tinkering with distributive mechanisms or outcomes. This has become clearer than ever today when owners and producers relocate or threaten environmental, and tax policies which are not to their liking. There is an indissoluble link between ownership, production, and equity on the one hand and equity and sustainability on the other.

The world ascendancy of globalist classes has provoked a serious social crisis affecting wage workers, peasants, employees, and the self-employed throughout the world (Petras and Morley, 1995). Precisely the growth and penetration of globalist policies have engendered a significant increase in inequality between the minority within the globalist loop and those exploited by it. While the growth of inequality of income between social classes is one consequence of the globalist ascendancy, there are several other inequalities the cut across national and cultural boundaries. Taxes have become increasingly regressive: government tax revenues are increasingly coming from wage and salaried groups, while the percentage from multinational corporate capital is declining. This is in part because of the numerous legal loopholes as well as the capacity of the corporate tax lawyers to devise tax shelters and to shift the focus of earnings to countries with lower tax rates (what is called transfer pricing). Parallel to the regressive tax system is the increasingly regressive state subsidy or spending programs. Corporate entitlement in the form of low interest loans, export incentives, subsidies for plant construction, land grants, infrastructure development, research and development, etc., has been accompanied by sharp reductions in social transfers to wage and salaried people. State subsidies for multinational corporate capital grows while the share for wage workers, pensioners, low wage families, the ill and injured, single parent families, and children declines.

These social inequalities are the result of two structural factors: the growing concentration and centralization of ownership through mergers, buyouts, joint ventures; the tight integration of the state and the globalist corporate elite. The centralization of political decisions is an essential element in the concentration of state resources toward further strengthening the profits and growth of concentrated capital. Today the pattern of asset ownership in the advanced imperial centers resembles the pattern of land ownership in what used to be called pejoratively the banana republics: less than five percent of the population owns close to 90 percent of the privately held assets. Moreover, a handful of brokers and banking investors reap the multibillion dollar fees that accompany the buying and selling of firms, and stocks that are transacted by private and nonprivate investment funds.

The greatest social crisis is precisely in the countries that have advanced furthest in globalization. The number of workers without medical coverage, nonunionized workers, temporary or part-time labor force with no or minimum social benefits (vacations, pensions) is greatest in the United States, followed by England. The much vaunted low unemployment rate of the United States in contrast to Europe is counterbalanced by the highest rate of low wage, vulnerable workers — conditions unacceptable to the European labor movements.

A similar process is occurring in the Third World. Argentina and Brazil have unemployment rates of 18 percent and 15 percent, rates that multiplied with the globalization of their economies. Similar processes have occurred in Eastern Europe where living standards have fallen between 30 and 80 percent since the transition to capitalism began in the late 1980s. The model Third World country, Mexico, has seen wage earning income levels plummet to 30 percent of their levels a decade and a half earlier (Veltmeyer and Petras, 1997).

The specific mechanisms by which the globalist classes perform this income and property counterrevolution is through an ideology (neoliberal or free market) and legislative packets, so-called structural adjustment policies, including the privatization of lucrative public resources and the development of a New Statism, which finances and directs the whole process.

The neoliberal ideology provides an intellectual gloss to the process of growing inequality through several conceptual devices: it emphasizes the individual as the basic unit of analysis and the notion of individual responsibility in obfuscating the concentrated economic activities and adverse social consequences. By obscuring the centrality of the concentration of institutional power and the impact that it has on living standards it depoliticizes the problem of power and socioeconomic inequality, while shifting the burden of dealing with the globalist-induced problems to the family, individual or local community. This in turn frees up personnel and funds to promote global expansion and accumulation.

The ideology of neoliberalism argues for free markets when in fact most exchanges of global firms take place within the enterprises. The free market ideology obscures the tight relations between imperial states and overseas investors, the increasing interdependence of state to global firm and the interrelation between global firms that shape political agendas.

The structural power of the globalist classes is cause and consequence of the so-called structural adjustment policies (SAP) that have been informally or formally implemented. The SAP is in reality a process of income reconcentration through cuts in social spending, corporate tax reductions, and increased subsidies. The concentration of power in the hands of employers at the expense of wage workers (dubbed flexibilization of labor) leads to rigidities in the hierarchy of the corporate organization. The employers unilaterally fix terms for hiring, firing, outsourcing, subcontracting, and other forms of increasing the rate of exploitation, lowering labor costs, and increasing profits for more global ventures.

The advance of SAP is directly related to the resistance of labor. And the resistance of labor is tied to the internal structure of the unions, the ideology of the union leaders and the accessibility and rotation of leaders. Where there are democratic structures within the unions, where the leaders confront organized oppositoin, where the leaders are imbued with anticapitalist ideology or at least see the union as a movement rather than a business and where leaders are challenged or replaced by legitimate rank and file alternative leaders, the unions have been more successful in blocking the implementation of SAP and the full globalist agenda. This is the case in France, Italy, and Germany. In contrast, in the United States where union leaders run oligarchical organizations, in which millionaire union officials run the union as a business through bureaucratic machines that marginalize the members and manage pension funds and lucrative real estate holdings, the unions have been totally incapable of opposing the globalist agenda. It is no wonder that President Clinton can gloat over his success in implementing the regressive economic reforms: he doesn't have democratic, radical trade unionists to contend with.

The U.S. economy is the prototype of the globalist ascendancy. Clinton's administration even speaks of it as a model. But it is a model for globalist classes and firmly rejected by labor everywhere else. Even the European leaders frown on its application, fearing that the rigid pursuit of its implementation would provoke a major social upheaval.

The theoretical issue is that the globalist project is reaching its political limits in many parts of the world: the resolution of the contradiction between empire or republic involves breaking the social organizations that sustain the beliefs and interests of millions of wage workers, families, and retirees. We are entering a period of prolonged crisis and possible upheaval. The so-called Anglo-Saxon model of globalization may be exportable only if the internal social relations between classes (capital/labor) are drastically transformed. The process of gradual or piecemeal change is underway: cuts in social budgets and plant relocations in Germany; privatization and the ending of wage indexation in Italy; high rates of unemployment and segmented labor conditions in Spain.

The defensive struggles of European labor reflect a belief that the choice is between the residue of the previous welfare state or globalist capital. What is clear is that the ascendancy of globalism has not been accompanied by the retention of the welfare state, let alone its expansion. Clearly the social polarization of interests and conditions and the fundamentally contrasting structural positions requires the rethinking of the productive system and more fundamentally of the nature of ownership. To deny the centrality of private profits in its most organized and extended form (multinational corporate enterprise) is to lose sight of the possible solution. To focus on policies and immediate outcomes as the politics of the day, and not the state structure and internal composition of the state (the powerful nexus between globalist classes and the executive) is to ignore the essential tool for transforming the ownership and property forms that direct the globalist project.

The irrationality of the privatization effort is undermining the environmental conditions for the reproduction of globalist expansion. New classes, new regions, new recreation and breathing areas are being voraciously exploited: Antarctica, Amazon, George's Banks, the major cities, the ozone cover. The privatization policy is not only the massive transfer of public wealth to the billionaire super rich globalists, but it is a license to exploit without constraint. To speak of sustainable growth, while the imperial state, the World Bank and their counterpart globalist investors and politicians promote privatization and pillage is an obscenity: nowhere has privatization been accompanied by conservation, it always has been and is associated with heightened pillage, exhaustion and abandonment of people and lands.

Privatization has taken place on a world scale but nowhere has it led to the dynamic development of the productive forces. If we discount population growth, per capita growth in the United States is under one percent and in Europe and Japan close to zero. Privatization is the private skimming or pillage of *existing* wealth and assets. It is a substitute for creating new firms, products, and discovering new markets. The boom in the stock markets parallels the declining growth of the real economy. Speculative growth feeds off of stagnation. The greatest growth is from mergers, firings, and reduction of better paid jobs. Apart from the abnormal case of the United States with its hyper-bloated oligarchical unions, the sociopolitical revolts against globalization are under way.

**National Policies and Globalization**

Probably the most widespread misconception circulated by globalization ideologues is the notion that the nation-state is anachronistic (or that it is weak) before the onslaught of globalizing corporations and new international actors. The reality is otherwise; *never has the nation-state played a more decisive role, intervened with more vigor and consequence in shaping economic exchanges and investment at the local, national, and international level* (Weiss, 1997; Rodrick, 1997; Petras and Morley, 1995). It is impossible to conceive of the expansion and deepening involvement of multinational banks and corporations without the prior political, military, and economic intervention of the nation-state. Nor is it possible to understand the expansion of the market in the ex-U.S.S.R., China, and Eastern Europe and former radical Third World Countries without acknowledging the vital political role of the imperial nation-states, particularly the United States in financing propaganda activity, fueling an arms race, subsidizing cultural and religious propaganda. The most elementary and important trade agreements (GATT, NAFTA, ASEA) and trading blocs (EEC, NAFTA, MERCOSUR) were formulated, codified, and implemented by nation-states. The major policies stimulating vast tax windfalls, providing massive subsidies, and lowering domestic labor costs have all been formulated by the nation-state. The scale and scope of nation-state activity has grown to such a point that one needs to refer to it as the New Statism rather than the free market. Globalism is in the first instance a product of the New Statism and continues to be accompanied and sustained by direct state intervention.

Too often glib commentators, business journalists, and publicists have argued that the state, as we knew it, has been superseded by a new kind of international order in which multinationals have become autonomous from the state. Other ideologues have argued that the market has replaced state functions and reduced its role to the minimum compatible with law and order. Not surprisingly, many ex-leftists or self-styled new thinkers have argued that a third economy is coming into being based on NGOs and local community-based organizations rooted in what they dub civil society. Finally a group of fringe thinkers believe that something labeled the world system has bypassed the nation-state and is the process of establishing a suprastate entity, which has yet to be fully disclosed, perhaps for absence of data.

The pervasiveness of the ideology of the dissolution of the nation-state is matched by the ignorance of its advocates of the major events and forces that shape and continue to propel the international flows of CGT.

The centerpiece of globalization is the overarching political framework: the architecture of which is built on the role of the state in eliminating the welfare state, diminishing the regulations on overseas flows, and demolishing political and economic constraints in overseas markets. These building blocks set in place by the nation-state have been followed by the linear column in the form of the nation-state appointees to the IFI who design, implement and enforce the extension of the policies throughout the world via the so-called SAP. The cupola of globalism is the short-term, day-to-day, micromanagement of the global economy by the middle-level functionaries who supervise individual investments, sectoral exchanges, and monthly commercial balances.

The political-economic role of the state is accompanied by the deep penetration of the police, military an intelligence agencies of dominated nations by the U.S. imperial state. Former domestic agencies like the Federal Bureau of Investigation and the Drug Enforcement Agency, now freely circulate in the highest levels of overseas state structures. U.S. drugs certification programs further extend U.S. power to shape appointments in the Ministries, Armed Forces, and Police. The legal principle of extraterritoriality is promoted by Washington asserting the supremacy of its laws over that of supposedly sovereign nations — as in the case of the Helms-Burton Law. All this suggests very forcefully that the imperial nation-states are pushing to the outer limits their capacity to bolster the role of multinational corporations and, more important, to increase the world market share of international flows that accrues to their ruling classes.

If the ideology and rhetoric of the globalists regarding the supposedly weak or anachronistic state does not reflect realities, what purpose does it serve? First it serves to disarm critics — to discourage opposition social forces from seizing upon the first and most essential element in creating an alternative to globalist dominated capital. Second, it has a politico-psychological purpose to disorient the struggle, for if it not over the state which is nonexistent, then what could the struggle be about? Third, by encouraging political and social groups to focus on operating in the interstice of the dominant system in the areas small-scale economic acitvity of reciprocity. The purpose is to create dependent links to the macro-economic system dominated by the globalist classes. The great majority of NGOs in fact are neither nongovernmental in funding or in their local collaborative activities.

Finally, the purpose is to create an open-ended category, such as civil society, which is inhabited by the harshly exploitative global sweatshop owners and to describe it as a locus for political democracy and private local economic initiative. This discourse ignores the multiplicity of links between the main actors of civil society (the ruling classes) with the apex of the state institution.

By identifying the dynamic and central role of the nation-state in the current phase of globalization allows us to envision the tremendous potentialities of the state as a center for alternative forms of economic organization. This can take the form of public enterprises, self-managed cooperatives, and decentralized planning in the reallocation and redistribution of income, credit, land, and technical assistance. Investment reallocation by the state presupposes fundamental changes in ownership in which state power plays a powerful role both in a juridical, political, and economic sense. National-state power (NSP) is the basis for shifting production and consumption from the centrality of the global markets to the local, turning global exchanges into *supplemental* activities. NSP is the basis for innovation and technological organization rooted in deepening social solidarity, and community ties and tying productivity increases to greater free time.

NSP is essential in educating and deepening self-management style transformative leadership in the running of enterprises and returning productivity and competitive gains back to the collectivity of producers.

NSP is the essential link to a new internationalism: as a successful example of an alternative to globalism, and by providing political, educational, and cultural activities that deepen links between movements across the world — creating greater integration from below as a prelude to the emergence of other alternatives.

NSP redefines the issue of markets by inserting it in a new socio-political context in which social relations give primacy to the producer classes. The market of the popular notion-state is based on exchanges guided by political criteria of *social profits* — gains that accrue to the general social wage and not to individual or firm profit takers. The local and national markets are shaped by the new configuration of popular power that shape global exchanges — the inverse of today's globalization process.

The search for alternatives to globalization involves a profound rethinking of the comparative advantages of privatization and socialization in historical perspective. It is clear that the tendency under socialization was for more working people (wage, salaried, self-employed) to have more free time, greater job security, wider health coverage, and more access to higher public education. The tendency was toward greater gender concern than is occurring under the privatization juggernaut. Comparative data on living standards in the countries currently experiencing privatization show a sharp decline in the quality of life, in particular for the younger generation. As the age of retirement recedes, exploitation is extended in the life cycle into old age. As managerial prerogatives increase, job-related stress and insecurity intensifies and work benefits (health, vacations, etc.) shrink. Objective observers can argue that the obsession with the needs of the CEOs and their profits (disguised by the term *competitiveness*) means that working class becomes degraded. Workers in Europe who retain 4–6 week vacations are described by the *N.Y. Times* as "coddled". CEOs in Europe who have 40/1 salary ratio to workers are described as underpaid or behind the times by *Forbes* because they are far below the 240/1 ratio of U.S. CEOs.

The privatization ethos is an ill-disguised effort to create a type of Western despotism rooted in the absolute power of capital to control the state, impose the singular ideology, and intimidate the labor force. The advance model is the United States.

Socialization provides an alternative democratic model in which capital becomes social capital by its formal subordination to the new organization of state power and the decentralization of authority to the constituent committees of production, consumption, and environmental protection. Productivity increases health fund plans for everyone; public education is open to those who academically qualify, retirement and alternative careers are open at 55 or 50 years; work hours are reduced to 25 or 30 hours. The advantages of socialization are not only the redistribution of wealth but the reorientation of production and media to serve democratically decided social values. It is a qualitative deepening and extension of the social values enunciated by the golden age of the welfare state. It is a post-globalist socialism built on democratic and internationalist principles.

**Resistance on a World Scale**

A review of resistance to globalist politics must take into account the great variety of social forces that have taken the lead in different socioeconomic settings, with varying degrees of intensity and with a broad gamut of strategies. Nonetheless, certain general tendencies are evident beyond the national and regional specificities.

In the first instance, while electoral vehicles have been one source of opposition, extraparliamentary action has been the most widespread and effective approach to blocking or limiting the application of globalist policies. Since most antiglobalist electoral opposition is confined to the legislature, and a minority at that, the globalist policies continue to be applied by executive decree and/or through globalist influence over the legislature. The Electoral fraud, as in the case of the election of President Salinas or the executive's blatant purchase of Congressional votes as in Brazil under Cardoso debilitate the role of electoral institutions as points of opposition. Secondly, center-left electoral opposition has almost uniformly assimilated the globalist ideology, once elected to office, in order to conform to the demands of the leading classes, the IFIs and the preexisting state institutions. The most recent example is the FMLN elected Mayor of San Salvador Hector Silva who sees the arch proponents of globalization, the IMF and the World Bank, as allies in the development process. Former revolutionary groupings in the seventies and eighties, upon turning to electoral politics and entering political office have almost always abandoned their opposition to globalization and accepted its postulates. As a result, all the groups adversely affected by globalization have turned toward extraparliamentary activities and organization: general strikes in France, Italy, Argentina, Brazil, Bolivia, South Korea, etc. Land occupations in Brazil, Paraguay, El Salvador, Mexico, Colombia, Peru, Zaire, etc. The extraparliamentary movements have become the chosen from of expression in the face of the impotence and cooptation of the electoral parties (Petras, 1997; Veltmeyer and Petras, 1997).

The second characteristic marked by the opposition is that they all *start* as *defensive movements* of existing rights and interests threatened by the globalist ruling classes. Whether it is to protest loss of employment, privatization of public enterprise, cuts in social security programs, living standards, pension plans, public educational facilities, etc., the initial point of confrontation is over the aggressive roll-back. Provoked by the globalist appropriation of new sources of profits and the reduction of fiscal costs, the movements respond. Within this common defense of past popular gains, some of the movements have taken the offensive and sought to advance toward structural changes: the peasant movements of Chiapas, Mexico, the MST in Brazil, the FARC-peasant movements in Colombia, the cocoa farmers in Chapare, Bolivia, have created co-ops, and established community-based economies that are in opposition to globalism and are oriented toward developing the domestic market. As yet a minority, there is a growing antiglobalist and even incipient anticapitalist consciousness among the mass movements currently engaged in defensive struggles.

The third characteristic of the opposition to globalism is the general tendency of all movements to form coalitions with or incorporate environmental, gender, ethnic, or racial groups and struggles. The globalist project has a multiplicity of negative impacts, exploiting and polluting, impoverishing and excluding that worsens living conditions and standards and deepening interclass as well as intraclass inequalities. The confluence of groups is a challenge in the face of the efforts by the IFI and local regimes to fragment and depoliticize the different identities into a series of self-serving, isolated, cultural entities divorced from class based political struggles.

Apart from the common features of the resistance to globalization, there are several general points that have to be kept in mind. First, the process of opposition is *uneven* between countries and within countries. Opposition in Europe and, in particular France, is obviously more advanced than say the United States. Brazil, and Mexico are more advanced than Chile and Peru. What distinguishes the level of struggle is the level of political organization, the tradition of struggle, the internal structure of the mass organizations, and the insurgent or bureaucratic origins of the opposition.

Within countries some sectors, regions, classes, ethnic groups demonstrate greater resistance than others. In Argentina, the provinces have been in the forefront of opposition, while Buenos Aires lags behind. In Brazil, the landless workers are far more combatative than the urban slum dwellers or the trade unions. In Venezuela, the urban poor of Caracas have been more active than the official trade unions. In general, public sector workers have been more active than private sector (Chile, Argentina, Brazil, Mexico). In general, with some notable exceptions, the center of the more radical struggle has been the rural areas and the provinces, while the urban industrial sectors have been basically engaged in the defensive phase. But these are not hard and fast distinctions. In Europe and Asia it has been the workers from the most advanced sectors (transport in France and metal workers in South Korea) who have spearheaded the struggle. The spread of opposition and its growing depth outside of the electoral arenas has created a firm base for a systemic alternative. Conversely, apart from electoral politics, the social base of globalist politicians and economic elites has become more fragile. The ideological and institutional center of globalism is the United States.: it is here that it stands unchallenged because of the longstanding oligarchical nature of the trade unions (which sets them apart from most workers) and the co-opted leadership of the major ethnic, gender, and conservationist groups who function as mere pressure groups on the dominant globalist parties. Once one moves away from the United States., the picture changes dramatically, particularly in Europe and in Latin America and Asia. A similar process occurs in examining the dynamic of the internal politics of the countries: a superficial view that looks only at the electoral process gives the impression of the solidity of globalist perspectives. Moving beyond electioneering to the everyday mass struggles and organizations and individual preference one finds a broad swathe of opposition to various or all elements of globalist politics.

The basic question that hasn't been resolved or is constantly posed is: if there is such general opposition, why hasn't globalism been overthrown? The answer is twofold: more groups have been thrown back onto limited resources and as a result are largely engaged in defensive struggles; secondly, while various alternatives are being elaborated, none have achieved general acceptance or they remain embedded in sectoral or local settings.

## Alternatives to Globalization

For years the critics of globalization repeatedly evoked the need to create an alternative. While some intellectuals continue to do so and many others continue their passive and impotent reflections on the impermeability of the globalist onslaught, a few have begun to examine the real world of emerging alternative created by militants and activists.

The new alternative should be understood not only in terms of what they are creating but also in what they reject. This can be succinctly summed up as "neither free market nor bureaucratic statism." Within these parameters, the emerging alternative needs to be further analyzed to distinguish them from the small-scale projects that the globalist IFIs fund to absorb the discontent generated by their management of the macroeconomy.

The alternatives that exist today are found in the local projects of insurgent groups or in the programmatic transformation of movements in struggle. In the first case, there are a variety of alternative forms of socioeconomic organizations ranging from the Brazilian rural cooperative network organized by the MST, which includes over 150,000 families, to the self-governing Indian communities under Zapatista leadership in Chiapas, the municipal enterprises organized in China, the emerging socialist-led regional rural producers in Colombia and Bolivia, to the proposals to democratize the universities in Chile and Argentina, to the self-management proposals set forth by the radical wing of the trade unions in France, South Korea, and Italy. What differentiates these sectoral or small-scale activities from the IFI and NGO local projects of alternative development is that *they are part of a larger political project of social transformation.* They are initiated by insurgent groups in confrontation with the globalist state and classes and they usually are internally democratic. The leaders are elected by and responsible to the local communities (unlike the NGOs dependent on and responsible to their foreign donors). Thus the small-scale alternatives are building blocks to large-scale transformation; the alternatives are born of struggles that increase class and national consciousness and they point toward the creation of an antiglobalist hegemonic bloc based on democratic collectivist alternatives. What unites these alternatives is their struggle for a social economy, one that combines sustainable growth, entrepreneurship, and economic democracy. The difference among the alternatives abound: labor relations, the scope of private ownership, the reliance on the market, etc. What is clear, however, is that social interests condition market exchanges: and the markets are essentially local or national, with external exchanges subordinated to deepening the internal market. The principal programmatic issue is the systematic elaboration of the microinstitutional relations to the macro level, the translation of programmatic transformation into specific institutional settings. The principal political problem is the struggle against technocratic intellectuals tied to globalist conceptions who seek to amalgamate popular social program to liberal economics (market socialism), and rigid collectivists who fail to understand the variety of forms of popular production (co-op, cooperative, public, household). The image that some intellectuals have that there is a need to create an alternative is, of course, an expression of their ignorance of existing alternatives in the process of creation or their unconscious acceptance of the globalist argument that there are no alternatives. Instead of repeating time-worn cliches about the need for alternatives, it is more appropriate to relate to the alternatives now in the process of elaboration by movements in struggle.

The alternatives are there to be given greater substance, coherence, and projection into the larger nation-state and beyond. Even now international links are being forged between movements in national struggle against the globalist classes, each with its local economy and programmatic transformations. If nothing else they add another affirmative element to the critique of globalist ideology: there is an alternative in the very struggle to overthrow the dominant globalist classes.

*Note*

---

[1] Heads of state in the United States, Argentina, Brazil, Peru, France, Italy, and Venezuela.

# BIBLIOGRAPHY

Abraham, D. (1986) *The Collapse of the Weimar Republic: Political Economy and Crisis*. New York: Holmes and Meier.

Achebe, C. et al. (1990) *Beyond Hunger in Africa*. Portsmouth, NH: James Currey, London, and Heinemann.

Aghion, P., and Howitt, P. (1998) *Endogenous Growth Theory*. Cambridge, MA: MIT Press.

Alavi, H. (1964) "Imperialism: Old and New," *Socialist Register*. London: Merlin.

Alavi, H. (1972) "The State in Post-Colonial Societies: Pakistan and Bangladesh," *New Left Review*, 74: 59–70.

Altvater, E., and Mahnkopf, B. (1997) "The World Market Unbound," *Review of International Political Economy*, 4, 3: 448–471.

Alvarez, S., and Escobar, A. (1992) "Conclusion: Theoretical and Political Horizons of Change in Contemporary Latin American Social Movements," in their *The Making of Social Movements in Latin America: Identity, Strategy and Democracy*. Boulder: Westview.

Alvarez, S., Dagnino, E., and Escobar, A. (1998) "Introduction: The Cultural and the Political in Latin American Social Movements," in their *Cultures of Politics: Politics of Cultures. Re-Visioning Latin American Social Movements*. Boulder: Westview.

Amin, A. (1997) "Placing Globalization," *Theory, Culture and Society*, 14 (2): 123–137.

Amin, S. (1974) *Accumulation on a World Scale: A Critique of the Theory of Underdevelopment*. 2 vols. New York: Monthly Review Press.

Amin, S. (1976) *Unequal Development.* New York: Monthly Review Press.

Amin, S. (1977) *Imperialism and Unequal Development.* New York: Monthly Review Press.

Amin, S. (1980) *Class and Nation, Historically and in the Current Crisis.* Susan Kaplow, trans. New York: Monthly Review Press.

Amin, S. (1985) "Modes of Production: History and Unequal Development," *Science & Society,* 49: 194–207.

Amin, S. (1989a) *Eurocentrism.* New York: Monthly Review.

Amin, S. (1989b) *La faillite du developpement en Afrique et dans le Tiers Monde.* Paris: L'Harmattan In English: *1990 Maldevelopment, Anatomy, of a Global Failure.* London: ZED Books.

Amin, S. (1992) "On Jim Blaut's Fourteen Ninety-Two," *Political Geography,* 11: 394–396.

Amin, S. (1993a) *Itineraire intellectuel, Regards sur le demi siècle 1945– 1990.* Paris: L'Harmattan. In English: *1994, Re-reading the Post War Period, An intellectual Itinerary.* New York: Monthly Review Press.

Amin, S. (et al.) (1993b) *Mondialisation et accumulation.* Paris: L'Harmattan.

Amin, S. (1995) *La gestion capitaliste de la crise.* Paris: L'Harmattan.

Amin, S. (1996a) *Les defis de la mondialisation.* Paris: L'Harmattan.

Amin, S. (1996b) *Capitalism in the Age of Globalisation.* London: ZED.

Amin, S. (Forthcoming) "Regionalisation in the Third World, in response to the polarisation in the global system," in Bjorn Hettne (ed.), *The New Regionalism.* Wider-Helsinki: Macmillan.

Amin, S. (ed.) (1982) *Dynamics of the Global Crisis.* Macmillan.

Amoore, L., Dodgson, R., Gills, B., Langley, P., Marshall, D., and Watson, I. (1997) "Overturning Globalisation: Resisting the Teleological, Reclaiming the Political," *New Political Economy,* 2 (1): 179–195.

Amsden, A. (1989) *Asia's Next Giant.* Oxford: Oxford University Press.

Anderson, B. (1983) *Imagined Communities: Reflections on the Origin and Spread of Nationalism.* London: Verso.

Anderson, P. (1974a) *Lineages of the Absolutist State,* London: Verso and New Left Books.

Anderson, P. (1974b) *Passages from Antiquity to Feudalism*. London: New Left Books.

Anderson, P. (1987) "The Figures of Descent", *New Left Review*, 161.

Anderson, P., and Nairn, T. (1964) "Origins of the Present Crisis," *New Left Review*, 23, Jan.–Feb.

Arendt, H. (1951) *The Origins of Totalitarianism*. New York: Harcourt, Brace, and World, 1966.

Arrighi, G. (1978) *The Geometry of Imperialism: The Limits of Hobson's Paradigm*. Patrick Camiller, trans. London: New Left Books.

Arrighi, G. (1983) *The Geometry of Imperialism: The Limits of Hobson's Paradigm*, London: Verso.

Arrighi, G. (1994) *The Long Twentieth Century: Money, Power and the Origins of Our Times*. London and New York: Verso.

Arthur, W. (1994) *Increasing Returns and Path Dependency in the Economy*. Ann Arbor: University of Michigan Press.

Aston, T., and Philpin, C. (eds.) (1985) *The Brenner Debate: Agrarian Class Structure and Economic Development in Pre-Industrial Europe*. Cambridge: Cambridge University.

Avineri, S. (ed.) (1969) *Karl Marx on Colonialism and Modernization*. New York: Anchor Books.

Bachaus, J. (1992) "Fredrich List and the Political Economy of Protective Tariffs," in T. Lowry (ed.), *Perspectives on the History of Economic Thought, Volume VII*, 142–56, Aldershot: Edward Elgar.

Backhouse, R. E. (1994) "Mummery and Hobson's *The Physiology of Industry*," pp. 78–99 in John Pheby (ed.), *J. A. Hobson after Fifty Years: Freethinker of the Social Sciences*, ed. New York: St. Martin's.

Bailey, A., and Llobera, J. (eds.) (1981) *The Asiatic Mode of Production: Science and Politics*. London: Routledge and Kegan Paul.

Bailey, D., Harte, G., and Sugden, R. (1994) *Transnationals and Governments: Recent Politices in Japan, France, Germany, the United State and Britain*. New York: Routledge.

Bairoch, P. (1993) *Economics and World History*. Chicago: University of Chicago Press.

218

Bairoch, P. (1994) *Mythes et paradoxes de l'histoire economique*. Paris: La decoverte.

Banaji, J. (1983) "Gunder Frank in Retreat?" In Peter Limqueco and Bruce McFarlane (eds.), *Neo-Marxist Theories of Development*. London: Croom Helm.

Baran, P. A. (1957) *The Political Economy of Growth*, New York: Monthly Review Press and Harmondsworth: Penguin, 1973.

Bardhan, P. (1997) "Corruption and Development: A Review of the Issues," *Journal of Economic Literature*, 35: 1320–46.

Barratt Brown, M. (1963) *After Imperialism*. London: Heinemann.

Barratt Brown, M. (1970) *After Imperialism*. London: Merlin.

Barratt Brown, M. (1972a) "A Critique of Marxist Theories of Imperialism," in Roger Owen and Bob Sutcliffe, *Studies in the Theory of Imperialism*, London: Longman.

Barratt Brown, M. (1972b) *Essays on Imperialism*. Nottingham: Spokesman.

Barratt Brown, M. (1974) *The Economics of Imperialism*. London and Baltimore: Penguin.

Barratt Brown, M. (1984) *Models in Political Economy*. London: Penguin.

Barratt Brown, M. (1988) "Away with all the Great Arches: Anderson's History of British Capitalism," *New Left Review*, 167.

Barratt Brown, M. (1989) "Commercial and Industrial Capital in England: A Reply to Geoffrey Ingham," *New Left Review*, 178.

Barratt Brown, M. (1993) *Fair Trade: Reform and Reality in the International Trading System*. London: Zed Books.

Barratt Brown, M. (1995) *Africa's Choices: After 30 Years of the World Bank*. London: Penguin.

Barratt Brown, M. (1997) "An Africa Road to Development: Are we all Romantics?" *African Studies Lecture*, Leeds.

Barratt Brown, M., and Tiffen, P. (1992) *Short Changed: Africa and World Trade*. London: Pluto Press.

Basu, K. (1997) *Analytical Development Economics*. Cambridge, MA: The MIT Press.

Bauer, Otto. (1907) *Die Nationalitätenfrage und die Sozialdemokratie*. Vienna: Ignaz Brand.

Bawtree, V. See Rahnema, M. and Bawtree (1997).

Beach, W. E. (1935) *British International Gold Movements and Banking Policy, 1881–1913*. Cambridge, MA: Harvard University Press.

Beard, C., and Smith, G. H. E. (1934) *The Idea of the National Interest*. New York: Macmillan.

Beaud, M. (1989) *L'economie monde dans les annees* 80. Paris: La decouverte.

Becker, D. G. et al. (1987) *Postimperialism, International Capitalism, and Development in the Twentieth Century*. Boulder: Lynne Rienner.

Bernal, M. (1987) *Black Athena*, Vol. 1, *The Fabrication of Ancient Greece*. London: Free Association Books.

Bernstein, R., and Munro, R. (1997) *The Coming Conflict with China*. New York: Knopf.

Bertram, C. (1990) "International Competition in Historical Materialism," *New Left Review*, 183: 116–28.

Bhagwati, J. (1982) "Directly Unproductive, Profit-seeking (DUP) Activities," *Journal of Political Economy*, 90: 988–1002.

Blackstock, P., and Hoselitz, F. (eds.) (1953) *The Russian Menace to Europe*. London: Allen and Unwin.

Blaut, J. (1976) "Where Was Capitalism Born?" *Antipode*, 8, 2: 1–11.

Blaut, J. (1987) *The National Question: Decolonizing the Theory of Nationalism*. London: Zed Books.

Blaut, J. (1989) "Colonialism and the Rise of Capitalism," *Science & Society*, 53, 3: 250–296.

Blaut, J. (1993) *The Colonizer's Model of the World: Geographical Diffusionism and Eurocentric History*. New York: Guilford.

Blaut, J. (1994) "Robert Brenner in the Tunnel of Time," *Antipode*, 26, 4: 351–374.

Blaut, J. (1997) "Evaluating Imperialism," *Science & Society*, 61: 382–393.

220

Blaut, J., Amin, S., Dodgson, R., Frank, A. G., Palan, R., and Taylor, P. (1992) *Fourteen Ninety-Two: The Debate on Colonialism, Eurocentrism, and History*, Trenton, NJ: Africa World Press.

Bleaney, M. (1976) *Underconsumption Theory: A History and Critical Analysis*. London: Lawrence and Wiseheart.

Block, F. L. (1977) *The Origins of International Economic Disorder: A Study of United States International Monetary Policy from World War II to the Present*. Berkeley: University of California Press.

Boone, C. (1992) *Merchant Capital and the Roots of State Power in Senegal, 1930–1985*. Cambridge: Cambridge University Press.

Booth, D. (1985) "Marxism and Development Sociology: Intepreting the Impasse," *World Development*, 13 (7): 761–787.

Bourdieu, P. (1986) "The Forms of Capital," in J. Richardson (ed.), *Handbook of Theory and Research for the Sociology of Education*, New York: Greenwood Press.

Braudel, F. (1979) *Civilisation matérielle, economie et capitalisme. XV – XVII siecles*, 3 vols. Paris: Armand Colin.

Brenner, R. (1977) "The Origins of Capitalist Development: A Critique of Neo-Smithian Marxism," *New Left Review*, 104: 25–93.

Brewer, A. (1980) *Marxist Theories of Imperialism. A Critical Survey*. London: Routledge.

Brewer, A. (1990) *Marxist Theories of Imperialism: A Critical Survey*, 2nd ed. London and New York: Routledge.

Brezezinski, Z. et al. (1996) *Foreign Policy into the 21st Century: The US Leadership Challenge*. Washington, DC: Center for Strategic and International Studies.

Brown, B. H. (1943) *The Tariff Reform Movement in Great Britain 1881–1895*. New York: Columbia University Press.

Brundtland, G. H. (1987) *Our Common Future*. Oxford and New York: Oxford University Press.

Bukharin, N. (1915) *Imperialism and the World Economy*. London: Merlin, 1972, and New York: Monthly Review Press, 1929.

Bukharin, N. (1917) *Imperialism and World Economy*. English translation. London: Merlin, 1972.

221

Cain, P. J. (1978) "J.A. Hobson, Cobdenism, and the Radical Theory of Economic Imperialism," *Economic History Review*, 33, 4: 463–490.

Cain, P. J. (1985) "Hobson, Wilshire, and the Capitalist Theory of Capitalist Imperialism," *History of Political Economy*, 17, 3: 455–560.

Cain, P. J. (1990) "Variations on a Famous Theme: Hobson, International Trade, and Imperialism," pp. 31–53 in Michael Freeden (ed.), *Reappraising J. A. Hobson: Humanism and Welfare*. London: Unwin Hyman, pp. 31–53.

Cain, P. J., and Hopkins, A. G. (1986) "The Political Economy of British Expansion Overseas, 1750–1914," *Economic History Review*, November.

Cain, P. J., and Hopkins, A. G. (1987) "Gentlemanly Capitalism and British Expansion Overseas: II New Imperialism, 1850–1914," *Economic History Review*, February.

Cain, P. J., and Hopkins, A. G. (1993a) *British Imperialism: Crisis and Deconstruction, 1914–1990*. London and New York: Longman.

Cain, P. J., and Hopkins, A. G. (1993b) *British Imperialism: Innovation and Expansion, 1688–1914*. London and New York: Longman.

Cairncross, A. K. (1953) *Home and Foreign Investment 1870–1913: Studies in Capital Accumulation*. Cambridge: Cambridge University Press.

Calderón, F., Piscitelli, A., and Reyna, J. L. (1992) "Social Movements: Actors, Theories, Expectations," in Antonio Escobar and Sonia Alvarez (eds.), *The Making of Social Movements in Latin America*. Boulder: Westview.

Calderón, F. (1986) "Los movimientos sociales ante la crisis," in Fernando Calderón (ed.), *Los movimientos sociales ante la crisis*. Buenos Aires: CLACSO.

Caldwell, M. (1977) *The Wealth of Some Nations*. London: Zed Press.

Cammack, P. (1997) "Cardoso's Political Project in Brazil: The Limits of Social Democracy," in Leo Panitch (ed.), *Socialist Register 1997*. New York: Monthly Review Press.

Caputo, O., and Pizzaro, R. (1974) *Dependencia y Relaciones Internacionales*. Costa Rica: Ediciones Educa.

Cardoso, F. H. (1972) "Dependency and Development in Latin America," *New Left Review*, 74 (July–August): 83–95.

Cardoso, F. H. (1977) "The Consumption of Dependency Theory in the U.S." *Latin American Research Review*, 12 (3): 7–24.

Cardoso, F. H. (1993) "North-South Relations in the Present Context: A New Dependency?" in Martin Carnoy, Manuel Castells, Stephen Cohen and Fernando Henrique Cardoso (eds.), *The New Global Economy in the Information Age*. University Park: Pennyslvania State University Press.

Cardoso, F. H., and Faletto, E. (1979) *Dependency and Development in Latin America*. Berkeley: University of California Press.

Casanova, P. G. et al. (ed.) (1994) *Etat et politique dans le tiers monde*. Paris: L'Harmattan.

Castañeda, J., and Hett, E. (1981) *El economismo dependentista*. Mexico: Siglo XXI.

Castells, M. (1993) "The Informational Economy and the New International Division of Labor," in Martin Carnoy et al., *The New Global Economy in the Information Age: Reflections on Our Changing World*. University Park: Pennsylvania State University Press.

Castells, M. (1996) *The Information Age. Economy, Society and Culture, I: The Rise of the Network Society*. Oxford: Blackwell.

Castells, M. (1997) *The Information Age. Economy, Society and Cultur. 2: The Power of Identity*. Oxford: Blackwell.

Castells, M. (1998) *The Information Age: Economy, Society and Culture. 3: End of Millenium*. Oxford: Blackwell.

Castley, R. J. (1996) "The Role of Japanese Foreign Investment in South Korea's Manufacturing Sector," *Policy Development Review*, 14, 1.

Cerny, P. (1999) "The Dynamics of Financial Globalization: Technology, Market Structure and Policy Response," *Policy Sciences*, 27, 4: 24.

Chesnais, F. (1994) *La mondialisation du capital*. Paris: Syros.

Chick, V. (1996) "Equilibrium and Determination in Open Systems: the Case of the General Theory," *History of Economics Review*, 25, (Winter–Summer) 184–189.

Chilcote, R. H. (1984) *Theories of Development and Underdevelopment*. Boulder, CO: Westview.

Chilcote, R. H. (1994) *Theories of Comparative Politics: The Search for a Paradigm Reconsidered*, 2nd ed. Boulder, CO: Westview Press.

Chilcote, R. H. (ed.) (1981) *Dependency and Marxism. Toward a Resolution of the Debate*. Boulder, CO: Westview Press.

Chomsky, N. (1991) *Deterring Democracy*. London: Verso.

Chomsky, N. (1993) *Year 501, The Conquest Continues*. New York: Black Rose Books.

Chomsky, N. (1996) *World Orders Old and New*. New York: Columbia University Press.

Clarke, P. (1990) "Hobson and Keynes as Economic Heretics," pp. 100–115 in Michael Freeden (ed.), *Reappraising J. A. Hobson: Humanism and Welfare*. London: Unwin Hyman.

Cohen, B. J. (1973) *The Question of Imperialism: The Political Economy of Dominance and Dependence*. New York: Basic Books.

Cohen, S. F. (1973) *Bukharin and the Bolshevik Revolution*. New York: Alfred A. Knopf.

Cole, G. D. H., and Postgate, R. (1946) *The Common People, 1746–1946*. Methuen.

Cole, W. A. See Phyllis Deane.

Collins, R. M. (1981) *The Business Response to Keynes, 1929–1964*. New York: Columbia University Press.

Comfort, A. (1976) *Man and Society*. London: Mitchell Beasley, Joy of Knowledge Library.

Corrigan, P., and Sayer, D. (1985) *The Great Arch*, Oxford.

Cottrell, P. L. (1991) "Great Britain," pp. 25–47 in *International Banking, 1870–1914*, Rondo Cameron and V. I. Bovykin (eds.).

Court, W. H. B. (1938) *The Rise of the Midland Industries, 1600–1838*. Cambridge.

Cox, R. W. (1994) *Power and Profits: U.S. Policy in Central America*. Lexington, KY: University Press of Kentucky.

Cox, R. W. (ed.) (1996) *Business and the State in International Relations*. Boulder, CO: Westview Press.

Crafts, N. J. R. (1997) "Some Dimensions of the 'Quality of Life' during the Industrial Revolution," *Economic History Review*, 50, 4.

Crosby, A. (1986) *Ecological Imperialism: the Biological Expansion of Europe, 900–1900*. Cambridge: Cambridge University Press.

224

Cumings, B. (1996) "The Political Economy of the Pacific Rim" in R. A. Palat, *Pacific Asia and the Future of the World System*. New York: Macmillan.

Daniels, P., and Lever, W. F. (ed.) (1996) *The Global Economy in Transition*. New York: Longman.

Darity, W. Jr. (1992) "A Model of 'Original Sin': Rise of the West and Lag of the Rest," *American Economic Review*, Papers and Proceedings of the 104th Annual Meeting, 82, 2: 163–167.

Darity, W. Jr., and Horn, B. L. (1988) *The Loan Pushers: The Role of Commercial Banks in the International Debt Crisis*. Cambridge, MA: Ballinger.

Dasgupta, B. (1998) *Structural Adjustment, Global Trade, and the New Political Economy of Development*. London: Zed Books.

Daunton, M. J. (1989) "Gentlemanly Capitalism and British Industry, 1820–1914," *Past and Present*, Oxford, February.

Davidson, B. (1978) *Africa in Modern History*. London: Allen Lane/Penguin.

Davidson, B. (1984) *The Story of Africa*. London: Mitchell Beasley.

Davidson, B. (1992) *The Black Man's Burden and the Curse of the Nation State*. Times Books and James Currey.

Davidson, B. (1995) *The Search for Africa*. New York: Times Books.

Davidson, P. (1991) *Post Keynesian Macroeconomic Theory: A Foundation for Successful Economic Policies for the Twenty-first Century*. London: Edward Elgar.

Davis, H. (1978) *Toward a Marxist Theory of Nationalism*. New York: Monthly Review Press.

Davis, L. E., and Huttenback, R. A. (1986) *Mammon and the Pursuit of Empire: The Political Economy of British Imperialism, 1860–1912*. Cambridge: Cambridge University Press.

De la Peña, S. (1994) "Las transfiguraciones del capitalismo en América Latina," *Revista Mexicana de Sociología*, 1 (Jan–March): 183–193.

De Ste Croix, G. (1981) *The Class Struggle in the Ancient Greek World*. New York: Cornell University.

Deane, P., and Cole, W. A. (1964) *British Economic Growth, 1688–1959*. Cambridge.

Debray, R. (1977) "Marxism and the National Question: Interview with Régis Debray," *New Left Review*, 105: 25–41.

Derrida, J. (1994) *Spectres of Marx. The State of Debt, the Work of Mourning*, and *the New International*. New York: Routledge.

Deutscher, I. (1954) *The Prophet Armed: Trotsky 1879–1921*. London: Oxford University Press.

Deutscher, I. (1959) *The Prophet Unarmed: Trotsky, 1921–1929*. London: Oxford University Press.

Diamond, J. (1997) *Guns, Germs and Steel*. London: Cape.

Dobb, M. (1946) *Studies in the Development of Capitalism*. London: Routledge.

Domar, E. D. (1947) "Expansion and Employment," *American Economic Review*, 37: 34–55.

Dos Santos, T. (1970) The Structure of Dependence," *American Economic Review*, 60: 231–236.

Dos Santos, T. (1996) "Latin American Underdevelopments Past, Present and Future. A Homage to Andre Gunder Frank," in Sing Chew and Robert Denemark (eds.), *The Underdevelopment of Development, Essays in Honor of Gunder Frank*. London: Sage Publications.

Dos Santos, T. (1998) "The Theoretical Foundations of the Cardoso Government: A New Stage of the Dependency Theory Debate," *Latin American Perspectives*, 25 (1): 53–70.

Edelstein, M. (1981) "Foreign Investment and Empire 1860–1914," in Roderick Floud and Donald McCloskey (eds.) *The Economic History of Britain since 1700*, v. 2. Cambridge: Cambridge University Press.

Edelstein, M. (1982) *Overseas Investment in the Age of High Imperialism: The United Kingdom 1850–1914*. New York: Columbia University Press.

Edelstein, M. (1994) "Imperialism: Cost and Benefit," pp. 197–216 in Roderick Floud and Donald McCloskey (eds.) *The Economic History of Britain since 1700*, 2nd ed. Cambridge: Cambridge University Press.

Edwards, S. (1995) *Crisis and Reform in Latin America. From Despair to Hope*. New York: Oxford University Press.

Ehrenreich, J. (1983) "Socialism, Nationalism, and Capitalist Development," *Review of Radical Political Economics,* 15: 1–40.

Elvin, M. (1973) *The Pattern of the Chinese Past.* Stanford: Stanford University.

Emmanuel, A. (1972a) *Unequal Exchange: A Study of the Imperialism of Trade.* London and New York: New Left Books and Monthly Review Press.

Emmanuel, A. (1972b) "White Settler Colonialism and the Myth of Investment Imperialism," *New Left Review,* 73.

Engels, F. (1884) *The Origin of the Family, Private Property and the State.* Stuttgart: Dietz.

Engels, F. (1974) "What Have the Working Classes To Do with Poland?" in D. Fernbach (ed.), *Karl Marx: Political Writings.* Vol. 3. New York: Vintage.

Erlich, A. (1960) *The Soviet Industrialization Debate, 1924–1928.* Cambridge MA: Harvard University Press.

Escobar, A. (1984) "Discourse and Power in Development: Michel Foucault and the Relevance of his Work to the Third World," *Alternatives,* 10, 3: 377–400.

Esteva, G. (1992) "Development" in Wolfgang Sach (ed.), *The Development Dictionary.* London: Zed Books.

Etherington, N. (1982) "Reconsidering Theories of Imperialism," *History and Theory,* 21: 1–36.

Etherington, N. (1983) "The Capitalist Theory of Capitalist Imperialism," *History of Political Economy,* 15, 1: 38–62.

Etherington, N. (1984) *Theories of Imperialism: War, Conquest, and Capital.* London: Croom Helm.

Evans, P. (1995) *Embedded Autonomy: States and Industrial Transformation.* Princeton: Princeton University Press.

Evans, P., Rueschemeyer, D., and Skocpol, T. (eds.) (1985) *Bringing the State Back In.* Cambridge: Cambridge University Press.

Feinstein, C. (1972) *National Expenditure and Output of the United Kingdom — 1855–1965.* Cambridge.

Feis, H. (1930) *Europe: The World's Banker, 1870–1914.* New York: Augustus M. Kelley.

Feldstein, M., and Horioka, C. (1980) "Domestic Saving and International Capital Flows," *Economic Journal*, 90: 314–29.

Ferguson, T. (1995) *The Golden Rule: The Investment Theory of Party Competition and the Logic of Money-driven political systems*. Chicago: University of Chicago Press.

Fieldhouse, D. K. (1961) "Imperialism: An Historiographical Revision," *The Economic History Review*, Second Series, 14, 2: 187–209.

Fieldhouse, D. K. (1973) *Economics and Empire, 1830–1914*. Weidenfeld.

Filtzer, D. (1979) "Introduction," *The Crisis of Soviet Industrialization: Selected Essays* by E. A. Preobrashensky. White Plains, NY: M.E. Sharpe.

Finley, M. (1981) *Economy and Society in Ancient Greece*. Harmondsworth: Penguin.

Fischer, F. (1974) *World Power or Decline — The Controversy over Germany's Aims in the First World War*. New York: Norton.

Floud, R. C. See D. McCloskey.

Fordham, B. (1998) *Building the Cold War Consensus*. Ann Arbor. MI: University of Michigan Press.

Foster, J. B. (1986) *The Theory of Monopoly Capitalism*. New York: Monthly Review Press.

Foucault, M. (1979) *Discipline and Punish*. New York: Vintage.

Frank, A. G. (1966) "The Development of Underdevelopment," *Monthly Review* (September): 17–31.

Frank, A. G. (1967) *Capitalism and Underdevelopment in Latin America*, New York: Monthly Review Press and Harmondswork: Penguin, 1971.

Frank, A. G. (1969a) *Capitalism and Underdevelopment in Latin America*. New York: Modern Reader Paperbacks.

Frank, A. G. (1969b) *Latin America: Underdevelopment or Revolution*. New York: Monthly Review Press.

Frank, A. G. (1971) *Capitalism and Underdevelopment in Latin America*. New York: Monthly Review Press, and London: Penguin.

228

Frank, A. G. (1977) "Dependence Is Dead, Long Live Dependence and the Class Struggle: An Answer to Critics," *World Development*, 5 (4).

Frank, A. G. (1978a) *Dependent Accumulation and Underdevelopment*. London: Macmillan.

Frank, A. G. (1978b) *World Accumulation 1492– 1789*. New York: Monthly Review Press.

Frank, A. G. (1984) *Critique and Anti-Critique: Essays on Dependence and Reformism*. London: Macmillan.

Frank, A. G. (1991) "The Underdevelopment of Development," *Scandinavian Journal of Development Alternatives*, 10, 3.

Frank, A. G. (1992) "Fourteen Ninety-Two Once Again," *Political Geography*, 11: 386–393.

Frank, A. G. (1998) *Re-Orient*. Berkeley: University of California Press.

Franklin, J. (1989) *A Gentleman's Country House and Its Plan, 1835–1914*, quoted in Saville (1988).

Freeden, M. (1994) " J.A. Hobson as a Political Theorist," pp. 19–33 in *J. A. Hobson after Fifty Years*, ed. John Pheby, New York: Saint Martin's Press.

Freyer, T. (1992) *Regulating Big Business: Antitrust in Great Britain and America, 1880–1990*. Cambridge: Cambridge University Press.

Friedman, G., and Friedman, M. (1996) *The Future of War*. New York: Crown.

Friedman, G., and Lebard, M. (1991) *The Coming War With Japan*. New York: St. Martins Press.

Fukuyama, F. (1992) *The End of History and the Last Man*. New York: Free Press.

Furedi, F. (1994) *The New Ideology of Imperialism. Renewing the Moral Imperative*. London: Pluto Press.

Galeano, E. (1972) *The Open Veins of Latin America*. New York: Monthly Review Press.

Gallagher, J., and Robinson, R. (1953) "The Imperialism of Free Trade," *Economic History Review*, 2nd series, 6, 1: 1–15.

García Canclini, N. (1995) *Culturas híbridas. Estrategias para entrar y salir de la modernidad.* Buenos Aires: Editorial Sudamericana.

Garten, J. (1992) *A Cold Peace: America, Japan, Germany and the Struggle for Supremacy.* New York: Random House.

Gellner, E. (1983) *Nations and Nationalism.* Ithaca: Cornell University Press.

George, S. (1988) *A Fate Worse Than Debt.* Harmondsworth: Penguin.

George, S. (ed.) (1992) *The Debt Boomerang.* London: Pluto Press.

Gerschenkron, A. (1966) *Economic Backwardness in Historical Perspective.* Cambridge, MA: Harvard University Press.

Gibbs, D. N. (1991) *The Political Economy of Third World Intervention: Mines, Money, and U.S. Policy in the Congo Crisis.* Chicago: University of Chicago Press.

Gibson-Graham, J. K. (1996) *The End of Capitalism (as We Knew It). A Feminist Critique of Political Economy.* Oxford: Blackwell.

Giddens, A. (1981) *A Contemporary Critique of Historical Materialism.* Berkeley: University of California Press.

Giddens, A. (1987) *The Nation State and Violence.* Berkeley: University of California Press.

Gilpin, R. (1981) *War and Change in World Politics.* Cambridge: Cambridge University Press.

Godelier, M. (1969) *El modo de producción asiático.* Barcelona: Martínez Roca.

Godelier, M. (1981) "The Asiatic Mode of Production," in Bailey, A., and Llobera, J. (eds.), *The Asiatic Mode of Production: Science and Politics.* London: Routledge and Kegan Paul.

Gompert, D., and Larabee, F. (eds.) (1997) *America and Europe: A Partnership for a New Era.* Cambridge: Cambridge University Press.

González Casanova, P. (1969) "Internal Colonialism and National Development." In Irving Louis Horowitz et al. (eds.), *Latin American Radicalism.* New York: Vintage Books.

Gramsci, A. (1988) *Selected Writings, 1916–1935,* edited by D. Forgacs. New York: Schocken.

Griffin, K., and Gurley, J. (1985) "Radical Analyses of Imperialism, the Third World, and the Transition to Socialism: A Survey Article," *Journal of Economic Literature,* 23: 1089–1143.

Gronemeyer, M. (1992) "Helping" in Wolfgang Sachs (ed.), *The Development Dictionary.* London: Zed Books.

Grosvenor, W. M. (1885) *American Securities: the Causes Influencing Investment and Speculation and the Fluctuations in Values from 1872 to 1885.* NY: Daily Commercial Bulletin.

Habermas, J. (1995) "Jürgen Habermas: A Philosophical-Political Profile," *New Left Review*, 151: 75–105.

Habib, I. (1969) "Problems of Marxist Historical Analysis," *Enquiry* 3, 2(n.s.):52–67.

Hall, J. (1986) *Powers and Liberties: The Causes and Consequences of the Rise of the West,* Harmondsworth: Penguin.

Hamilton, H. (1947) *History of the Homeland.* Boston: Allen and Unwin.

Hampden-Turner, C., and Trompenaars, F. (1993) *The Seven Cultures of Capitalism.* New York: Doubleday.

Hargreaves Heap, S. (1989) *Rationality in Economics.* Oxford: Blackwell.

Hargreaves Heap, S., and Varoufakis, Y. (1995) *Game Theory.* London: Routledge.

Harris, N. (1968) *Beliefs in Society.* Harmondsworth: Penguin.

Harris, N. (1986) *The End of the Third World.* London: Penguin.

Harris, N. (1987) *The End of the Third World.* Harmondsworth: Penguin.

Harris, N. (1990) *National Liberation.* Harmondsworth: Penguin.

Hauchler, I., and Kennedy, P. (1993) *Global Trends.* New York: Continuum.

Hayes, C. (1960) *Nationalism: A Religion.* New York: Macmillan.

Held, D. (1995) *Democracy and the Global Order.* Cambridge: Polity Press.

Henwood, D. (1997) *Wall Street: How it Works and for Whom.* New York: Verso.

Herman, E. S. (1997) "Globalization in Question?" *Z Magazine* (April): 8–11.

Hilferding, R. (1910) *Finance Capital: a Study of the Latest Phase in Capitalist Development*. London: Routledge & Kegan Paul, 1981.

Hill, C. (1972) *God's Englishman: Cromwell and the English Revolution*. Penguin.

Hilton, R. (ed.) (1976) *The Transition from Feudalism to Capitalism*. London: New Left Books.

Hirschman, A. (1982) "Rival Interpretations of Market Society," *Journal of Economic Literature*, 20: 1463–1484.

Hirschman, A. O. (1958) *The Strategy of Economic Development*. New Haven: Yale University Press.

Hirst, P., and Thompson, G. (1996) *Globalization in Question*. Cambridge: Polity Press.

Hobsbawm, E. (1962) *The Age of Revolution: 1789–1848*. New York: World and Mentor.

Hobsbawm, E. (1968) *Industry and Empire*. Harmondsworth: Penguin.

Hobsbawm, E. (1975) *The Age of Capital: 1848–1875*. New York: New American Library.

Hobsbawm, E. (1977b) "Some reflections on *The Break-Up of Britain*," *New Left Review*, 105: 1–14.

Hobsbawm, E. (1983) *The Age of Empire, 1875–1914*, London: Weidenfeld, and Terry Ranger (eds.). *The Invention of Tradition*. Cambridge.

Hobsbawm, E. (1990) *Nations and Nationalism Since 1780: Programme, Myth, Reality*. Cambridge: Cambridge University Press.

Hobsbawm, E. J. (1987) *The Age of Empire 1875–1914*. London: Weidenfeld and Nicolson.

Hobsbawm, E. (1977a) *The Age of Capital*. London: Abacus.

Hobsbawm, E. (1987) *The Age of Empire*. New York: Pantheon.

Hobsbawm, E. (1995) *The Age of Extremes*. New York: Pantheon.

Hobson, J. A. (1894) *The Evolution of Modern Capitalism*. London: Walter Scott Publishing, 1906.

Hobsom, J. A. (1900) *The War in South Africa: Its Causes and Effects*. New York: Macmillan.

Hobson, J. A. (1902) *Imperialism: a Study*. Ann Arbor: University of Michigan Press, 1965. Page numbers are to the most recent (1965) edition given.

Hobson, J. A. (1927) *The Conditions of Industrial Peace*. New York: Macmillan.

Hobson, J. A., and Mummery, A. F. (1889) *The Physiology of Industry: Being an Exposure of Certain Fallacies in Existing Theories of Economics*. New York: Kelley and Millman, 1956.

Hollander, S. (1996) "Malthus and Keynes: Some Recent Secondary Literature," *History of Economics Review*, 25: 127–128.

Holmes, C. See Sidney Pollard.

Hoogvelt, A. (1997) *Globalization and the Postcolonial World: The New Political Economy of Development*. London: Macmillan.

Hopkins, A. G. See P. J. Cain.

Howard, M., and King, J. (1985) *The Political Economy of Marx*. Harlow: Longman.

Howard, M., and King, J. (1989) *A History of Marxian Economics, Volume I, 1883–1929*. Princeton: Princeton University Press.

Howard, M., and King, J. (1992) *A History of Marxian Economics Volume II, 1929–1990*. Princeton: Princeton University Press.

Howard, M., and King, J. (eds.) (1976) *The Economics of Marx*. Harmondsworth: Penguin.

Howard, M., and Kumar, R. (1999) "Classical Liberalism in an Environment of Rational Choice Involving Commitment and Security as Well as Greed," in S. Dow and J. Hillard (eds.), *Keynes Knowledge and Uncertainty*. Aldershot: Edward Elgar.

Howells, J., and Wood, M. (1993) *The Globalization of Production and Technology*. London: Belhaven Press.

Hoy, D. (1996) "Splitting the Difference: Habermas's Critique of Derrida." in Manizlo Passerin D'Entreves and Seyla Behhabib (eds.), *Habermas and the Unfinished Project of Modernity*. Cambridge: Polity Press.

Huntington, S. (1996) *The Clash of Civilizations*. New York: Touchstone.

Huttenback, R. See L. E. Davis.

IMF (1997) *World Economic Outlook (May), Globalization: Opportunities and Challenges.* Washington DC: IMF.

Imlah, A. H. (1958) *Economic Elements in the Pax Britannica.* Cambridge, MA: Harvard University Press.

Ingham, G. (1984) *Capitalism Divided: The City and Industry in British Social Development.* Macmillan.

James, C. L. R. (1936) *The Black Jacobins: Toussaint L'Ouverture and the San Domingo Revolution.* London: Secker and Warburg.

James, C. L. R. (1970) "The Atlantic Slave Trade and Slavery: Some Interpretations of their Significance in the Development of the United States and the Western world," pp. 119–164 in J. Williams and C. Harris (eds.), *Amistad I.* New York: Vintage.

James, P. (1997) "Postdependency? The Third World in an Era of Globalism and Late Capitalism," *Alternatives,* 22: 205–226.

Jessop, B. (1990) *State Theory.* University Park: Pennsylvania State University Press.

Jones, E. L. (1981) *The European Miracle.* Cambridge: Cambridge University Press.

Kadish, A. (1994) "The Non-Canonical Context of *The Physiology of Industry*," pp. 53–57 in John Pheby (ed.), *J. A. Hobson after Fifty Years.* New York: Saint Martin's Press.

Kalecki, M. (1952) *Theory of Economic Dynamics: An Essay on Cyclical and Long-Run Changes in Capitalist Economy.* New York: Augustus M. Kelley, 1969.

Kalecki, M. (1972) "Fascism of Our Time." in *The Last Stage in the Transformation of Capitalism.* New York: Monthly Review Press.

Kalmanowitz, S. (1983) *El desarollo tardío del capitalismo. Un enfoque crítico de la teoría de la dependencia.* Bogotá: Siglo XXI.

Kapstein, E. (1996) *Governing the Global Economy: International Finance and the State.* Cambridge, MA: Harvard University Press.

Kates, S. (1996) "Say's Law and the Theory of the Business Cycle," *History of Economics Review,* 25: 119–126.

Kay, C. (1989) *Latin American Theories of Development and Underdevelopment.* London: Routledge.

Kay, G. (1975) *Development and Underdevelopment: A Marxist Analysis*. Macmillan.

Kedourie, E. (1970) *Nationalism in Asia and Africa*. New York: World.

Kelly, K. (1997) "The Network Economy," *Wired*, September.

Kennedy, P. (1989) *The Rise and Fall of Great Powers*. London: Fontana.

Kennedy, P. (1993) *Preparing for the Twenty-First Century*. New York: Harper-Collins.

Kennedy, W. P. (1987) *Industrial Structure, Capital Markets and the Origins of British Economic Decline*. Cambridge: Cambridge University Press.

Key, V. O. (1942) *Politics, Parties, and Pressure Groups*. New York: Crowell.

Keynes, J. M. (1919) *The Economic Consequences of the Peace*. New York: Penguin, 1971.

Keynes, J. M. (1936) *General Theory of Employment, Interest, and Money*. New York: Harcourt Brace Jovanovich, 1964.

Kiely, R. (1995) "Third World Relativism: A New Form of Imperialism," *Journal of Contemporary Asia*, 25: 159–78.

Knapp, J. (1957) "Capital Exports and Growth," *Economic Journal*, 67, 267.

Kolko, G. (1988) *Confronting the Third World*. New York: Pantheon.

Kolko, G. (1994) *Century of War: Politics, Conflicts, and Society Since 1914*. New York: The New Press.

Korzeniewicz, R., and Smith, W. (eds.) (1997) *Latin America in the World-Economy*. Westport, CT: Praeger.

Kreye, O., Frobel, F., and Henrichs, J. (1980) *The New International Division of Labor*. Cambridge: Cambridge University Press.

Krugman, P. (1991) *Geography and Trade*. Cambridge, MA: MIT Press.

Krugman, P. (1995) *Development, Geography, and Economic Theory*. Cambridge, MA: MIT Press.

Krugman, P. (1996) *Pop Internationalism*. Cambridge, MA: MIT Press.

Kubálková, V. and Cruickshank, A. (1989) *Marxism and International Relations*. Oxford: Oxford University Press.

Laclau, E. (1977) *Politics and Ideology in Marxist Theory*. London: New Left Books.

LaCoste, Y. (1965) *Ibn Khaldoun: naissance de 'histoire passé du tiers monde*. Paris: Maspero.

Landes, D. (1966) "Technological Change and Development in Western Europe, 1750–1914," in *Cambridge Economic History of Europe*. Cambridge.

Landes, D. (1969) *Unbound Prometheus*. Cambridge.

Landes, D. (1998) *The Wealth and Poverty of Nations*. New York: Norton.

Lang, T., and Hines, C. (1993) *The New Protectionism*. Earthscan.

Larrain, J. (1989) *Theories of Development: Capitalism, Colonialism and Dependency*. Cambridge: Polity Press.

Lattimore, O. (1951) *Inner Asian Frontiers of China*. Oxford (1940).

Lavoie, M. (1992) *Foundations of Post-Keynesian Economic Analysis*. Aldershot, England: Edward Elgar.

Lebow, R. N., and Risse-Kappen, T. (eds.) (1995) *International Relations Theory and the End of the Cold War*. New York: Columbia University Press.

Lefort, C. (1978) "Marx: From One Vision of History to Another," *Social Research*, 615–665.

Lenin, V. (1915a) Notes for a Lecture on "Imperialism and the Right of Nations to Self-Determination," pp. 735–742 in *Collected Works*, 39 (*Notebooks on Imperialism*).

Lenin, V. (1915b) "The Revolutionary Proletariat and the Right of Nations to Self-Determination," pp. 407–414 in *Collected Works*, 21.

Lenin, V. (1916a) *Imperialism, The Highest Stage of Capitalism*, pp. 185–304 in *Collected Works*, 22. Moscow, Foreign Languages Publishing House, 1960–70.

Lenin, V. (1916b) "The Nascent Trend of Imperialist Economism," *Collected Works*, 23: 13–21.

Lenin, V. (1916c) "A Caricature of Marxism and Imperialist Economism," *Collected Works*, 23: 28–76.

Lenin, V. (1916d) "The Discussion on Self-determination Summed Up," *Collected Works*, 23: 320–360.

Lenin, V. (1921a) "Preliminary Draft Theses on the National and Colonial Questions," *Collected Works*, 31: 144–151.

Lenin, V. (1921b) "Report of the Commission on the National and the Colonial Questions," *Collected Works*, 31: 240–245.

Lenin, V. I. (1899) *History of Capitalism in Russia*. Moscow: Foreign Languages Publishing House.

Lenin, V. I. (1917) *Imperialism, the Highest Stage of Capitalism*, in *Selected Works*, vol. I, Moscow: Foreign Languages Publishing House, 1950, and Progress Publishers, 1977: 633–731.

Lenin, V. I. (1939) *Imperialism: The Highest Stage of Capitalism*. New York: International Publishers.

Lenin, V. I. (1960) *Collected Works, vol. 3: The Development of Capitalism in Russia*, Moscow: Progress Publishers.

Leroi, A. M. (1997) "Why Rhino-mounted Bantu Never Sacked Rome," *London Review of Books*, September 4.

Levathes, L. (1994) *When China Ruled the Seas*. New York: Simon and Schuster.

Lewis, W. A. (1954) "Economic Development with Unlimited Supplies of Labor," *The Manchester School*, 22: 139–191.

Lewis, W. A. (1983) *Selected Economic Writings of W. Arthur Lewis*. New York: New York University Press.

Leys, C. (1996) *The Rise and Fall of Development Theory*. James Currey, and Indiana.

Lichtheim, G. (1971) *Imperialism*, New York: Praeger Publishers.

Light, M. (1988) *The Soviet Theory of International Relations*, London: Wheatsheaf.

Linklater, A. (1990) *Beyond Realism and Marxism*, London: Macmillan.

Lipson, E. (1934) *Economic History of England*. London: Black.

Long, D. (1996) *Towards a New Liberal Internationalism: the International Theory of J. A. Hobson*. Cambridge: Cambridge University Press.

Luard, E. (1990) *The Globalization of Politics: The Changed Focus of Political Action in the Modern World*. New York: New York University Press.

Lubbock, P. (1922) *Earlham*. London.

Lucas, R. (1995) "Making a Miracle," *Econometrica*, 61: 251–272.

Lukes, S. (1973) *Power: A Radical Analysis*. London: Macmillan.

Luxemburg, R. (1908–1909) "The National Question and Autonom," in H. Davis (ed.), *The National Question: Selected Writings of Rosa Luxemburg*. New York: Monthly Review.

Luxemburg, R. (1913) *The Accumulation of Capital*. London: Routledge and Kegan Paul 1951 and New York: Monthly Review, 1951.

Lyotard, J. F. (1984) *The Post-Modern Condition*. Manchester: Manchester University Press.

Mackenzie, R. (1998) "The United States and the Taliban," in William Maley (ed.), *Fundamentalism Reborn? Afghanistan and the Taliban*. London: Hurst.

Macrosty, H. W. (1907) *The Trust Movement in British Industry: A Study of Business Organization*. New York: Agathon Press, 1968.

Maddison, A. (1994) "Explaining the Economic Performance of Nations, 1820–1989," pp. 91–132 in W. J. Baumol, R. R. Nelson and E. N. Wolff (eds.), *Convergence of Productivity: Cross National Studies and Historical Evidence*, Oxford: Oxford University Press, pp. 20–61. Also in A. Maddison (1995), *Explaining the Economic Performance of Nations*. Cambridge: Edward Elgar.

Maddison, A. (1995) *Monitoring the World Economy, 1820–1992*. Paris: OECD.

Magdoff, H. (1969) *The Age of Imperialism: The Economics of U.S. Foreign Policy*. New York: Monthly Review Press.

Magdoff, H. (1978) *Imperialism: From the Colonial Age to the Present*. New York: Monthly Review Press.

Magdoff, H. (1992) *Globalization: To What End?* New York: Monthly Review Press.

Magnusson, L. (1994) "Hobson and Imperialism: An Appraisal," pp. 143–162 in *J. A. Hobson after Fifty Years: Freethinker of the Social Sciences*, ed. John Pheby. New York: Saint Martin's.

Mahan, A. T. (1890) *The Influence of Sea Power upon History*. New York: Dover, 1987.

Malthus, T. (1966) *First Essay on Population 1798*. London: Macmillan.

Mandel, E. (1975) *Late Capitalism*. London: New Left Books.

Mander, J., and Goldsmith, E. (eds.) (1996) *The Case against the Global Economy and for a Turn Toward the Local*. San Francisco: Sierra Club Books.

Manfred, A. (ed.) (1974) *A Short History of the World*. 2 vols. Translated by K. Judelson. Moscow: Progress.

Mann, M. (1986) *The Sources of Social Power*, vol. 1, *A History of Power from the Beginning to A.D. 1760*. Cambridge: Cambridge University Press.

Mann, M. (1988) *States, War and Capitalism*. Oxford: Balckwell.

Mann, M. (1993) *The Sources of Social Power, Vol. 2*, Cambridge: Cambridge University Press.

Mann, M. (1997) "Has Globalization Ended the Rise of the Nation State," *Review of International Political Economy*, 4, 3 (Autumn): 472–496.

Manzo, K. (1991) "Modernist Discourse and the Crisis of Development Theory," *Studies in Comparative International Development*, 26 (2): 3–36.

Marable, M. (1983) *How Capitalism Underdeveloped Black America*. Boston: South End Press.

Marchand, M., and Parpart, J. (eds.) (1995) *Feminism, Postmodernism, Development*. London: Routledge.

Marini, R. M. (1978) "World Capitalist Accumulation and Sub-Imperialism," *Two Thirds*, 1 (Fall): 29–39.

Marx, K. (1972a) *The Ethnological Notebooks of Karl Marx*. Edited by L. Krader. Assen: Van Gorcum.

Marx, K. (1972b) "The Future Results of British Rule in India," pp. 583–588 in *The Marx-Engels Reader*, Robert Tucker (ed.). New York: W.W. Norton.

Marx, K. (1976) *Capital, vol. 1: A Critique of Political Economy*, London: Penguin Books.

Marx, K. (1978) *Capital*, vol. 2. London: Penguin Books.

Marx, K., and Engels, F. (1844–1894) *Ireland and the Irish Question*. Moscow: Progress Publisher, 1971.

Marx, K., and Engels, F. (1850–88) *On Colonialism*. Moscow, Foreign Languages Publishing House, n.d.

Marx, K., and Engels, F. (1972) pp. 331–362 in "The Communist Manifesto," *The Marx-Engels Reader*, Robert Tucker (ed.). New York: W.W. Norton.

Marx, K., and Engels, F. (1975) *Selected Correspondence*. Moscow: Progress.

Mayer, A. (1981) *The Persistence of the Old Regime*. New York: Pantheon.

McCloskey, D. C., and Floud, R. C. (1981) in McCloskey and Floud (eds.), *The Economic History of Britain since 1870*, vol. 2. Cambridge.

Mearsheimer, J. (1990) 'Back to the Future: Instability in Europe After the Cold War," *International Security*, 15: 5–56.

Melotti, U. (1977) *Marx and the Third World*. London: Macmillan.

Melucci, A. (1996) *Challenging Codes, Collective action in the Information Age.* Cambridge: Cambridge University Press.

Milgate, M., and Eatwell, J. (1983) "Unemployment and the Market Mechanism," pp. 260–280 in *Keynes' Economics and the Theory of Value and Redistribution*, eds. John Eatwell and Murray Milgate. London: Gerald Gutworth and Co.

Mill, J. S. (1900) *Principles of Political Economy*. New York: The Colonial Press.

Milonakis, D. (1993–1994) "Prelude to the Genesis of Capitalism: The Dynamics of the Feudal mode of Production," *Science & Society*, 57: 390–419.

Mohanty, C. (1988) "Under Western Eyes: Feminist Scholarship and Colonial Discourses," *Feminist Review*, 30, 61–88.

Mohri, K. (1989) "Marx an Underdevelopment," *Monthly Review* 41 (October): 1–17.

Moore, B. (1966) *Social Origins of Dictatorship and Democracy*. Harmondsworth: Penguin.

Munck, R. (1984) *Politics and Dependency in the Third World: The Case of Latin America.* London: Zed Books.

Munck, R. (1999) "Deconstructing Development Discourses: Of Impasses, Alternatives and Politics." In Ronaldo Munck and Denis O'Hearn (eds.), *Critical Development Theory: Contributions to a New Paradigm.* London: Zed Books.

Munck, R. (forthcoming) "Labour in the Global: Discourses and Practices." in Robin Cohen and Shirin Rai (eds.), *Social Movements in a Global Age.* London: Routledge.

Muñoz, H. (ed.) (1981) *From Dependency to Development. Strategies to Overcome Underdevelopment and Inequality.* Boulder, CO: Westview Press.

Myrdal, C. (1968) *Asian Drama: An Inquiry into the Poverty of Nations.* New York: Twentieth Century Fund.

Nairn, T. (1977) *The Break-Up of Britain.* London: New Left Books.

Nairn, T. See Anderson and Nain, 1964.

Nassan Adams, *World Apart: The North South Divide and the International System.* London: Zed Books.

Needham, J. et al. (1954–1984) *Science and Civilization in China.* 6 vols. Cambridge: Cambridge University Press.

Nemmers, E. E. (1956) *Hobson and Underconsumption.* New York: Kelley and Millmann.

Nivola, P. (ed.) (1997) *Comparative Disadvantage?: Social Regulations and the Global Economy.* Washington, D.C.: Brookings Institution Press.

North, D. (1981) *Structure and Change in Economic History.* New York: Norton.

North, D. (1990) *Institutions, Institutional Change and Economic Performance.* Cambridge: Cambridge University Press.

Northern Marxists' Historians' Group (1988) *The Development of British Capitalist Society.* Manchester.

Nove, A. (1969) *An Economic History of the USSR.* London: Allen Lane.

Nowell, G. P. (1990) "The Air Quality Debate in California: Should Gasoline Be Banned?" *Energy Policy,* 18, 7: 662–660.

Nowell, G. P. (1994) *Mercantile States and the World Oil Cartel, 1900–1939.* Ithaca, New York: Cornell University Press.

Nurkse, R. (1953) *Problems of Capital Formation in Underdeveloped Countries.* New York: Oxford University Press.

Nye, J. (1990) *Bound to Lead, The Changing Nature of American Power.* New York: Basic Books.

O'Brien, P. (1975) "A Critique of Latin American Theories of Dependency," in Ivor Oxaal, Tony Barnett, and David Booth (eds.), *Beyond the Sociology of Development.* London: Routledge.

O'Brien, P. (1982) "European Economic Development: The Contribution of the Periphery," *Economic History Review*, 35: 1–18.

O'Brien, P. (1988) "The Costs and Benefits of British Imperialism, 1846–1914," *Past and Present*, 120: 163–200.

Olson, M. (1982) *The Rise and Decline of Nations: Economic Growth, Stagflation, and Social Rigidities.* New Haven, CT.: Yale University Press.

Olson, M. (1993) "Dictatorship, Democracy and Development," *American Political Science Review*, 87: 567–576.

Oman, C. (1996) *The Policy Challenges of globalization and Regionalization*, Policy Brief, 11. Paris: OECD Development Center.

Owen, R., and Sutcliffe, B. (1972) *Studies in the Theory of Imperialism.* London: Longman.

Padgug, R. (1976) "Problems in the Theory of Slavery and Slave Society," *Science & Society*, 40: 3–28.

Palat, R. A. (1996) *Pacific Asia and the Future of the World System.* MacMillan.

Palley, T. I. (1996) *Post-Keynesian Economics: Debt, Distribution, and the Macro Economy.* New York: St. Martin's Press.

Palloix, C. (1975) *L'Internalisation du capital.* Paris: François Maspero.

Palma, G. (1978) "Dependency: a Formal Theory of Underdevelopment or a Methodology for the Analysis of Concrete Situations of Underdevelopment?" *World Development*, 6: 881–924.

Palma, G. (1991) "Dependency and Development: A Critical Overview," in Dudley Seers (ed.), *Dependency Theory. A Critical Reassessment.* London: Francis Pinter.

Parpart, J. (1996) "Post-Modernism, Gender and Development," in Jonathan Crush (ed.), *Power of Development.* London: Routledge.

Parry, J. (1981) *The Discovery of the Sea.* Berkeley: University of California Press.

Pastré, O. (1992) *Les nouveaux piliers de la finance.* Paris: La decouverte.

242

Patnaik, P. (1986) "On the Economic Crisis of World capitalism," in P. Patnaik (ed.), *Lenin and Imperialism*. Delhi: Orient Longman.

Patnaik, P. (1995a) "The Nation-State in the Era of Globalisation," *Economic and Political Weekly* (Bombay), August 19.

Patnaik, P. (1995b) *Whatever Happened to Imperialism and Other Essays*. New Delhi: Tolika, 102–104.

Patnaik, P. (1997) *Accumulation and Stability Under Capitalism*. Oxford: Clarendon Press.

Patnaik, P., and Chandrashekhar, C. P. C. (1998) "India: *Dirigisme*, Structural Adjustment and the Radical Alternative," in D. Baker, G. Epstein, and R. Pollin (eds.), *Globalisation and Progressive Economic Policy*. Cambridge: Cambridge University Press.

Patnaik U. (1996) "Export-Oriented Agriculture and Food Security in India and Developing Countries," *Economic and Political Weekly* (Bombay), Special Number: 2429–49.

Peacock, A., and Wiseman, J. (1961) *The Growth of Public Expenditure in the United Kingdom*. Oxford.

Perelman, M. (1996) *The End of Economics*. London: Routledge.

Petras, J. (1997) "Latin America: The Resurgance of the Left," *New Left Review*, 223: 17–47.

Petras, J., and Morley, M. (1980) "The U.S. Imperial State," *Review*, 4, 2: 171–222.

Petras, J., and Morley, M. (1995) *Empire or Republic: American Global Power and Domestic Decay*. New York: Routledge.

Petras, J., and Vieux, S. (1996) "The Decline of Revolutionary Politics: Capitalist Detour and the Return of Communism," in Chronis Polychroniou and Harry Targ, *Marxism Today: Essays on Capitalism. Socialism and Strategies for Change*. Westport, CT: Praeger Publishers.

Piven, F. F., and Cloward, R. A. (1998) "Eras of Power," *Monthly Review*, 49: 11–23.

Polanyi, K. (1957/1944) *The Great Transformation: The Political and Economic Origins of Our Time*. Boston: Beacon Press.

Pollard, S., and Holmes, C. (1972) *Documents of European History: Industrial Power and National Rivalry, 1870–1914*. Oxford.

Porter, B. (1994) *War and the Rise of the State*. New York: Free Press.

Porter, R. (1997) *The Greatest Benefit to Mankind: a Medical History of Humanity from Antiquity to the Present*. London: Harper Collins.

Postgate, R. See G. D. H. Cole.

Prebisch, R. (1959) "Commercial Policies in Underdeveloped Countries," *American Economic Review*, 49.

Preobrazhensky, E. A. (1979) *The Crisis of Soviet Industrialization: Selected Essays*. White Plains, NY: M.E. Sharpe.

Pritchett, L. (1997) "Divergence, Big Time," *Journal of Economic Perspectives*, 11: 3–17.

Przeworski, A. (1990) *The State and Economy under Capitalism*. London: Harwood.

Quijano, A. (1995) "Modernity, Identity and Utopia in Latin America," in John Beverley, Michael Aronna, and José Oviedo (eds.), *The Postmodernism Debate in Latin America*. Durham: Duke University Press.

Rahnema (1997) See Rahnema and Bawtree (1997).

Rahnema, M., and Bawtree, V. (eds.) (1997) *The Post-Development Reader*. London: Zed Books.

Ranger, T. (1983) "The Invention of Tradition in Colonial Africa," in Eric Hobsbawm and Terry Ranger (eds.), *The Invention of Tradition*. Cambridge.

Reich, R. (1992) *The Work of Nation*. New York: Vintage.

Reynolds, L. (1985) *Economic Growth in the Third World, 1850–1980*. New Haven: Yale University Press.

Ricardo, D. (1951) *Works of David Ricardo, vol. I: Principles of Political Economy*, Piero Sraffa (ed.). Cambridge: Cambridge University Press.

Robinson, C. (1989) *Hungry Farmers*. London: Christian Aid.

Robinson, J. (1949) "Mr. Harrod's Dynamics," *Economic Journal*, 59: 68–85.

Robinson, J. (1951) "Introduction," *The Accumulation of Capital* by Rosa Luxemburg. New York: Monthly Review Press.

Robinson, R. (1972) "Non-European Foundations of European Imperialism, Sketch for a Theory of Collaboration," in Owen and Sutcliffe (1972).

244

Robinson, R. (1986) "The Excentric Idea of Imperialism, With or Without Empire," in W. Mommsen and J. Osterhammel (eds.), *Imperialism and After; Continuities and Discontinuities*. London: Allen and Unwin.

Robinson, R., and Gallagher, G. (1961) (with A. Denny) *Africa and the Victorians: the Official Mind of Imperialism*. London: Macmillan.

Robinson, W. I. (1996) *Promoting Polyarchy: Globalization, U.S. Intervention, and Hegemony*. Cambridge: Cambridge University Press.

Rodney, W. (1974) *How Europe Underdeveloped Africa*. Washington DC.: Howard University Press.

Rodrick, D. (1997) "Sense and Nonsense in the Globalization Debate," *Foreign Policy*, 107: 20–30.

Roemer, J. (1982) *A General Theory of Exploitation and Class*. Cambridge: Harvard University Press.

Rosenberg, J. (1994) *The Empire of Civil Society*. London: Verso.

Rosenberg, J. (1996) "Isaac Deutscher and the Lost History of International Relations," *New Left Review*, 215: 3–15.

Rosenberg, N., and Birdzell, L. (1986) *How the West Grew Rich*. New York: Basic Books.

Rostow, W. W. (1970) *The Stages of Economic Growth: A Non-Communist Manifesto*. Cambridge.

Rothschild, K. (ed.) (1971) *Power in Economics*. Harmondsworth: Penguin.

Royal Institute of International Affairs (1937) *The Problem of International Investment*. Oxford.

Rubinstein, W. D. (1987) *Elites and the Wealthy in Modern British History*. Brighton.

Sachs, J. (1997) "The Limits of Convergence, Nature, Nurture and Growth," *The Economist* (London), June 14.

Sachs, W. (ed.) (1992) *The Development Dictionary*. London: Zed Books.

Said, E. (1979) *Orientalism*. New York: Random House.

Said, E. (1993) *Culture and Imperialism.* Knopf and Chatto and Windus.

Said, E. (1994) *Culture and Imperialism.* London: Vintage.

Sassen, S. (1997) "The Spatial Organization of Information Industries: Implications for the role of the State," in James Mittelman (ed.), *Globalization: Critical Reflections.* Boulder, CO: Lynne Rienner Publisher.

Saville, J. (1988) "Some Notes on Anderson's 'Figures of Descent'" in Northern Marxists' Historians' Group, *The Development of British Capitalist Society,* Manchester.

Say, J.-B. (1803) *A Treatise on Political Economy, or the Production, Distribution, and Consumption of Wealth,* trans. C. R. Prinsep. New York: Augustus M. Kelley, 1971.

Sayer, D. See Peter Corrigan.

Schaeffer, R. (1997) *Understanding Globalization: The Social Consequences of Political, Economic and Environmental Change.* Landham, MD: Rowman and Littlefield Publishers.

Schattschneider, R. E. (1935) *Politics, Pressures, and the Tariff.* New York: Prentice-Hall.

Schneider, M. (1994) "Modelling Hobson's Underconsumption Theory," pp. 100–123 in *J. A. Hobson after Fifty Years: Freethinker of the Social Sciences,* ed. John Pheby. London: Macmillan.

Schumpeter, J. (1919) *Imperialism and Social Classes.* New York: Meridan, 1955.

Schumpeter, J. (1942) *Capitalism, Socialism and Democracy.* London: Allen and Unwin.

Schumpeter, J. (1954) *History of Economic Analysis.* New York: Oxford University Press.

Semmell, B. (1970) *The Rise of Free Trade Imperialism.* Cambridge.

Sen, G. (1995) *The Military Origins of Industrialization and International Trade Rivalry.* London: Pinter.

Shanin, T. (1997) "The Idea of Progress" in Rahnema and Bawtree, *The Post-Development Reader.* London: Zed Books.

Siegelman, P. (1965) "Introduction" in *Imperialism: A Study* by J. A. Hobson, Ann Arbor, MI: University of Michigan Press.

Skidmore, D., and Hudson, V. M. (eds.) (1993) *The Limits of State Autonomy: Societal Groups and Foreign Policy Formulation*. Boulder, CO: Westview Press.

Skocpol, T. (1979) *States and Social Revolutions*. Cambridge: Cambridge University Press.

Skocpol, T. (1992) *Protecting Soldiers and Mothers*. Cambridge, MA: Harvard University Press.

Skocpol, T. (1994) *Social Revolutions in the Modern World*. Cambridge: Cambridge University Press.

Smith, A. (1910) *An Inquiry into the Nature and Causes of The Wealth of Nations*. London: J.M. Dent.

Smith, D. (1992) "Conflict and War," in Susan George (ed.), *The Debt Boomerang*. London: Pluto Press.

Smith, M. (1992) "The Value Abstraction and the Dialectic of Social Development," *Science & Society*, 56: 261–290.

Snyder, L. (1954) *The Meaning of Nationalism*. New Brunswick: Rutgers University.

Solow, B., and Engerman, S. (eds.) (1987) *British Capitalism and Caribbean Slavery: The Legacy of Eric Williams*. Cambridge: Cambridge University Press.

Sousa Santos, B. (1995) *Toward a New Common Sense, Law, Science and Politics in the Paradigmatic Transition*. New York: Routledge.

Stalin, J. (1913) *Marxism and the National Question. Collected Works*, 3: 300–384.

Stern, S. J. (1988) "Feudalism, Capitalism and the World-System in the Perspective of Latin America and the Caribbean," *American Historical Review*, 93: 211–222.

Strachey, J. (1959) *The End of Empire*. London: Victor Gollanz.

Susjan, A., and Lah, M. (1997) "Inflation in the Transition Economies: the post-Keynesian View," Review of Political Economy, 9, 4: 381–393.

Sutcliffe, B. (1999) "The Place of Development in Theories of Imperialism and Globalisation," in Ronaldo Munck and Denis O'Hearn (eds.), *Critical Development Theory: Contributions to a New Paradigm*. London: Zed Books.

Sutcliffe, B. See Roger Owen.

Svennilson, I. (1954) *Growth and Stagnation in the European Economy*. Geneva.

Sweezy, P. M. (1942) *The Theory of Capitalist Development: Principles of Marxian Political Economy*. New York: Monthly Review Press, 1970.

Sylos-Labini, P. (1956) *Oligopoly and Technical Progress*. Trans. Elizabeth Henderson. Cambridge, MA: Harvard University Press, 1962.

Szentes, T. (1985) *Theories of World Capitalist Economy*. Budapest: Akademiaikiado.

Tabb, W. K. (1997) "Globalization Is *An* Issue, The Power of Capital Is *The* Issue," *Monthly Review*, 49, 2: 20–30.

Tarbell, I. M. (1936) *The Nationalizing of Business, 1878–1898*. New York: Macmillan.

Tarbuck, K. (1989) *Bukharin's Theory of Equilibrium*. London: Pluto Press.

Tiffen, P., and Zadek, S. (1996) "Can Fair Trade Take on the Mainstream?" *New Economics*, London, Summer, and see Barratt Brown, 1992.

Tomlinson, J. (1997) "Cultural Globalisation: Placing and Displacing the West," in Vincent Tucker (ed.), *Cultural Perspectives on Development*. London: Frank Cass.

Toulemon, R. (1994) *La construction europeenne*. Paris: Livre de Poche, References.

Turgeon, L. (1997) *Bastard Keynesianism: The Evolution of Economic Thinking and Policy-Making Since World War II*. Westport, CT: Praeger.

UNCTAD (1996) *Handbook of International Trade and Development Statistics*. New York: UN.

UNCTAD (1997) *Trade and Development Report. Globalisation, Distribution and Growth*. New York, United Nations.

UNDP (1997) *Human Development Report, 1997*, New York: UNDP.

Usher, D. (1998) "How Dreadful Life Used to Be," mimeo, Queen's University, Canada.

Veltmeyer, H., and Petras, J. (1997) *Neoliberalism and Class Conflict in Latin America*. London: Macmillan.

Von Laue, T. (1987) *The World Revolution of Westernization*. Oxford: Oxford University Press.

Wade, R. (1990) *Governing the Market*. Princeton: Princeton University Press.

Wallerstein, I. (1974) *The Modern World System*, l. New York: Academic Books.

Wallerstein, I. (1976) *The Modern World System, Vol. 1: Capitalist Agriculture and the Origins of the European Economy in the Sixteenth Century*. New York: Academic Press.

Wallerstein, I. (1980) *The Modern World System, Vol. 2: Mercantilism and the Consolidation of the European World-Economy, 1600–1750*. New York: Academic Press.

Wallerstein, I. (1982) contribution to Samir Amin, *Dynamics of Global Crisis*. MacMillan.

Wallerstein, I. (1983) *Historical Capitalism*. London: Verso.

Wallerstein, I. (1984) *The Politics of the World Economy*. Cambridge: Cambridge University Press.

Wallerstein, I. (1989) *The Modern World-System, Vol. 3: The Second Era of Great Expansion of the Capitalist World-Economy, 1730–1840s*. New York: Academic Press.

Wallerstein, I. (1997) "Eurocentrism and Its Avatars: The Dilemmas of Social Science," *New Left Review*, 226: 104–5.

Warren, B. (1973) "Imperialism and Capitalist Industrialization," *New Left Review*, 81: 3–44.

Warren, B. (1980) *Imperialism: Pioneer of Capitalism*. London: New Left Books and Verso.

Waters, M. (1995) *Globalization*. London: Routledge.

Weber, M. (1948) *From Max Weber*, H. Gerth and C. W. Mills (eds.). London: Routledge.

Weber, M. (1968) *Economy and Society*, 2 vols., eds. Claus Wittich and Guenther Roth. Berkeley, CA: University of California Press.

Weber, M. (1983) *Max Weber on Capitalism, Bureaucracy and Religion*, S. Andreski (ed.). London: Allen and Unwin.

Weiss, L. (1997) "Globalization and the Myth of the Powerless State," *New Left Review*, 225: 3–27.

Whitaker's *Almanac*. 1963 London.

Whitman, J. (1984) "From Philology to Anthropology in Mid-Nineteenth-Century Germany," in G. Stocking (ed.), *Functionalism Historicized.* Madison: University of Wisconsin.

Wickham, C. (1988) "The Uniqueness of the East," in J. Baechler, J. Hall, and M. Mann (eds.), *Europe and the Rise of Capitalism*. Oxford: Basil Blackwell.

Williams, E. (1944) *Capitalism and Slavery*. Chapel Hill: University of North Carolina.

Williams, R. (1981) *Culture*. Glasgow: Fontana.

Willoughby, J. (1995) "Evaluating the Leninist Theory of Imperialism," *Science and Society*, 59, 3.

Wilshire, G. H. (1900) *The Significance of the Trust*. New York: Wilshire's Magazine.

Wittfogel, K. (1957) *Oriental Despotism*. New Haven: Yale University.

Wolf, E. (1982) *Europe and the People Without History*. Berkeley: University of California Press.

Woods, E. M. (1988) *Peasant-Citizen and Slave: The Foundations of Athenian Democracy*. London: Verso.

World Bank (1997) "Bulletin," October–December, Washington, DC.

Yachin, F., and Amin, S. (1988) *La Mediteranee dans la systeme mondial*. Paris: La decouverte.

Yergin, D., and Stanislaw, J. (1998) *The Commanding Heights*. New York: Simon and Schuster.

Zadek, S. See Pauline Tiffen.

Zevin, R. (1992) "Are World Financial Markets More Open? If So, Why and With What Effects?" in Tariq Banuri and Juliet Schor (eds.), *Financial Openness and National Autonomy*. Oxford: Clarendon Press.

# BIOGRAPHIES

**Samir Amin** is author of many books on the Third World, including *Accumulation on a World Scale* (1974), *Unequal Development* (1976), and *Capitalism in the Age of Globalism* (1997). He directs the Third World Forum in Dakar, Senegal.

**Michael Barratt Brown** taught industrial studies at Sheffield University and has lectured on industrial development in many countries. He is a director of the Bertrand Russell Peace Foundation and was founding principal of Northern College and chair of Twin Trading. His books include *After Imperialism* (1963), *Economics of Imperialism* (1972), *Models in Political Economy* (1984, revised 1995), *Fair Trade* (1993), and *Africa's Choices: After Thirty Years of the World Bank* (1995).

**James M. Blaut** is professor of geography and anthropology at the University of Illinois at Chicago. He was educated at the University of Chicago, the University of the West Indies, and Louisiana State University. He is the author of *The Colonizer's Model of the World: Geographical Diffusionism and Eurocentric History* (1993) and three other books dealing with the historical and political geography of the Third World. He was awarded the Distinguished Scholarship Honors for 1997 from the Association of American Geographers.

**Anthony Brewer** is professor of the history of economics at the University of Bristol. He has written several books, including *Marxist Theories of Imperialism: A Critical Survey* (1990) and is currently working on eighteenth- and nineteenth-century theories of economic growth.

**Ronald H. Chilcote** is professor of economics and political science at the University of California, Riverside. He is the author and editor of numerous books and scholarly journal articles, including *Theories of Comparative Political Economy* (2000), an edited anthology of previously published writing, *Imperialism: Theoretical Directions* (2000), *Theories of Comparative Politics: The Search for* *a Paradigm Revisited* (1994), and *Power and the Ruling Classes in Northeast Brazil* (1990). He is a founder and currently managing editor of the bimonthly journal *Latin American Perspectives*. His research has focused on Portuguese-speaking Africa, Brazil, and Portugal.

**M. C. Howard** was born in Gloucestershire in 1945. Educated at the universities of Lancaster and Leicester in England, he has held academic positions in the United Kingdom, United States, and Canada. He has published extensively in Marxian economics, economic theory, and economic systems, and is currently professor of economics at the University of Waterloo, Canada.

**J. E. King** was born in London in 1947. Educated at Oxford University, he has held academic positions at the University of Lancaster in England and La Trobe University in Australia, where he is currently reader in economics. He has published extensively in Marxian economics, history of economic thought, labor economics, and post-Keynesianism.

**Ronaldo Munck** is an Argentinian sociologist, currently based at the University of Liverpool. He has written extensively in the field of political sociology, especially on labor and development issues. He has written ten books including *Politics and Dependency in the Third World: The Case of Latin America* (1984) and *Marx @ 2000: Late Marxist Perspectives* (1999). He has also coedited several volumes and is currently working on globalization, labor flexibility, and worker organizations in Latin America.

**Gregory P. Nowell** is associate professor of political science at the State University of New York at Albany, where he teaches international relations and international political economy. He is author of *Mercantile States and the World Oil Cartel* (1994) and has published articles on the politics of international oil on academic journals and the popular press. Nowell has also been active as a consultant in the politics of air quality and alternative transportation fuels.

**Prabhat Patnaik** is professor at the Centre for Economic Studies and Planning, Jawaharlal Nehru University, New Delhi, writing on political economy and macroeconomic issues concerning developing countries. His books include *Economics and Egalitarianism* (1991), *Whatever Happened to Imperialism and Other Essays* (1995), and *Accumulation and Stability under Capitalism* (1997).

**James Petras** is professor of sociology at SUNY-Binghampton. He is the author or editor of more than thirty books and more than 200 referred articles. He has contributed to *The British Journal of Sociology, The American Sociological Review,* and *Le Monde Diplomatique*. His latest publication is *Neoliberalism and Class Conflict in Latin America* (1997).

**John Willoughby** is associate professor of economics at American University in Washington, D.C. and at the American University of Sarjah, United Arab Emirates. He received his Ph.D. from the University of California at Berkeley in 1979. He has written extensively on the Marxian theory of imperialism, the political economy of capitalist competition, and the history of American imperialism. He has recently begun a study of the institutional organization of American foreign economic assistance.

# INDEX

Abraham, D., 103
accumulation, primitive: Luxemburg on, 117–118, 125; Marx on, 115; socialist, 121–124
acquisitiveness, of capitalism, 21–22, 24
Africa: agriculture in, 175; colonial domination on, 45; European contacts with, 68; famines in, 172–175; scramble for, 66, 70
agriculture, 5
agriexports versus food crops, 173–175
alternatives to globalization, 166–167, 199–200, 209, 211–213
Alvarez, Sonia, 152
Amin, Ash, 148
Amin, Samir, 9
antipatriotic cosmopolitanism, 161
Arrighi, Giovanni, 6–7, 57
Asia, European penetration into, 68
Association of South East Asian Nations (ASEAN), 164

Bagú, Sergio, 9
banking, British, 52
banking concentration, in Britain, 4
Baran, Paul, 5, 7, 8, 20, 32
Becker, 12–13
Bernal, Martin, 46
big push, 200–201

Bolshevik Revolution, 118–119
bourgeois internationalism, 169–179; African famines and, 172–175; agriexports versus food crops in, 173–175; components of, 169; definition of, 169; food security in, 175–176; fundamentalism and, 176–177; interimperialist rivalry in, 178–179; internecine conflicts in, 176; labor reserves for, 171–172; Marx, Lenin, Luxemburg and, 170–171; outlying regions in, 172; resource conflicts from, 177–178; subjugation in, 172; subnational conflicts and, 176; summary critique of, 170; terms of trade in, 173, 175
Braudel, Fernand, 12
Brenner, Robert, 12, 133, 135–136
Bretton Woods institutions, 173, 175
Brewer, Anthony, 6
British colonialism, 6, 41–43
British Empire, 44–45; Barratt Brown on, 43–44; commerce and industry in, 50–53; "gentlemanly capitalism" in, 53–56; industrial capitalism and, 49–50; nature of, 41–43; new imperialism in, 58–63; North–South divide in, existence of, 56–57; North–South divide in, geography of, 46–49; political and cultural imperialism in, 44–46
British Industrial Revolution, 49–50, 51

and economic nationalism in, 145; in
Latin America, 141–154; limitations of,
11; methodological approach to, 144; in
noncapitalist world, 1–2; radical approach to, 144; reformist approach to,
144; versus socialism, 145; as stagnationist, 11, 142–143; statistics on, 149–
150; totalizing perspective of, 145–146
Derrida, Jaques, 141, 154
development, 2; core and periphery in, 9;
Euro-Marxism and, 10–11; gap in, 71;
historical stages in, 7; inward-directed,
9; market and relations of exchange in,
10; metropole and satellite in, 8–9; in
Mexico, 8–9; old versus new imperialism and, 7–8; revolution as prerequisite
for, 32; value of, 61. *See also* capitalist
development
development economics, 113–115
development theory, 6–11; Arrighi on,
6–7; Baran on, 7; Brewer on, 6; Cardoso
on, 7; Marini on, 7; Patnaik on, 7; Warren on, 7
Diamond, Jared, 46–49
diffusionism, Eurocentric: doctrine of,
128–129; Marxism and, 127–139
diffusionist theory of nationalism, Stalin's,
134–135
disease, Old World, effect on New World
population, 67–68
distribution, 203–206
distributional coalitions, 89
divergence, economic, 33; dos Santos,
Theotônio, 8

Eatwell, J., 89
economic development, socialist, 119–121
economic equalities, political independence and, 79
economic gains, 73–76
economics: development, 113–115; in imperialism, 4; politics and, 159
economy, imperialist capitalist world, 88
Edelstein analysis, 98–100
effects, of imperialism, 72–78; gainers in,
73–76; losers in, 76–78

Emmanuel, Arrighi, 9
empire: economic basis of, 4; fall of, 6; unequal class benefits of, 42. *See also* British Empire
employment, full, market-driven, 89
*enfoque totalizador,* 145–146
Escobar, Arturo, 151, 152
ethnic conflicts, 176
EU-ACP association, 164
Eurocentric diffusionism, 128–129
Eurocentric diffusionism, Marxism and,
127–139; ancient society and, 129–131;
background on, 127–128; colonialism
and, 135–137; doctrine in, 128–129;
Euro-Marxism in, 128; imperialism and,
138–139; national question and, 134–
135; rise of capitalism and, 132–133
Euro-Marxism, 10–11, 128
Europe, dominant position of, 6
European capitalism, on Third World,
138–139
European imperial territories, 65–66
European Union, 164, 165
exploitation of noncapitalist world, 1

fall of imperialism, 78–79
famines, African, 172–175
feminism, 151
feudal mode of production, 132
Fieldhouse, D. K., 100–102
finance capital, in world capitalism, 7
financialization, 163
financial markets, 202–203
Fordham, B., 103
foreign investment, 70, 87; from maldistribution of wealth, 89; profits from, 75,
77; as toxic/imperialistic, 89
Foucault, Michel, 151
Fourth World, 148
Frank, André Gunder, 5, 20, 32, 57, 143,
149
free trade, 4
free trade phenomenon, imperialism as,
97–98
Frondizi, Silvio, 9

89–90; underconsumption in, 86–88,
91–92; war cycle in, 93–94
Hopkins, 50–53; "gentlemanly capitalism"
of, 53–56

imperfectionism, 87, 88–89
imperialism: classic theories of, 26–31; as
expansion of capitalism, 41; history of,
2–3; Marx on, 23–26; Marxist theory of,
138–139; meanings of, 2–3, 19; new,
149; new, in Latin America, 147–149;
old versus new, 2–3, 7–8
imperialist capitalist world economy, 88
India, independence of, 78
industrial capitalism, empire and, 49–50
industrial concentration, 86–87
Industrial Revolution, 42; in Britain, 49–
50, 51
industry, commerce and, 50–53
inevitability, of globalization, 196–197
information accumulation, 194–195
intelligence agencies, 207–208
intelligence operations, 184–185
interimperialist rivalry, 178–179
International Monetary Fund, 2, 60
internationalism: bourgeois, 169–179; liberal, 104
internecine conflicts, 176
investment, foreign, 70, 87; from maldistribution of wealth, 89; profits from, 75,
77; as toxic/imperialistic, 89

James, C. L. R., 136

Kalmanovitz, Salomón, 145–146
Kautsky, Karl, 3–4, 28–29; ultraimperial-
ism of, 138
Kay, Geoff, 41
Keynesian theory, 89; versus Say's Law,
86–87
Kolko, G., 96

labor, wage, 130
labor reserves, for capitalism, 171–172
Latin America, 79–80; dependency and
imperialism in, 141–154; beyond, 154;

entrance of, 141–143; exit from, 153–
154; globalization versus new imperialism in, 147–149; postdependency,
149–153; social movements in, 152
Lenin, V. I., 3–4, 9, 20, 70; on capitalism,
171; on capitalist development, 115–
117, 125–126; on colonialism in capitalism, 137; on Eurocentric diffusionism,
128; on imperialism, 90, 141; on Kautsky, 29; on monopoly capitalism, 125;
nondiffusionist theory of nationalism of,
134–135
Lewis, W. Arthur, 113–114
liberal internationalism, 104
logocentrism, development theory and, 146
Luxemburg, Rosa, 3, 8; on capitalism, 171;
on capitalist development, 117–118; on
Eurocentric diffusionism, 128; on imperialism, 141–142; on primitive accumulation, 117–118, 125
Lyotard, J. F., 151

Magdoff, Harry, 7
Malaya rubber industry, 77
Malthus, Thomas, 113–114
Mandel, Ernest, 9–10
Marini, Rui Mauro, 7
market forces/coercion dichotomy, 32
Marx, Karl, 5, 9, 20, 70; on capitalism, 1,
21–23; on capitalism as closed system,
170–171; on capitalist development,
115; on imperialism, 23–26
Marxian critics, 36–37
Marxism: Euro-, 10–11, 128; Eurocentric
diffusionism and, 127–139; Eurocentrism in, 139; on nation and nation-state
formation, 134–135; stages of history in,
130
Marxist capitalist development, 113–126
Marxist theorists, 19–20, 141
materialism, historical, 35
mercantilism, imperialism under, 3
merchant capitalism, 41–42
metropole, 8–9
Mexico, development versus imperialism
in, 8–9